C++

No experience required.

C++

No experience required.™

Paulo Franca

SYBEX®

San Francisco • Paris • Düsseldorf • Soest

Associate Publisher: Gary Masters
Acquisitions Manager: Kristine Plachy
Acquisitions & Developmental Editor: Peter Kuhns
Editor: Ronn Jost
Project Editor: Kim Wimpsett
Technical Editor: Dale Wright
Book Designers: Patrick Dintino, Catalin Dulfu
Graphic Illustrator: Andrew Benzie
Electronic Publishing Specialist: Robin Kibby
Production Coordinator: Amy Eoff
Indexer: Ted Laux
Cover Designer: Ingalls + Associates

Screen reproductions produced with Collage Complete.

Collage Complete is a trademark of Inner Media Inc.

SYBEX is a registered trademark of SYBEX Inc.

No experience required. is a trademark of SYBEX Inc.

TRADEMARKS: SYBEX has attempted throughout this book to
distinguish proprietary trademarks from descriptive terms by
following the capitalization style used by the manufacturer.

Library of Congress Card Number: 97-61957
ISBN: 0-7821- 2111-X

Manufactured in the United States of America

10 9 8 7 6 5 4 3 2 1

*To
Julia Arentz
and
Eunhee Kim*

Acknowledgments

Where should I start? I suppose I should thank my dear notebook computer! It is now three years old and ready for retirement. It has been with me in several classrooms and has been exposed to X-rays of all kinds in several airports in the Northern and Southern Hemispheres. Not to mention a few virus attacks! Yet, it has performed reliably enough to allow me to produce about 80 percent of this text and software.

Professor C.V. Ramamoorthy—Ram—with his always inspiring presence, was the first to encourage me to write this book. Professor Daniel Lewis was very helpful when I started writing. Many of the ideas for the software and presentation were developed in our discussions.

I also wish to acknowledge the continued support from the Brazilian Research Council (CNPq) and the Federal University of Rio de Janeiro (UFRJ). This university, especially the computer science department and the Computing Laboratory (NCE-UFRJ), has given me ample support and encouragement. I am especially grateful to Professor Adriano Cruz, Chair of the Computer Science Department. It is very difficult for me to name just a few of the faculty and staff at UFRJ, since many have been supportive of my work.

Thanks to everyone at Sybex, especially Kristine Plachy and the editorial team—Peter Kuhns, Ronn Jost, Kim Wimpsett, and Dale Wright—and the production team—Amy Eoff, Robin Kibby, and Andrew Benzie.

Special thanks to Andrea Franca and Frederico Arentz. This work has required several long trips, and, during each of them, they sacrificed their already busy lives to provide me with their help.

Eunhee Kim played a very special role. In any long-term endeavor, there are many times when one feels frustrated and tempted to quit. Whether we were near each other or thousands of miles apart, she never allowed that to happen. I had constant encouragement, motivation, and inspiration to proceed.

Santa Clara, not only the school, but also the saint herself—both significantly contributed to the start and finish of this work.

Finally, my list would not be complete without an acknowledgment to the local cafes, especially to the unbeatable Coffee Society in Cupertino, where a significant part of my work was done. I deeply thank the management, friendly crew, and crowd at this very special place. May they all live long and prosper!

Cupertino, July 24, 1997

Contents at a Glance

Table of Contents

Introduction

Once Upon a Time. . .

…and not too long ago, teaching C++ and object-oriented programming (OOP) to beginners was not an easy task. The language is not friendly, and most of the textbooks available were designed to teach C++ to those people who already knew C.

Advocates of object-oriented programming argue, and I agree, that it is better for a beginner to learn in the object-oriented paradigm from the start than it is to learn with the traditional approach and then switch to OOP. Also, it was already known that the wide use of C and the increasing popularity of C++ would make C++ the language of choice for computer specialists in the near future.

On the other hand, I had always been interested in developing teaching material that would make the process more interesting and challenging. How could this be done with C++ and object-oriented programming?

At that time, I was a visiting associate professor at Santa Clara University, and I had several enlightening discussions with Professor Daniel Lewis, Chair of the Computer Engineering Department. I thought of writing a textbook. Daniel pointed out that I should either go for something revolutionary, or forget it. Use a new teaching paradigm to teach a new programming paradigm.

The Support Software

This is how the idea of developing multimedia programs was born. Readers shouldn't have to learn boring input/output stuff just to see what happens with their programs. If I could provide them with a suitable class library, they could learn how to manipulate these objects to produce sounds, pictures, and animations.

The resulting software provides an interface with the Windows graphic environment and several program objects that are used throughout the text to teach the reader how to build programs. These objects simulate people, robots, circles, squares, boxes for messages, and other things. They significantly simplify the learning of computer programming, because the reader can practice immediately, without having to understand all the complicated input/output procedures. Also, with the available objects, readers can work on algorithm development using simple and intuitive examples and, later on, interesting geometric examples, instead of the usual arithmetic examples. This software makes the learning experience so easy that it makes no sense to use this book without the software.

I knew it was beyond my power to develop this support software for a universal platform. This is the price that had to be paid for the exciting learning tools. I decided to develop this software for IBM-compatible machines because they are cheap enough for students to have at home (as opposed to workstations), and for the Microsoft Windows environment because it is the direction in which most PC software is going.

Still, I had to choose a compiler. Although I started with Borland's Turbo C++ (which is friendly and cheap), the software now runs with later versions of Borland's compilers and with Microsoft's Visual C++.

Developing a book while integrating it with software is much more of a complex task than I anticipated at first. It becomes even worse when you decide to develop software to run under Windows—worse yet, software that allows the support software to run under Windows. I should add at this point that I am not a Windows specialist!

Anyway, it is now done, and I hope readers will enjoy it.

NOTE Visit the Sybex Web site at http://www.sybex.com. Click the No experience required link, then the C++: No experience required link, and then, finally, Download to get all the code and software for this book.

What Else Is Innovative?

Besides the support software, this book offers other innovative features. It is divided into 10 Parts, numbered 0 through IX. Why start at zero? It will help the reader remember that, in C++, array subscripts always start at zero. Besides, the material in Part 0 is designed to get the reader ready for the real action. In Part 0, I explain a few things about computers and programmers. I also explain how to set up the compilers (Turbo C++, Borland C++, and Visual C++) to use the supplied software.

N NOTE It is important that readers check their ability by completing the exercises in Part 0 before they read on.

In Parts I–III, I discuss and illustrate basic programming concepts without burdening readers with syntax details. More complete syntax rules are presented at the end of each Part. This enables readers to understand the purpose of the rules before they study the intricacies. One important feature, seldom found in similar books, is the early introduction of functions. I tested this approach in classrooms and was very satisfied with the results. Programmers who learn early how to use functions can develop solutions easier and usually split the code into functions with which it is easier to deal. From the first example in the book, readers are also exposed to objects.

At the same time, the reader must learn how to develop projects. It cannot be left for the final chapter. For this reason, short projects are developed beginning in Part III. One of these projects evolves with the reader throughout the book, from a very simplified version of a point-of-sale terminal to a relatively complex one involving catalogs, disk files, and so on.

Part IV deals with decisions and recursion. Again, I tried to approach recursion using graphical and intuitive examples.

Arithmetic manipulation is purposely postponed until Part V. The use of simple expressions is introduced earlier, but readers will only be required to work with numeric computations when they really have something interesting to do with them. The material in Part V brings all numeric computation to the geometric domain. Students are able to simulate planets, atoms, billiard balls, and cannonballs, and draw function graphs.

Objects are used from the very first Skill. Creating and deriving classes are not covered until Part VI, however.

In Part VII, arrays are introduced in a nontraditional way. First, they are introduced as collections of Screen Objects: objects representing people (athletes), circles, and so on. Then, they are introduced as sequences of numbers and characters.

There is no need to use input/output (i/o) to start programming. Readers will manipulate objects that appear on the screen according to instructions. Animations can be produced from Skill 1. Input/output using the Windows graphic interface is introduced as needed, and the real issues of i/o, including formatting and files, are discussed in Part VIII.

Part IX presents a discussion of common software-development techniques, and explores a more complete project.

Subjects are introduced when readers are able to use and understand them. Some subjects are discussed in more than one Part so that readers are able to see how a particular feature can be used in different circumstances. In almost every Part, there is a short project in which design options are discussed. Exercises to test the reader's learning are found throughout the text, under the heading "Try These for Fun…".

Additional hints and suggestions, and further material for this book, can be found on the Sybex Web site at `http://www.sybex.com`.

Paulo Bianchi Franca, Ph.D.
Home page: `http://www.franca.com`

PART 0

Getting Set Up

The purpose of Part 0 is just to get you used to the C++ compiler and the special software for this book. There is a brief introduction to programming, operating the C++ compiler, and executing programs using our special software. The software for this book was specially developed to help you learn C++ in a faster and more pleasant way.

This text was designed for readers with no experience in programming. However, some computer literacy is expected. If you have been able to browse the Web, download files, and use electronic mail, you should be able to learn computer programming.

Although learning becomes much easier and rewarding with this software, you should not fear getting dependent on it. In the last Skills of this book, after you are proficient in programming with C++, you will learn how to survive without this special software.

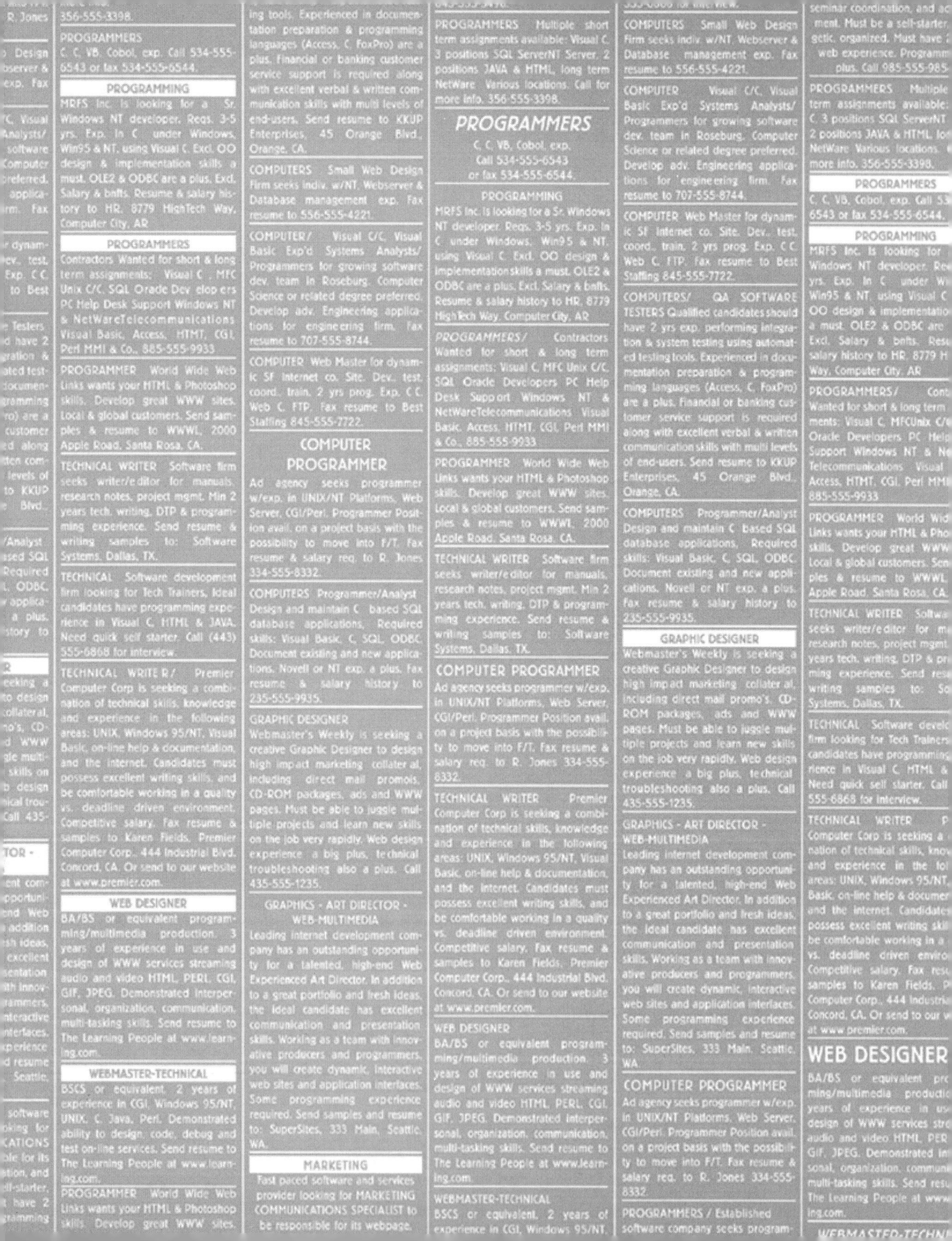

356-555-3398.

PROGRAMMERS
C, C, VB, Cobol, exp. Call 534-555-6543 or fax 534-555-6544.

PROGRAMMING

MRFS Inc. is looking for a Sr. Windows NT developer. Reqs. 3-5 yrs. Exp. In C under Windows, Win95 & NT, using Visual C. Excl. OO design & implementation skills a must. OLE2 & ODBC are a plus. Excl. Salary & bnfts. Resume & salary history to HR, 8779 HighTech Way, Computer City, AR

PROGRAMMERS

Contractors Wanted for short & long term assignments; Visual C, MFC Unix C/C, SQL Oracle Dev elop ers PC Help Desk Support Windows NT & NetWareTelecommunications Visual Basic, Access, HTMT, CGI, Perl MMI & Co., 885-555-9933

PROGRAMMER World Wide Web Links wants your HTML & Photoshop skills. Develop great WWW sites. Local & global customers. Send samples & resume to WWWL, 2000 Apple Road, Santa Rosa, CA.

TECHNICAL WRITER Software firm seeks writer/editor for manuals, research notes, project mgmt. Min 2 years tech. writing, DTP & programming experience. Send resume & writing samples to: Software Systems, Dallas, TX.

TECHNICAL Software development firm looking for Tech Trainers, Ideal candidates have programming experience in Visual C, HTML & JAVA. Need quick self starter. Call (443) 555-6868 for interview.

TECHNICAL WRITER/ Premier Computer Corp is seeking a combination of technical skills, knowledge and experience in the following areas: UNIX, Windows 95/NT, Visual Basic, on-line help & documentation, and the internet. Candidates must possess excellent writing skills, and be comfortable working in a quality vs. deadline driven environment. Competitive salary. Fax resume & samples to Karen Fields, Premier Computer Corp., 444 Industrial Blvd. Concord, CA. Or send to our website at www.premier.com.

WEB DESIGNER

BA/BS or equivalent programming/multimedia production. 3 years of experience in use and design of WWW services streaming audio and video HTML, PERL, CGI, GIF, JPEG. Demonstrated interpersonal, organization, communication, multi-tasking skills. Send resume to The Learning People at www.learning.com.

WEBMASTER-TECHNICAL

BSCS or equivalent, 2 years of experience in CGI, Windows 95/NT, UNIX, C, Java, Perl. Demonstrated ability to design, code, debug and test on-line services. Send resume to The Learning People at www.learning.com.

PROGRAMMER World Wide Web Links wants your HTML & Photoshop skills. Develop great WWW sites.

ing tools. Experienced in documentation preparation & programming languages (Access, C, FoxPro) are a plus. Financial or banking customer service support is required along with excellent verbal & written communication skills with multi levels of end-users. Send resume to KKUP Enterprises, 45 Orange Blvd., Orange, CA.

COMPUTERS Small Web Design Firm seeks indiv. w/NT, Webserver & Database management exp. Fax resume to 556-555-4221.

COMPUTER/ Visual C/C, Visual Basic Exp'd Systems Analysts/ Programmers for growing software dev. team in Roseburg. Computer Science or related degree preferred. Develop adv. Engineering applications for engineering firm. Fax resume to 707-555-8744.

COMPUTER Web Master for dynamic SF Internet co. Site. Dev., test, coord., train. 2 yrs prog. Exp. C C. Web C. FTP. Fax resume to Best Staffing 845-555-7722.

COMPUTER PROGRAMMER

Ad agency seeks programmer w/exp. in UNIX/NT Platforms, Web Server, CGI/Perl. Programmer Position avail. on a project basis with the possibility to move into F/T. Fax resume & salary req. to R. Jones 334-555-8332.

COMPUTERS Programmer/Analyst Design and maintain C based SQL database applications, Required skills: Visual Basic, C, SQL, ODBC. Document existing and new applications. Novell or NT exp. a plus. Fax resume & salary history to 235-555-9935.

GRAPHIC DESIGNER
Webmaster's Weekly is seeking a creative Graphic Designer to design high impact marketing collater al, including direct mail promos, CD-ROM packages, ads and WWW pages. Must be able to juggle multiple projects and learn new skills on the job very rapidly. Web design experience a big plus, technical troubleshooting also a plus. Call 435-555-1235.

GRAPHICS - ART DIRECTOR - WEB-MULTIMEDIA
Leading internet development company has an outstanding opportunity for a talented, high-end Web Experienced Art Director. In addition to a great portfolio and fresh ideas, the ideal candidate has excellent communication and presentation skills. Working as a team with innovative producers and programmers, you will create dynamic, interactive web sites and application interfaces. Some programming experience required. Send samples and resume to: SuperSites, 333 Main, Seattle, WA.

MARKETING

Fast paced software and services provider looking for MARKETING COMMUNICATIONS SPECIALIST to be responsible for its webpage.

PROGRAMMERS Multiple short term assignments available: Visual C, 3 positions SQL ServerNT Server, 2 positions JAVA & HTML, long term NetWare. Various locations. Call for more info. 356-555-3398.

PROGRAMMERS

C, C, VB, Cobol, exp.
Call 534-555-6543
or fax 534-555-6544.

PROGRAMMING
MRFS Inc. is looking for a Sr. Windows NT developer. Reqs. 3-5 yrs. Exp. In C under Windows, Win95 & NT, using Visual C. Excl. OO design & implementation skills a must. OLE2 & ODBC are a plus. Excl. Salary & bnfts. Resume & salary history to HR, 8779 HighTech Way, Computer City, AR

PROGRAMMERS/ Contractors Wanted for short & long term assignments: Visual C, MFC Unix C/C, SQL Oracle Developers PC Help Desk Support Windows NT & NetWareTelecommunications Visual Basic, Access, HTMT, CGI, Perl MMI & Co., 885-555-9933

PROGRAMMER World Wide Web Links wants your HTML & Photoshop skills. Develop great WWW sites. Local & global customers. Send samples & resume to WWWL, 2000 Apple Road, Santa Rosa, CA.

TECHNICAL WRITER Software firm seeks writer/editor for manuals, research notes, project mgmt. Min 2 years tech. writing, DTP & programming experience. Send resume & writing samples to: Software Systems, Dallas, TX.

COMPUTER PROGRAMMER
Ad agency seeks programmer w/exp. in UNIX/NT Platforms, Web Server, CGI/Perl. Programmer Position avail. on a project basis with the possibility to move into F/T. Fax resume & salary req. to R. Jones 334-555-8332.

TECHNICAL WRITER Premier Computer Corp is seeking a combination of technical skills, knowledge and experience in the following areas: UNIX, Windows 95/NT, Visual Basic, on-line help & documentation, and the internet. Candidates must possess excellent writing skills, and be comfortable working in a quality vs. deadline driven environment. Competitive salary. Fax resume & samples to Karen Fields, Premier Computer Corp., 444 Industrial Blvd. Concord, CA. Or send to our website at www.premier.com.

WEB DESIGNER
BA/BS or equivalent programming/multimedia production. 3 years of experience in use and design of WWW services streaming audio and video HTML, PERL, CGI, GIF, JPEG. Demonstrated interpersonal, organization, communication, multi-tasking skills. Send resume to The Learning People at www.learning.com.

WEBMASTER-TECHNICAL
BSCS or equivalent, 2 years of experience in CGI, Windows 95/NT,

COMPUTERS Small Web Design Firm seeks indiv. w/NT, Webserver & Database management exp. Fax resume to 556-555-4221.

COMPUTER Visual C/C, Visual Basic Exp'd Systems Analysts/ Programmers for growing software dev. team in Roseburg. Computer Science or related degree preferred. Develop adv. Engineering applications for engineering firm. Fax resume to 707-555-8744.

COMPUTER Web Master for dynamic SF Internet co. Site. Dev., test, coord., train. 2 yrs prog. Exp. C C. Web C. FTP. Fax resume to Best Staffing 845-555-7722.

COMPUTERS/ QA SOFTWARE TESTERS Qualified candidates should have 2 yrs exp. performing integration & system testing using automated testing tools. Experienced in documentation preparation & programming languages (Access, C, FoxPro) are a plus. Financial or banking customer service support is required along with excellent verbal & written communication skills with multi levels of end-users. Send resume to KKUP Enterprises, 45 Orange Blvd., Orange, CA.

COMPUTERS Programmer/Analyst Design and maintain C based SQL database applications, Required skills: Visual Basic, C, SQL, ODBC. Document existing and new applications. Novell or NT exp. a plus. Fax resume & salary history to 235-555-9935.

GRAPHIC DESIGNER

Webmaster's Weekly is seeking a creative Graphic Designer to design high impact marketing collater al, including direct mail promo's, CD-ROM packages, ads and WWW pages. Must be able to juggle multiple projects and learn new skills on the job very rapidly. Web design experience a big plus, technical troubleshooting also a plus. Call 435-555-1235.

GRAPHICS - ART DIRECTOR - WEB-MULTIMEDIA
Leading internet development company has an outstanding opportunity for a talented, high-end Web Experienced Art Director. In addition to a great portfolio and fresh ideas, the ideal candidate has excellent communication and presentation skills. Working as a team with innovative producers and programmers, you will create dynamic, interactive web sites and application interfaces. Some programming experience required. Send samples and resume to: SuperSites, 333 Main, Seattle, WA.

COMPUTER PROGRAMMER
Ad agency seeks programmer w/exp. in UNIX/NT Platforms, Web Server, CGI/Perl. Programmer Position avail. on a project basis with the possibility to move into F/T. Fax resume & salary req. to R. Jones 334-555-8332.

PROGRAMMERS / Established software company seeks program-

seminar coordination, and a
ment. Must be a self-starter
getic, organized. Must have
web experience. Programm
plus. Call 985-555-985

PROGRAMMERS Multiple
term assignments available
C, 3 positions SQL ServerNT
2 positions JAVA & HTML, lo
NetWare. Various locations.
more info. 356-555-3398.

PROGRAMMERS

C, C, VB, Cobol, exp. Call 53
6543 or fax 534-555-6544.

PROGRAMMING

MRFS Inc. is looking for
Windows NT developer. Re
yrs. Exp. In C under W
Win95 & NT, using Visual C
OO design & implementatio
a must. OLE2 & ODBC are
Excl. Salary & bnfts. Res
salary history to HR, 8779 H
Way, Computer City, AR

PROGRAMMERS/ Con
Wanted for short & long term
ments: Visual C, MFCUnix C/
Oracle Developers PC Hel
Support Windows NT & Ne
Telecommunications Visual
Access, HTMT, CGI, Perl MM
885-555-9933

PROGRAMMER World Wid
Links wants your HTML & Pho
skills. Develop great WWW
Local & global customers. Sen
ples & resume to WWWL
Apple Road, Santa Rosa, CA.

TECHNICAL WRITER Softw
seeks writer/editor for m
research notes, project mgm
years tech. writing, DTP & pr
ming experience. Send res
writing samples to: So
Systems, Dallas, TX.

TECHNICAL Software devel
firm looking for Tech Trainer
candidates have programmin
rience in Visual C, HTML &
Need quick self starter. Call
555-6868 for interview.

TECHNICAL WRITER P
Computer Corp is seeking a
nation of technical skills, kno
and experience in the fo
areas: UNIX, Windows 95/NT
Basic, on-line help & documer
and the internet. Candidates
possess excellent writing skil
be comfortable working in a
vs. deadline driven enviro
Competitive salary. Fax res
samples to Karen Fields. P
Computer Corp., 444 Industri
Concord, CA. Or send to our
at www.premier.com.

WEB DESIGNER

BA/BS or equivalent pr
ming/multimedia productio
years of experience in us
design of WWW services stre
audio and video HTML, PER
GIF, JPEG. Demonstrated in
sonal, organization, commun
multi-tasking skills. Send res
The Learning People at www
ing.com.

WEBMASTER-TECHN

Setting Up Your Software

- ❑ Understanding what programmers do
- ❑ Understanding files and directories
- ❑ Installing and using the software
- ❑ Using specific compilers (read the section that applies to you)
- ❑ Running programs

Contrary to popular belief, computer programming can be fun and provide you with an excellent opportunity to exercise your mind, creativity, and imagination. Most people involved in computer programming got into the profession because they like to program. True, as in any other profession, some parts are interesting and others are boring. We cannot choose to do only the interesting parts all the time.

Programming is exciting. It gives you the power to instruct the computer to do anything you want! Only your knowledge and imagination can limit what you do.

Nevertheless, learning how to program is not always exciting. It amazes me that we can use computers to make learning so much more interesting in math, astronomy, physics, geography, and so on, but when it comes to teaching how to seriously program, most of us are still in the chalk age!

But don't despair! There is hope! Some of us do believe that we must capture the interest of students while they are enthusiastic, and the way to do that is by making the subject ever more interesting and rewarding. This is the purpose of this book and its accompanying software, available from the Sybex Web site.

THE SYBEX WEB SITE

The URL for the Sybex Web site is `http://www.sybex.com`. You will find complete information on Sybex books as well as the software downloads. See "Installing the Book Software" below for more detailed instructions.

I would like to make one important recommendation before we get started: Use your computer! The more time you spend with it, the more you are likely to learn. If you ever think of another way to make a program, just go ahead and try it! If you have ideas about how to do something interesting, go on; nothing is stopping you.

Be curious: Don't ask your instructor what you can find out by yourself!

Skill 0 contains introductory material about programming languages, files, and so on. If you are familiar with these topics, you might want to skip to the section "Installing and Using the Software."

WHAT DOES PROGRAMMING MEAN?

Programming is the art of explaining exactly how a specific task is to be performed, so that the task can be successfully accomplished in our absence. Most likely, we will be referring to tasks to be performed by computers. Sometimes, however, humans execute a sequence of steps precisely to perform a given task, such as following a recipe. The person who writes a recipe must give a detailed explanation, because the cook must be able to follow the steps without consulting the author.

NOTE   Be sure you know how to execute a program as explained in this section before you start Skill 1.

How Do I Make Programs with C++?

Computers are not yet able to understand our language. It is still necessary to use a special *programming language* to explain to them what we want them to do. Computers are faster and more reliable than we humans, but by no means smarter! It may strike you as odd to hear that programming languages are much simpler than natural languages, but this is indeed the case.

Although programming languages are simpler than our languages, they are not the language a computer can understand! When operating, computers need to use a simple *machine language*. Unfortunately, this kind of language is so elementary that it is extremely boring to humans, and we are error prone when we use it.

Developing and Running a Program

Under the directions of special programs called *compilers*, computers can translate a programming language into machine language. Compilers are programs that explain to the computer how to translate directions written in a programming language (such as C++) into the machine language.

The process of developing a program involves several steps:

1. Write the program in a programming language, such as C++.

2. Use a compiler to translate your program into the *object* (.OBJ) form.

3. Often the compiler will notice some mistakes and notify you. You may have to fix the program and repeat step 2.

4. Use your compiler to link your program to other programs that may be needed to make it work. This generates your program in the *executable* (.EXE) form. Some compilers perform this step automatically, and you are not even aware of it.

5. Run the program. Often the program is wrong, due to logic errors, and doesn't behave as you expect. You may have to revise it and rewrite parts of it. You then have to redo steps 1 through 5.

Why Would I Link My Programs to Others?

Several programming tasks that may seem simple are, in fact, complex. Displaying a sentence on the computer screen, locating where the mouse is clicked, and many other tasks all involve many steps. Writing programs to perform all these tasks would take considerable time.

For this reason, several program pieces are already developed, and we will incorporate them into your programs to make your work easier and faster. In addition, I developed a special set of programs for the purpose of helping you learn how to program. We will bind these together with your programs.

What Do I Need to Use C++?

Many programming languages are currently in use. They all provide means of writing programs to tell computers what to do. The C++ programming language is growing in popularity and is powerful enough to deal with complex applications.

Skill 0

C++ is no kid's stuff! It was developed for professional programmers who deal with complex applications. C++ was not designed with the beginning programmer in mind. Indeed, it presents a challenge both for you (trying to learn) and for me (trying to help). Nevertheless, I believe you can become an almighty C++ programmer! I am providing you with a learning approach that will get you started not only painlessly, but, I hope, even with some excitement.

Turbo C++, Visual C++

Turbo C++ is software developed by Borland International to assist computer programmers in writing C++ programs. Borland also provides another product, Borland C++, which is a more complete (and expensive) version.

Visual C++ is software developed by Microsoft with the same purpose. Other C++ compilers are also available.

WARNING   The C++ compilers that you need to use are *not* included in the software. You must purchase one of the compilers and install it on your computer.

To use the material in this book, you need one of the following compilers:

- Turbo C++ for Windows 4.5 (Borland)
- Borland C++ 4 or 5 (for Windows)
- Microsoft Visual C++ for Windows 1.56, 4, or 5

TIP   Check this book's Web page to see if any other compilers were added to the list since publication.

Windows 3.1 or Windows 95

To run your compiler, you need an operating system. You must have Windows, either version 3.1 or Windows 95, running on your computer.

Unfortunately, there are some differences in using these compilers and using Windows 3.1 or Windows 95. This Skill explains how to get your programs up and running in each of those environments.

Do I Need a CD-ROM?

Absolutely no! Many people nowadays associate multimedia with CD-ROM. Multimedia involves several communications media, including animations and sounds. CD-ROMs are convenient for running multimedia applications, but in this course you will be developing your own multimedia programs.

Do I Really Need to Use These Programs?

Can you learn to ride a bike without using one? I would guess not. There is no way you can learn how to program computers without really trying. It is imperative that you have access to a computer and have enough time to run your programs.

Why Does This Book Require Specific Software?

This is the only way I could find to let you learn in an interesting way and avoid the boredom of having to learn many things before seeing some results. If you use the software I provide, you will soon be able to work on some interesting problems. The purpose of this software is to make the learning experience more enjoyable and challenging.

Quick Start—Files and Directories

I am providing several programs for your use. You will also be creating your own programs. In addition, your computer has several other programs. Each of those programs is stored in the computer as a *file*. In order for the computer to locate a particular program, every time we store a program, we give it a name. *File names* may have several characters, but it is a good idea to restrict your names to eight characters. For example:

```
MYPROG
PROG1
XX354
```

Optionally, you can include a period (usually called a dot by programmers), followed by an additional three characters that may result in something like the following file names:

```
MYPROG.CPP
XYZ.H
MYPROG.EXE
```

These three additional characters are called the *extension* and have a special meaning: They identify the purpose of the file. For example, programs written in C++ use the extension .CPP.

Often, in this book, we will use a set of programs that make up what we call a *project*. Projects are useful when you need to use multiple files—more than one piece of a program at the same time. You will see that I am supplying some programs that must be used with those you develop, and for that reason, we will use projects.

> **NOTE** Using ready-made pieces of programs is a clever technique that can substantially reduce the time needed to generate a new program. The main purpose of using my programs with yours is to provide a more interesting environment without the need to build it all from scratch.

Directories

It is important to give each file a unique name because the computer can use only the names to differentiate among files. To make managing file names easier, you can group files in a *directory*. A directory is similar to a drawer in a file cabinet. If you want to share one file cabinet with somebody else, the safest and simplest thing to do is to assign a different drawer to each person. Every time you create a file, you place it in your drawer, and when you look for your files, you will find them in your drawer.

Computer directories, however, have a substantial advantage over drawers in a file cabinet. There is no practical limit, except for disk space, on the number of drawers you can use! As long as you can provide a unique name for each drawer, you can create them at will.

If you tell the computer to store a file with a name that already belongs to another file, the contents of the old file will be lost! However, you can have files with the same name if you store them in different directories.

Using Directories

For most of the work we will do in this book, we can store all our programs in one directory. You can build your own programs and leave them in this same directory. Of course, you can also use your own directories if you like.

All our programs will be in the directory named FRANCA (this way you will remember me). Since this directory will likely reside on drive C: (your hard disk drive), you will see this directory referred to as C:\FRANCA on your computer screen.

> **N** **NOTE**   You may install the software in a different directory. The book suggests and assumes that you install it in C:\FRANCA.

* Means Anything . . .   You will soon see that you can use the asterisk (*) in operations involving the file name. The asterisk stands for any possible name—it is also called a *wildcard*. For example, *.CPP means all files that have the extension .CPP; *.* means all possible files.

Directory Hierarchies

Suppose you like the idea of directories, and you create a directory named MYDIR in which to store all your files. After working for a while, you discover that you are storing too many files in this directory and may end up confusing them, because you have files that relate to computing classes, files that relate to physics classes, personal files, and so on.

Putting these files into separate "drawers" may be a good idea. The good news is that you can create a directory (called a *subdirectory*) within another directory. This is similar to creating a drawer inside another drawer. Inside the MYDIR directory, you can create three subdirectories: COMPUT, PHYSICS, and PERSONAL, for example.

You would then have a *directory hierarchy*. Of course, you can expand your hierarchy by creating further subdirectories inside the subdirectories you just created; there are no practical limitations for that. Figure 0.1 illustrates a possible organization of your hard disk. Disk drives are designated by the letters A:, B:, C:, and so on. Most likely, your hard drive is drive C:. You can divide drive C: into several directories. Two such directories are shown, FRANCA and TCWIN. Inside the FRANCA directory is the OBJFILES directory. Although Figure 0.1 shows only those directories, your hard drive may include several others.

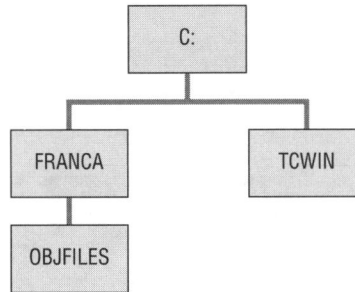

FIGURE 0.1:   A directory hierarchy

Since you can have files with the same name in different directories, you could, for example, have a file named OHBOY.CPP in the FRANCA directory and in the TCWIN directory. How does the computer differentiate between them? Well, you usually work in one directory at a time (just as you open one drawer of the file cabinet at a time). The directory you are working with is called the *current directory*. The computer always assumes that you are using files in the current directory. Sometimes, though, you may have to specify a file completely by including the directory hierarchy. This is called the *fully qualified file name* or *full path* to the file.

In this example, the full paths of the files are as follows:

```
C:\FRANCA\OHBOY.CPP
C:\TCWIN\OHBOY.CPP
```

Moving through the Directory Hierarchy

Suppose you want to open a file that is in your PERSONAL directory. Remember, this directory is in the MYDIR directory. If you try to open this file using a compiler such as Turbo C++ 4.5, you will see a screen similar to the one in Figure 0.2.

If you do so using a Windows 95 compiler, you may see a screen such as that in Figure 0.3.

The list of files in this directory (empty)

Selected directory (drive C:)

To select a directory, double-click its name.

List of directories and files in drive C:

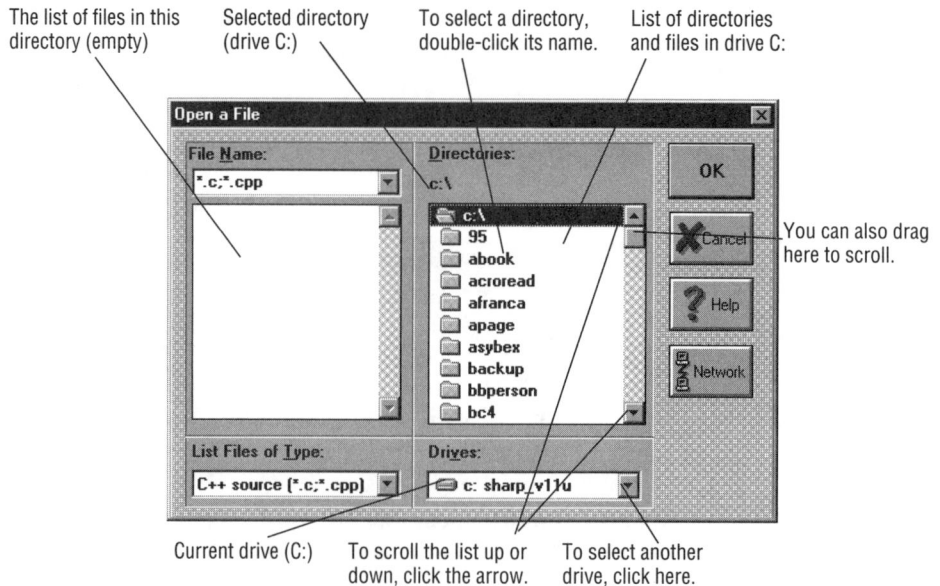

You can also drag here to scroll.

Current drive (C:)

To scroll the list up or down, click the arrow.

To select another drive, click here.

FIGURE 0.2:   Directories in drive C: (Turbo C++ 4.5)

Now, you select the MYDIR directory and then the PERSONAL directory. But the problem is, Where is the MYDIR directory?

In this example (and most likely in your computer, too), there are many directories besides MYDIR. Therefore, the entire list cannot be displayed at once. What do you do? Use the slide bar (or the arrows) to scroll through the list until you can see the directory you want. At some point, you will see the list as shown in Figure 0.4 or 0.5.

The list of files and
directories in drive C:

Selected directory
(drive C:)

Click here to
scroll left.

Drag here to
scroll the list.

Click here to
scroll right.

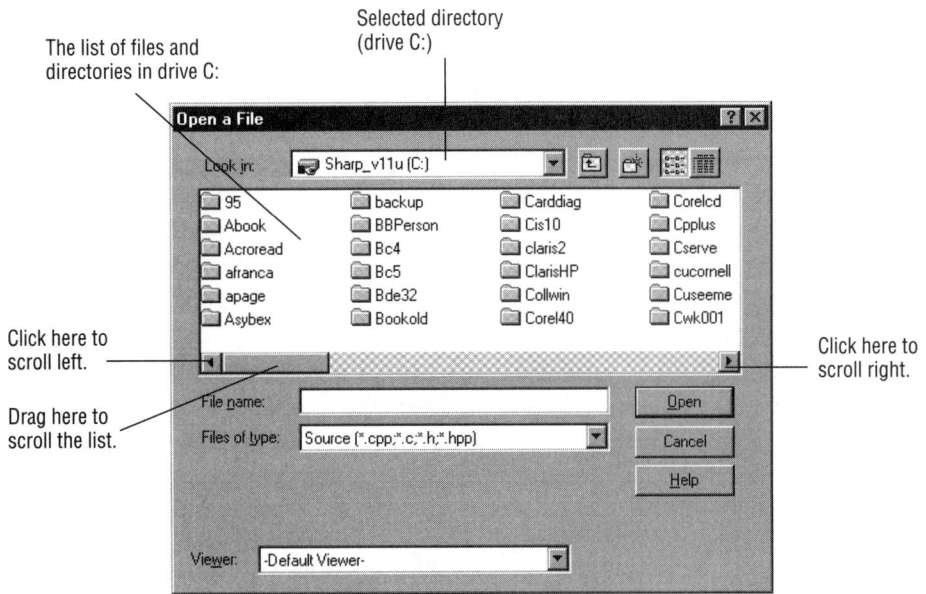

FIGURE 0.3:   Directories in drive C: (Borland C++ 5)

Here is the directory
you want.

Notice that the cursor
has moved.

FIGURE 0.4:   Finding the MYDIR directory (Turbo C++ 4.5)

Here is the directory
you want.

Notice that the cursor
has moved.

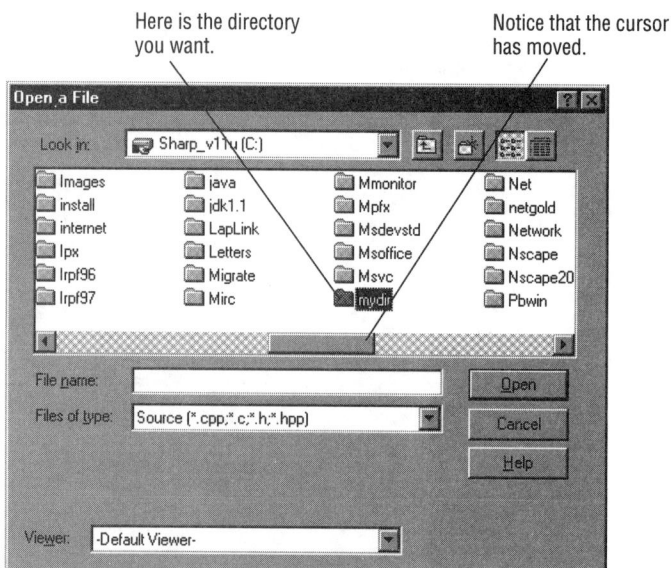

FIGURE 0.5:   Finding the MYDIR directory (Borland C++ 5)

All you have to do now is double-click MYDIR. You will see a new screen, either that in Figure 0.6 or 0.7.

YOUR PROGRAMS AND MINE

As you develop programs or modify those that are supplied, you will want to store them so that you can look at them and use them at any time.

Avoid using program names that already exist in your directory. Also, whenever you look at one of these programs and modify it, try to store it back with a different name (or else not store it); otherwise, you will lose the original program. Of course, if you do that and still want to use the original program, you can always restore it from the Sybex Web site.

It is good programming practice to keep copies of your programs. You may accidentally erase them, and your work will be lost.

The list of files in
MYDIR directory
(empty)

Selected directory
(MYDIR)

One directory up in the
hierarchy (C:)

Directories down in
the hierarchy

The types of files for which
you are looking (C or CPP)

To look for other file
types, click here.

FIGURE 0.6:   The contents of the MYDIR directory (Turbo C++ 4.5)

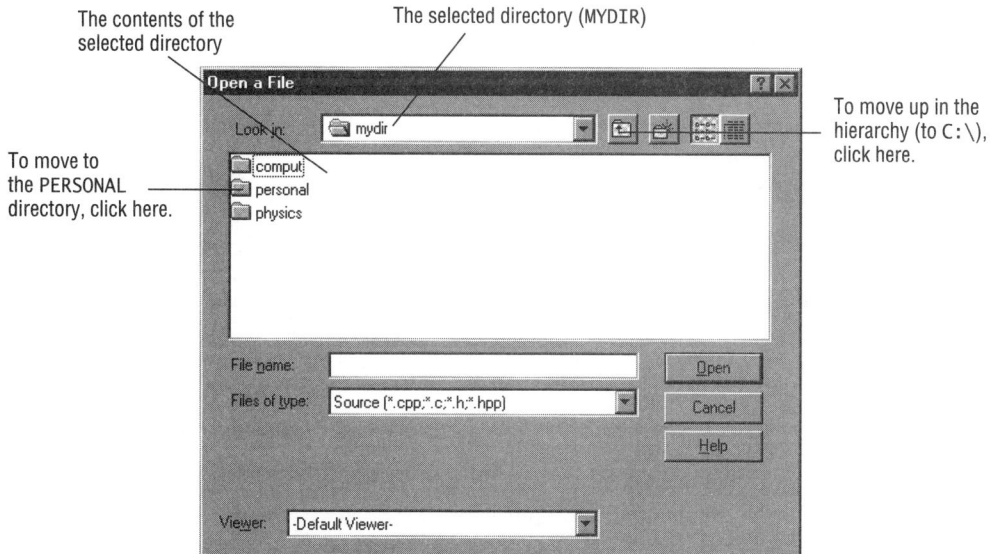

The contents of the
selected directory

The selected directory (MYDIR)

To move up in the
hierarchy (to C:\),
click here.

To move to
the PERSONAL
directory, click here.

FIGURE 0.7:   The contents of the MYDIR directory (Borland C++ 5)

Installing and Using the Software

The purpose of this book is to teach you how to program and how to use the computer to solve your problems. Only the essential information regarding the compiler environment is discussed here. In the menu bar, click Help for additional material.

You can also check this book's home page for more instructions and hints.

Installing the C++ Compiler

Install the C++ compiler (Borland or Microsoft) according to the manufacturer's instructions. It is important that you find out and note in which directory the compiler files are installed.

Installing the Book Software

The software installation consists of the following steps:

- Create a directory on your hard drive.
- Download the files.
- Decompress the files.

Creating a Directory

Before downloading the software, you should create a directory on your hard drive. I recommend that you create a directory FRANCA in the root directory of your hard drive—C:.

You can do this with the Windows Explorer, or you can use File Manager in Windows 3.1.

In the Windows Explorer window, click once on drive C:, then select File ➤ New ➤ Folder. Type **FRANCA** and then click OK.

Downloading the Software

Here is how you download the software from the Internet:

1. Open your Internet browser and go to www.sybex.com. You should see Sybex's home page.

2. Click the No experience required link. You will see another screen listing all the books in the *No experience required* series.

3. Click the C++: No experience required link. This will bring you to this book's Web page. This page may include last-minute information about software compatibility and installation, and hints. It will be clear how to download the software from this Web page.

4. As you request the software to be downloaded, the browser will ask you for the location where you want the file placed on your hard drive. Select FRANCA in your directory hierarchy and click OK.

After a successful download, you should have an executable file (CPPNER.EXE) in your FRANCA directory. You can verify this using the Windows Explorer.

Decompressing the Files

The software is in compressed form so that you can download all of it at once and save time during the downloading process.

The downloaded file CPPNER.EXE contains all the software in compressed form. If you execute this file, it will decompress itself and create all the files.

You can decompress the files using the Windows Explorer:

- Double-click the downloaded program CPPNER.EXE.

Your C:\FRANCA directory will then contain several files and a subdirectory sounds.

You are now ready. You can delete the original downloaded file CPPNER.EXE, but it may be a good idea to keep it in case you need to restore your files.

NOTE FOR NETWORK USERS (ADVANCED)

If the software is in a read-only network drive, it may be necessary to copy it to a read/write drive (such as the local hard drive). The project file *must* be located in a read/write drive as well as the programs that you will develop. It is possible to modify the project file so that you can use object and resource files in the read-only drive.

Throughout this book, you will see references to software being installed in the FRANCA directory on drive C:. You may, however, copy the files to another directory.

Running Your Programs

To run the programs in this book, you will need to use your compiler and the software. The way you work may be a bit different if you are using a Microsoft or a Borland C++ compiler. You can find more specific instructions in the next sections.

(W) WARNING   A specific project file is supplied for each possible environment. If you use the wrong file, chances are you will not be able to run your programs.

Essentially, these are the operations you perform with your compiler:

- Start the compiler environment.
    - You need the compiler running to run your programs.
- Open, edit, and close a project.
    - A project is a set of programs that are linked and executed together. For the most part, you will link your programs with the programs in C:\FRANCA.
    - Most of the programs that you will execute are part of a project. You will have to know how to select a project so that you can work with it. This is what we call *opening a project*.
    - Generally speaking, your projects will contain three files: PAULO.RC, FRANxxx.OBJ (xxx varies according to the compiler you are using), and one source program (initially C_SAL.CPP).
    - Since the project is a set of programs, you will often need to remove (or delete) programs from inside a project or insert (or add) other programs to it. You will always be using the same project. You will replace (delete one, add another) the appropriate source program that tells the computer what you want to do each time.
- Open, edit, and save a program file.

- • The project contains program files. Some of them will remain unchanged, but you will replace and modify others. You must know how to look into a source program file and modify it. You must also know how to save a program that you either create or modify.

- • Execute a project.

  - • When you need to see a program running, you execute the project. Execution of the project causes all the project components to be linked together and execute. If this operation is successful, you will see the results of your program on the computer screen.

  - • If you execute the initial project that contains the file C_SAL.CPP, you'll see a screen like the one shown in Figure 0.8.

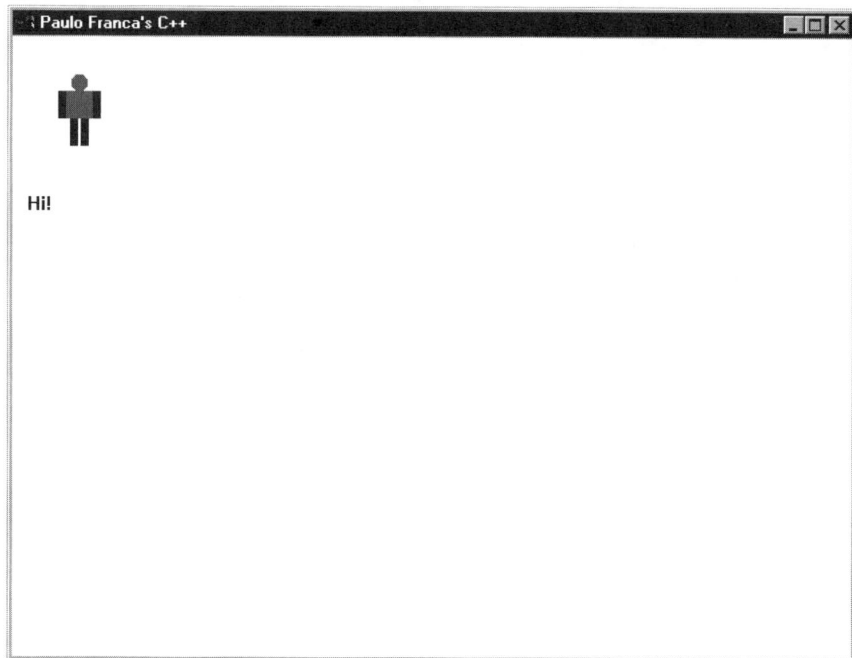

FIGURE 0.8:   The result of C_SAL.CPP

> **NOTE**   Do not proceed to Skill 1 until you know how to perform the operations above.

FILES IN A PROJECT

Out of the files that are part of a project, the one with the extension .CPP is the one that determines what the program will do. This is like a "personality module" in the project. To execute different tasks, you will remove this .CPP file and insert another .CPP file in its place. These .CPP files can be either sample programs or programs that you build. The other files remain to support your work. The PAULO.RC file is called a resource file and is required by Windows to support input dialogs; the .OBJ file is the graphic support for the programs you write. Every time you change the .CPP file in the project, you do a "brain transplant" in the project.

This is how you make programs do different things: write a program to do what you want and put this program in the project as the "personality module."

Using Specific Compilers

The following sections tell you how to use specific compilers. Choose the section that applies to your compiler and read it. Disregard the sections that deal with the other compilers.

The following compilers have been tested and their use is explained in the following sections:

- Turbo C++ 4.5 for Windows

- Borland C++ 4 for Windows

- Borland C++ 5 for Windows

- Microsoft Visual C++ 1.56 for Windows

- Microsoft Visual C++ 4 for Windows

- Microsoft Visual C++ 5 for Windows

> **NOTE**   Check the Sybex Web site at http://www.sybex.com for updated information on compatible compilers and further instructions.

Using Borland Turbo C++ 4.5

If you are using Borland Turbo C++ 4.5, follow the instructions in this section.

Starting the Compiler Environment

To start the compiler, double-click the Turbo C++ 4.5 icon. You'll see the screen shown in Figure 0.9.

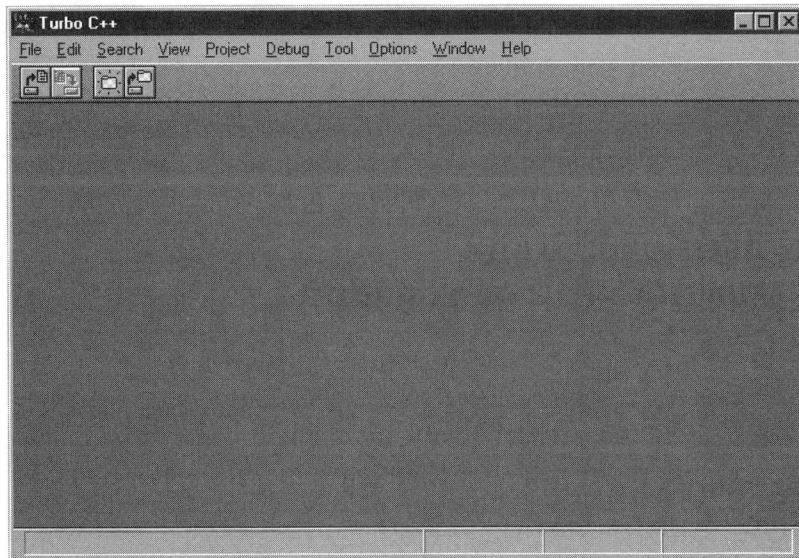

FIGURE 0.9: The Turbo C++ 4.5 screen

Opening a Project

At the top of the compiler screen, you'll see a menu bar:

File Edit Search View Project Debug Tool Options Window Help

Choose Project ➤ Open Project to open the Open Project File dialog box, as shown in Figure 0.10.

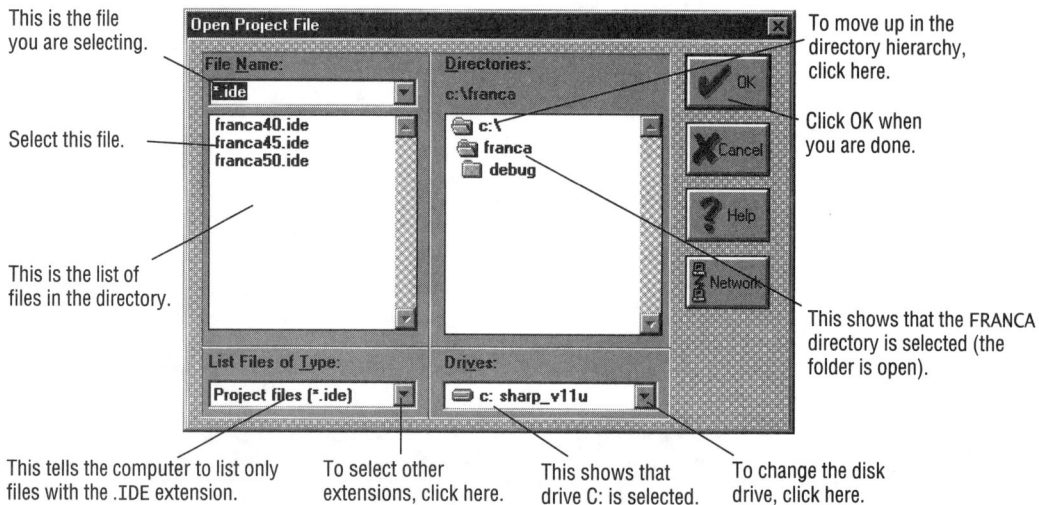

This is the file you are selecting.

Select this file.

This is the list of files in the directory.

Open Project File

File Name:
*.ide

franca40.ide
franca45.ide
franca50.ide

Directories:
c:\franca

c:\
franca
debug

OK

Cancel

Help

Network

To move up in the directory hierarchy, click here.

Click OK when you are done.

This shows that the FRANCA directory is selected (the folder is open).

List Files of Type:
Project files (*.ide)

Drives:
c: sharp_v11u

This tells the computer to list only files with the .IDE extension.

To select other extensions, click here.

This shows that drive C: is selected.

To change the disk drive, click here.

FIGURE 0.10:   Selecting the project to open in Turbo C++ 4.5

Be sure that the directory box contains the directory where the book software is contained (C:\FRANCA). If this is not the case, you can either type it in the File Name box and click OK, or you can select the appropriate directory in the list by clicking your mouse.

Project FRANCA45 is prepared to work in this environment. Select the project by double-clicking it (you can also click the project once and then click OK).

WARNING   Be aware that there are other projects in the list! Each works with a different compiler.

Once the project is open, you should be able to see the project information on the screen.

The project should initially contain the following modules:

- PAULO.RC

- FRANCA45.OBJ

- C_SAL.CPP

The first two files (PAULO.RC and FRANCA45.OBJ) should always remain in your project. The last one (C_SAL.CPP) will be replaced by whatever program you want to execute. The order in which those programs are listed is not important.

CHECK YOUR SKILL!

Make sure you understand how to work with your compiler:

1. Start your compiler.

2. Determine which project you are supposed to use with the compiler.

3. Open the appropriate project for your compiler.

4. Check which files are in your project. Are they the same ones as listed in the text?

5. Close the project.

Editing the Project

The project should contain only one program with the extension .CPP. This is the program in C++ that you really want to execute. All the others are accessories to it. Throughout this book, you will remove one program and insert another in the project so that you can see it running. As a start, the project contains one program that you can view and execute.

Removing (Deleting) a Program from the Project   To remove a file from the project, right-click it to open the shortcut menu, and then select Delete Node.

Click the program you want to remove—*do not* click FRANCA.EXE. Otherwise, you may need to restore the project file.

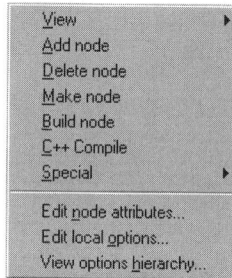

```
View                    ▶
Add node
Delete node
Make node
Build node
C++ Compile
Special                 ▶

Edit node attributes...
Edit local options...
View options hierarchy...
```

Adding a Program to the Project   To add a program to the project, right-click the project name (FRANCA45.IDE) and then select Add Node from the shortcut menu:

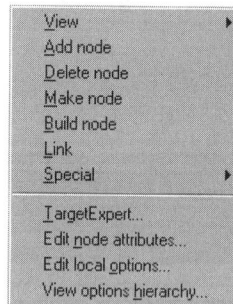

```
View                    ▶
Add node
Delete node
Make node
Build node
Link
Special                 ▶

TargetExpert...
Edit node attributes...
Edit local options...
View options hierarchy...
```

This opens the Add to Project List dialog box, as shown in Figure 0.11. Select the project you want to add.

Type the name you want here, or select if from the list.

Drag this square to scroll through the list.

The selected directory

Add to Project List

File Name:
c_sound.cpp

c_sal.cpp
c_sound.cpp
c1clock.cpp
c1robot1.cpp
c1robot2.cpp
c2change.cpp
c2cinout.cpp
c2clkcpy.cpp
c2input.cpp
c2jmpbd1.cpp
c2jmpbdy.cpp
c2jmpjck.cpp

Directories:
c:\franca

c:\
franca
debug

OK
Cancel
Help
Network

List Files of Type:
C++ source (*.c;*.cpp)

Drives:
c: sharp_v11u

To see other file types, click here.

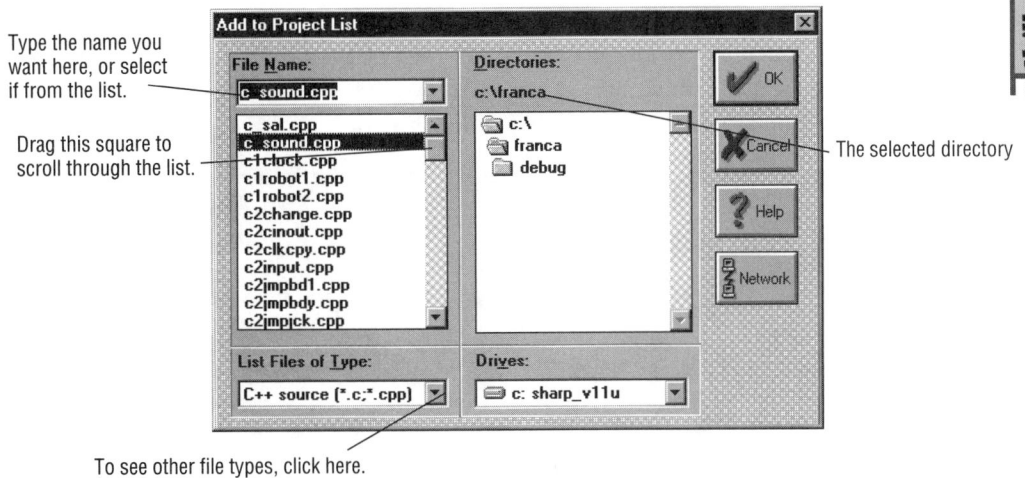

FIGURE 0.11:   Selecting a program to add to a project

Executing a Project

To execute a project, the project must be open. Be sure that your project has one (and only one) program with the extension .CPP. To execute your program, in the menu bar choose Debug ➤ Run:

Debug

Run	Ctrl+F9
Step over	F8
Trace into	F7
Toggle breakpoint	F5
Find execution point	
Pause program	
Terminate program	Ctrl+F2
Add watch...	Ctrl+F5
Add breakpoint...	
Evaluate/Modify...	Ctrl+F7
Inspect...	
Load symbol table...	

Skill 0

If you execute a project with the program C_SAL.CPP, you'll see a screen like the one in Figure 0.8, earlier in this Skill.

After a program is executed, it remains on the screen until you close it. To close the screen if you are using Windows 3.1, double-click the upper-left square . If you are using Windows 95, click the upper-right corner.

CHECK YOUR SKILL!

Here are some practice steps involving C_SAL.CPP:

1. If the project is not open, open it.

2. Execute the project and see the results. Does it look like what is shown in Figure 0.8?

3. Close the window that displays your program.

4. Look at the list of files in your project:

   • Remove the program C_SAL.CPP.

   • Insert the program C_SOUND.CPP.

5. Execute your project. If you have a sound board, you should hear something.

6. Close the window that displays your program.

7. Remove C_SOUND.CPP and insert C_SAL.CPP again in the project.

8. Close your project.

Editing Programs

Often, you may need to modify a program or type in a new program.

Creating a New Program   To type a new program, from the menu bar choose File ➤ New to open a new screen in which you can type your program (see Figure 0.12).

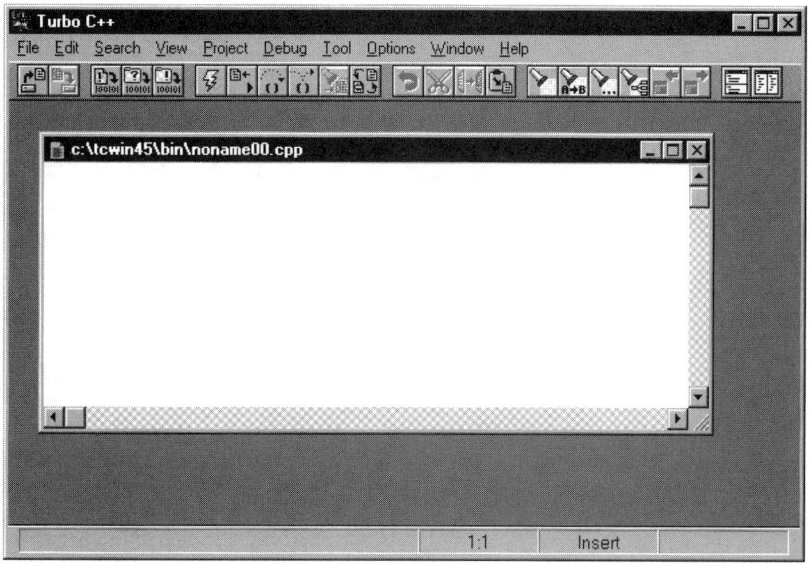

FIGURE 0.12:   The new program screen

The new program receives the default name of NONAME.CPP and is assumed to be placed in the compiler directory. Type your program and then choose File ➤ Save As to open the Save File As dialog box, as shown in Figure 0.13. As you can see, the file name is NONAME00.CPP and points to the compiler directory. In the File Name box, type the name that you want for your file and move it to the correct directory; otherwise, all your new programs will be left in the compiler directory.

Editing Existing Programs   To view and edit a program that is not a part of the currently open project, go to the menu bar and choose File ➤ Open to open the File Open dialog box. If you see the file you want, double-click its name. If you don't see the file you want, be sure that you are in the correct directory. Usually, the compiler displays the .CPP files (source files). To open files with different suffixes, indicate that in this window.

To view and edit a program that belongs to an open project, all you have to do is to double-click its name (C_SAL.CPP, for example), and a new window will pop up showing the program. Do this only with the .CPP program files. Once the program window is showing, click where you want to start typing, as shown in Figure 0.14. The program window appears on top of the project window. To move any window, click the upper rectangle and move it around while keeping the left button pressed. You can also move a window to the top by clicking anywhere on it.

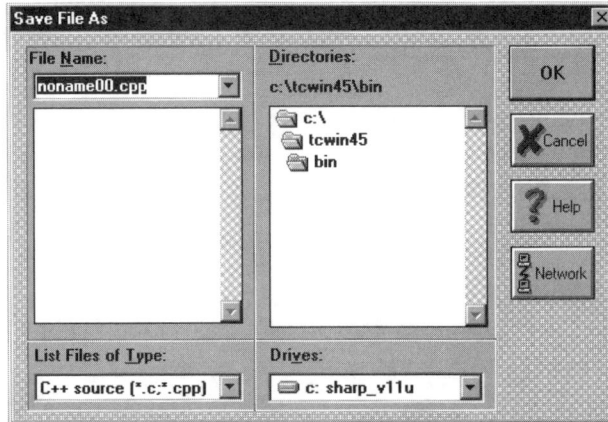

FIGURE 0.13:   Choosing a name and a directory for your program

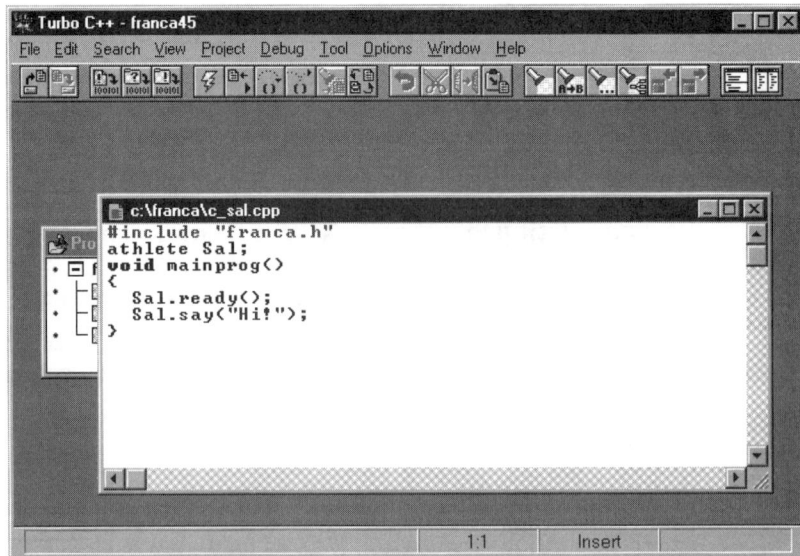

FIGURE 0.14:   Editing an existing program

WARNING Once you modify a program, you will lose the original! If you don't want that to happen, open the program window, choose File ➤ Save As, and then save the program with a new name.

CHECK YOUR SKILL!

Here are some practice steps involving C_SAL.CPP:

1. If the project is not open, open it.

2. Check the files in your project and make sure that C_SAL.CPP is the only .CPP file. If not, remove the other .CPP file and insert C_SAL.CPP instead.

3. Open a window to see the C_SAL.CPP program.

4. The next-to-last line reads, Sal.say("Hi!");. Change Hi! to Hello! (place your cursor right before the *H* and click the left button. Then, type **Hello** and hit Del a couple of times to delete the original *Hi*).

5. Save the new version of the program with a new name, C_SALNEW.CPP. Make sure you save this program in the same directory as the other programs (C:\FRANCA). If you execute your project now, what do you think Sal will say? *Hi* or *hello*? Sal should still say *Hi!* because C_SALNEW.CPP is not part of your project. If you don't believe me, run it.

6. Remove C_SAL.CPP from the project and insert C_SALNEW.CPP.

7. Execute the project. Does Sal now say *hello*?

8. Remove C_SALNEW.CPP from the project and insert C_SAL.CPP.

Using Borland C++ 4

If you are using Borland C++ 4, follow the instructions in this section.

Starting the Compiler Environment

To start the compiler, double-click the Borland C++ 4 icon to open the screen shown in Figure 0.15.

FIGURE 0.15:   Borland C++ 4 screen

Opening a Project

At the top of the compiler screen, there is a menu bar.

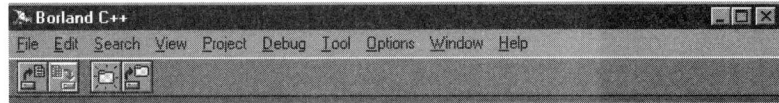

Choose Project ➤ Open Project to open the dialog box shown in Figure 0.16.

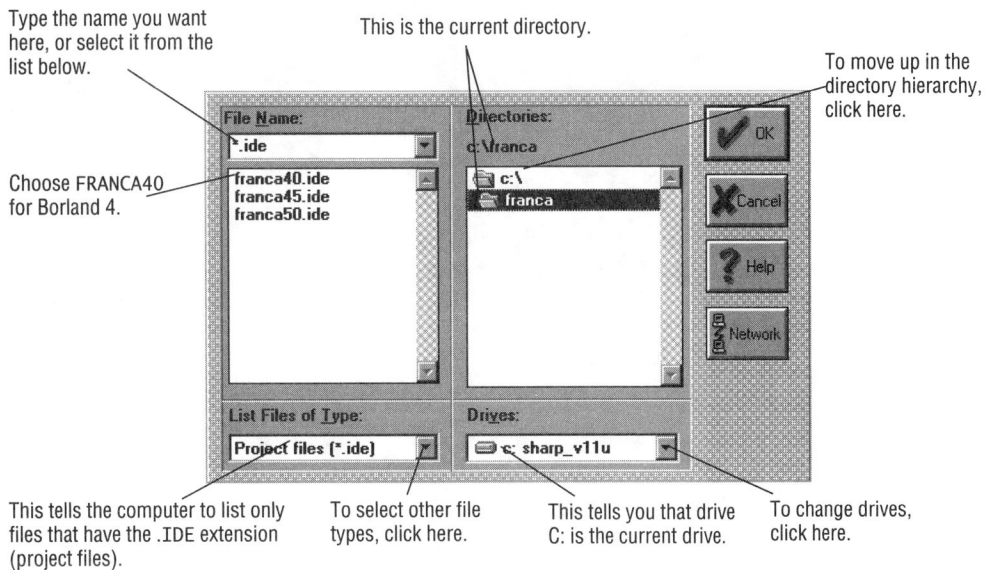

Type the name you want here, or select it from the list below.

This is the current directory.

To move up in the directory hierarchy, click here.

Choose FRANCA40 for Borland 4.

This tells the computer to list only files that have the .IDE extension (project files).

To select other file types, click here.

This tells you that drive C: is the current drive.

To change drives, click here.

FIGURE 0.16:   The open project window in Borland C++ 4

Be sure that the directory box contains the directory where the book software is contained (C:\FRANCA). If this is not the case, you can either type it in the File Name box and click OK, or you can select the appropriate directory in the list.

Project FRANCA40 is prepared to work with the Borland C++ 4 environment. To select this project, double-click it (you can also click once on the project and then click OK).

Once the project is open, you can see the project information on the screen, as shown in Figure 0.17.

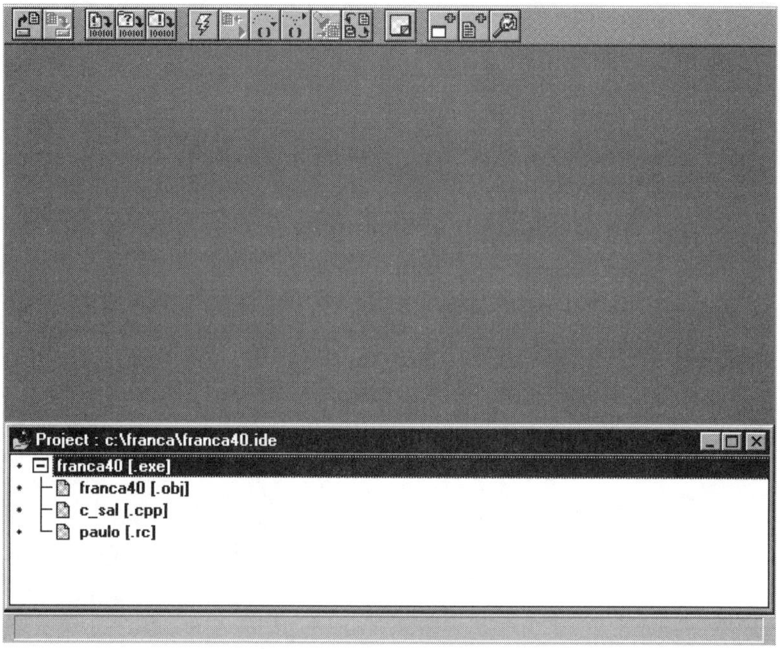

FIGURE 0.17: Open project FRANCA40 for Borland C++ 4

The project should initially contain the following modules:

- PAULO.RC
- FRANCA40.OBJ
- C_SAL.CPP

The first two files (PAULO.RC and FRANCA40.OBJ) should always remain in your project. The last one (C_SAL.CPP) will be replaced by whatever program you want to execute. The order in which those programs are listed is not important.

CHECK YOUR SKILL!

Make sure you understand how to work with your compiler:

1. Start your compiler.
2. Determine which project you are supposed to use with this compiler.
3. Open the appropriate project for your compiler.
4. Check which files are in your project. Are they the same ones as listed in the text?
5. Close the project.

Editing the Project

The project should contain only one program with the extension .CPP. This is the program in C++ that you really want to execute. All the others are accessories to it. Throughout this book, you will remove one program and insert another in the project so that you can see it running. As a start, the project contains one program that you can view and execute.

Removing (Deleting) a Program from the Project   To remove a file from the project, right-click it to open the shortcut menu, and select Delete Node:

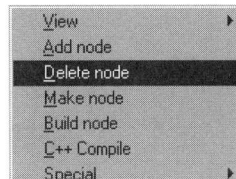

```
View            ▶
Add node
Delete node
Make node
Build node
C++ Compile
Special         ▶
```

WARNING   Be sure to select the actual module that you want to remove. *Do not* select FRANCA40.EXE. If you do, the entire project will be erased, and you will have to restore it.

Adding a Program to the Project   To add a program to the project, right-click the project name (FRANCA40.EXE) to open the shortcut menu and select Add Node:

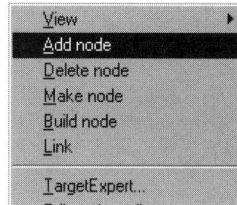

Now, select from a list of files to add to your project.

TIP   When adding a program, be sure to select FRANCA40.EXE before clicking Add.

Executing a Project

To execute a project, the project must be open. Be sure that your project has one (and only one) program with the extension .CPP. To execute your program, in the menu bar choose Debug ➤ Run.

If you execute a project with the program C_SAL.CPP, you'll see a screen like the one in Figure 0.8, earlier in this Skill.

After a program is executed, it will remain on the screen until you close it. To close the screen using Windows 3.1, double-click the upper-left square. If you are using Windows 95, click the upper-right corner of the screen.

CHECK YOUR SKILL!

Here are some practice steps involving C_SAL.CPP:

1. If the project is not open, open it.

2. Execute the project and see the results. Does it look like what is shown in Figure 0.8?

continued ▶

3. Close the window that displays your program.

4. Look at the list of files in your project:

    - Remove the program C_SAL.CPP.
    - Insert the program C_SOUND.CPP.

5. Execute your project. If you have a sound board, you should hear something.

6. Close the window that displays your program.

7. Remove C_SOUND.CPP and insert C_SAL.CPP again in the project.

8. Close your project.

Editing Programs

Often, you may need to modify a program or type in a new program.

Creating a New Program   To type a new program, in the menu bar choose File ➤ New to open the screen shown in Figure 0.18. Simply type your program, and then choose File ➤ Save As to save it to disk.

Editing Existing Programs   To view and edit a program that is not part of the currently open project, choose File ➤ Open. A window should pop up with a list of available files in the current directory. Double-click the name of the file you want. If you don't see the file you want, be sure you are in the correct directory. Usually, the compiler will show you the .CPP files (source files). To open files that have different extensions, indicate that in this window.

To view and edit a program that belongs to an open project, double-click its name; a new window pops up showing the program. Do this only with the .CPP program files. Once the program window is showing, click the mouse where you want to start typing. Figure 0.19 shows what happens if you double-click C_SAL.CPP.

The program window appears on top of the project window. You can move any window by clicking the upper rectangle and moving it around while keeping the left button pressed. You can also move a window to the top by clicking anywhere on it.

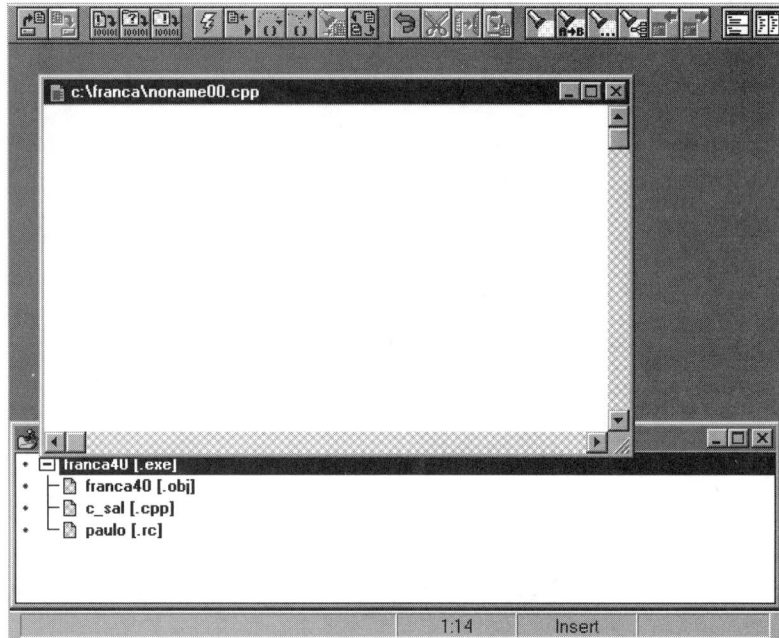

FIGURE 0.18:   The new program (NONAME00.CPP) window

WARNING   Once you modify a program, you will lose the original! If you don't want that to happen, open the program, choose File ➤ Save As, and then save the program with a new name.

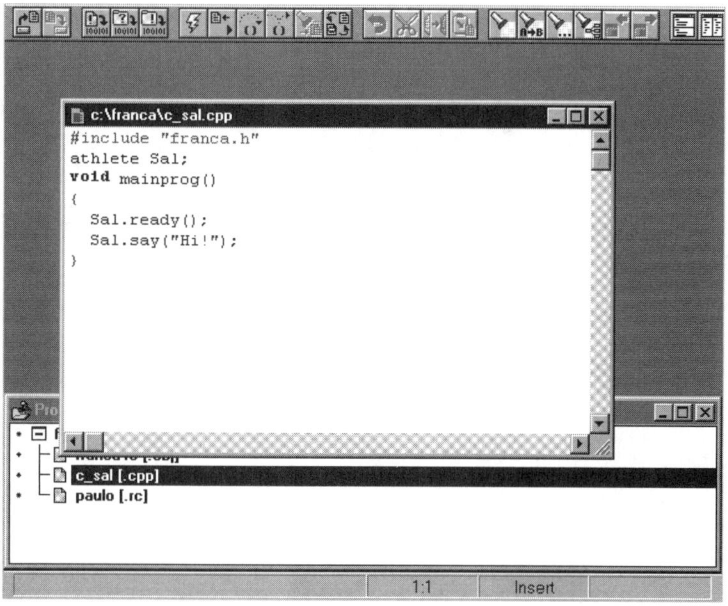

```
c:\franca\c_sal.cpp                                    _ □ ×
#include "franca.h"                                         ▲
athlete Sal;
void mainprog()
{
   Sal.ready();
   Sal.say("Hi!");
}
```

```
Pro                                                _ □ ×
  □
     franca [.obj]
     c_sal [.cpp]
     paulo [.rc]
```

```
1:1        Insert
```

FIGURE 0.19:   Open the file C_SAL.CPP.

CHECK YOUR SKILL!

Here are some practice steps involving C_SAL.CPP:

1. If the project is not open, open it.

2. Check the files in your project and make sure that C_SAL.CPP is the
    only .CPP file. If not, remove the other .CPP file and insert C_SAL.CPP
    instead.

3. Open a window to see the C_SAL.CPP program.

4. The next-to-last line reads, Sal.say("Hi!");. Change Hi! to Hello!
    (place your cursor right before the *H* and click the left button. Then,
    type **Hello** and hit Del a couple of times to delete the original *Hi*).

continued ▶

5. Save the new version of the program with a new name, C_SALNEW.CPP. Make sure you save this program in the same directory as the other programs (C:\FRANCA). If you execute your project now, what do you think Sal will say? *Hi* or *hello*? Sal should still say *Hi!* because C_SALNEW.CPP is not part of your project. If you don't believe me, run it.

6. Remove C_SAL.CPP from the project and insert C_SALNEW.CPP.

7. Execute the project. Does Sal now say *hello*?

8. Remove C_SALNEW.CPP from the project and insert C_SAL.CPP.

Using Borland C++ 5

If you are using Borland C++ 5, follow the instructions in this section.

Starting the Compiler Environment

To start the compiler, double-click the Borland C++ 5 icon to open the window shown in Figure 0.20.

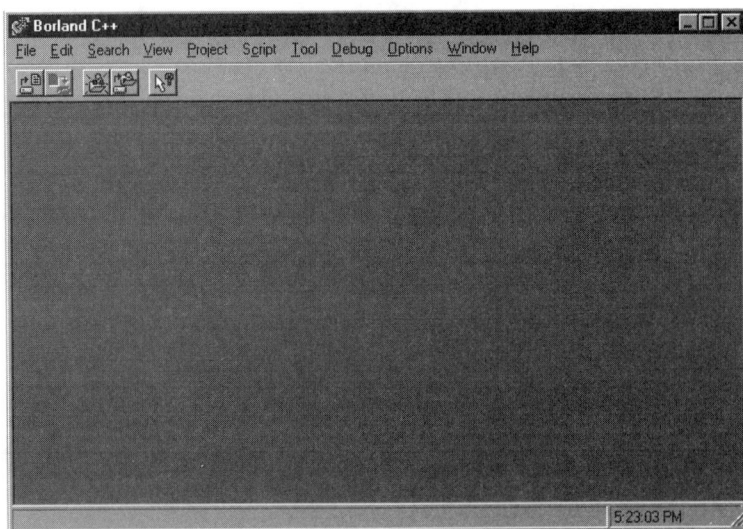

FIGURE 0.20:   The Borland C++ 5 screen

Opening a Project

At the top of the compiler screen, you'll see the following menu bar:

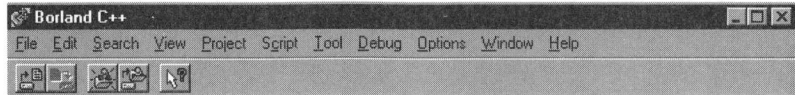

Choose Project ➤ Open Project to open the Open Project File dialog box, as shown in Figure 0.21.

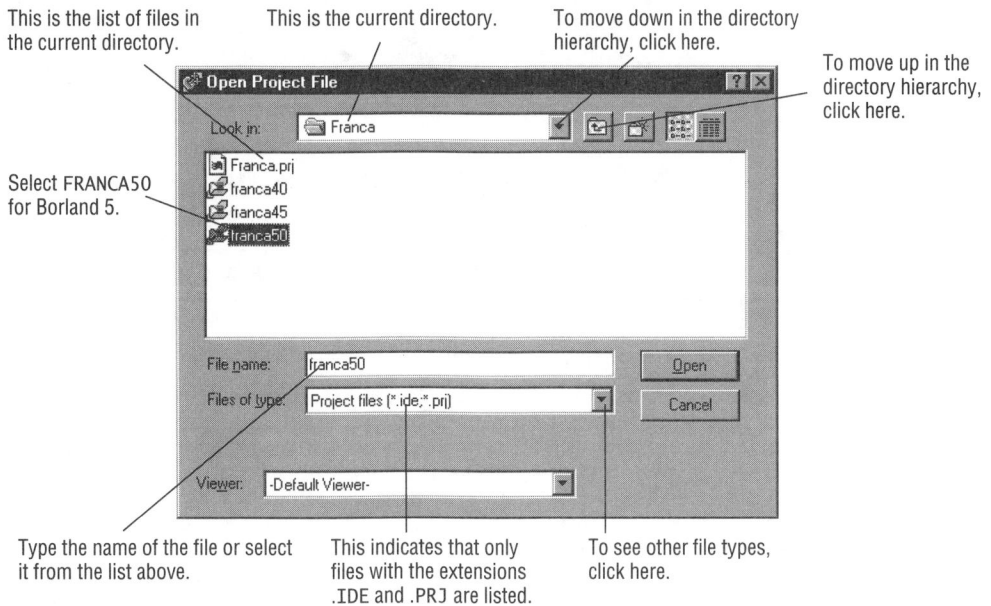

This is the list of files in the current directory.

This is the current directory.

To move down in the directory hierarchy, click here.

To move up in the directory hierarchy, click here.

Select FRANCA50 for Borland 5.

Type the name of the file or select it from the list above.

This indicates that only files with the extensions .IDE and .PRJ are listed.

To see other file types, click here.

FIGURE 0.21:   The open project window in Borland C++ 5

Be sure that the directory box contains the directory where the book software is contained (C:\FRANCA). If this is not the case, you can either type it in the File Name box and click OK, or you can select the appropriate directory in the list.

Project FRANCA50 is prepared to work with the Borland C++ 5 environment. To select this project, double-click it (you can also click once on the project and then click OK) to open the window shown in Figure 0.22.

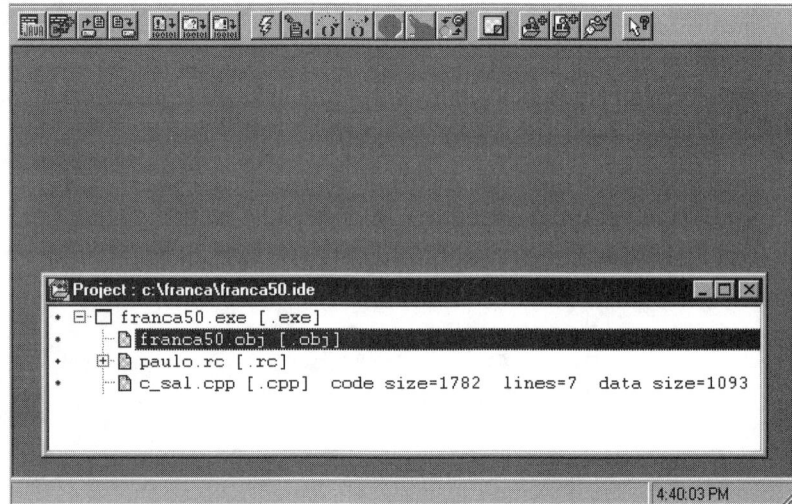

FIGURE 0.22:   Open the project FRANCA50 for Borland C++ 5

The project should initially contain the following modules:

- PAULO.RC

- FRANCA50.OBJ

- C_SAL.CPP

The first two files (PAULO.RC and FRANCA50.OBJ) should always remain in your project. The last one (C_SAL.CPP) will be replaced by whatever program you want to execute. The order in which those programs are listed is not important.

CHECK YOUR SKILL!

Make sure you understand how to work with your compiler:

1. Start your compiler.

2. Determine which project you are supposed to use with this compiler.

3. Open the appropriate project for your compiler.

4. Check which files are in your project. Are they the same ones as listed in the text?

5. Close the project.

Editing the Project

The project should contain only one program with the extension .CPP. This is the program in C++ that you really want to execute. All the others are accessories to it. Throughout this book, you will remove one program and insert another in the project so that you can see it running. As a start, the project contains one program that you can view and execute.

Removing (Deleting) a Program from the Project   To remove a file from the project, right-click it to open the shortcut menu, and select Delete Node:

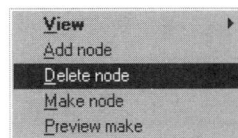

```
View              ▶
Add node
Delete node
Make node
Preview make
```

WARNING   Be sure to select the actual module that you want to remove. *Do not* select FRANCA50.EXE. If you do this, the entire project will be erased, and you will have to restore it.

Adding a Program to the Project   To add a program to the project, right-click the project name (FRANCA50.EXE) to open the shortcut menu, and select Add Node:

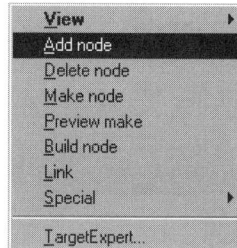

This opens the Add to Project List dialog box, as shown in Figure 0.23. Select the file you want.

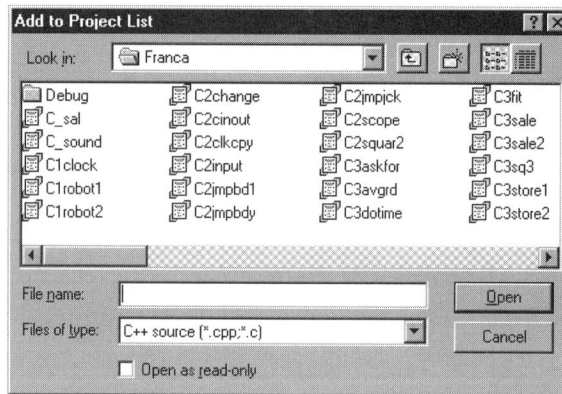

FIGURE 0.23:   Selecting the program to add to a project

WARNING   When adding a program, be sure to select FRANCA50.EXE before clicking Add.

Executing a Project

To execute a project, the project must be open. Be sure that your project has one (and only one) program with the extension .CPP. To execute your program, in the menu bar choose Debug ➤ Run.

If you execute a project with the program C_SAL.CPP you should see a screen like the one in Figure 0.8, earlier in this Skill.

After a program is executed, it will remain on the screen until you close it. To close the screen in Windows 3.1, double-click the upper-left square. If you are using Windows 95, click the upper-right corner to close the screen.

CHECK YOUR SKILL!

Here are some practice steps involving C_SAL.CPP:

1. If the project is not open, open it.

2. Execute the project and see the results. Does it look like what is shown in Figure 0.8?

3. Close the window that displays your program.

4. Look at the list of files in your project:

   - Remove the program C_SAL.CPP.
   - Insert the program C_SOUND.CPP.

5. Execute your project. If you have a sound board, you should hear something.

6. Close the window that displays your program.

7. Remove C_SOUND.CPP and insert C_SAL.CPP again in the project.

8. Close your project.

Editing Programs

Often, you may need to modify a program or type in a new program.

Creating a New Program   To type a new program, in the menu bar choose File ➤ New ➤ Text Edit to open the window shown in Figure 0.24. Type your program, and then choose File ➤ Save As to save it to disk. When doing so, remember to place the file in the directory of your choice (usually C:\FRANCA) and choose whatever name you like by typing it in the File Name box, as shown in Figure 0.25.

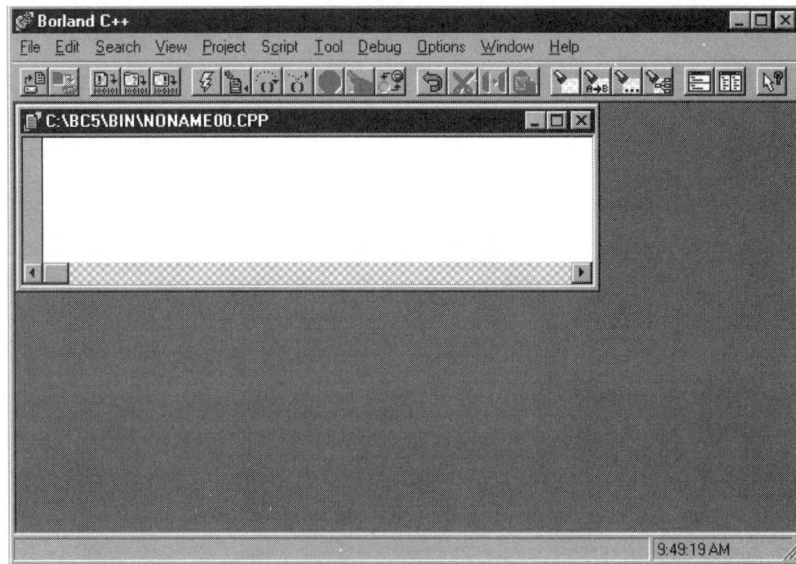

FIGURE 0.24:   The new program window

Editing Existing Programs   To view and edit a program that is not a part of the currently opened project, in the menu bar, choose File ➤ Open. A window should pop up with a list of available files in the current directory. Double-click the file you want. If you don't see the file you want, be sure that you are in the correct directory. Usually, the compiler will show you the .CPP files (source files). To open files with different extensions, indicate that in this window.

Be sure that the directory you want is selected.

To move up in the directory hierarchy, click here.

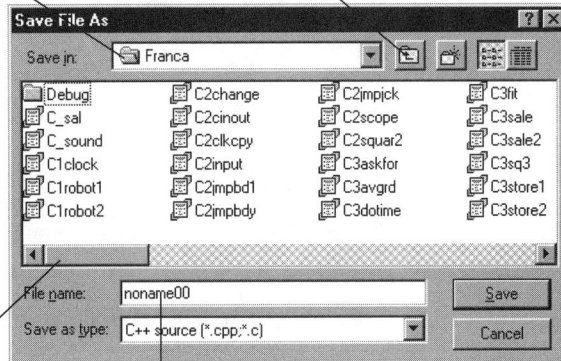

Save File As `? ✕`

Save in: 📁 Franca ▾ 📤 🗂 🔡 🏛

📁 Debug	🖹 C2change	🖹 C2jmpjck	🖹 C3fit
🖹 C_sal	🖹 C2cinout	🖹 C2scope	🖹 C3sale
🖹 C_sound	🖹 C2clkcpy	🖹 C2squar2	🖹 C3sale2
🖹 C1clock	🖹 C2input	🖹 C3askfor	🖹 C3sq3
🖹 C1robot1	🖹 C2jmpbd1	🖹 C3avgrd	🖹 C3store1
🖹 C1robot2	🖹 C2jmpbdy	🖹 C3dotime	🖹 C3store2

File name: `noname00` `Save`

Save as type: `C++ source (*.cpp;*.c)` ▾ `Cancel`

To see more files or directories, drag here.

Type the file name of your program here.

FIGURE 0.25: Saving a program

To view and edit a program that belongs to an open project, all you have to do is double-click its name, and a new window pops up showing the program. Do this only with the .CPP program files. Once the program window is showing, click the mouse where you want to start typing. Figure 0.26 shows what happens if you double-click C_SAL.CPP.

The program window appears on top of the project window. To move any window, click the upper rectangle and move it around while pressing the left mouse button. You can also move a window to the top by clicking anywhere on it.

WARNING Once you modify a program, you will lose the original! If you don't want that to happen, after opening the program window choose File ➤ Save As, and then save the program with a new name just like you save a new program.

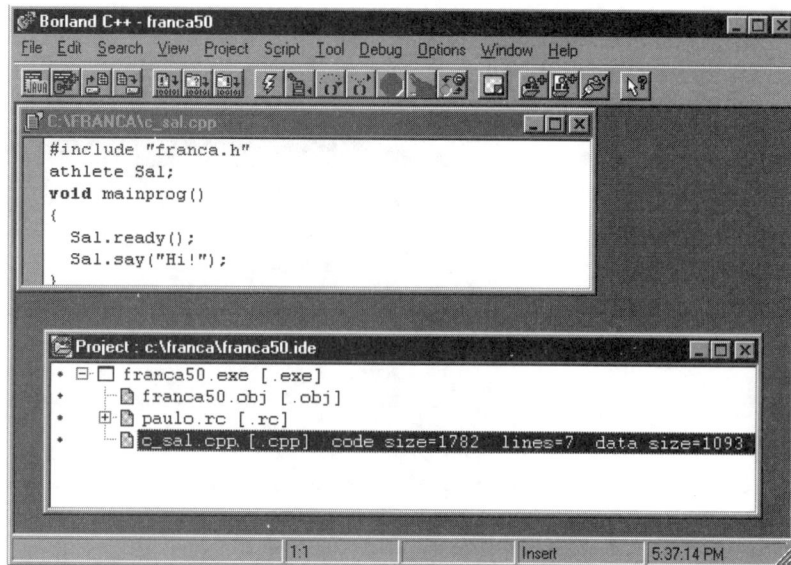

FIGURE 0.26:   Opening the file C_SAL.CPP in Borland C++ 5

CHECK YOUR SKILL!

Here are some practice steps involving C_SAL.CPP:

1. If the project is not open, open it.

2. Check the files in your project and make sure that C_SAL.CPP is the only .CPP file. If not, remove the other .CPP file and insert C_SAL.CPP instead.

3. Open a window to see the C_SAL.CPP program.

4. The next-to-last line reads, Sal.say("Hi!");. Change Hi! to Hello! (place your cursor right before the *H* and click the left button. Then, type **Hello** and hit Del a couple of times to delete the original *Hi*).

continued▶

5. Save the new version of the program with a new name, C_SALNEW.CPP. Make sure you save this program in the same directory as the other programs (C:\FRANCA). If you execute your project now, what do you think Sal will say? *Hi* or *hello*? Sal should still say *Hi!* because C_SALNEW.CPP is not part of your project. If you don't believe me, run it.

6. Remove C_SAL.CPP from the project and insert C_SALNEW.CPP.

7. Execute the project. Does Sal now say *hello*?

8. Remove C_SALNEW.CPP from the project and insert C_SAL.CPP.

Using Microsoft Visual C++ 1.5

If you are using Visual C++ 1.5 for Windows, follow the instructions in this section.

Starting the Compiler Environment

To start the compiler, double-click the Microsoft Visual C++ 1.5 icon to open the window shown in Figure 0.27.

Opening a Project

At the top of the compiler screen, you will see a menu bar:

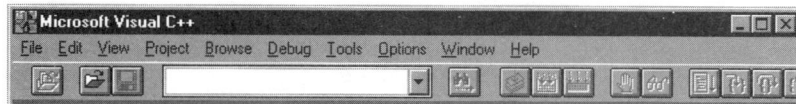

Choose Project ➤ Open Project to open the Open Project dialog box, shown in Figure 0.28.

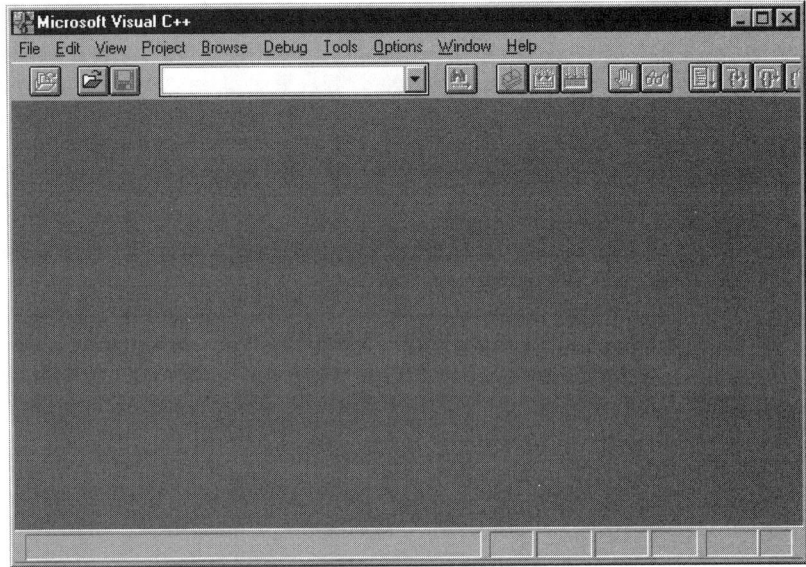

FIGURE 0.27:   The Microsoft Visual C++ 1.5 screen

In the File Name box, type the name of the file you want, or select it from the list below.

The selected directory

To move up in the directory hierarchy, click here.

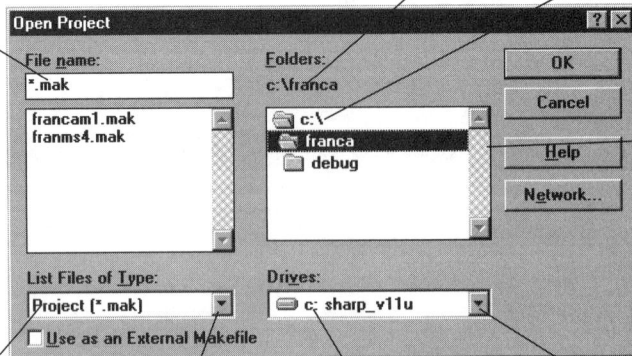

To select more directories, if available, scroll this list.

Only files with the .MAK extension are listed.

To see other file types, click here.

This indicates that drive C: is selected.

To select another drive, click here.

FIGURE 0.28:   The Open Project dialog box in Visual C++ 1.5

Be sure that the directory box contains the directory where the book software is contained (C:\FRANCA). If this is not the case, you can either type it in the File Name box and click OK or select the appropriate directory in the list.

Project FRANCAM1 is prepared to work with the Visual C++ 1.5 environment. To select this project, double-click it (you can also click once on the project and then click OK).

Once the project is open, there is no change to the main screen. To see the files included in the project, choose Project ➤ Edit to open the Edit dialog box shown in Figure 0.29.

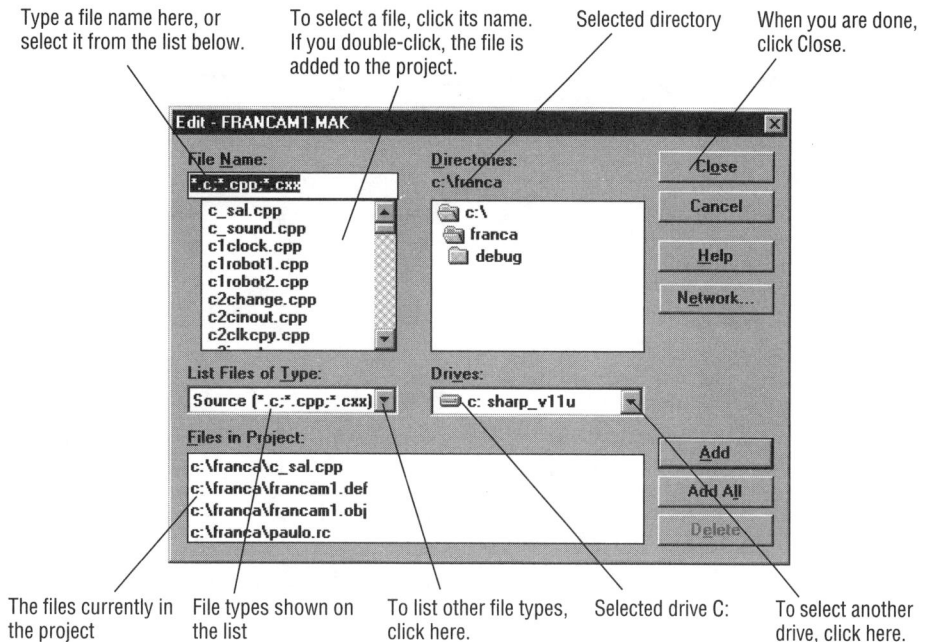

Type a file name here, or select it from the list below.

To select a file, click its name. If you double-click, the file is added to the project.

Selected directory

When you are done, click Close.

Edit - FRANCAM1.MAK

File Name:
`*.c;*.cpp;*.cxx`

c_sal.cpp
c_sound.cpp
c1clock.cpp
c1robot1.cpp
c1robot2.cpp
c2change.cpp
c2cinout.cpp
c2clkcpy.cpp

Directories:
c:\franca

c:\
franca
debug

Close
Cancel
Help
Network...

List Files of Type:
Source (*.c;*.cpp;*.cxx)

Drives:
c: sharp_v11u

Files in Project:

c:\franca\c_sal.cpp
c:\franca\francam1.def
c:\franca\francam1.obj
c:\franca\paulo.rc

Add
Add All
Delete

The files currently in the project

File types shown on the list

To list other file types, click here.

Selected drive C:

To select another drive, click here.

FIGURE 0.29: The project editing screen

The project should initially contain the following modules:

- PAULO.RC
- FRANCAM1.OBJ
- FRANCAM1.DEF
- C_SAL.CPP

The first three files (PAULO.RC, FRANCAM1.OBJ, and FRANCAM1.DEF) should always remain in your project. The last one (C_SAL.CPP) will be replaced by whatever program you want to execute. The order in which those programs are listed is not important.

CHECK YOUR SKILL!

Make sure you understand how to work with your compiler:

1. Start your compiler.
2. Determine which project you are supposed to use with this compiler.
3. Open the appropriate project for your compiler.
4. Check which files are in your project. Are they the same ones as listed in the text?
5. Close the project.

Editing the Project

The project should contain only one program with the extension .CPP. This is the program in C++ that you really want to execute. All the others are accessories to it. Throughout this book, you will remove one program and insert another in the project so that you can see it running. As a start, the project contains one program that you can view and execute. To add or remove files to or from a project, you must have the project opened. Then, in the main menu choose Project ➤ Edit.

Removing (Deleting) a Program from the Project   To remove a file from the project, in the main menu choose Project ➤ Edit. In the window that opens, the lower-left box contains a list of the files that are part of the project. To remove any of these, double-click it. Figure 0.30 shows an example that selects C_SAL.CPP for removal.

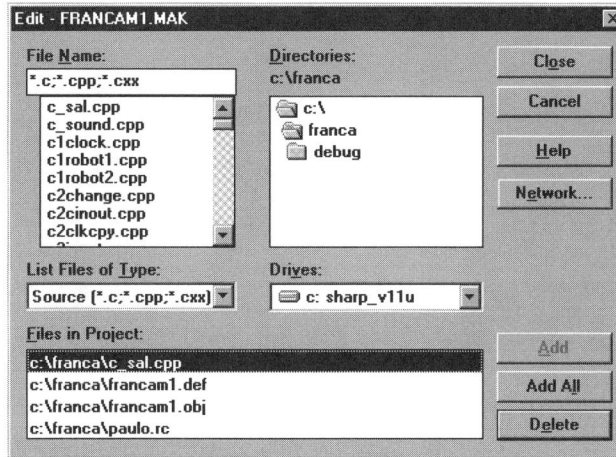

FIGURE 0.30:   Selecting C_SAL.CPP for removal

> **WARNING**   Remove only the source file. The files FRANCAM1.OBJ and PAULO.RC should always be part of the project.

After removing C_SAL.CPP, the Edit dialog box should be like Figure 0.31.

Adding a File to the Project   To add a program to the project, you must have the project open. From the main menu choose Project ➤ Edit. You'll see an Edit window, as shown in Figure 0.31. The upper-left box contains a list of the files in the current directory. Select the one you want to include and double-click it. For example, if you want to include C_SOUND.CPP, select it (as shown in Figure 0.32), and click Add. You'll then see the new project contents, as shown in Figure 0.33.

FIGURE 0.31: The project after deleting C_SAL.CPP

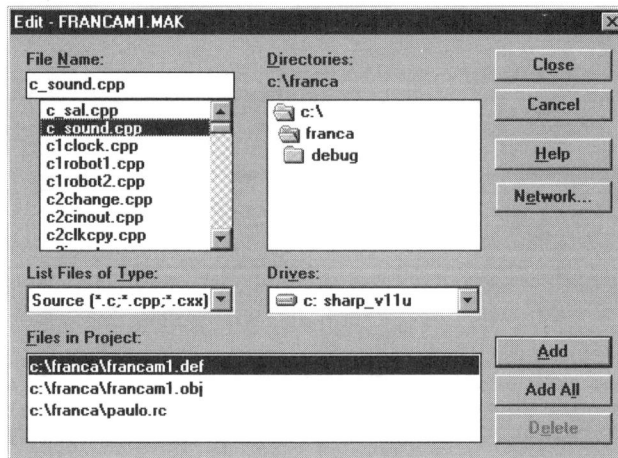

FIGURE 0.32: Selecting C_SOUND.CPP for inclusion in the project

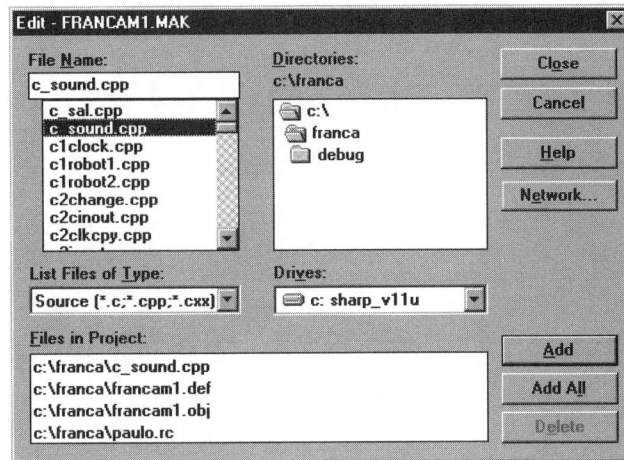

FIGURE 0.33:   The file C_SOUND.CPP is now included in the project.

Executing a Project

To execute a project, the project must be open. Be sure that your project has one (and only one) program with the extension .CPP.

Visual C++ first builds the project (puts all its program files together) and then lets you run it. To build a project, from the main menu choose Project ➤ Build. When the project is built, choose Debug ➤ Go.

NOTE   You can also simply choose Debug ➤ Go to execute a project. However, Visual C++ will ask if you want to build the project (which, of course, you do) and will stop after building it so that you still have to choose Debug ➤ Go.

If you execute a project with the program C_SAL.CPP, you should see a screen similar to the one in Figure 0.8, earlier in this Skill, and Sal will greet you with a sound. Try it!

After a program is executed, it remains on the screen until you close it. To close the screen in Windows 3.1, double-click in the upper-left square of the screen. If you are using Windows 95, click the upper-right corner.

Check Your Skill!

Here are some practice steps involving C_SAL.CPP:

1. If the project is not open, open it.

2. Execute the project and see the results. Does it look like what is shown in Figure 0.8?

3. Close the window that displays your program.

4. Look at the list of files in your project:

   • Remove the program C_SAL.CPP.

   • Insert the program C_SOUND.CPP.

5. Execute your project. If you have a sound board, you should hear something.

6. Close the window that displays your program.

7. Remove C_SOUND.CPP and insert C_SAL.CPP again in the project.

8. Close your project.

Editing Programs

Often, you may need to modify a program or type in a new program.

Creating a New Program   To type a new program, from the menu bar choose File ➤ New to open a new screen, as shown in Figure 0.34. Type in your program, and then choose File ➤ Save As to save it to disk. When saving your file, place it in the directory of your choice, and type the name you want for your program in the File Name box, as shown in Figure 0.35.

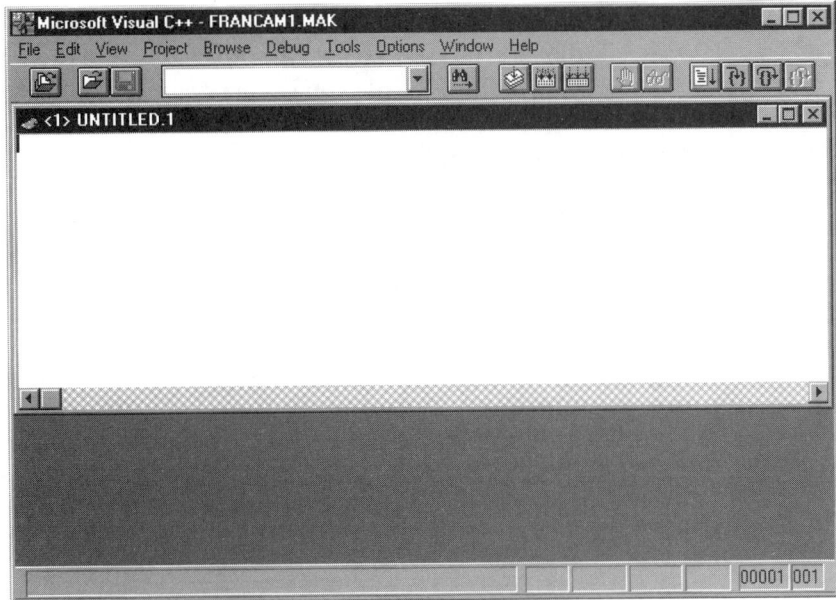

FIGURE 0.34: The new program window

FIGURE 0.35: Saving a program

Editing Existing Programs   To view and edit a program that is not a part of the currently opened project, from the menu bar, choose File ➤ Open to open the Open File dialog box, as shown in Figure 0.36. If you see the file you want, double-click it. If you don't see the file you want, be sure that you are in the correct directory. Usually, the compiler displays the `.CPP` files (source files). To open files with different extensions, indicate that in this window.

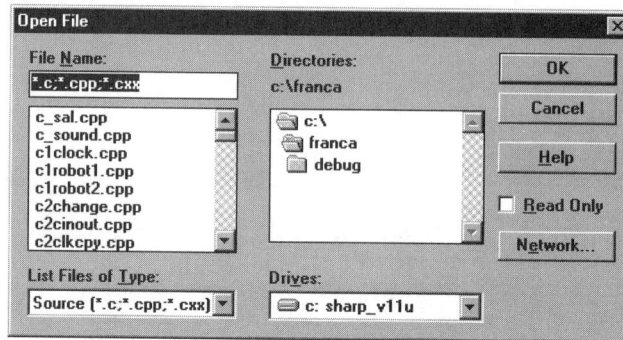

FIGURE 0.36:   Selecting the program file to open

To view and edit a program that belongs to an open project, all you have to do is to double-click its name, and a new window pops up showing the program. Do this only with the `.CPP` program files. Once the program window is showing, click where you want to start typing. Figure 0.37 shows what happens if you double-click `C_SAL.CPP`.

The program window appears on top of the project window. To move any window, click the upper rectangle and move it around while pressing the left mouse button. You can also move a window to the top by clicking anywhere on it.

Once you modify a program, you will lose the original. If you don't want that to happen, open the program window, and choose File ➤ Save As to open the Save As dialog box, as shown in Figure 0.38. Move your cursor to the File Name box, and replace the old name (`C_SAL.CPP`) with a new one of your choice (for example, `NEWSAL.CPP`), and then click OK.

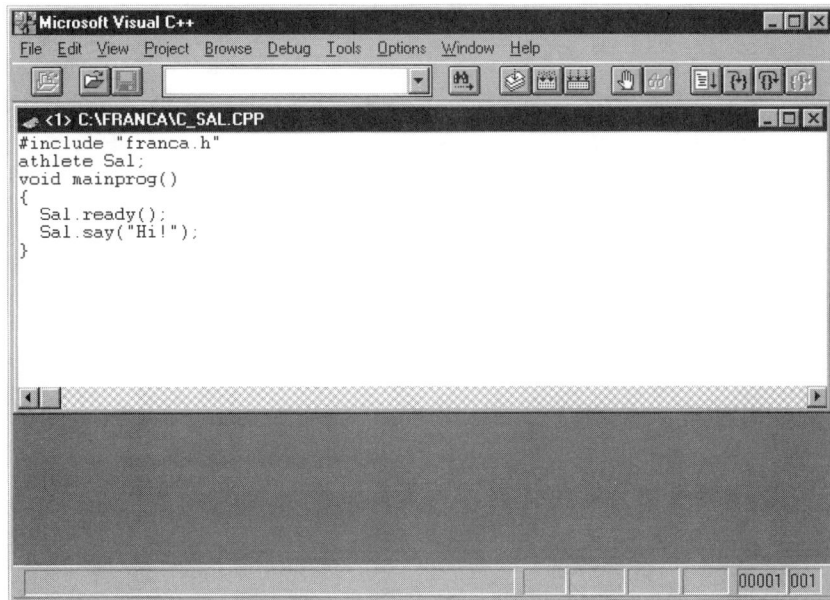

FIGURE 0.37:   Opening the file C_SAL.CPP in Visual C++ 1.5

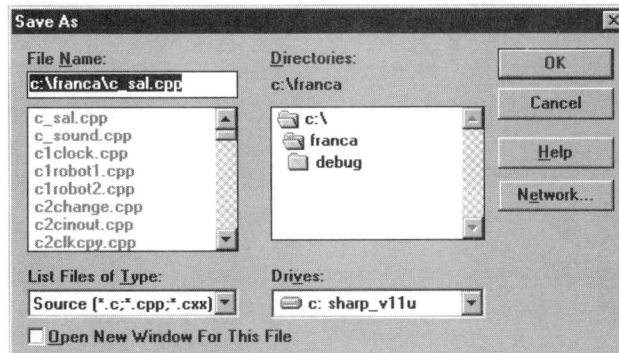

FIGURE 0.38:   Saving a program with a new name

Check Your Skill!

Here are some practice steps involving C_SAL.CPP:

1. If the project is not open, open it.

2. Check the files in your project and make sure that C_SAL.CPP is the only .CPP file. If not, remove the other .CPP file and insert C_SAL.CPP instead.

3. Open a window to see the C_SAL.CPP program.

4. The next-to-last line reads, Sal.say("Hi!");. Change Hi! to Hello! (place your cursor right before the *H* and click the left button. Then, type **Hello** and hit Del a couple of times to delete the original *Hi*).

5. Save the new version of the program with a new name, C_SALNEW.CPP. Make sure you save this program in the same directory as the other programs (C:\FRANCA). If you execute your project now, what do you think Sal will say? *Hi* or *hello*? Sal should still say *Hi!* because C_SALNEW.CPP is not part of your project. If you don't believe me, run it.

6. Remove C_SAL.CPP from the project and insert C_SALNEW.CPP.

7. Execute the project. Does Sal now say *hello*?

8. Remove C_SALNEW.CPP from the project and insert C_SAL.CPP.

Using Microsoft Visual C++ 4

If you are using Visual C++ 4 for Windows, follow the instructions in this section.

Starting the Compiler Environment

To start the compiler, double-click the Microsoft Visual C++ 4 icon to open the Microsoft Developer Studio window shown in Figure 0.39.

Skill 0

The project workspace window

The program listing window

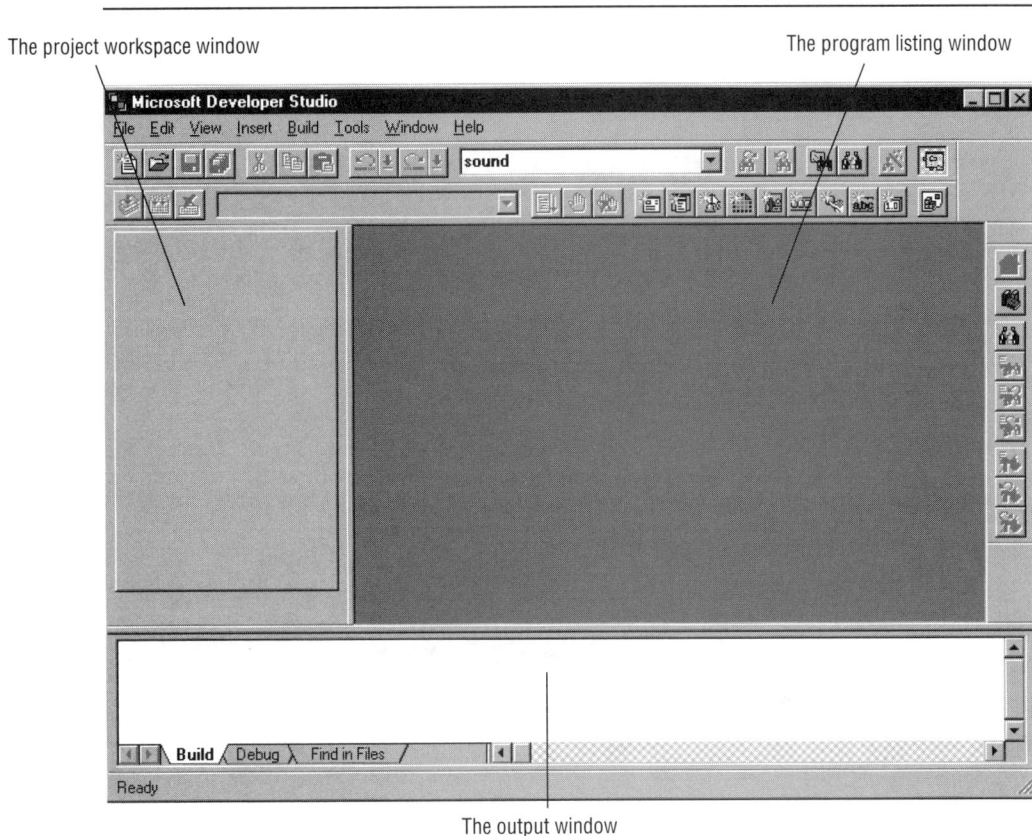

The output window

FIGURE 0.39:   The Microsoft Developer Studio window

The Microsoft Developer Studio window is divided into three windows:

- The project workspace window
- The output window
- The program listing window

You can resize any window by dragging it with your mouse. You can also hide any window by right-clicking it and selecting Hide from the shortcut menu. To view a window as maximized, right-click it and deselect Docking View in the shortcut menu. If you hide any window, to make it visible again, choose View and then from the shortcut menu choose Project Workspace or Output, depending on the window you want visible.

Opening a Project

At the top of the compiler screen, you will see a menu bar:

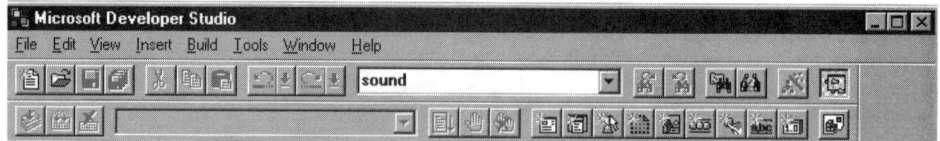

Choose File ➤ Open Workspace to open the Open Project Workspace dialog box, as shown in Figure 0.40.

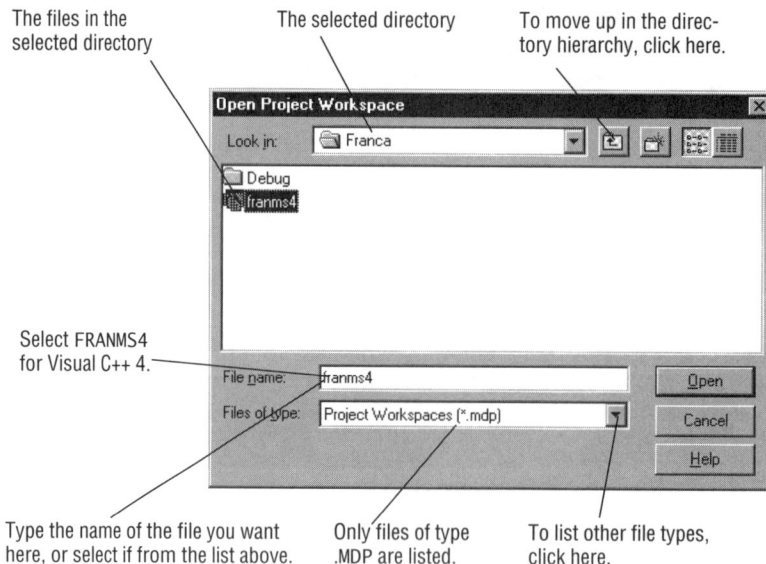

The files in the selected directory

The selected directory

To move up in the directory hierarchy, click here.

Select FRANMS4 for Visual C++ 4.

Type the name of the file you want here, or select if from the list above.

Only files of type .MDP are listed.

To list other file types, click here.

FIGURE 0.40:   The Open Project Workspace dialog box in Visual C++ 4

Be sure that the Look In box contains the directory where the book software is contained (C:\FRANCA). If this is not the case, click the appropriate directory in the list.

Project FRANMS4 is prepared to work with the Visual C++ 4 environment. To select this project, double-click it (you can also click once on the project and then click OK).

Once the project is open, the project workspace window displays some information about it, as shown in Figure 0.41.

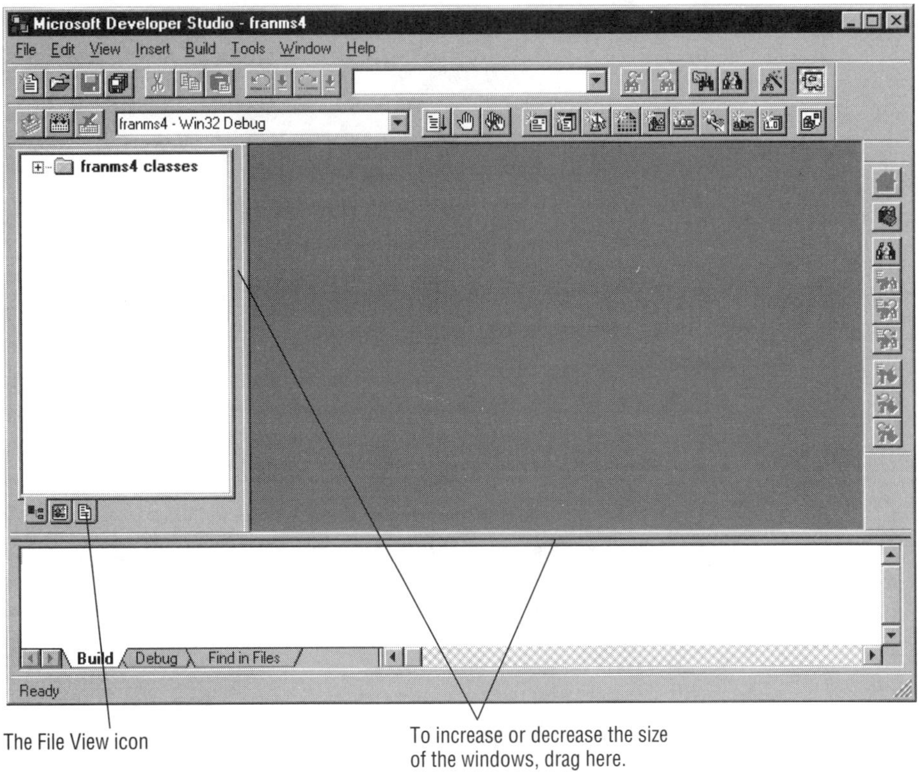

The File View icon

To increase or decrease the size of the windows, drag here.

FIGURE 0.41:   Project FRANMS4 is open.

By default, the project workspace window displays information on classes used in the project. This is not useful information at this stage. To display the files that are part of the project in this window, click the File View icon at the bottom of this window. Now this pane is similar to Figure 0.42.

To see the list of project files, click here.

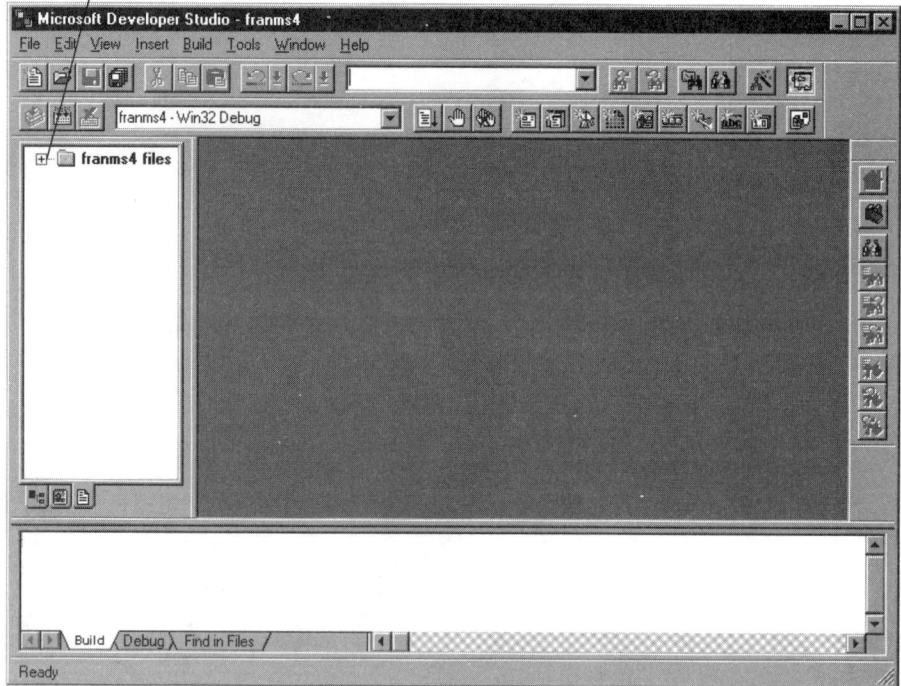

FIGURE 0.42:   The project workspace window in File view

Still, all you see is one name representing the project, not the list of files. Now, click the little square with the plus sign to the left of the project file name (FRANMS4 FILES), and voilà! A list of the files is expanded right there, as you can see in Figure 0.43.

The project should initially contain the following modules:

- PAULO.RC

- FRANCMS4.OBJ

- C_SAL.CPP

The first two files (PAULO.RC and FRANCMS4.OBJ) should always remain in your project. The last one (C_SAL.CPP) will be replaced by whatever program you want to execute. The order in which those programs are listed is not important.

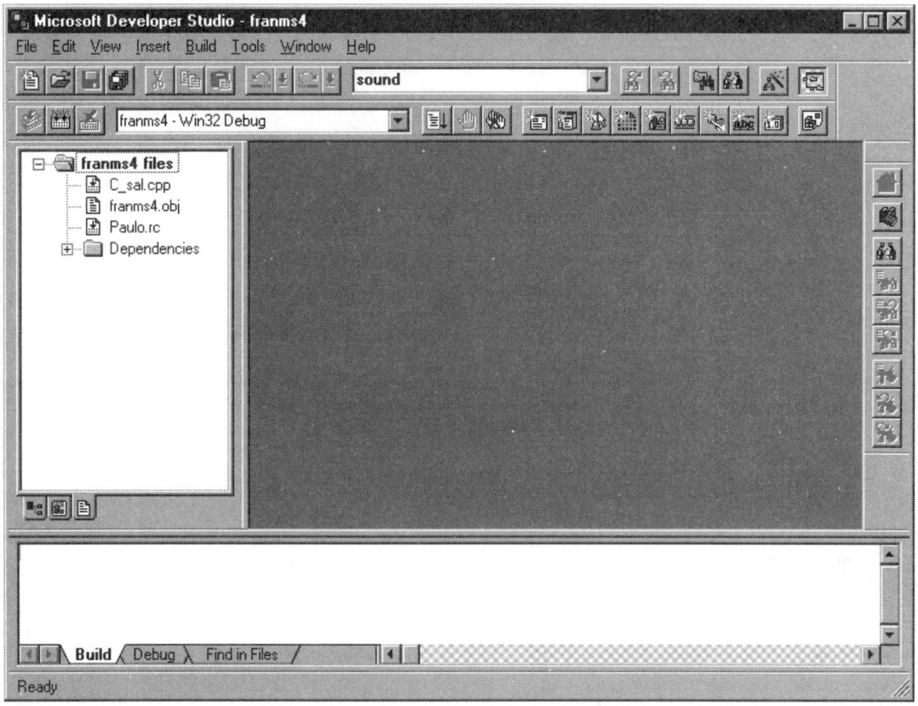

Skill 0

FIGURE 0.43: A list of the project files

CHECK YOUR SKILL!

Make sure you understand how to work with your compiler:

1. Start your compiler.

2. Determine which project you are supposed to use with this compiler.

3. Open the appropriate project for your compiler.

4. Check which files are in your project. Are they the same ones as listed in the text?

5. Close the project.

Editing the Project

The project should contain only one program with the extension .CPP. This is the program in C++ that you really want to execute. All the others are accessories to it. Throughout this book, you will remove one program and insert another in the project so that you can see it running. As a start, the project contains one program that you can view and execute (C_SAL.CPP). To add or remove files to or from a project, you must have the project open.

Removing (Deleting) a Program from the Project   To remove a file from the project, select it in the project workspace window by clicking once on it (if you click twice, the compiler displays the program listing), and choose Edit ➤ Delete.

NOTE   The removed file is not deleted from the disk. It is simply removed from your project.

WARNING   Remove only the source file. The files FRANMS4.OBJ and PAULO.RC should always be part of the project.

Adding a File to the Project   To add a program to an open project, from the main menu choose Insert ➤ Files into Project to open the Insert Files into Project dialog box, as shown in Figure 0.44. Select the file you want.

Executing a Project

To execute a project, the project must be open. Be sure that your project has one (and only one) program with the extension .CPP. To execute the project, from the main menu choose Build ➤ Debug ➤ Go. If you execute a project with the program C_SAL.CPP, you should see a screen like the one in Figure 0.8, earlier in this Skill.

After a program is executed, it remains on the screen until you close it. To close the screen in Windows 3.1, double-click the upper-left square of the screen. If you are using Windows 95, click the upper-right corner.

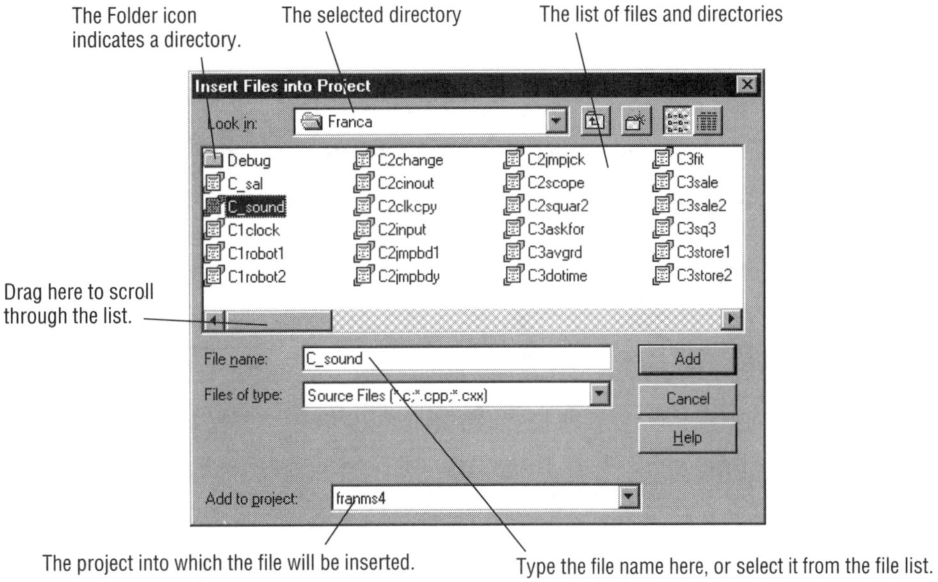

The Folder icon indicates a directory.　　The selected directory　　The list of files and directories

Insert Files into Project　　　　　　　　　　　　　　　　　　 ☒

Look in:　　　🗀 Franca　　　　　　▾　🔼　🗂　🔳 🔳

🗀 Debug　　　📄 C2change　　📄 C2jmpjck　　📄 C3fit
📄 C_sal　　　📄 C2cinout　　　📄 C2scope　　　📄 C3sale
📄 C_sound　　📄 C2clkcpy　　　📄 C2squar2　　📄 C3sale2
📄 C1clock　　📄 C2input　　　📄 C3askfor　　📄 C3sq3
📄 C1robot1　📄 C2jmpbd1　　📄 C3avgrd　　📄 C3store1
📄 C1robot2　📄 C2jmpbdy　　📄 C3dotime　　📄 C3store2

Drag here to scroll through the list.

File name:　　　C_sound　　　　　　　　　　　　　Add

Files of type:　Source Files (*.c;*.cpp;*.cxx)　▾　　Cancel

　　　　　　　　　　　　　　　　　　　　　　　　Help

Add to project:　franms4　　　　　　　　　▾

The project into which the file will be inserted.　　　Type the file name here, or select it from the file list.

FIGURE 0.44: Selecting a file to be inserted

CHECK YOUR SKILL!

Here are some practice steps involving C_SAL.CPP:

1. If the project is not open, open it.

2. Execute the project and see the results. Does it look like what is shown in Figure 0.8?

3. Close the window that displays your program.

4. Look at the list of files in your project:

  • Remove the program C_SAL.CPP.

  • Insert the program C_SOUND.CPP.

continued ▶

5. Execute your project. If you have a sound board, you should hear something.

6. Close the window that displays your program.

7. Remove C_SOUND.CPP and insert C_SAL.CPP again in the project.

8. Close your project.

Editing Programs

Often, you may need to modify a program or type in a new program.

Creating a New Program   To type a new program, from the main menu choose File ➤ New to open the New dialog box, shown in Figure 0.45.

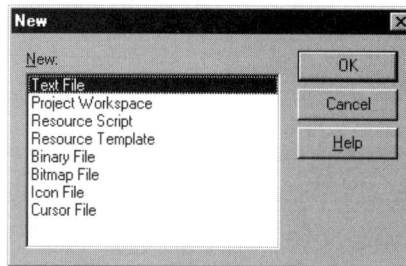

FIGURE 0.45:   Selecting a text file

Click OK to open the window shown in Figure 0.46. Type in your program, and then choose File ➤ Save As to save it to disk. When saving your new program, be sure the directory you want to place it in is selected and then type the new program name in the File Name box.

Editing Existing Programs   To view and edit a program that is not a part of the currently open project, from the main menu, choose File ➤ Open to open the File Open dialog box. If you see the file you want, double-click it. If you don't see the file you want, be sure that you are in the correct directory. Usually, the compiler displays the .CPP files (source files). To open files with different extensions, indicate that in this window.

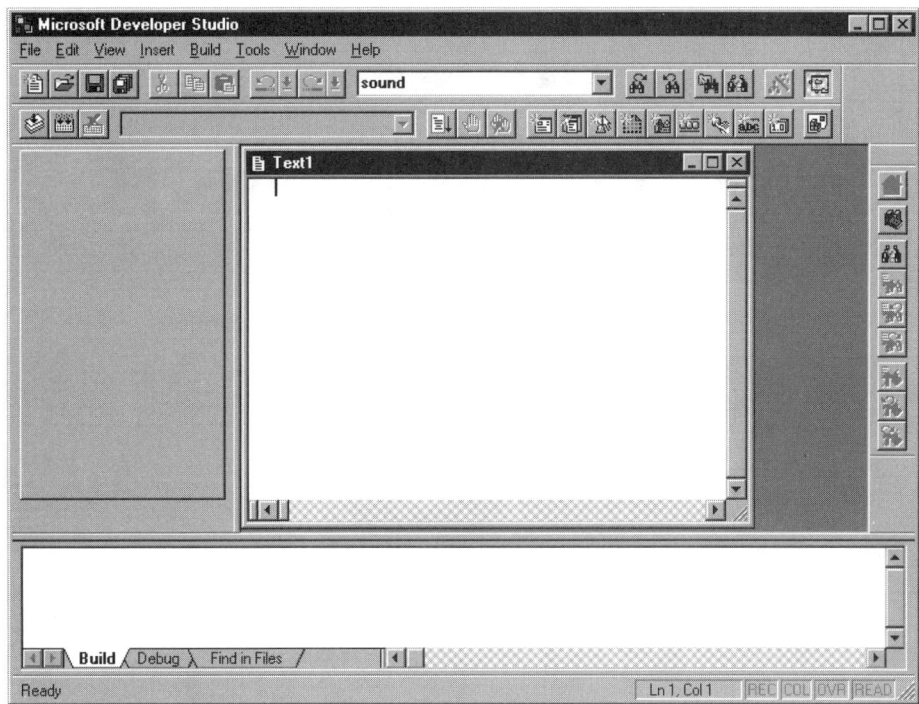

FIGURE 0.46: The new program window

To view and edit a program that belongs to an open project, all you have to do is to double-click its name, and a new window pops up showing the program. Do this only with the .CPP program files. Once the program window is showing, click where you want to start typing. Figure 0.47 shows what happens if you double-click C_SAL.CPP.

The program window appears on top of the project window. To move any window, click its upper rectangle and move it around while pressing the left mouse button. You can also move a window to the top by clicking anywhere on it.

Be aware that once you modify a program, you will lose the original. If you don't want that to happen, open the program window, and from the main menu choose File ➤ Save As to open the Save As dialog box, as shown in Figure 0.48. Now save the program with a new name. Move your cursor to the File Name box, replace the old name (C_SAL.CPP) with a new one of your choice (for example, NEWSAL.CPP), and then click OK.

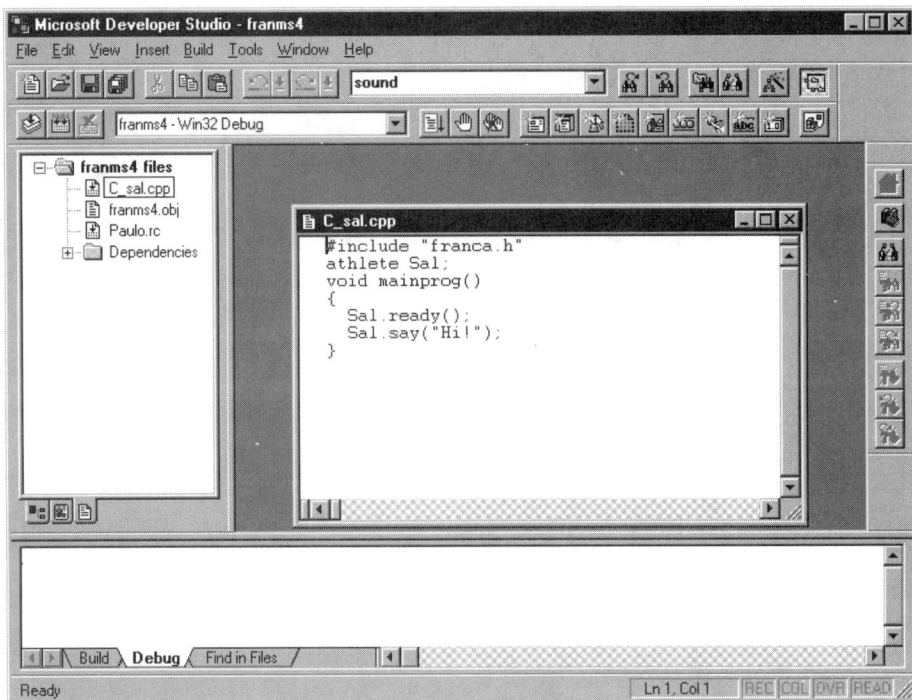

FIGURE 0.47: The file C_SAL.CPP open in Microsoft Visual C++ 4

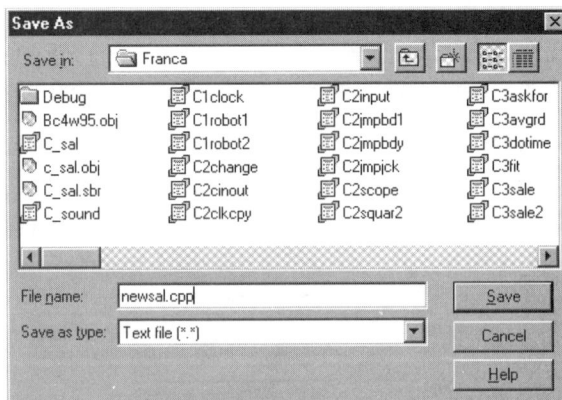

FIGURE 0.48: Saving a program with a new name

CHECK YOUR SKILL!

Here are some practice steps involving C_SAL.CPP:

1. If the project is not open, open it.

2. Check the files in your project and make sure that C_SAL.CPP is the only .CPP file. If not, remove the other .CPP file and insert C_SAL.CPP instead.

3. Open a window to see the C_SAL.CPP program.

4. The next-to-last line reads, Sal.say("Hi!");. Change Hi! to Hello! (place your cursor right before the *H* and click the left button. Then, type **Hello** and hit Del a couple of times to delete the original *Hi*).

5. Save the new version of the program with a new name, C_SALNEW.CPP. Make sure you save this program in the same directory as the other programs (C:\FRANCA). If you execute your project now, what do you think Sal will say? *Hi* or *hello*? Sal should still say *Hi!* because C_SALNEW.CPP is not part of your project. If you don't believe me, run it.

6. Remove C_SAL.CPP from the project and insert C_SALNEW.CPP.

7. Execute the project. Does Sal now say *hello*?

8. Remove C_SALNEW.CPP from the project and insert C_SAL.CPP.

Using Microsoft Visual C++ 5

If you are using Visual C++ 5 for Windows, follow the instructions in this section.

Starting the Compiler Environment

Microsoft
Visual C++ 5.0

To start the compiler, double-click the Microsoft Visual C++ 5 icon to open the Microsoft Developer Studio window shown in Figure 0.49.

You can click any of these book
icons to read about the subject.

The project workspace window

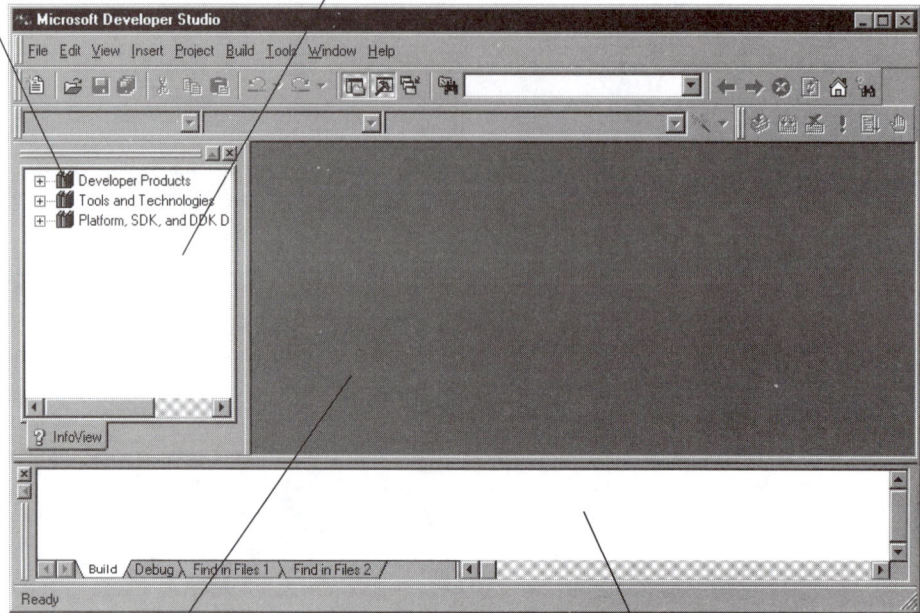

The program listing window

The output window

FIGURE 0.49:   The Microsoft Developer Studio window in Visual C++ 5

The Microsoft Developer Studio window is divided into three windows:

- The project workspace window

- The output window

- The program listing window

You can resize any window by dragging it with your mouse. You can also hide any window by right-clicking it and selecting Hide from the shortcut menu. To change a window's appearance, right-click it and deselect Docking View in the shortcut menu. If you hide any window, to make it visible again, choose View and then from the shortcut menu, choose Project Workspace or Output, depending on the window you want visible.

Opening a Project

At the top of the compiler screen, you will see a menu bar:

File Edit View Insert Project Build Tools Window Help

Choose File ➤ Open Workspace to open the Open Workspace dialog box, as shown in Figure 0.50.

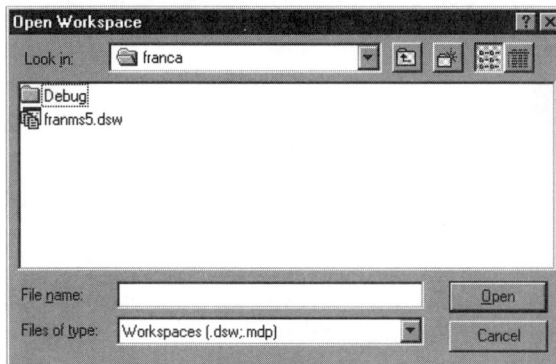

FIGURE 0.50:   The Open Workspace dialog box in Visual C++ 5

Be sure that the Look In box contains the directory where the book software is contained (C:\FRANCA). If this is not the case, click the appropriate directory in the list.

Project FRANMS5 is prepared to work with the Visual C++ 5 environment. To select this project, double-click it (you can also click once on the project and then click OK).

Once the project is open, the project workspace window displays some information about it, as shown in Figure 0.51.

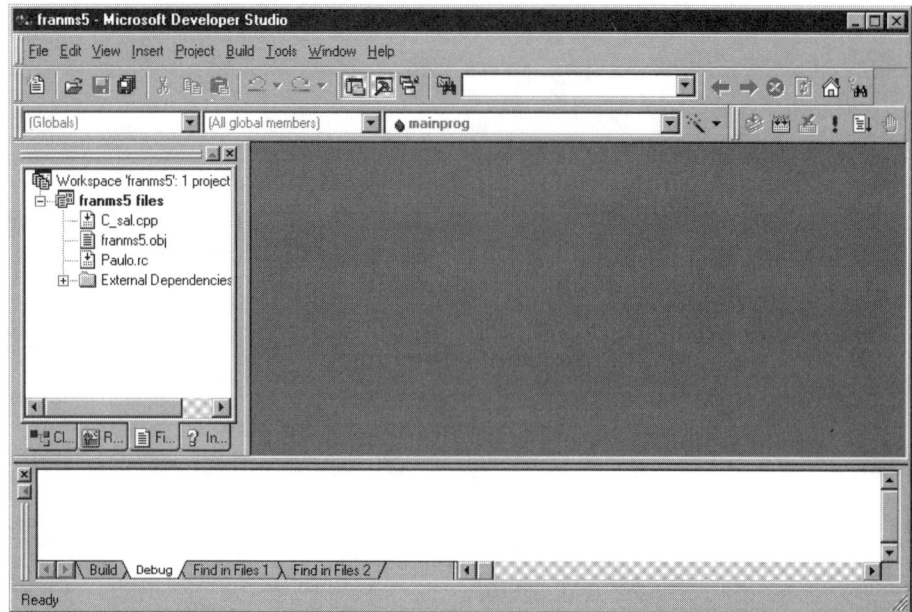

FIGURE 0.51: Project FRANMS5 is open.

By default, the project workspace window displays the files that are part of the project. However, to display other information, click the appropriate icon at the bottom of this window. For now, keep this window showing the files.

The project should initially contain the following modules:

- PAULO.RC

- FRANMS5.OBJ

- C_SAL.CPP

The first two files (PAULO.RC and FRANMS5.OBJ) should always remain in your project. The last one (C_SAL.CPP) will be replaced by whatever program you want to execute. The order in which these programs are listed is not important.

CHECK YOUR SKILL!

Make sure you understand how to work with your compiler:

1. Start your compiler.

2. Determine which project you are supposed to use with this compiler.

3. Open the appropriate project for your compiler.

4. Check which files are in your project. Are they the same ones as listed in the text?

5. Close the project.

Editing the Project

The project should contain only one program with the extension .CPP. This is the program in C++ that you really want to execute. All the others are accessories to it. Throughout this book, you will remove one program and insert another in the project so that you can see it running. As a start, the project contains one program that you can view and execute (C_SAL.CPP). To add or remove files to or from a project, you must have the project open.

Removing (Deleting) a Program from the Project   To remove a file from the project, select it in the project workspace window by clicking once on it (if you click twice, the compiler displays the program listing), and choose Edit ➤ Delete.

NOTE   The removed file is not deleted from the disk. It is simply removed from your project.

WARNING   Remove only the source file. The files FRANMS5.OBJ and PAULO.RC should always be part of the project.

Adding a File to the Project   To add a program to an open project, from the main menu choose Project ➤ Add To Project ➤ Files to open the Insert Files into Project dialog box, as shown in Figure 0.52. Select the file you want. You can achieve the same effect by right-clicking the project name (FRANMS5) and then selecting Add Files To Project.

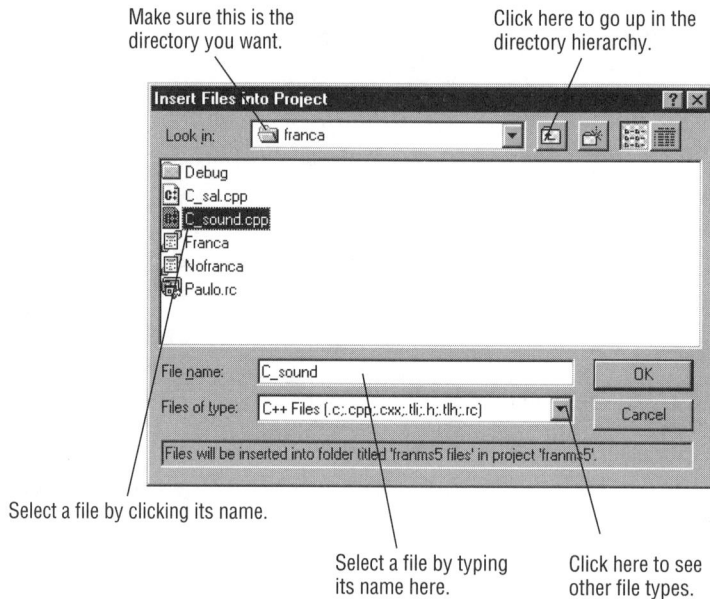

Make sure this is the directory you want.

Click here to go up in the directory hierarchy.

Select a file by clicking its name.

Select a file by typing its name here.

Click here to see other file types.

FIGURE 0.52:   Selecting a file to be inserted

Executing a Project

To execute a project, the project must be open. Be sure that your project has one (and only one) program with the extension .CPP.

To execute the project, from the main menu choose Build ➤ Execute or Build ➤ Start Debug ➤ Go.

If you execute a project with the program C_SAL.CPP, you should see a screen like the one in Figure 0.8, earlier in this Skill.

Before a project can be executed, the source (.CPP) program has to be compiled. If the project is not ready, the compiler will notify you that some files are out of date or do not exist, and will ask if you want to rebuild the project. Just click Yes. Then, again choose Build and Execute.

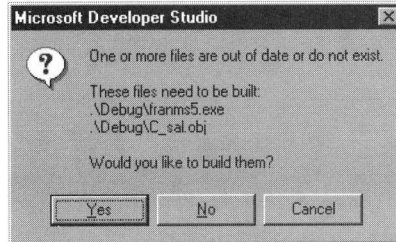

After a program is executed, it remains on the screen until you close it. To close the screen in Windows 3.1, double-click the upper-left square of the screen. If you are using Windows 95, click the upper-right corner.

CHECK YOUR SKILL!

Here are some practice steps involving C_SAL.CPP:

1. If the project is not open, open it.

2. Execute the project and see the results. Does it look like what is shown in Figure 0.8?

3. Close the window that displays your program.

4. Look at the list of files in your project:
    - Remove the program C_SAL.CPP.
    - Insert the program C_SOUND.CPP.

5. Execute your project. If you have a sound board, you should hear something.

6. Close the window that displays your program.

7. Remove C_SOUND.CPP and insert C_SAL.CPP again in the project.

8. Close your project.

Editing Programs

Often, you may need to modify a program or type in a new program.

Creating a New Program   To type a new program, from the main menu choose File ➤ New to open the New dialog box, as shown in Figure 0.53.

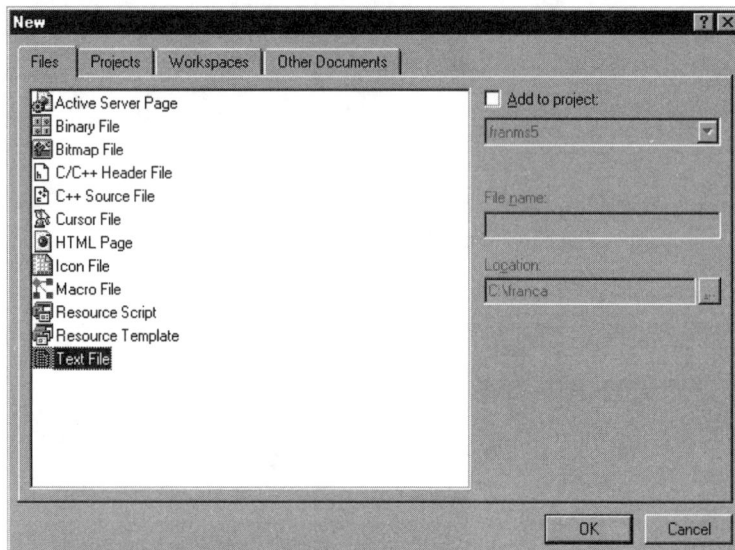

FIGURE 0.53:   Selecting a text file

Click OK to open the window shown in Figure 0.54. Type in your program, and then choose File ➤ Save As to save it to disk. When saving your new program, be sure the directory you want to place it in is selected and then type the new program name in the File Name box.

Editing Existing Programs   To view and edit a program that is not a part of the currently open project, from the main menu, choose File ➤ Open to open the File Open dialog box. If you see the file you want, double-click it. If you don't see the file you want, be sure that you are in the correct directory. Usually, the compiler displays the .CPP files (source files). To open files with different extensions, indicate that in this window.

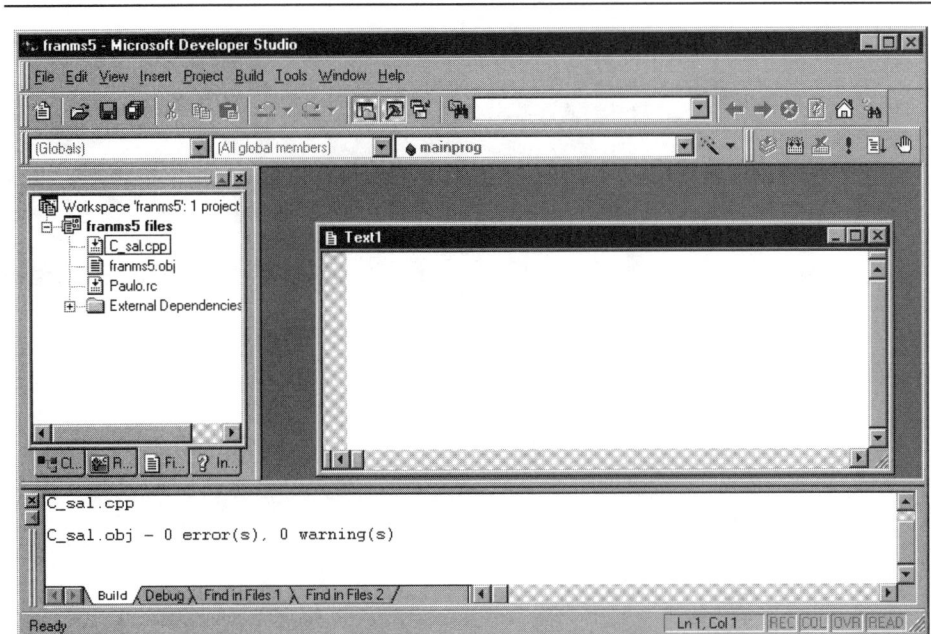

FIGURE 0.54:   The new program window

To view and edit a program that belongs to an open project, all you have to do is to double-click its name, and a new window pops up showing the program. Do this only with the .CPP program files. Once the program window is showing, click where you want to start typing. Figure 0.55 shows what happens if you double-click C_SAL.CPP.

Be aware that once you modify a program, you will lose the original. If you don't want that to happen, open the program window, and from the main menu choose File ➤ Save As to open the Save As dialog box, as shown in Figure 0.56. Now save the program with a new name. Move your cursor to the File Name box, replace the old name (C_SAL.CPP) with a new one of your choice (for example, NEWSAL.CPP), and then click OK.

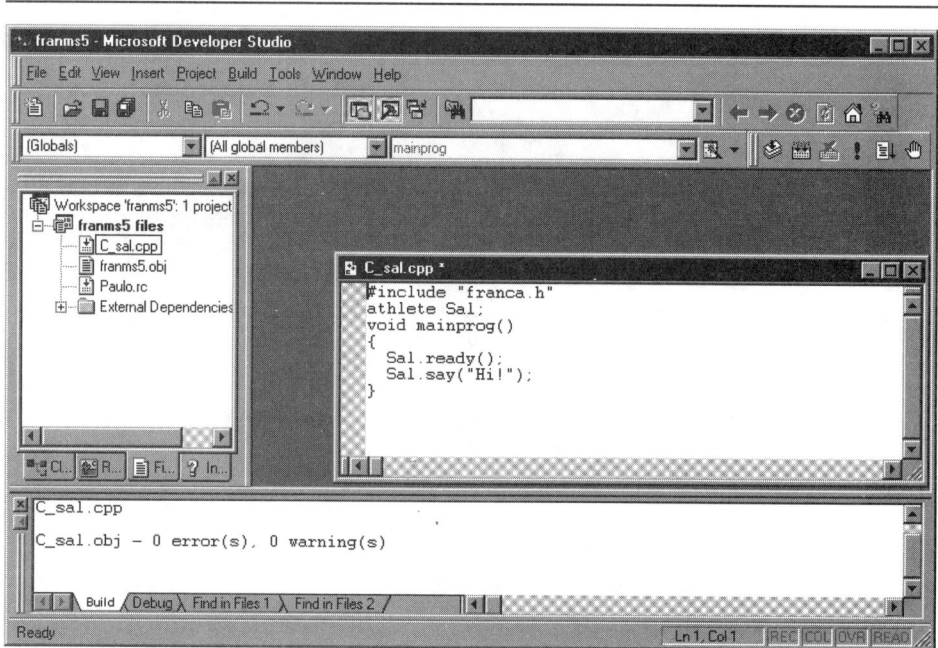

FIGURE 0.55: The file C_SAL.CPP open in Microsoft Visual C++ 5

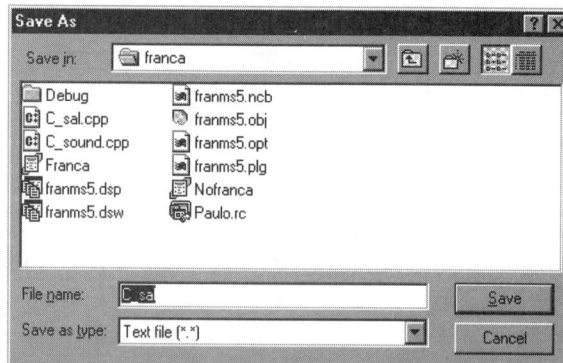

FIGURE 0.56: Saving a program with a new name

Check Your Skill!

Here are some practice steps involving C_SAL.CPP:

1. If the project is not open, open it.

2. Check the files in your project and make sure that C_SAL.CPP is the only .CPP file. If not, remove the other .CPP file and insert C_SAL.CPP instead.

3. Open a window to see the C_SAL.CPP program.

4. The next-to-last line reads, Sal.say("Hi!");. Change Hi! to Hello! (place your cursor right before the *H* and click the left button. Then, type **Hello** and hit Del a couple of times to delete the original *Hi*).

5. Save the new version of the program with a new name, C_SALNEW.CPP. Make sure you save this program in the same directory as the other programs (C:\FRANCA). If you execute your project now, what do you think Sal will say? *Hi* or *hello*? Sal should still say *Hi!* because C_SALNEW.CPP is not part of your project. If you don't believe me, run it.

6. Remove C_SAL.CPP from the project and insert C_SALNEW.CPP.

7. Execute the project. Does Sal now say *hello*?

8. Remove C_SALNEW.CPP from the project and insert C_SAL.CPP.

Problems?   If you are able to perform all the steps correctly, but the program fails to run, there is a good chance that the compiler could not find the file FRANCA.H or one of the other files it needed.

NOTE   Your project should be in the same directory as all the book software (C:\FRANCA).

USING SOUNDS

You can include sounds in your programs. You don't really need a sound board, but, in that case, you must install a sound driver to use your computer speaker. I am not encouraging the use of sound, because you can imagine what will happen in a computer lab! However, it may be a good idea to produce your own sounds and play them with the programs you develop.

To use sounds in your programs, you need sounds stored in .WAV format. Most sound boards can record a sound and store it in this format.

To test your computer ability, run the program C_SOUND.CPP listed below:

```
#include "franca.h"
athlete Sal;                    // c_sound.cpp
void mainprog()
{
  Sal.ready();
  sound("hello.wav");
}
```

Are You Experienced?

Now you can. . .

☑ Understand the problems involved in computer programming

☑ Open projects and replace programs in projects

☑ Modify programs

☑ Create new program files

☑ Save program files

☑ Run a sample program that uses the book's software by using your C++ compiler

PART I

Getting Ready

In Part I, you will develop your basic skills in understanding and writing simple programs. By now, you should know how to use the C++ compiler as described in Part 0.

Computer programs are directions that tell the computer how to solve a problem. The simplest kinds of problems can be solved in a straight sequence of steps. These sequential programs do not check for any conditions, nor do they contain any repetitions. We will be dealing with these kinds of programs in Part I.

By the end of Part I, you will be able to understand, modify, and create simple programs; to communicate with the user; and to solve simple problems.

Making and Modifying Programs

- ❑ Understanding program statements
- ❑ Sending messages to objects
- ❑ Understanding arguments
- ❑ Using *athlete* objects
- ❑ Adding comments

This Skill will help you understand how simple computer programs are written. We'll use a friendly "athlete" named Sal in several programs. You'll be able to display Sal on the screen, where he will perform some exercises and "say" a few words.

A Simple First Program

We start with a simple computer program that you can immediately run on your computer. Try this program as soon as possible, because later you'll need to know how to use your computer to run other programs. To run this program, you use the project facility of your C++ compiler.

> **NOTE**   See Skill 0 for instructions on the appropriate way to run programs in your environment.

This program, c_sal.cpp, displays a picture on the screen. Here is the actual content of the program:

```
#include "franca.h"
athlete Sal;
void mainprog()
    {
        Sal.ready();
        Sal.say("Hi!");
    }
```

Let's look at what each line does.

#include ...   This line tells the computer to fetch other lines that I, the author, have prepared, and include them in your program. These extra lines contain instructions for the computer to make your programs easier and more interesting. The computer knows these lines by the file name franca.h. As a matter of fact, this line does not belong to the C++ language. It instructs the compiler (more specifically, a part of the compiler called the *preprocessor*) to locate these previously prepared program parts and pretend they were inserted at that point in your program.

It is possible to use pieces of programs that either you or somebody else developed in your programs. This is a real time saver! Several actions that we need to perform frequently may be provided with the compiler, bought from an independent vendor, or made available by colleagues. We then use the #include directive to incorporate them in our programs.

athlete Sal;   We are going to use one particular object to help you write your first programs. This object creates a picture in which one person performs fitness exercises. In franca.h, we explain to the computer that we will use one particular kind, or *class*, of object; we call this class athlete.

We named our athlete Sal. This line simply explains that Sal is an object of the class athlete. Since objects of the class athlete have pictures in several positions, Sal will have these, too.

void mainprog( )   This line begins to describe the main set of actions you want the computer to perform. These actions consist of the instructions enclosed within the opening and closing braces ({ }) shown on the next line and a few lines below.

NOTE   In C++, braces delimit a set of actions.

Actually, in C++, the main set of actions is denoted by main or winmain. The name mainprog is used only with the software for this book. Later Skills explain this distinction in detail.

NOTE   Using mainprog to name the main function is an educational trick. The actual winmain function is embedded in the supplied software. This software, which interfaces with Windows' graphic environment, has to be known by this name to the system. However, our programs will call the main function mainprog, so that you can explain what you want done. We will be naming our programs mainprog until we reach Part VIII.

Sal.ready( );   This line says that we want Sal to be ready (ready means to assume the initial position for the exercise). To do this, we send a message (ready) to our object (Sal). The usual format for sending messages is the object name (Sal), a dot, and the message name (ready). The message name is followed by parentheses.

Sal.say("Hi!");   This is another message we send to Sal. We want Sal to say "hi," and this is an easy way to do that. Will Sal actually speak? Well, not yet, but you will get his message! Notice that, in this case, something is inside the parentheses—what we want Sal to say. Enclose Sal's word in double quotes.

You can run this program right now if you like. Put your C++ compiler to work, and open the appropriate project. Examine the program and run it! Figure 1.1 shows the result.

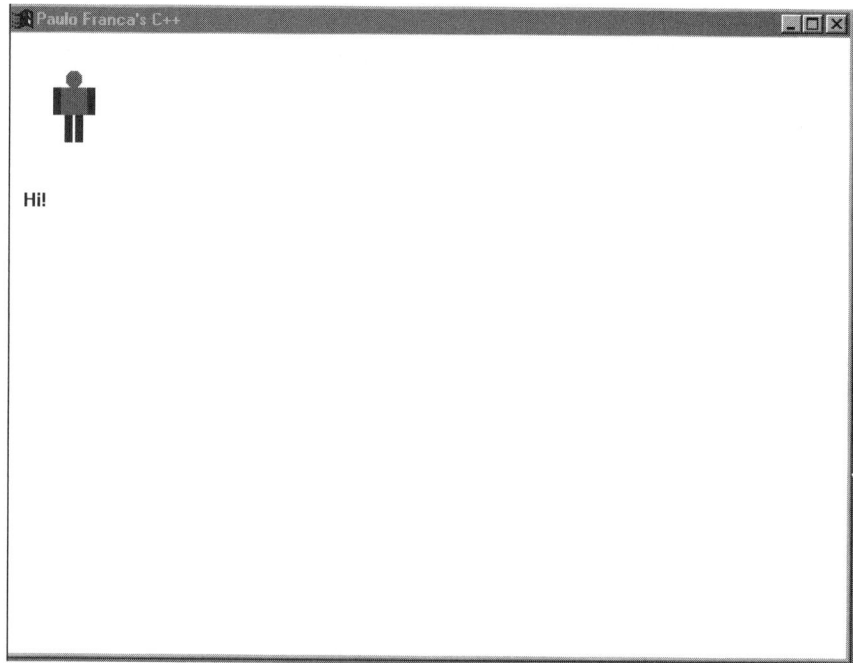

FIGURE 1.1:   The result of executing the project with `c_sal.cpp`

RUNNING YOUR C++ PROGRAMS

If you have not read Skill 0 yet, please do so now. It explains how to run the programs you create in this book in your C++ compiler. Skill 0 shows you in detail how to use some of the most popular C++ compilers.

Sending Messages

Now that you know how to run a program, let's get started writing some. You will tell the computer to work with things called *objects*.

To get going in an easy and interesting way, I have provided some objects for your use. You already met the first one, Sal. Sal will be our companion during the first skills. Sal is an object that can be displayed in several positions:

ready

up

left

right

We have to send Sal the appropriate message so that he appears in the desired position. You may have already guessed that we have built our athlete so that he understands messages such as ready, up, left, and right and can respond to them by assuming the corresponding position.

> **NOTE**
>
> In the generic programming literature, we say that we send a message to an object when we want that object to do something. In the more specific C++ literature, we say that we use one of that object's *member functions* when we want it to do something. Both descriptions refer to the same thing. The term *message* may seem more appropriate at this stage, but you will get a better understanding of why you should use member functions instead of messages when you learn about functions and classes in later Skills.

In the first program, we simply instructed Sal to assume the ready position and to say "hi." Before we go to the computer and send Sal some messages, however, let's look at a few programming basics.

Write One Statement per Line

Statements are instructions to your computer. Some statements are messages to objects. *Messages* are instructions that objects know how to obey. A computer (and its objects) can obey one instruction at a time. You can write more than one instruction left to right in the same line. However, computer programmers have long established that it is more convenient and understandable to place each instruction on a separate line.

You Can Only Use Messages That Your Objects Understand.   In this case, you can use only messages such as ready, up, left, and right. If you tell Sal to go down, for example, he won't obey, because he doesn't know how to do that yet!

NOTE   The class `athlete` objects were designed to respond only to these specific messages (in other words, only these member functions were included in the class).

Figure 1.2 summarizes the actions that Sal can perform.

ready   up   left   right

FIGURE 1.2:   The only instructions the `Sal` class understands (at the moment)

You Must Specify Which Object Is Supposed to Obey Your Messages.
Some programs may deal with several objects. For example, you might have two athletes, Sal and Sally. If you simply say *up*, who do you want to move up? Sal? Sally? Both? You must precede the message with the object name, and you must place a dot between the object name and the message name, as in the following line:

```
Sal.ready();
```

You must let the computer know which objects you are using and what class (what kind) of objects they are.

The C++ compiler differentiates between uppercase and lowercase letters. *Sal* is not the same as *sal*. This is called *case sensitivity,* and you must take it into consideration.

WARNING   Be sure your commands and class names are the same throughout your program. Using *Sal* in one place and *sal* in another can cause errors.

Each instruction in your program must end with a semicolon (there are a few exceptions, such as the `include` and `void mainprog` instructions).

To send a message to an object, you use the object name, a dot, and the message followed by opening and closing parentheses (later we may include something inside the parentheses). For example:

```
Sal.ready();
```

tells the object `Sal` to position itself as ready.

Bugs?

You may have already noticed that any minor mistake (such as misspelling a name, missing a dot, and so on) causes the computer either to send you an error message or to act improperly (if you have not seen this yet, do not despair—you will see it sooner than you expect). This is a great time to learn that the computer always does as it is told.

If the computer is not doing the right thing, it is because you told it to do the wrong thing! You may sometimes feel that the computer is crazy, but if you carefully examine your instructions, chances are you will find you did something wrong. These mistakes are called *bugs* in programming jargon.

The *athlete* Class

You can declare objects of the class `athlete` and use them with your programs. All objects of this class have the following characteristics (summarized in Figure 1.2).

Each object occupies a square on the screen. The first object occupies the upper-left square, and each succeeding object you declare occupies a square to the right.

These objects have a shape that is drawn in response to the messages:

ready

up

left

right

In addition, athletes pretend to "say" something to you. To make this happen, send the message `say` to the athlete (enclose the message in parentheses and enclose the words you want spoken in double quotes).

Understanding Arguments

Arguments modify the effect of a message. For example, it is possible to alter the speed at which the athlete works by specifying how many seconds the athlete remains in the requested position. The `say` message also has an argument that specifies what you want the athlete to say.

Movements can be performed faster or slower. To modify the speed, all you have to do is to include the number of seconds as an argument inside the parentheses. For example, the following lines:

```
Sal.left(5);
Sal.up(8);
```

cause Sal to remain in the left position for 5 seconds and then switch to the up position and stay like that for 8 seconds.

The `ready`, `up`, `left`, and `right` arguments can be a number with a fractional part. For example:

```
Sal.left(0.5);
```

If you do not provide an argument, 1 second is assumed. If you use zero as an argument, the action is performed as fast as the computer can manage to do it. (You probably won't even be able to notice the movements!)

`Ready`, `up`, `left`, and `right` can use numeric arguments, that is, a number that specifies a length of time. On the other hand, `say` can use either a number or a sequence of characters, digits, and signs, and will display them on the screen exactly as they appear inside the double quotes.

WARNING   Please don't forget! If you save the modified program, you may lose the original! To preserve the old program, choose File ➤ Save As, and give the file a new name.

Why is it that when we want Sal to say something, we enclose that "something" in quotes? Well, suppose you want Sal to say hello. Sending your message like this:

```
Sal.say(hello);
```

causes a problem. *Hello* is a valid name for an object, and the computer cannot tell whether you want to write the letters *h-e-l-l-o* on the screen or write the contents of the object `hello`. Therefore, the quotes tell the computer that you want to display exactly what is inside the quotes.

> **NOTE**   You must always use quotes ("") in C++ to denote text that will appear on the screen. C++ compilers differentiate between hello and "hello".

Keeping Your C++ Programs Nice and Neat

A good programmer is always concerned that others can understand what he or she has done. Never assume that all you have to do is have your program running. You or someone else may have to use and modify it. Worse still, you may have to understand and modify a program written by someone else! In any case, it is important that someone else can read and understand your program without too much trouble.

One of the ways you help someone else understand your programs is to use *comments,* explanatory lines that you insert in your code. These lines have nothing to do with how the program works, and the computer ignores them. They simply explain to someone else what you are doing in the program. (At a later time, they can also serve to remind you of what you were doing.)

You may feel reluctant to use comments in the programs you are working on right now because they are small and (hopefully) easy to understand, but don't be fooled! Your programs will grow in size and complexity. Start using comments now!

You add comments in C++ by preceding the text with two slashes (//). If you do this, all text to the end of the line is considered a comment.

For example, our first program could look like this after adding comments:

```
// ************************************************
//                    Program C_SAL.CPP
// This program shows an athlete on the screen.
// Programmed by Paulo Franca, 08/21/94
// Last revision on 08/21/94
// ************************************************
//
#include "franca.h"    // Use textbook programs
athlete Sal;           // Declare Sal to be an athlete
void mainprog()        // The program starts here
{
  Sal.ready();         // Tell Sal to appear in the
                       //     Ready position.
  Sal.say("Hi!");       // Tell Sal to say "Hi!"
}                      // Program ends here
```

You can write anything you like after the two slashes. If the text does not fit on one line, no problem. Use the next line, as I've done in the `Sal.ready()` statement. You can use the slashes at the beginning of the line or in any place you please. Just don't forget to use them!

> **TIP** Besides explanatory comments, it's always a good idea to include your name, the date you wrote the program, the date when you last changed it, and a brief description of what the program does. The description is helpful when you're later looking for a particular program.

Notice that between the comments:

```
The program starts here
```

and

```
Program ends here
```

all comments are indented to the right. This makes it easier for you to readily identify where actions start and finish. Use this same structure for program statements (notice that, inside the braces, all statements are indented).

Understanding Sequence

To execute a task, you must explain to the computer the steps involved. Of course, you must know how to accomplish the task to explain it.

An *algorithm* is a detailed, precise description of how to execute a task, and it can be expressed in any language. A *program* is an algorithm in a form that the computer can understand.

Here, we are going to explore only *sequential* algorithms, which involve a sequence of steps that are executed one after the other. In later Skills, we'll look at how to include repetitions and decisions.

Taking One Step at a Time

If you can write the recipe for cooking Eggs Benedict or if you can write the directions to get to the downtown theater, there is no reason you can't explain to a computer how to solve a problem. Just remember a couple of things:

- You cannot explain what you don't know. You can't tell someone how to find the downtown theater if you don't know where it is. No matter what you want to explain to a person or to a computer, be sure you know what you are talking about.

- Nothing is obvious to a computer. A human is never as dumb as a computer. The computer has no judgment. If you don't explain all the details, the computer may get stuck.

Giving Sal Some Instructions

Let's start by telling Sal to perform some fitness exercises. For example:

        ready

        up

        ready

Do you think you can write a program to do that? All you have to do is to send Sal the appropriate messages. Why don't you simply take the original program and include the new messages you want Sal to receive? Go on! Try it! Remember though:

- Write one instruction in each line.

- Don't forget the semicolon.

- Be sure that messages to Sal include his name, a dot, and the message followed by (). For example, `Sal.right()`, `Sal.left()`, and so on.

If you do this exercise correctly, you should be able to see Sal move his arms up and then down.

Do you want to try another one? How about this:

        ready

        up

        left

        up

        ready

        up

        right

        up

        ready

If you write these programs properly, you can see Sal exercising. If you want to try some other exercises before proceeding, be my guest! I want to make sure you understand that things happen because the computer looks at the instructions and executes them one at a time.

Try These for Fun. . .

- Change the previous program to make the fitness exercises go slower. Place a number, such as 5, inside the parentheses for the messages `ready`, `up`, `left`, and `right`.

- Change the program to make the exercises go faster. Place a zero inside the parentheses this time.

- Change the program `c_sal.cpp` so that Sal says "Sal" instead of "Hi!"

- Declare an object in addition to Sal, let's say Sally. Have each object say his or her name.

- Have Sal and then Sally perform the following fitness exercise:

    ready

    up

    left

    up

    right

    up

    ready

- Have Sal say what he is doing (ready, up, left, up, right, up, done!) while he exercises.

Are You Experienced?

Now you can...

- ☑ Identify program statements inside a C++ code list

- ☑ Send messages to objects of different types, including strings (text) such as "Hello!" and numbers

- ☑ Understand sequential algorithms

- ☑ Use *athlete* objects

- ☑ Use comments

Skill 1

S K I L L

two

2

Displaying Information to the User

- ❑ Using *Clock* objects
- ❑ Using *Box* objects
- ❑ Using *Robot* objects

In this Skill, you'll learn how to keep track of the time elapsed while running your programs and how to make the computer wait for a specific time. You do this with objects of the class Clock.

This Skill also allows you to make the computer communicate with you or any other user. Often, you will need to display some values or some words that reflect what your program is doing or its result. Box objects are convenient for this purpose. You can use a box to display a value or a message. Each box can also have a label that identifies its purpose.

To develop more interesting programs, you will learn how to use another class of objects, the Robot class. Objects of this class are useful for drawing simple shapes on the screen. (Later, we'll use them to illustrate more complex problems.)

Using *Clock* Objects

You declare objects of the type Clock (notice the first character is uppercase) to keep track of time in your programs. Just like any other object used in the program, you have to declare an object by giving it an identifier:

```
Clock mywatch;      // mywatch is a Clock
```

After you declare this object, you can use it to do the following things:

- Keep track of the time elapsed since the object was declared

- Wait for a specific time period before continuing the program

You can restart the clock at any time.

Sending Messages to *Clock*

Clock objects can respond to the following messages:

```
wait(seconds);
time();
reset();
```

The wait(seconds); message instructs the computer to wait for the number of seconds specified as an argument inside the parentheses. This number can include a fractional part.

The `time();` message causes `Clock` to produce a result that is the time (in seconds) elapsed since `Clock` was initialized or created (you'll see how to use this later).

The `reset();` message resets Clock. Each clock is automatically reset (to zero) at declaration, so you don't need to reset your clock before using it.

Putting Words in Sal's Mouth with *Clock*

Suppose you want to use a clock to make Sal say, "Hello!" and, then after 3 seconds, say, "How are you?" All you have to do is the following:

1. Send a message for Sal to say "Hello!"

2. Send a message to your `Clock` object to wait 3 seconds.

3. Send a message for Sal to say "How are you?"

You must, however, declare an object of class `athlete` (`Sal`) and declare an object of class `Clock` so that you can use it. Also, you must send a message for Sal to show himself (`ready`); otherwise, he will be invisible!

In the program below, `C1CLOCK.CPP`, an object named `mywatch` functions as the clock.

```
// This program illustrates the use of Clocks
// Programmed by: Paulo Franca, 10/19/94
#include "franca.h"                    C1CLOCK.CPP
void mainprog()
{
  Clock mywatch;
  athlete Sal;
  Sal.ready();          // Show Sal...
  Sal.say("Hello!");    // Say Hello!
  mywatch.wait(3);      // wait 3 second before
                        // doing what is next
  Sal.say("How are you?"); // now say "how..."
  mywatch.wait(1);      // wait 1 second...
}
```

The actual arguments to the `Clock` object are numbers that can contain a fractional part. The time returned by the `time()` message also has a fractional part. You can, therefore, specify a wait of a half second by using a statement such as the following:

```
mywatch.wait(0.5);
```

The `mywatch` object was automatically reset to zero when the program started execution. We could, at any moment, display the elapsed time in seconds by including a statement such as the following one:

```
Sal.say(mywatch.time());
```

We could see the actual elapsed time since the beginning of the program, because `mywatch.time()` causes `Clock` to return the value of the elapsed time. So far, the only way we know to show a value is to have the athlete "say" the value.

Getting Started

When you have to develop a new program, you sometimes feel stuck and stare at the computer screen without a hint of how to get started. This is a common beginner's symptom. I suggest you consider developing the habit of writing down some of the actions that are needed in plain English. If you like, use the computer, and enter those actions as comments. As you do so, your mind will get organized, and you'll start to understand the problem.

For example, you want to display one athlete (Sal) who says, "Sally! Where are you?" Then, after 5 seconds, you want to display another athlete (Sally) who says, "Here I am!"

An athlete can say only short words, because there isn't much space provided in the display box. You can, however, have the athlete say a longer sentence by breaking it into smaller pieces. Thus, instead of Sal's saying "Sally! Where are you?" all at once, he can say this sentence a few words at a time, with a 2-second interval between words.

If you follow my suggestion about writing the actions as comments, you might have the following comments:

```
// Declare two athletes
// Show Sal on the screen
// Have Sal say "Sally! Where are you?"
//      waiting 2 seconds for each word
// Wait 5 seconds
// Show Sally
// have Sally say "Here I am"
//      waiting 2 seconds for each word
```

These comments actually describe the algorithm of the program. You might look at them and feel ready to write the program. If not, change them or provide better explanations until you can see the program completely explained.

You might not like the comment that tells Sal to say a sequence of words, waiting 2 seconds between each word. Perhaps you want to explain this better. No problem—simply change that comment to something like the following comment.

```
// Have Sal say "Sally!"
// Wait 2 seconds
// Have Sal say "Where"
// Wait 2 seconds
// Have Sal say "are you?"
```

Insert these comments in the appropriate place, and the complete algorithm will be as follows:

```
// Declare two athletes
// Show Sal on the screen
//         Have Sal say "Sally!"
//         Wait 2 seconds
//         Have Sal say "Where"
//         Wait 2 seconds
//         Have Sal say "are you?"
// Wait 5 seconds
// Show Sally
// Have Sally say "Here I am"
//         Waiting 2 seconds for each word
```

> **NOTE**   The *indentation* makes it clear that the purpose of those actions is to perform the complete action in the line above (have Sal say the words...). You might want to provide similar comments to explain how Sally will say her part, or you can leave the algorithm as it stands.

Adding Statements to Your Comments

Now that you have a good description of your program, you can leave each comment exactly where it is and start to include the actual C++ statements. For example, just below the following line:

```
// Declare two athletes
```

include something like this:

```
athlete Sal, Sally;
```

Add all the statements, and your program is ready. Try to adopt the practice of outlining the steps of your program as comments and then adding the statements. It can be especially useful if you don't know how to get started.

As an exercise, try to complete this program and run it.

Using *Box* Objects

Suppose in one of the programs above you want to display how long it takes for the program to complete. You can easily get this information from the `Clock` object. But where do you display this value?

The only option we have covered so far is to have Sal "say" the value of the time. If you want to display this information in a different manner, you need a different object.

`Box` objects are similar to `athlete` objects. Once you declare a `Box` object (notice the uppercase B), you can use it to "say" whatever you like, just as you did with an `athlete` object. `Box` objects differ from `athlete` objects in the following two ways:

- No athlete is associated with them.

- The `Box` object can have a label.

Boxes are automatically located one below the other on the right side of the screen.

For example, to display the time, you can declare a `Box` object as follows:

```
Box display ("Time:");
```

At any point, you can now use this box to display the value of the time, which is kept by an existing clock, `mywatch`:

```
display.say(mywatch.time());
```

In this case, the word *Time:* is the label of the box, as stated in the declaration. The time value is shown as the content of the box.

If you declare more than one box, the next boxes appear one below the other. In Skill 14, you will learn how to move boxes to other locations.

The Great Escape—Part 1

You use `Robot` objects to simulate a situation in which you and your master are lost in a maze and explore the alternatives.

Robot Objects

Robot objects consist of a robot inside a room that may or may not have walls blocking the way. Standard Robot objects are placed in an empty room in the upper-left corner of the screen. It is a good idea to force the robot to face a specific direction, say east, when you start. Figure 2.1 illustrates a robot in this situation.

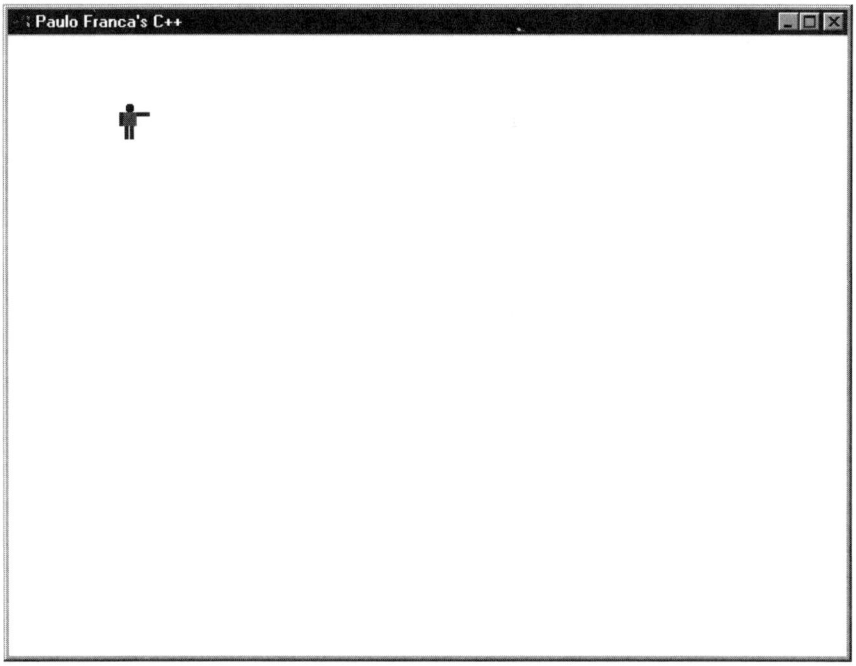

FIGURE 2.1:   Using a Robot object

To use a Robot object in your program, you must declare one (and only one) Robot object. Throughout this book, all the examples declare a Robot object named Tracer.

The program c1robot1.cpp, listed below, was used to generate the screen in Figure 2.1.

```
#include "franca.h"
// c1robot1.cpp
```

```
Robot Tracer;
void mainprog()
    {
        Tracer.face(3);
        Tracer.step();
    }
```

What Can the Robot Do?

Tracer, as well as any other `Robot` object you use in your programs, knows how to respond to the following messages.

step()   Takes one step ahead. Optionally, you can specify a number of steps inside the parentheses. The robot does not check for a wall. Each step takes a standard amount of time, as set by `timescale` (see below). The default time is 1 second.

left()   Turns 90 degrees to the left.

right()   Turns 90 degrees to the right.

seewall()   Checks for a wall ahead (next square). (We'll use this message in Skill 8.) This message returns a one if there is a wall, and zero otherwise.

seenowall()   Checks for no wall ahead (next square). (We'll use this message in Skill 8.) This message returns a one if there is no wall ahead, and zero otherwise.

face(integer)   Turns the robot to face the specified direction. Direction is an integer (0, 1, 2, or 3), specifying north, west, south, or east. If any other value is given, the remainder of the division by 4 is used.

mark()   Marks the next square in the map using a given color. If no value is specified, two is used (green). Table 2.1 shows the colors and their corresponding values.

say("message")   Displays the "message" on the screen, as if the robot had said it. The message can be either an integer (in which case, omit the quotes) or a few words (enclosed in quotes). Avoid exceeding 12 characters in a string.

TABLE 2.1:   The Colors and Their Values

Color	Its Value
White	0
Red	1
Green	2
Blue	3
Light Blue	4
Pink	5
Yellow	6
Black	7

timescale(value)   Changes the `timescale`. You don't need to use this unless you want to change the default value, in which each step takes 0.1 seconds. For example, if you want to slow down Tracer so that she spends 0.5 seconds in each step, you can do this as follows:

```
Tracer.timescale(0.5);
```

The C++ syntax for handling all objects is exactly the same whether you are dealing with athletes, clocks, or robots. To send a message to an object, you use the object name, a dot, and then the message followed by parentheses. Therefore, as shown in the `c1robot1.cpp` program, to have Tracer step ahead, you use a statement such as the following one:

```
Tracer.step();
```

Tracer appears on the screen with her arm pointing in the direction in which she just stepped. In the following examples, Tracer will move in an empty room, so you don't need to check for her bumping into the walls. Later, you will learn how to check for walls on the way and how to avoid crashing.

Moving Your Robot

Now, let's modify `c1robot1.cpp` and experiment. To start, have her step four times. You can do this by repeating these steps:

```
Tracer.step();
Tracer.step();
```

```
Tracer.step();
Tracer.step();
```

or by indicating the number of steps inside the parentheses:

```
Tracer.step(4);
```

This will do for the time being. Later, you will learn how to tell the computer to repeat a sequence of statements.

Marking Tracer's Way

Now, let's paint the squares as Tracer moves so that you can clearly see her path. A robot can mark the square that is immediately in front in a given color. Can you modify the program so that Tracer marks the squares as she goes?

Remember, Tracer cannot mark the square she is stepping in. Only the one immediately ahead of her.

If we don't care about the first square, the following program will do:

```
Tracer.mark();
Tracer.step();
Tracer.mark();
Tracer.step();
Tracer.mark();
Tracer.step();
Tracer.mark();
Tracer.step();
```

With this program, Tracer marks and steps four times. The initial square remains blank.

Turning Tracer

A robot can turn to the left or to the right and can face any of four directions. Directions are represented by an integer number, as shown in Table 2.2.

TABLE 2.2:   The Directions and Their Values

Direction	Its Value
North, facing the top of the screen	0
West, facing the left side of the screen	1
South, facing the bottom of the screen	2
East, facing the right side of the screen	3

Suppose, for example, that after Tracer steps and marks four squares, we want her to turn back to the original position.

How can we do that? Well, you have to make Tracer turn around and then step four times. This should bring her back to the original square. How do you turn back? Either you turn to one of the sides twice, or, in this case, since Tracer was facing east, have her face west:

```
Tracer.face(1);
```

Putting Words in Tracer's Mouth

At any point, the robot can inform you of what's happening in the program. As can athletes, robots can say something. For example:

```
Tracer.say("Done!");
```

By the way, did you notice that robots and athletes look alike? Hmm, maybe they are related! Who knows?

Now you can modify your program so that Tracer says "going" as she steps and marks the four squares ahead. When Tracer turns back, she says "coming back" and then steps back to the original square.

Helping Your Master

Imagine that you, your master Ram, and Tracer are lost in a maze built with rectangular squares. You are now in a position to start helping Ram explore the maze. As an introductory exercise, Ram has suggested that the robot be instructed to walk, describing a square of size 3. As you know, Tracer has to step 3 times, turn to the right, step 3 times, and so on.

This was the algorithm:

step

step

step

turn right

step

step

step

turn right

step

step

step

turn right

step

step

step

turn right

We can easily transcribe this into a C++ program:

```cpp
// Program c1robot2.cpp
#include "franca.h"  // c1robot2.cpp
Robot Tracer;
void mainprog()
{
Tracer.face(3);
Tracer.mark();
Tracer.step();
Tracer.mark();
Tracer.step();
Tracer.mark();
Tracer.step(); // Done with one side
Tracer.right();
Tracer.mark();
Tracer.step();
Tracer.mark();
Tracer.step();
Tracer.mark();
Tracer.step(); // Done with one side
Tracer.right();
Tracer.mark();
Tracer.step();
Tracer.mark();
Tracer.step();
Tracer.mark();
Tracer.step(); // Done with one side
Tracer.right();
Tracer.mark();
Tracer.step();
Tracer.mark();
Tracer.step();
Tracer.mark();
Tracer.step(); // Done with last side
Tracer.right();
}
```

I'm sure you're upset about writing all these steps. Hold on until the next Skill! Figure 2.2 illustrates the result of running this program.

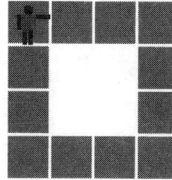

FIGURE 2.2:   The robot's journey around the square

Is there anything wrong with this program? Of course, there is! Why does the square measure 4 steps instead of 3? Well, it turns out that the program is wrong! In this program, the original square was not counted as part of the square. Therefore, stepping 3 times for each side actually results in a square of size 4, as shown in Figure 2.2. To draw a square of size 3, step 2 more times beyond the current square.

Are You Experienced?

Now you can. . .

☑ **Keep track of time using a *Clock* object**

☑ **Display data using a *Box* object**

☑ **Use a *Robot* object**

three

Solving Problems

- ❑ Devising solutions to simple problems
- ❑ Understanding syntax and rules

The purpose of this Skill is to start developing your ability to work on problem solving. As you work through this book, you will no doubt improve on this ability, as you will throughout your programming life. I cannot teach you how to devise a solution to any problem. I can give you some hints on how to do that yourself.

At the end of this Skill, you will find a more formal discussion of the rules for writing programs. I purposely omitted most of the rules so that you could concentrate on the concepts: what is the purpose of a statement, why do we use it, and so on. However, rules must be very strict for the compiler, and, therefore, we'll now take a look at them.

Facing and Solving Problems

The most difficult part is to overcome the fear of starting. Write down any explanation that comes to your mind. If your explanation is wrong, no problem. It is easier to correct an explanation once it is written. If the explanation is vague, just go on and add more detail to it.

Write Anything

Never trap yourself by staring at a blank piece of paper (or at a blank screen, for that matter). You will never get anywhere that way.

Once you have written some explanation of how to solve your problem, read it a few times. Is it correct? It's all right if it isn't precise. For example, the following explanation:

draw a square of size 3

is correct. That is what you want to do. However, it is not precise. It won't do for the computer. You need to explain what you mean by drawing a square of size 3!

Break Down the Problem

You must go on explaining your problem until the computer is able to understand how to solve it. The general idea is to identify smaller problems that you already know how to solve. This will get you closer to the solution. Try to break the problem down into easier ones, but, if possible, into problems for which you already have a solution. For example, to draw a square, you might think of drawing a line at a time:

> draw a line
>
> turn right
>
> draw a line
>
> turn right
>
> draw a line
>
> turn right
>
> draw a line
>
> turn right

It would be great if your computer already knew how to draw a line. But that is no problem. You can now explain how to draw a line:

> mark
>
> step
>
> mark
>
> step

This explanation gives you the proposed algorithm.

Reuse Simpler Problems

Finally, let me stress that, while breaking down your problem into simpler ones, try to identify simpler problems that you can reuse. What do I mean by reuse? If you can fit a solution that you already have, you are reusing that solution. The more you reuse, the more time you save. Sometimes, though, you don't have a reusable piece of software available. What do you do?

Well, in that case, you will have to build it yourself. Nonetheless, whenever you build a piece of software, try to evaluate how it could be reused in the future. Try to build your software, or , most likely, your functions (as you will see in the next Skill), in such a way that they can be reused without any change.

Why Are Computers So Dumb?

Why are computers puzzled by so little? This next exercise introduces some intentional mistakes in the program. It is designed to get you used to some of the most common error messages. Notice that, in many cases, the error message does not explain the problem well enough.

Take the program `c_sal.cpp` and try the following things one at a time:

- Remove the semicolon at the end of a statement:

    ```
    Sal.ready()
    ```

- Remove one opening parenthesis:

    ```
    Sal.ready);
    ```

- Remove the opening braces.

- Remove the `#include` line.

- Remove the following line:

    ```
    Sal.say("Hi!");
    ```

Most likely, you will receive an error message indicating that the compiler got confused and could not understand what you wanted. Try to understand why these messages show up and what caused the confusion. For example, removing a semicolon causes the compiler to think that the statement has not ended, and so the computer continues in the following line. Now, since

```
Sal.ready() Sal.say("Hi!");
```

does not represent anything the computer can recognize, the compiler does not know what to do. This may seem like a small mistake that you can easily fix, but the computer has to work with strict rules and is unable to find out what was wrong.

Most of the cases above fall into the category of *syntax errors,* which are violations of simple rules for constructing statements. For example, for each opening parenthesis, there must be a closing parenthesis; all object names must be declared; and so on.

The last error in the list, however, does not generate an error message. You may be able to run your program, but the program will not be correct because "Hi!" will not be displayed under the picture. In this case, the compiler could not find anything wrong. The syntax rules were respected. Nevertheless, the program is not correct, because it does not do what you intended in the original version.

Keep in mind that the computer always does what it is told to do. If something is not done correctly, chances are you did not issue the correct instructions. Unfortunately, because computers have a simple "mind," the rules have to be strictly observed. A minor mistake can cause a completely different action to take place!

Rules and Regulations

Thus far, I have loosely explained the rules for constructing programs. I was more interested in making sure you understand the purpose of the programming elements, rather than the actual rules to use them. However, the rules are important, and I'll summarize them in this section. Hopefully, it will be easier for you to understand the rules after you are familiar with the purpose of each programming construct.

Identifier Names

To identify objects you use in a program, you designate them by an *identifier*, which is simply a name for the object. You can choose the identifier as you wish, subject to the following rules:

- Begin with a letter or an underscore (_).
- Use letters, digits (0 through 9), and an underscore.
- Use a maximum of 32 characters (you can use more, but the compiler will look at only the first 32).
- Do not use blank spaces.
- Do not use a keyword as an identifier (keywords are explained below).

It is a good idea to use names that remind you of the purpose of the object you are naming.

> **WARNING**   Long names may bore you after a while.

The following identifiers are not valid:

- 2waystop (It starts with a digit.)
- my number (It contains a blank.)
- this-number (The minus sign is not valid.)
- "Sal" (The quotes are not valid.)

Skill 3

On the other hand, the following identifiers are valid:

- `twowaystop`
- `mynumber`
- `thisnumber`
- `Sal`

Keywords

Keywords have a special meaning for the compiler. You might have noticed that we have used a few of them, `void`, for example. You cannot use keywords to name your objects. As you go through this book, you will be learning keywords. Most compilers have a *syntax highlight* feature. All keywords are displayed in boldface as soon as you type them.

Types and Classes

Types and classes serve similar purposes, and, for the time being, we will use the two terms interchangeably. I'll explain the technical difference in a later Skill.

Types or classes denote the general characteristics of a group of objects. As you will see shortly, there is a type of data designed to contain and operate with integer numbers. This is the type `int`, which contains a number without a decimal part. You can perform some arithmetic operations on an `int`. You also learned how to deal with other kinds of data, athletes, for example. Athletes can be set to ready, up, left, and right, and they can "say" something. All data of the same type have similar characteristics. All athletes know exactly the same tricks.

It is important that you tell the compiler the class of each object that you are using so that the compiler can verify that you are doing the correct operations with that object.

You can also create your own classes. For example, `athlete` is a class I created for your use. In later Skills, you will see how you can create your own classes, either using an existing class such as `athlete` or starting from scratch.

Declarations

The declaration simply consists of the class of the object, followed by the identifier. The declaration has the following syntax:

```
class name   object name;
```

The *class name* entry is a valid class name existing in your program (`athlete` and `Clock` are defined in `franca.h`), and *object name* is an identifier of your choice that denotes the object you want to use. You can declare more than one object by separating their identifiers with commas, as follows:

```
athlete Sal, Sally;
```

You can use the identifier only after it has been declared, and you can declare objects and variables anywhere in your program. Here is an example:

```
Clock mywatch       ;  // mywatch is a Clock
int number_of_times;  // number_of_times is an integer
```

Messages

You can instruct the objects you use in your program to perform certain actions. To do so, your program sends a "message" to the object. Objects can respond only to messages to which they are prepared to respond.

To send a message to an object, you must include the object name (identifier), a dot, and the message name followed by parentheses. If the message requires arguments, enclose them in the parentheses. Here is the syntax:

```
object name . message ();
```

The following example sends the message up to the object `Sal`:

```
Sal.up();
```

The following example sends the message up to the object `Sal` with an argument of 2:

```
Sal.up(2);
```

The argument indicates that you want to execute the next instruction after 2 seconds have elapsed.

Technically speaking, C++ uses the term *member function* instead of the term *message*. We'll look at member functions in Skill 16.

Comments

You include comments in your program to make it easier for you or someone else to understand. The computer does not use comments. You can include comments in C++ programs in two ways:

- Enter two slashes (//) and then your text.

- Enter /*, type your text, and then finish with */.

The latter method allows you to include several lines as a comment:

```
/* This is
a comment that
occupies 3 lines */
```

It also allows you to include a comment in the middle of a statement:

```
int /* this is a comment */ lapcount;
```

Try These for Fun. . .

Let's look at some examples.

Find the Error

The following program is a "wrong" copy of our first program c_sal.cpp:

```
include "franca.h"
athlete Sal;
void mainprog()
{
sal.ready();
Sal.say(Hi);
}
```

This copy has three mistakes. Compare the program with the original and locate the mistakes. Then, try to run the wrong program and notice the error messages.

Write a Couple of Programs

First, write a program that displays three athletes and their names. Declare three athletes (with names of your choice), and send messages to each one to get "ready" and to "say" their name.

Second, write a program that displays a picture such as that in Figure 3.1 (Sal and his shapes). You need to declare four athletes and send a different message to each.

ready   up   left   right

FIGURE 3.1: Sal and his shapes: your first programming job!

Find Some More Mistakes

The following program is another "wrong" copy of c_sal.cpp:

```
#include "franca.h"
void mainprog()
{
ready;
Sal.say("Hi!");
}
```

This program also has three mistakes. Locate the mistakes, and run the program to see the error messages.

Find the Valid Identifiers

Indicate which of the identifiers below are valid:

2ndTime

apollo-13

apollo13

BigTime

my friend

my.friend

my_friend

void

Draw a Picture

Write a program that instructs your robot to produce a drawing such as the one in Figure 3.2.

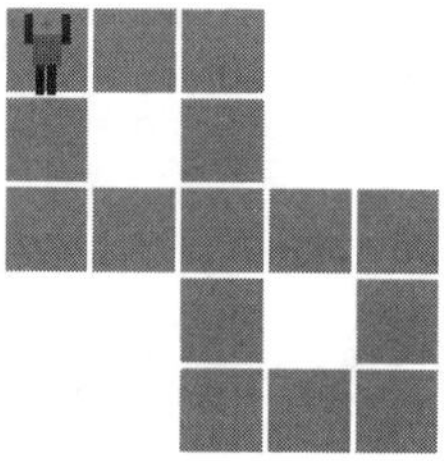

FIGURE 3.2:   Your robot is an artist!

You can draw this picture in a couple of ways:

- Draw a square, move to the lower-right position of this square, and then draw the other square.

- Draw all the lines in a continuous movement.

Each move takes one second. Can you figure out which solution is the fastest? If the robot knew how to draw a square, which solution would be easier?

Find Some More Identifiers

Examine the following program. Which identifiers are invalid? Which identifiers were not declared?

```
void mainprog()
{
  athlete bill, john doe, ann3;
  Clock 3days, my-clock, O'Hara,other;
  Box show;
  show.say(thetime);
  bill.say(other.time());
  Marie.ready();
  Robert.up();
}
```

Are You Experienced?

Now you can...

- ☑ Devise solutions to simple problems
- ☑ Understand syntax and rules

PART II

Getting Smart

In Part II, you will develop the skills of using functions and simple arithmetic expressions. You will learn how to use functions and arguments to make your computer smarter and how to manipulate values in functions to return a result. Also, you will further develop your problem-solving skills by using functions.

At the end of Part II, you will find a formal discussion of the rules that regulate the use of functions and numeric expressions.

S K I L L

four

Using Functions

- ❑ Creating functions
- ❑ Using arguments to add versatility to functions
- ❑ Creating header files
- ❑ Understanding scope and scope rules

4

With the help of Sal, our tireless athlete, you will learn how to build simple functions. Any fitness exercise you may want Sal to perform can become a function. For example, once you teach Sal how to do a jumping jack, you will not have to teach him again. All you will have to do is create a function that explains how to do a jumping jack.

Next, you will use arguments to increase the usefulness of functions. You will also learn how to keep useful functions stored in header files, so that you can use them with any of your programs.

Finally, an important concept will be covered: scope. Because each function is treated by the compiler as a separate entity, the names you choose for your variables and objects are valid in that function's scope. This feature is a nice feature because it relieves you of having to keep track of all the names used in the program. However, scope rules must be clearly understood to avoid confusion.

What Is a Function?

Sometimes, a group of orders constitutes a distinctive action. You may want to simply refer to that group, instead of having to list, one by one, all the instructions needed to perform that action.

For example, take the following group of orders:

```
Sal.up();
Sal.left();
Sal.up();
Sal.right();
Sal.up();
Sal.ready();
```

We can see that this group constitutes one particular fitness exercise. If we let the computer recognize this sequence by a name—for example, leftright—whenever we say *leftright*, we actually want Sal to perform the sequence specified above. Generally speaking, we define a sequence of statements like this one as a function that explains how to perform that sequence. A similar feature in other languages may be called a procedure or a subroutine. Although C++'s nomenclature gives these pieces of programs the name *function*, the generic term *procedure* may still be used.

NOTE A *function* is a group of statements to which you give a name. These statements can be performed by calling the function name.

When you use functions, you make the computer smarter. Once you have explained the function, you don't need to repeat the orders: Your computer now knows how to carry out these orders! The program will look more understandable, too.

Did you notice that the sequence of movements Sal performed constitutes one particular exercise? Sometimes fitness instructors will give a name to an exercise such as the one that consists of the following movements:

> ready
>
> up
>
> ready

Fitness instructors have named this sequence of actions *jumping jack.* So, when the instructor wants the class to perform a jumping jack, he or she doesn't have to reexplain the steps.

For example, once the instructor has explained how to do a leftright and a jumping jack, they may give orders as follows:

> jumping jack
>
> leftright
>
> jumping jack

Notice how much simpler the directions have become! Instead of giving a one-by-one description of all the steps involved, the instructor simply names what exercises they want performed.

This strategy applies to computer programming, as well: You may group several instructions and give them a name. When you want that function to be performed, you, the almighty programmer, merely need to mention the function name and the computer will perform each order described in the function.

Skill 4

Creating a Function

We can create a function right away. It is always a good idea to know exactly what you want to do before you start writing any program. So, let's get started by writing a description of what we want to do in plain English:

> Here is the function for a jumping jack:
>
>> Make Sal go up.
>
>> Make Sal return to the ready position.
>
> That's all, folks!

In C++ language, this description would become

```
void JumpJack()
{
    Sal.up();
    Sal.ready();
}
```

Naming the Function

We want to tell the computer that we are explaining how to perform a function, and we want to give the computer the name of that function. In the plain-English text, we used *This is the function for a jumping jack*. This sentence explains that the function for a jumping jack consists of the sequence of instructions that follows.

Delimiting the Function

Which instruction is the first and which is the last in the sequence that belongs to this function?

You must clearly indicate the answer to this question to the computer, because other instructions may not belong to the function. To specify the first and last instructions, we included opening and closing braces ({}) around the sequence in which we were interested. The function starts after the opening brace and ends with the closing brace. In addition to including opening and closing braces, we also indented the instructions inside the braces. Indenting is not useful to the computer, but it is very useful for us; it is a good programming practice.

In the program, the function name follows the word void. We will explain this convention later in this Skill. The function name is followed by (). There is no semicolon on the line that names the function.

Technically speaking, the whole function is regarded as a single compound statement (compound statements are explained later). If you insert a semicolon after the function header and before the opening brace, you will make the compiler believe that your statement ends there (before the actual function body).

Let's now look at the program c2jmpjck.cpp:

```
//                          c2jmpjck.cpp
// Programmed by: Paulo Franca
// Revised January 5, 1996.
// This program uses a function JumpJack that exercises
//     Sal once.
#include "franca.h"      // Include textbook programs
athlete Sal;             // Create an athlete Sal
void JumpJack()          // Function JumpJack starts here
{
  Sal.up();              // Up
  Sal.ready();           // Ready
}                        // Function ends here
void mainprog()          // Main program starts here
{
  Sal.ready();           // Ready
  JumpJack();            // Do a jumping jack!
}                        // Main program ends here
```

This program includes the code for the function JumpJack and the code for the function mainprog. Notice that mainprog is the name of the function in which you explain what you really want the computer to do. This function is like any other, except that it has to be present in every program you create. The mainprog function may use other functions, in the same way that it used the JumpJack function in the example above .

NOTE   You must include the function before you can use it in the program.

If we want to have a couple of additional jumping jacks performed, we can simply include two more statements. mainprog will look as follows:

```
void mainprog()          // Main program starts here
{
  Sal.ready();           // Ready
  JumpJack();            // Do a jumping jack!
  JumpJack();            // Another
  JumpJack();            // And another
}                        // Main program ends here
```

Remember that a function is, essentially, a collection of actions that you have named. By using a function, you make your programs easier to read, and you also avoid having to explain the whole sequence if you want to perform it again. You can also make different objects perform the actions specified by a function.

Managing Several Objects

Suppose we have more than one athlete, Sal and Sally. We can easily use more than one athlete by including the following declaration in the program:

```
athlete Sal,Sally;
```

This declaration tells the computer that we now have two objects that are of the type `athlete` and, therefore, we may show both of them:

```
Sal.ready();
Sally.ready();
```

Now, we want Sal to perform a jumping jack. We already know how to do that. What if we want Sally to do the same? It's of no use to call this function `JumpJack`, because `JumpJack` asks Sal to do all the exercises. (Would you like to try it? Go ahead!) What can you do? You may think of two simple solutions:

- You can make another `JumpJack` function specifically for Sally.

- You can list all the actions to make Sally perform the jumping jacks.

Both of these solutions are disappointing. We have already explained how to do jumping jacks, and they are not any different if performed by Sal, Sally, or anybody else. (After all, fitness instructors don't have to explain the exercises to one student at a time, do they?)

Using Arguments to Add Versatility

It would be great to rewrite the function to explain how *any* athlete performs a jumping jack. It is like explaining *this is the way somebody performs a jumping jack* without worrying who the *somebody* is that will actually perform the jumping jack.

In a sense, this is similar to a theater play. The author writes the play to consist of characters. The author seldom knows who will actually play the characters. When the play goes on stage, each actor takes the role of a character. However, you realize that characters and actors are not permanently tied together. The same character may be played by different actors, and a given actor plays the role of several characters in his or her professional life.

Arguments and Parameters

When we write a function, we don't know beforehand which objects will be used as arguments. Therefore, we refer to make-believe objects called *parameters*. When the function is called, an actual object will be used in place of the parameter. The actual objects, which you use when you execute the function, are called *arguments*. All this happens just like it does in the theater play.

In the `JumpJack` function of the `c2jmpjck.cpp` program, we want to be able to give orders to Sal or Sally (or any other athlete that may show up later), instead of giving orders only to Sal. This task can be accomplished by making the function work with an impersonal athlete, instead of personalizing the task for one athlete:

1. Tell the computer how to make a fictitious athlete perform the jumping jacks. You may give this athlete a name, such as *somebody*. Include all the instructions to make *somebody* do a jumping jack. There is nothing called *somebody*—there is only Sal and Sally. *Somebody* is just a parameter.

2. Once you have explained how *somebody* can perform a jumping jack, tell Sally (or Sal) to play the part of *somebody* in that function. Sally is an object that really exists in your programs (like actors exist in real life) and can be used in place of the fictitious *somebody*.

Let's see how this works in `c2jmpbdy.cpp`:

```
//                          c2jmpbdy.cpp
//
#include "franca.h"
athlete Sal,Sally;
void JmpJack(athlete somebody)
{
     somebody.up();
     somebody.ready();
}
void mainprog()
{
     Sal.ready();
     JmpJack(Sal);
     Sally.ready();
     JmpJack(Sally);
}
```

Inside the function, we use the object `somebody`, which, as we know, does not exist in reality. Nevertheless, we explain to this object what actions need to be done to have the jumping jack completed. If you look at the main part of the program, you will notice that the JumpJack function is used twice:

```
JmpJack(Sal);
JmpJack(Sally);
```

However, in the first instance, Sal is inside parentheses. What does this mean?

We want to execute JmpJack, but to actually use Sal as an argument in place of the fictitious parameter somebody. All the moves will be performed by Sal and not by the nonexistent *somebody*. The second time, we use Sally as an argument. Figure 4.1 shows the computer screen after this program is executed.

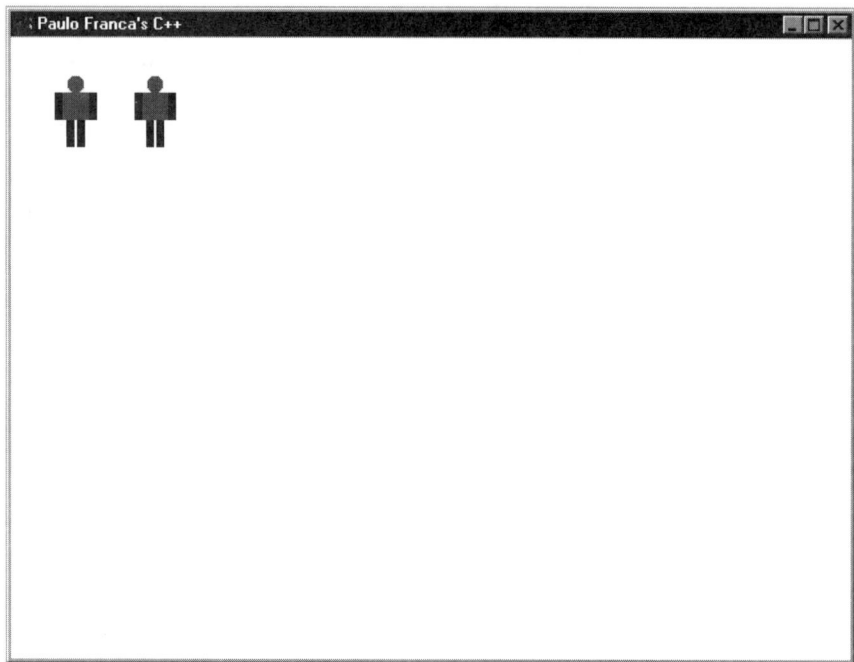

FIGURE 4.1: The result of executing c2jmpbdy.cpp

Give this new method for replacing arguments a try by declaring two athletes, Sal and Sally:

- Have them assume the ready position and say their names. Then, call the JmpJack function with each athlete as a parameter. Observe the action.

    - To do this, simply have Sal say "Sal" and have Sally say "Sally" before calling the JmpJack function.

- Now, call JmpJack first with Sally and then with Sal. Observe the result.

  - In other words, first call JmpJack(Sally); then call JmpJack(Sal);.

Default Values for Parameters

Sometimes, it may be desirable to specify a default value for a parameter. This is especially useful when you want to use the same (default) object as an argument most of the time.

For example, suppose that in most cases we want to perform a jumping jack with Sal, and only a few times with Sally. We can specify a default value for the parameter in the function definition by appending an assignment to the parameter. For example, if we change the function header JmpJack to

```
void JmpJack (athlete somebody=Sal)
```

will cause Sal to be used as the default athlete if no other athlete is specified in the function call. Therefore, a statement such as

```
JmpJack();
```

will cause the same result as if we had

```
JmpJack(Sal);
```

This simply allows us to omit the actual argument when calling the function. It is still possible to include the argument when needed. For example, if we want Sally to be used, we can use the following function call:

```
JmpJack(Sally);
```

TIP   When you specify a default argument, the object specified as the default must be previously defined and known to the function (see the section on scope later in this Skill).

Multiple Arguments

It is also possible to create functions that use more than one argument. For example, we can have another function that takes two athletes as arguments and has them both perform a jumping jack. In C++, it is possible to have two functions with the same name in the same program—provided that the functions have a different number of arguments or have different classes (or types) of arguments.

Let's develop a new `JmpJack` function that makes both athletes exercise. Of course, you may have thought of calling the existing `JmpJack` function for each of the athletes:

```
void JmpJack(athlete first, athlete second)
{
  JmpJack(first);
  JmpJack(second);
}
```

However, this will make the athletes exercise one at a time. Try it, if you'd like.

What can we do to make them both exercise simultaneously? Actually, it is impossible to perform two actions at the same time in this case, because the computer operates sequentially on your program. We have to control the time that the athlete remains in each position.

To give the illusion that both athletes are exercising at the same time, we can tell the first athlete to be ready for zero seconds, then tell the second athlete to be ready for 1 second, as usual. Then, we do the same with the other movements. Most computers nowadays will perform the movement so fast that you will hardly notice it. Only the picture that is kept for a long period (1 second) will actually be registered in your mind.

Here is the algorithm:

> Function JmpJack to make two athletes perform a jumping jack at the same time:
>
> > First athlete stays in *ready* for zero seconds.
> >
> > Second athlete stays in *ready* for 1 second.
> >
> > First athlete stays in *up* for zero seconds.
> >
> > Second athlete stays in *up* for 1 second.
> >
> > First athlete stays in *ready* for zero seconds.
> >
> > Second athlete stays in *ready* for 1 second.

Can you finish the function and see the results? You may start with the following statement:

```
void JmpJack(athlete first, athlete second)
```

Originals and Copies: Value vs. Reference

In general, when you use a function that has an argument, the function will use a copy of the argument. In other words, when you issue a statement such as

```
Jmpjack(Sally);
```

the computer makes a copy of the athlete `Sally` and then uses it in the `JmpJack` function. Your original athlete remains unaltered no matter what you do in the function. C++ usually does this when calling functions. You can be sure that the function does not tamper with your original object.

In the special case of an athlete, differences are small. Another athlete will be created in the exact position as your original athlete, and this new athlete will move according to the function instructions. By looking at the screen, you cannot tell whether the movements were performed by the original athlete or by its clone.

If you want to see the consequences of using a copy, you can use a `Clock` object. In the example that follows, we are going to use a `Clock` object called `timer`. We then invoke a function that resets the timer. Instead of resetting the original `Clock`, the function will reset the Clock's clone!

This can be easily observed by having a box "say" the time before, during, and after the function's execution. To do this, we can declare three boxes and label them `Before:`, `During:`, and `After:`. We can use each one to display the time at the appropriate moment. `c2clkcpy.cpp` illustrates the problem:

```cpp
#include "franca.h"        //      c2clkcpy.cpp
// This program illustrates how arguments are copied
//      when used in a function.
Box before("Before:"),during("During:"),after("After:");
void zero(Clock clone)
{
    clone.reset();          // Reset the Clock
    during.say(clone.time());// Show the time (0.)
}
void mainprog()
{
    Clock timer;
    timer.wait(1.);         // Make sure time>1
    before.say(timer.time());// Show the time
    zero(timer);            // Call the function
    after.say(timer.time()); // Show the time
}
```

If you run this program, you should see three numbers on the screen. The first number is the number of seconds that elapsed since the program started. This should be close to 1 second, since `wait(1)` was included.

The second number is the number of seconds that elapsed since the Clock was reset inside the `zero` function. This number should be zero.

The third number is the number of seconds that elapsed since the Clock was last reset. You might expect this to be close to zero, because the Clock was sent to the function as an argument and was reset. But this is not true! The actual value you'll see is probably 1 or a little more than that. This indicates that your Clock was not reset: A clone of your Clock was reset instead. Check out Figure 4.2.

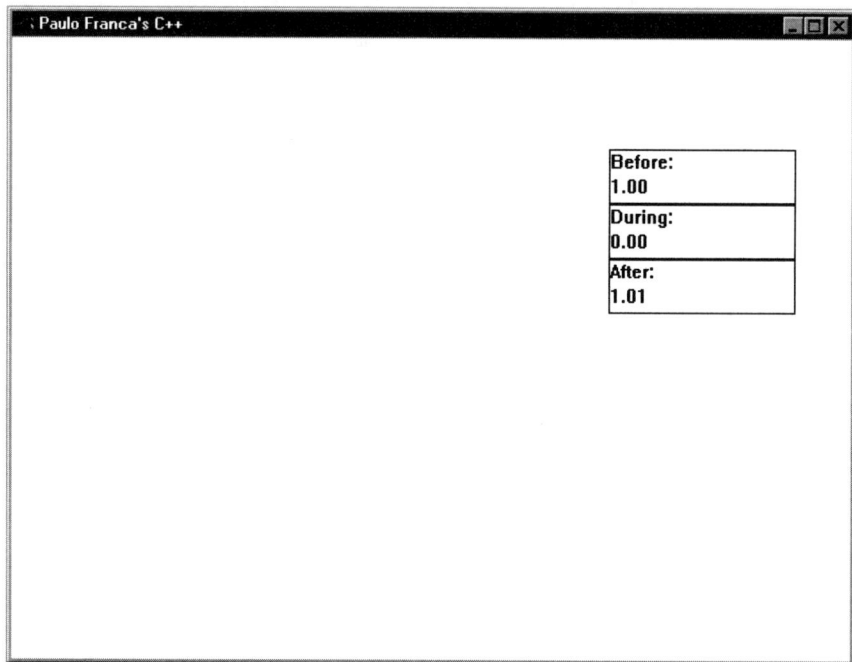

F I G U R E   4 . 2 :   The result of executing `c2clkcpy.cpp`

This seems like a great idea to prevent you from messing up the contents of your objects when you invoke functions. But what if you want to operate on the original object?

Passing by Reference or Passing by Value

C++ allows you to indicate that your function is supposed to operate on the original argument and not on a copy of it. This is referred to as a parameter passing by *reference*, as opposed to a parameter passing by *value*. Passing by reference is very simple. Indicate which parameters you want passed by reference (passing by value is the default). In C++, you simply precede the parameter name by the reference symbol &. In our example, the modified function would be as follows:

```
void zero(Clock & clone)
{
    clone.reset();          // Reset the Clock
    during.say(clone.time());// Show the time (0.)
}
```

This is the only change! The statements in the function remain the same, as do those in the main program. By simply including the reference symbol (&), you make sure that all operations will be performed on the original object. You can now modify the program and observe the results.

> **NOTE** If you have more than one parameter, you must use a reference symbol & for each parameter that you want passed by reference.

When Should We Use References?   Clearly, you must use a reference when you want to use the original argument. There may be other situations in which using a reference may be convenient as well.

When a clone object is used, the computer spends some time preparing a copy of the object. In most cases, this time is negligible. However, some objects consume more time while being copied. `athlete` objects, for example, are relatively complex. If you're sure you don't need protection against modifications to your original and your object complexity is significant, you may also consider passing by reference.

Teaching an Object

You may have noticed that there is a similarity between invoking a function and sending a message to an object. In both cases, a sequence of actions is executed. When you send a message to an object, you invoke a function that is restricted to that class of objects. These are called member functions. Member functions will be studied in detail in Skills 16 and 17.

When the `athlete` class was created, it was designed to respond to messages of `ready`, `up`, `left`, and `right`. This was done by including a member function for each of those actions. We might have included a function for a jumping jack, too, but we did not want to steal all the fun from you!

Member Functions and Non-Member Functions

Objects have functions that correspond to each message the objects are supposed to understand. For example, `athlete` objects have functions such as

```
ready

up

left

right

say
```

However, these functions are part of the objects and cannot be used independently. Formally speaking, these are *member functions* of the `athlete` class of objects. Member functions can be defined only when the class is being defined. We will learn how to do this in a later Skill. On the other hand, the `JmpJack` function does not belong to any class and, for that reason, we were able to create it at will. Functions such as `JmpJack` that are not part of a class are called *non-member functions*.

Header Files

If you have a function that you want to use in several programs, you may have to copy it to each new program in the place where you want to use it. This is not so smart! It would be good if you could tell the computer to grab the function that you want and copy it for you.

You may have stored the function in a file (just like any other program). You then use the `#include` directive to make a copy for you. This is the purpose of `#include`. I prepared several functions to make your life easier, but if you have to copy these programs one by one, you will soon give up. Instead, I stored these functions in a header file (`franca.h`), and when you use a statement such as

```
#include "franca.h"
```

you are telling the computer to find the file franca.h and copy it into your program. You can do this with your programs and functions, too!

If a function jumpjack.cpp is stored in a disk file, you can copy the function by including the following line in the program in which you want it to be copied:

```
#include "jumpjack.cpp"
```

As you look at the program, you will not see the function jumpjack (just like you don't see the functions of franca.h). You will only see #include. Nevertheless, just before the compiler starts translating your program into machine language, a copy of the requested program will be placed where #include was.

For the compiler to find your included file, this file should be in the same directory as the project with which you are currently working (for example, c:\franca). If this is not the case, you may also specify the full path to your header file:

```
#include "c:\franca\jumpjack.cpp"
```

When you want to include files that are located in your directories, the file name is enclosed in double quotes, as above. In other situations, you may want to include files that are located in the compiler directories (as you will learn how to do in later Skills). Then, instead of enclosing the file name in double quotes, you enclose it in angled brackets. For example:

```
#include <math.h>;
#include <iostream.h>;
```

What Is a Directive?

A *directive* is an instruction to the compiler. It specifies what you want done before your program is compiled. Directives are not part of the C++ language; they are mere directions that you provide to the compiler.

The compiler recognizes a directive by the pound sign (#) that is present as the first character in a line. There are several compiler directives, but we will only study include.

Creating Header Files

Files that contain pieces of programs to be copied to other programs are usually called *header files* (or *include files*) and are identified by the extension .h (instead of .cpp). You could include files with the .cpp extension, but to do the professional thing, you should store the file with the extension .h. You can do this by using

File ➤ Store As or File ➤ Save As in your C++ compiler. Type the name of the file with `.h` right after it (refer to additional material on this topic at the end of this Skill).

Try This for Fun. . .

- Transform the `JmpJack` function into a header file.

- Write a program that includes `jumpjack.h` and uses this function.

Understanding Scope

If you hear me saying, "I love Napoleon," chances are that you will understand I am a great admirer of the French general. However, if you are thinking about pastries, you may think instead that I am referring to the delicious pastry that bears the same name as the general.

This is what happens when we do not define our *scope*. You don't have to specify all the time whether you are talking about the general or the pastry, provided you are sure that you are in the right context—the same scope—as dictated by the conversation.

Scope is used in C++ and other programming languages to allow you to designate different objects using the same name, provided the objects are in different scopes.

If an object is defined in a function, it is not known outside of that function: it is *local* to that function. If the object is defined outside all functions, it is known by all functions that are defined after you have defined the object. It is then called a *global* object.

The `c2jmpjck.cpp` program contains a global object, `Sal`. The function `JmpJack()` simply used this global object to perform the exercise. This was a serious limitation, because only one object could be used with the function.

The later version, `c2jmpbdy.cpp`, offers two global objects, `Sal` and `Sally`. The function `JmpJack` uses the parameter `somebody` and, therefore, is able to exercise any athlete that is passed as an argument. `Sal` and `Sally` are still left as global objects in this program, but they don't have to be! `Sal` and `Sally` can be declared inside the `mainprog()` function to be local objects.

Although it is not wrong to use global objects, it is a good idea to avoid their use. A better implementation of `c2jmpbdy.cpp` is shown below as `c2jmbd1.cpp`.

```
//                        c2jmbd1.cpp
//
// This program uses a function JmpJack that exercises
//    a given athlete (parameter).
#include "franca.h"
void JmpJack(athlete somebody)
{
    somebody.up();
    somebody.ready();
}
void mainprog()
{
    athlete Sal,Sally;
    Sal.ready();
    JmpJack(Sal);
    Sally.ready();
    JmpJack(Sally);
}
```

Notice that, in this case, Sal and Sally are known only inside the mainprog() function. This is perfect, since no other function needs to know them.

Repeating Local Object Names

A slightly different implementation of this program can be seen below. The only difference between this program and c2jmbd1.cpp is the parameter name used in the JmpJack(athlete   Sal) function. Instead of using somebody to designate the parameter, this program uses Sal.

The following example has a scope of Sal:

```
void JmpJack(athlete Sal)
{
 Sal.up();
 Sal.ready();
}
```

This next example has a scope of Sal and Sally:

```
void mainprog()
{
 athlete Sal,Sally;
 Sal.ready();
 JmpJack(Sal);
 Sally.ready();
 JmpJack(Sally);
}
```

You should avoid using the same name to designate different things. However, the computer will not be confused if you forget. Inside the function, Sal will designate the parameter that will be substituted with a copy of the actual argument. This particular Sal plays the role of the other object Sal, which was declared in the mainprog function, and also plays the role of the Sally object.

This is the main benefit of scope: You don't have to keep track of all the names used in each function. Each name is only valid within the scope in which it was declared.

Another implementation (which should be avoided) is shown below. In this case, a global and a local object both share the name Sal. The program will still operate correctly, but inside the function JmpJack both objects have a valid scope. The locally declared object takes precedence over the global one. However, you may easily get confused when developing a program in which several objects have valid scope.

The following example has a scope of Sal:

```
athlete Sal;
```

This next example has a scope of another Sal and the original Sal:

```
void JmpJack(athlete Sal)
{
 Sal.up();
 Sal.ready();
}
```

The final example has a scope of Sally and Sal:

```
void mainprog()
{
 athlete Sally;
 Sal.ready();
 JmpJack(Sal);
 Sally.ready();
 JmpJack(Sally);
 }
```

N NOTE When two objects or variables that use the same name are valid in a given scope, the one with the most local scope is used. No two objects with the same name can be declared in the same scope.

A common mistake for beginners is to forget that the parameter is already declared in the parameter list. For example, in the function below, there is an athlete somebody declared in the parameter list. The second declaration for an athlete with the same name is incorrect.

```
void JmpJack(athlete somebody)
{
    athlete somebody; // This is wrong! Somebody exists!
    ...
```

Examples of Scope

The following example shows an invalid declaration of two objects with the same name. The first declaration of Sal occurs inside the mainprog function. The function scope is delimited by the closing brace at the end of this listing. Therefore, it is not possible to declare another object Sal before the delimiting closing brace.

```
void mainprog()
{
  athlete Sal;
  jmpjack(Sal);
  athlete Sal;     // This is incorrect:
  ...              //     first declaration of Sal is
}                  //     in the same scope!
```

As we will see later, other C++ constructs are also delimited by braces. In this case, a new scope is defined for each set of matching opening/closing braces. The example below is correct. The second declaration for Sal is within a new scope delimited by a new pair of braces. This new object will exist only within this inner scope. References to Sal within this inner scope use this new object instead of the first one. Any reference to Sal that occurs before or after the inner braces uses the first object.

```
void mainprog()          // c2scope.cpp
{
  athlete Sal;
  Sal.ready();           // This will use the first
  {
      athlete Sal;       // This is correct: new scope!
      athlete Sally;
      Sal.up();          // Another athlete is used
      Sally.left();
  }                      // End of scope here!
  Sal.right();           // This uses the first again
}
```

Skill 4

In the example above, another object, Sally, was also declared in the inner scope. References to this object are valid only within that scope (remember that a scope is delimited by a pair of braces). Any reference to Sally, either before the inner opening brace or after the inner closing brace, is an error.

Are You Experienced?

Now you can. . .

- ☑ **Write functions to simplify your programming tasks**
- ☑ **Use arguments to make functions reusable**
- ☑ **Choose between reference or value when passing arguments**
- ☑ **Create header files to use a function in different programs**
- ☑ **Understand Scope**

S K I L L

five

Using Numbers

- ❑ Storing integers, floating point numbers, and alphanumeric characters in variables

- ❑ Manipulating numeric variables

- ❑ Using arithmetic and relational operators in simple expressions

- ❑ Inputting and outputting values

In several situations, we have to use numbers in our programs. Numbers keep track of how many times we repeat something, note the time that has elapsed, and represent general quantities that we use in our programs.

As briefly mentioned in Part I, there are simple objects called variables. All they do is accommodate numbers.

> **NOTE** The name *variable* originated from the fact that the value stored in a variable may vary during program execution.

Understanding Numbers and Numeric Variables

Variables are identified in a program by an identifier. Variable identifiers obey the same rules as object identifiers. A *variable* is a location (or set of locations) in the computer memory in which we can store a number. Numbers can represent characters, colors, or just about anything we want. C++ recognizes three fundamental types of variables:

- Integer: this type represents numbers that do not include a decimal part. There are two types of integers, `int` and `long`.
    - The type `int` can hold an integer number ranging from –32,768 to +32,767.
    - The type `long` can hold an integer number ranging from –2,147,483,648 to +2,147,483,647.
- Floating point: this type represents numbers that include a decimal part. There are two types of floating point numbers, `float` and `double`.
    - The type `float` can hold a positive or negative floating point number ranging from 3.4×10^{-38} to 3.4×10^{38}. The number of significant digits is limited.
    - The type `double` can hold a positive or negative floating point number ranging from 1.7×10^{-308} to 1.7×10^{308}. The number of significant digits is also limited.

- Character: this type, although it stores an integer number, associates that number with a code that represents an alphanumeric character. This is the type char. A variable of type char can also be used as an integer.

Actual ranges for int and long may vary with your compiler.

To use a variable in your program, you have to declare it. You declare variables just like you declare objects. Remember that you declare an object by giving the object class followed by the object identifier. For example:

```
athlete Sal;
Clock mytime;
```

You declare a variable by giving the variable type followed by the variable identifier. For example:

```
int  count, howmanytimes;
float elapsedtime;
```

In addition, you can specify an integer to be *unsigned* if you don't need negative numbers. In this case, you will have twice as many positive values. For example:

```
unsigned int lapcount;
```

would declare an object lapcount that could accommodate integers from 0 to 65,535.

You may be wondering why these limits are strange numbers, instead of neat thousands or millions. This has to do with the way that computers store numbers in their memory.

Why Are There Different Types?   The main reason there are different types to represent numbers is that the different types make more efficient use of the computer's memory. Each type of variable is able to accommodate a given range of values. To represent a floating point number, we need four times the space needed to represent a character. Moreover, we cannot represent numbers that have an arbitrary number of digits. Each type has a specific limitation, as we shall see later.

Skill 5

All the numeric types obey similar syntax rules.

General Rules for Numeric Variables

Numeric variables obey the same rules that all objects obey:

- Use an identifier (a name) to designate the variable.

- Use these identifiers in the same way you have already used them for other objects.

- Declare the variable before you use it.

- As with any other object, declare a variable by preceding the variable name (identifier) with the type.

W WARNING   The declaration of a variable does not imply that it has been assigned a value. It only implies that you can use this object in your program. For example, when an int is declared, the computer simply saves a piece of memory to store the value, but does not set this value to zero or any other value.

Variables can be used in several ways:

- You can check the value of the variable.

- You can assign a new value to the variable.

- You can compare the variable to another.

Values

We will now experiment with the following code listing:

```
#include "franca.h"
void mainprog()
{                         // one, two, three program
   Athlete Sal;
   int one, two, three;
   Sal ready(5);
   Sal.say("one");
   Sal.say(one);
```

```
        Sal.say("two");
        Sal.say(two);
        Sal.say("three");
        Sal.say(three);
    }
```

What are the values of one, two, and three? If you try to run this program, you will probably notice some strange numbers when Sal tries to tell you the values of the integer variables. This is because we have not set the variables to any specific values.

WARNING   The computer's memory is always storing some information that was not cleared after use. If you use a variable without storing any value in it, the computer uses whatever information remains at that memory location.

Assigning a Value   Use the assignment operator (=) to assign a value to a variable. This symbol looks like the equal sign you know from math. To assign a value, give the variable identifier, followed by = and then the value that you want.
For example, to make a variable howmany assume the value 21, we could use

```
howmany=21;
```

Of course, the variable howmany must be declared before it is used:

```
int howmany;
```

It is important you understand that in C++ the symbol = means *becomes* or *receives the value of*—it represents an action that takes the value on its right side and stores it in the variable whose identifier is on its left side. This is not the same as an equation in math! For example, the following statement is not valid in C++:

```
21=howmany; // This will never work!
```

because the compiler would try to fetch the value of howmany and store it in 21. This does not make sense. 21 is not a variable and should always remain 21!
Here is another example: Suppose you have two integer variables in your program whose identifiers are new and old. Also, suppose new has a value of 15 and old has a value of 13. If you execute a statement such as

```
new=old;
```

both objects will now be equal to 13, because the computer takes the value on the right side and stores it in the variable whose identifier is on the left side of the assignment operator. If, in addition, you have a statement such as

```
old=new;
```

both objects will still have the value 13, because new just had its value changed to 13 with the previous statement.

If you have two variables, new and old, and you want to exchange their values, the following sequence is incorrect:

```
new=old;
old=new;
```

because when you copy the contents of old into new, the previous contents of new are lost. To correct this problem, you need an additional variable to keep the original value. For example:

```
temp=new;
new=old;
old=temp;
```

Initialization

It is also possible to assign a value at the time that the variable is declared. For example:

```
int maybe=21;
```

will not only create the integer variable maybe, but will also assign the value 21 to it.

In the *one, two, three* program, you can initialize the values by changing the declaration to

```
int one=1,two=2,three=3;
```

You can go ahead and try this now.

Using Arithmetic Operators in Simple Expressions

Variables can also be used in expressions by using the arithmetic operators for addition (+) and subtraction (–). These operators have the meaning you would expect. Variables can also be multiplied (*) and divided (/), but we will deal with these operators later.

You can combine integer variables and integer numbers in an expression to produce a result. This result can be stored in any variable if you use the = operator. For example:

```
int maybe,hisage,difference; // Declares int object
maybe=21;                     // Stores the value 21 in maybe
difference=5;                 // Stores the value 5 in difference
hisage=maybe+difference;      // Adds the value in maybe to
                              //     the value in difference and
                              //     stores the result in hisage
```

will result in the value 26 being stored in hisage.

Incrementing and Decrementing

You can also increment (add one) to your variables. This is very easy—you can use

```
maybe=maybe+1;
```

This is correct, since the computer picks up the current value of maybe, adds one to it, and stores the result in the same place again. (Can you see how this is different from a mathematical equation?) Similarly, you can decrement any value by using

```
maybe=maybe-1;
```

which is also correct.

The ++ and – – Operators

In C++, there is another possibility: You can increment a variable by following the identifier with the increment operator ++. For example:

```
maybe++;
```

There is one important difference with this increment operator: You can use it inside another expression.

```
maybe=25;
hisage=maybe++;
```

In this case, the value in maybe is used first, and only after this will maybe be incremented. In the example above, the values will be as follows after execution:

- maybe will be 26 (because it was incremented)

- hisage will be 25 (because it was copied from maybe before maybe was incremented)

If we have the following sequence instead:

```
maybe=25;
hisage=++maybe;
```

maybe will first be incremented to become 26. Then, this result will be assigned to hisage. This will cause both maybe and hisage to become 26.

A third possibility is the following sequence:

```
maybe=25;
hisage=++maybe++;
```

What do you think the values of maybe and hisage will be? maybe is incremented twice—once before and once after it is used in the expression!

N **NOTE**   Similar results can be obtained with the decrement operator (−−).

T **TIP**   ++ and −− can be used *before* or *after* a variable. If they are used before, the variable is first incremented (or decremented) and then used in the expression.

Try This for Fun. . .

- Consider that the following declaration is included in a program:

  ```
  int i=1, j=2, k=3;
  ```

  - Use the expressions below to indicate the value of k after the expression is executed. If the expression is incorrect, specify the reason. Assume that these statements are executed in sequence.

    ```
    k=++k+j;
    k=i+j++;
    k=i-j;
    i+j=k;
    k++=j;
    ```

Using Relational Operators

You can also compare values by using relational operators. In general, when you make a comparison, you want to know whether a value is

==	equal to another
!=	not equal to another
<	less than another
<=	less than or equal to another
>	greater than another
>=	greater than or equal to another

Comparisons are useful to control the number of repetitions (as we will see in the next section), and also to make decisions in programs (as we will see in a future Skill).

OBJECTS VS. VARIABLES

In many cases, we will refer to objects and variables in a similar manner. In fact, there is little difference between the two things. In the good old days of computing, there were only variables. Variables could hold information, and you could perform a limited number of operations using variables. Objects are a recent creation. Besides storing information in objects, you can specify the kinds of operations you perform with your objects. In other words, you can specify the kinds of messages to which your object will respond. Therefore, an object is a "smarter" kind of variable, because you can teach the object to do new things.

Inputting Values

Quite often, you may have to bring information into your computer. This information may be *input* through the keyboard by a human operator, may be read from a previously recorded disk file, or may be acquired by the computer from a sensor of some kind (for example, the clock). Information that comes from the real world outside the computer is valuable. Computers can respond to a variety of situations because of input.

Generally speaking, input occurs only when the program requests it. Input information is usually assigned to a variable or an object, so that the program can test it and use it.

In this Skill, we will study only means for inputting information from the keyboard. Input from disk files will be examined in Skill 23. The input methods studied in this Skill can be used only with the support software you downloaded from the Sybex Web site.

N **NOTE**   General techniques for inputting and outputting in C++ will be discussed in Part VIII.

It is possible to request that a value be input from the keyboard and then assigned to a variable. For example, when we want to make a purchase and receive some change, it is impractical to create a program each time we want to purchase something. Instead, we instruct the computer to request the value of the purchase and the amount paid.

We will examine two ways to input values:

- `ask` is an easy method that is available only with our software files.

- `Cin` is also available with our software files, but closely resembles the standard method used in C++.

The *ask* Input Function

The `ask` function generates a dialog box that asks the user to input a value from the keyboard. The value is then made available, so that you can assign it to a variable. The syntax is as follows:

```
ask ( question );
```

question represents the sentence that will be displayed to the user. For example:

```
Price=ask("Please enter the price:");
```

will cause a dialog box (such as the one shown in Figure 5.1) to be presented to the user. After the user types the value and clicks OK (or presses Enter), the dialog box disappears and the value is assigned to the variable—`Price` in this case.

The Cancel option is nonfunctional in this dialog box.

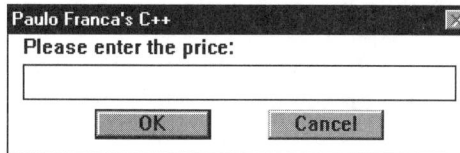

```
Paulo Franca's C++                              ▣
Please enter the price:

┌──────────────────────────────────────────┐
│                                            │
└──────────────────────────────────────────┘
        ┌──────────┐      ┌──────────┐
        │    OK    │      │  Cancel  │
        └──────────┘      └──────────┘
```

FIGURE 5.1:   Asking for input

The *Cin* Simulated Input Stream

The other alternative you can use to input values is the object Cin, which simulates the standard method for C++ input. The syntax in this case is a bit different from the ask function's syntax:

```
Cin >> variable name ;
```

variable name is the identifier of the variable in which you want the value to be stored. The main inconvenience of this approach is that there is not a question presented to the user. However, you can display a message before inputting the value (see the following section on outputting values).

The effect of Cin is similar to that of the ask function. A dialog box that instructs the user to input either an integer, a floating point number, or a sequence of characters will be displayed (see Figure 5.2).

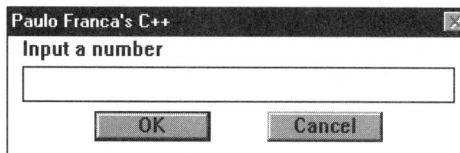

```
Paulo Franca's C++                              ▣
Input a number

┌──────────────────────────────────────────┐
│                                            │
└──────────────────────────────────────────┘
        ┌──────────┐      ┌──────────┐
        │    OK    │      │  Cancel  │
        └──────────┘      └──────────┘
```

FIGURE 5.2:   Inputting values with Cin

Skill 5

Outputting Values

In the same way that there are situations in which you want to input information to the computer from the outside world, there are other situations in which you need the computer to let you know something. Information that the computer provides to the outside world is called *output*.

Output can be received by writing numbers or characters to the screen or printer, recording information to a disk, displaying a picture on the screen, playing a sound, and many other ways. Some of these methods have been explored earlier in this book. In this section, we will examine only output that is written to the display screen as numbers or characters.

You already know how to display a value or a message by using athletes and boxes. Of course, the sentence that can be displayed is very limited in these cases. Although boxes are not generally available in standard C++ output, their functionality is similar to what you will find when you leave the standard text interface behind and move to real graphic-interface programming.

There is a Cout object to display program output that is similar to Cin. This, too, is implemented in our software as a simulation of the standard output used in C++.

The *Cout* Simulated Output Stream

The Cout output produces a wide rectangular box at the bottom of the screen and writes our output to that location. Each new output erases the previous one, since there is only one box to display.

The syntax of Cout is similar to that of Cin. However, the direction of the arrows is reversed. This will help you remember that the values go *from* the variable *to* Cout and *from* Cin *to* the variable. For example:

```
Cout<<  variable name ;
```

We can display the value of the variable Price by using:

```
Cout<<Price;
```

The program below uses ask and say (see Figure 5.3):

```
#include "franca.h"           // c2input.cpp
athlete Julia;
void mainprog()
{
  float Price;
  Julia.ready();
```

```
        Price=ask("Please enter the price:");
        Julia.say(Price);
    }
```

NOTE Standard C++ inputting and outputting is performed with cin and cout (lower-cased). They will be studied in Part VIII. It is not possible to use cin and cout while using the Windows graphic interface in the same program. Cin and Cout (capitalized) are included in the support software to use as an alternative while using the Windows graphic interface.

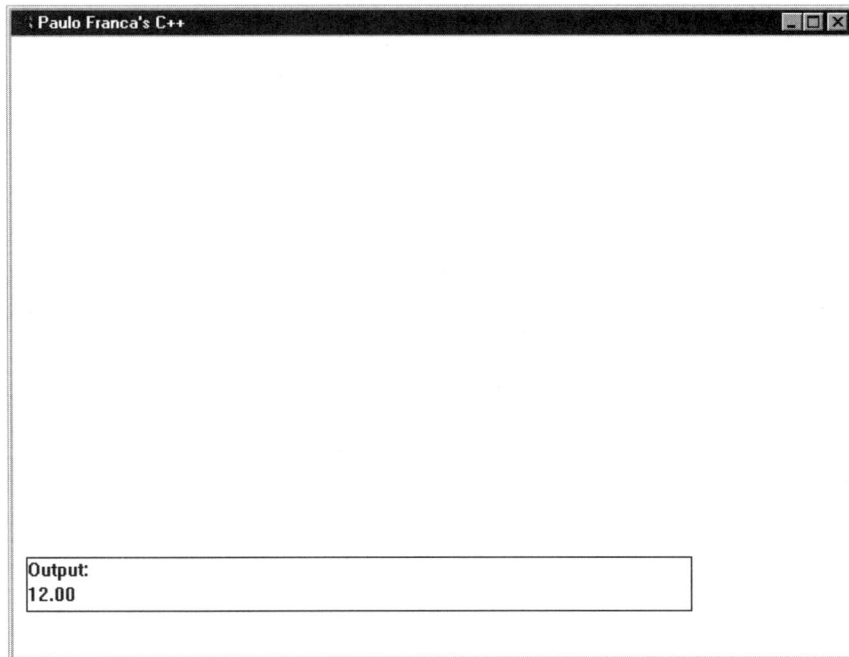

FIGURE 5.3:   The result of executing c2input.cpp

The next example uses Cin and Cout. (It is possible to mix all these functions in the same program.)

```
    #include "franca.h"              // c2cinout.cpp
```

```
void mainprog()
{
  float Price;
  Cout<<"Enter the price:";
  Cin>>Price;
  Cout<<Price;
}
```

In this program, since Cin makes no provision for a message, we used Cout to display a message to the user. It is always a good idea to tell the user what kind of input you are expecting. The final screen for this program is shown in Figure 5.3.

We can also use this program to illustrate the use of simple expressions. Let's suppose that first we want to compute the price after the sales tax is added. The program can be modified as follows:

```
#include "franca.h"
void mainprog()
{
  float Price,tax=8.25;             // New variable here
  Cout<<"Enter the price:";
  Cin>>Price;
  Price=Price+(Price*tax/100)    // Compute new price
  Cout<<Price;
}
```

There is a new variable, tax, initialized to 8.25, which assumes a sales tax of 8.25 percent. After reading Price, the program computes a new value for Price that includes the sales tax.

Are You Experienced?

Now you can. . .

☑ **Manipulate numeric variables**

☑ **Input numeric values from the keyboard**

☑ **Output numeric values to the computer screen**

S K I L L

six

6

Using Functions to Solve Problems

- ❑ Returning values in a function
- ❑ Using inline functions
- ❑ Solving problems

Now that you have learned how to handle numeric variables, you can make functions more useful. In this Skill, we will examine a few more techniques for writing and using functions, and we will reexamine the issue of problem solving. However, this time you have the powerful knowledge of using functions to simplify your problem-solving tasks.

In a real-world situation, it is unlikely that someone will tell you to "write a function to do this" or to "write a function to do that." You will be faced with a problem and you will have to do your best to solve it, using functions or not. In fact, most of the problems you will see in real life are not well defined at all!

A client may not know exactly what he or she wants (sometimes they may not even know what the problem really is). You may be responsible for studying the problem and offering a solution that will help you and your client.

Functions play an important role in problem solving. There are many benefits to using functions in your programs:

- Functions simplify the main body of the program.

- Functions make it easier to develop, understand, and modify the program.

- You may already have some functions available that can solve parts of the problem.

Always use what is available. Any new piece of program that you create will take time to develop and debug. If there is no function available to help you, start developing functions that can be used in the future to solve similar problems. You will be amazed by the amount of work you can save. Many problems in real life are variations of another problem.

It is up to you to choose how deeply into functions you want to go. In general, you should

- Deliver a program that solves the specified problem.

- Write as few lines of code as possible.

- Make your program reusable.

- Reuse whatever you can.

- Make your program easy to understand and modify.

- Deliver your program on time.

- Deliver your program as free of errors as possible.

In addition, it is important that you document all your programs and functions. Include a reasonable amount of comments with the code, and write separate documentation (like a user's manual), if necessary.

Returning Values in a Function

In general, every time you call a function, it causes some kind of result. The result may be an animation shown on the screen (such as in the jumping jack functions), a value that is obtained somehow (such as checking the time in a `Clock` object), or some combination of these.

Parameters are the primary means of communicating with a function. A parameter can be used to

- Input information to a function (as in the jumping jacks)

- Provide output from the function (in this case, the parameter must be passed as a reference)

As a simple example, let's consider a function that computes the difference between two floating point numbers to give the change for a purchase. For example, given the purchase price and the amount tendered, the function computes the change. This function needs three values to operate:

- The value of the purchase price—`theprice` (given)

- The amount tendered—`theamount` (given)

- The change to be returned—`thechange` (computed by the function)

You can write a function that takes three parameters like these, computes the difference between the first two, and places the result in the third parameter. Remember that this third parameter must be passed as a reference. The first two parameters are used as input to the function and the third one is used as output.

This function does not request any input from the keyboard, nor does it write any output to the screen. However, the values of the purchase price and the amount tendered are provided as input to the function (not to the computer) by means of the first two parameters, `theprice` and `theamount`. In a similar manner, the result obtained is passed back to the calling program by means of the third parameter, `thechange`.

NOTE   Input from the keyboard and output to the screen are done in the `mainprog` function.

In C++, you can implement this procedure with the code below:

```
void dif(float theprice,float theamount, float & thechange)

{
   thechange=theamount-theprice;
}
```

In this case, if you write a program that has values in amount and price, you can give the change by using

```
...
dif(price, amount, &change);
Cout<<change;
...
```

There is another way to communicate the result of a function so that the result can be used immediately in any expression. For example, you can use

```
Cout<<dif(price,amount,change);
```

This syntax is valid if the function returns a value as a result. Some programming languages differentiate between functions that return a result and those that do not. For example, in Pascal they are called functions if they return values; if they do not return values, they are called procedures.

How does the compiler know which functions return values and which do not? Why can't we issue a statement such as

```
Number=JumpJack(Sal);
```

but we *can* issue a statement such as

```
Price=ask("Please enter the price:");
```

What makes these functions different from each other?

Types of Return Values

In C++, the difference can be found in the function header—the first line, in which you give the name of the function. For example:

```
void dif(float theprice,float theamount, float & thechange)
```

The first thing that you write when defining a function is the type of the return value, if any. Do you remember that all our functions so far have had void preceding their names? This keyword meant that the function did not return a value.

To return a value, you must

- Specify the return type in the function header. A return type other than void will make the function return a result. If you omit the return type, C++ will assume you are returning an int.

- Include at least one statement in the function's body that specifies the result you want to return. This is done by using the keyword return.

For example, consider the simple case in which we want a modified dif function to return the difference between two floating point values that are passed as arguments. Since we want this function to return a floating point value as a result, the function header can be

```
float dif(float value1, float value2)
```

There is nothing new about the syntax. This header tells the compiler that the function whose name is dif will take two arguments, value1 and value2 (both are floating point numbers), and return a result that is also a floating point number. You no longer need a third parameter in which to store the result.

To finish the function's body, all we have to know is the syntax of the return. This is simple—it consists of the keyword return, followed by an expression:

```
return   expression ;
```

The expression is evaluated, and the result is returned by the function.

This example could then include the following function:

```
float dif(float value1, float value2)
{
    return value1-value2;
}
```

WARNING   If a return is executed, the function ends! No other statements in the function are executed after the return.

This function can be used as illustrated in the program c2change.cpp below. In this program, we request that the user input a price to be paid and the amount tendered. The program then computes the change.

This is an extremely simple application of a function that returns a value. In fact, you could do better without using a function by computing the difference in the program itself. However, we will take advantage of the simplicity of this application to further our knowledge of functions.

Skill 6

The algorithm for this program is quite simple:

- Declare the variables, price, amount, and change.

- Request that the user enter the purchase price.

- Request that the user enter the amount tendered.

- Compute the change (using the function dif).

- Inform the user of the value of the change.

Here is the program c2change.cpp (as illustrated in Figure 6.1):

```
#include "franca.h"              // c2change.cpp
float dif(float value1,float value2)
{
  return value1-value2;
}
void mainprog()
{
  float price, amount,change;
  Box given("Amount:"),thechange("Change:");
  price=ask("What is the price to pay?");
  amount=ask("How much are you giving me?");
  change=dif(amount,price);
  given.say(amount);
  thechange.say(change);
}
```

Notice that after we asked for the values for price and amount, we used the expression

```
change = dif (amount, price);
```

The value of this expression is obtained by the function dif. As we know, this function returns a value that is the difference between the first and second arguments. This returned value is then assigned to the variable change.

In this expression, we use the arguments amount and price, in that order. The function dif uses the parameters value1 and value2. When the program is executed and dif is invoked, the numeric value contained in the variable amount is copied to the variable value1 in the function. In a similar manner, the value in price is copied to value2. The resulting values will then be used, and the result will be returned.

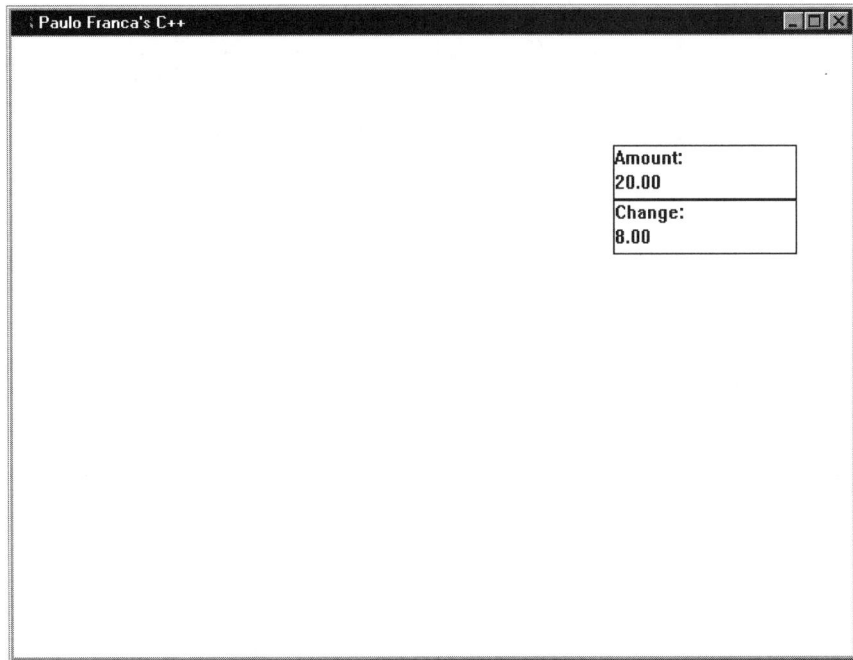

FIGURE 6.1:   The result of executing c2change.cpp

Remember that the correspondence between arguments is given solely by their order. If the expression were written as follows:

```
change = dif(price, amount);
```

the result would be completely wrong!

Originals and Copies

When you invoke a function that takes arguments, the original argument is not used. Instead, the function uses a copy of this variable (or object).

To use another example, modify the function dif so that the value in one of the arguments changes. For example, do as follows

```
float dif(float value1,float value2)
{
  value1=value1-value2;
  Cout<<value1;
  return value1;
}
```

In this case, we store the difference in `value1`, which is one of the arguments. `Cout` may be used to show the result that is stored in this variable. Still, the result is the same, because the function returns `value1`, which contains the difference.

If you include an output to display the value of the amount in the program, you will notice that this value was not changed.

> **TIP**   This output was included for teaching purposes only. In this example, `mainprog` uses this result and could possibly display it. Avoid unnecessary output in functions—it may limit the reusability of your functions.

Inline Functions

Every time your program calls a function, the computer takes some time to switch to the function and then back to the program. Most likely, the values in the arguments must be copied to the function's parameters. This consumes time.

While using different programming languages, it is not generally advisable to design functions that perform extremely simple tasks, because the time the computer spends switching back and forth offsets the benefits of using a function.

However, C++ has a distinct feature that enables you to handle this kind of function: *Inline functions* are functions whose code is placed right where the function was invoked. In other words, the compiler actually writes a copy of your instructions in every place that you call the function. There is no switching back and forth at the point in which you invoked the function. On the other hand, unlike with ordinary functions, the code will be repeated every time the function is called.

Not all functions can become inline functions, though. There are a few restrictions—the most important one is that you cannot have repetitions inside an inline function (repetitions will be studied in Skill 7).

Include the keyword `inline` in the function header to designate an inline function. Keep in mind, though, that this is strictly a C++ feature and is not available in other programming languages.

I will give an example of using an inline function in the next section of this Skill, in which we reexamine the problems seen in "The Great Escape—Part 1" in Skill 2 and use functions to simplify the solution.

The Great Escape—Part 2

Functions greatly simplify the task of having the robot move to draw squares. Notice how much easier this task becomes if the robot already knows how to draw a line!

If a function that makes the robot draw a line is available, the problem of drawing a square can be summarized as follows:

> draw a line
>
> turn right
>
> draw a line
>
> turn right
>
> draw a line
>
> turn right
>
> draw a line
>
> turn right

The last turn is not really necessary, but it is convenient, because you leave the robot facing the initial direction. You can use our robot, Tracer, to draw lines and squares.

Since we are not dealing with repetitions yet, we can think in terms of lines that are always three steps long. The algorithm is obvious:

> This is how you draw a line of size 3:
>
> mark
>
> step
>
> mark
>
> step

Since the robot can only mark the square ahead of her (and not the one she is in), the total length of the line, including the initial square and the last one, is three squares. Again, this leaves the first square blank. If this bothers you, you can always correct the situation:

> This is how you draw a line of size 3, including the first square:
>
> mark
>
> step
>
> right
>
> right   // Turn back
>
> mark   // Mark first square
>
> right   // Turn back

right

mark

step

It is easy to write a function that implements any of the algorithms above:

```
Robot Tracer;
void line3()
{
    Tracer.mark();
    Tracer.step();
    Tracer.mark();
    Tracer.step();
}
```

Nevertheless, when you design a function, try to make it as useful as possible. That way, you may be able to reuse it someday.

This function would be a lot more useful if you could specify the line size. This will be done later when you learn how to handle repetitions. Still, you can add a little more versatility to this function if you allow the color to be chosen by means of a parameter. For example:

```
void line3(int color)
{
    Tracer.mark(color);
    Tracer.step();
    Tracer.mark(color);
    Tracer.step();
}
```

Does it bother you that you have to specify a color every time you invoke the function? No problem! You can specify a default value for the color in the function header:

```
void line3(int color=2)
```

Once you have written the line function, you can easily draw a square or, for that matter, you can consider writing a function that draws squares, as well. By doing so, you collect solutions to common problems that you may face someday.

One possible implementation of the square function is

```
void square3(int color=2)
{
    line3(color);
```

```
      Tracer.right();
      line3(color);
      Tracer.right();
      line3(color);
      Tracer.right();
      line3(color);
      Tracer.right();
   }
```

When to Use a Function

To solve this simple square-drawing problem, functions can be used in several ways:

- Use two functions, line3 and square3. square3 draws a square by using another function, line3, which draws a line.

- Use three functions, paint, line3, and square3. You can use a function to mark and step to each square, because each time you want to paint a square, you have to mark and then step. This simplifies the code used for the line3 function.

- Don't use the square3 function. Use line3 to draw the square in the program.

- Don't use the line3 function. Use square3, which draws each line.

- Don't use functions at all. Write all the instructions to draw the square in the mainprog function.

Which Alternative Is Best?

There is no simple answer to this question. Several factors need to be considered to determine which alternative is best, and this may even vary from one person to another.

Clearly, the last alternative—not using functions at all—makes the program more difficult. Programmers who don't use functions typically spend more time developing and debugging, because

- The code ends up being more complex.

- No pieces were reused from previously developed software.

Some programmers maintain that using fewer functions makes their programs run faster. In general, this is a true statement. Each time a function is called, the computer spends additional time. However, not that many applications are so time-critical. In many situations, it may be preferable to finish your programs earlier and be able to change them easily upon request, instead of ending up with a high- speed application that is difficult to change and requires a long time to get ready.

The second alternative—using three levels of functions—may seem a little extreme. Functions that perform tiny tasks can become superfluous and steal time from your computer. This may or may not always be the case. But as far as you, the programmer, are concerned, this solution requires you to write the fewest lines of code! This makes it the ideal solution for the lazy programmer.

Is there anything wrong with being a lazy programmer? No, not at all! As long as you solve your problems while writing as little code as possible, you will actually climb the ladder of success. What is wrong with this solution then?

As I said before, it is questionable to use a function that is called a million times to do a puny job, because a lot more time is lost while switching than is used to do actual work. This leads to the natural conclusion that using functions in these cases should be avoided.

This is true in most programming languages, but is not completely true in C++—remember the inline functions?

Small pieces of program that do not contain a repetition and that are needed many times in the program are good candidates to become inline functions. However, remember that inline functions are specific to C++ and are not available in other languages. It remains a good practice to avoid using tiny functions!

The program c2squar2.cpp illustrates a solution that uses all three functions. In the mainprog function, the robot is instructed to take five steps toward the east then seven steps toward the south to start the drawing. Two squares are then built in different colors.

```
#include "franca.h"     // c2squar2.cpp
Robot Tracer;
inline void paint(int color=2)
{
  Tracer.mark(color);
  Tracer.step();
}
void line3 (int color=2)
{
  paint(color);
  paint(color);
}
void square3(int color=2)
{
```

```
    line3(color);
    Tracer.right();
    line3(color);
    Tracer.right();
    line3(color);
    Tracer.right();
    line3(color);
    Tracer.right();
}

void mainprog()
{
  Tracer.face(3);
  Tracer.step(5);
  Tracer.right();
  Tracer.step(7);
  Tracer.left();
  square3();
  Tracer.step(5);
  square3(3);
}
```

Rules and Regulations

Let's now summarize the syntax rules for the material covered so far.

Function Definition   The *function definition* is a piece of program that explains the actions to be performed each time you invoke the function. The definition includes a function header and the function body. In general, a function will look as follows

```
function header
{
    function body
}
```

Function Header   The *function header* contains

- The return type (functions that do not return a result use the type void)

- The function name (or identifier), and a list of parameters and their types enclosed in parentheses (if there are no parameters, the space inside the parentheses will be empty)

Skill 6

You may also see the keyword `void` inside the parentheses. For example, `float time(void)` is exactly the same as empty parentheses—`float time()`.

If there is more than one parameter, the parameters are separated by commas and each one must be preceded by its type or class. The parameters are already declared in the list itself.

For example, we have

```
void JmpJack( athlete somebody)
```

This is a header for a function that

- Does not return a result (`void`)

- Has a name (`JmpJack`)

- Takes one parameter of type `athlete`. This parameter will be known as somebody in the function. (Do not declare somebody to be of type `athlete` again in the function)

Function Body The *function body* contains the code that is executed when the function is called. This piece of program consists of one or more statements, which are placed inside braces.

For example, in the `JmpJack` function, the body is as follows:

```
somebody.up();
somebody.ready();
```

Therefore, the complete function is as follows:

```
void JmpJack( athlete somebody)
{
    somebody.up();
    somebody.ready();
}
```

Now, observe the following items:

- If some arguments have default values and others do not, those with default values must be shown last in the argument list. Values assigned to default arguments must be in a valid scope.

- A function cannot be called before it has been defined!

Type Matching   The *types* (or classes) of arguments must match those of the corresponding parameters when calling a function. If a function is defined as follows:

```
void jumps (Clock timekeeper, athlete somebody)
```

this function must be called using two arguments: the first must be `Clock` and the second must be `athlete`. The compiler checks whether this correspondence is done correctly and issues an error message if an error is found.

Function Overloading   Unlike many other programming languages, C++ allows for more than one function to have the same identifier. This can be done if either the number or the type of arguments is not the same. We call this *function overloading*.

For example, a function `JmpJack` with one argument and another function `JmpJack` with two arguments can both be included in the same program. However, no other function `JmpJack` with one or two arguments of class `athlete` can be included.

The compiler will be able to differentiate between calls of the form

```
JmpJack(Sal);
```

and those of the form

```
JmpJack(Sal, Sally);
```

and will use the appropriate function.

Value vs. Reference   By default, arguments are passed to a function *by value*. This means that a copy of the object or variable is made and is then used by the function. You can use and modify the parameter at will, without causing any modification to the original argument.

By including the & symbol before the parameter identifier, you indicate that all operations stated in the function involving that parameter are to use the original argument, instead of a copy.

Passing *by reference* can speed up your program if the object passed is complex. This will save the computer the time it needed to copy the object. It is not possible to pass a constant (e.g., a number) when the function expects a reference. For example, a function defined as follows:

```
float dif (float &value1,float &value2)
```

cannot be invoked as

```
change = dif(100.00 ,- price);
```

Skill 6

The reference would allow the function to modify the value of `value1` and, in this case, the constant, `100.00`, is not supposed to be altered. This would result in an error message.

Function Call   When you want to perform the set of actions you defined in a function, you can use a *function call* in your program. The function call consists of the function name followed by parentheses:

```
function_name ( argument_list )
```

If the function takes arguments, you must include the objects that will be used inside the parentheses. If the function takes more than one argument, the correspondence between the actual object and the parameter is established solely by the order in which they appear.

Function Prototype   There may be situations in which you need to use a function before the function is defined. Since the compiler examines the source code sequentially, it will think you are calling a function that does not exist. This is not a very common situation. However, if you are faced with this problem, you will have to notify the compiler that there is a function with a given name that takes certain parameters and returns a result of a certain type. This is the *function prototype.*

The function prototype looks very much like the function header, except that

- There is a semicolon at the end:

```
float change (float price, float amount);
```

- You may omit the parameter names:

```
float change (float, float);
```

WARNING It is a common mistake to include a semicolon after the function header—the compiler thinks this header is simply a prototype and never finds the function definition.

Function prototypes are not required unless you need to tell the compiler about a function that will be defined later in the code—but it is not a mistake to include them even when not needed.

Avoiding Multiple Inclusions of Header Files

When you use `include` to include files in your program, you may inadvertently copy the same file more than once. This may happen either because you have more than one `include` in your program or you included a file that also includes another file that was already requested.

For example, suppose you have a program that includes a program named `gymnast.h` as well as including `JumpJack.h`. As illustrated below, in this case the `gymnast.h` program also has an `include` for `JumpJack.h`.

Your program:

```
#include "gymnast.h"
#include "JumpJack.h"
```

The `gymnast.h` program:

```
#include "JumpJack.h"
```

If you want to do things right, you can prevent more than one copy from being included in your program by adding a few more lines to your header file. Add the following two lines at the beginning:

```
#ifndef    JUMPJACK_H
#define    JUMPJACK_H
```

and add this line at the end:

```
#endif
```

JUMPJACK_H should be replaced with a different name for each file. You can adopt the practice of using the name of the header file (`JumpJack`) in all upper-cased letters, followed by an underscore and an uppercased *H*.

Statements that start with the character # in the first position are not specifically part of the C++ language. They are instructions for the part of the compiler called the preprocessor. These statements are also called preprocessor directives.

Try your hand at preprocessor syntax by writing a piece of code that uses an `include` to include the `JumpJack.h` file twice. Then, include the preprocessor directives given above in the `JumpJack.h` file and execute the same program.

When you've mastered these tasks, write a header file that contains functions for jumping jacks and leftrights. These functions should be able to receive an athlete as a parameter. Call this header file `fitness.h` and store it in your computer.

Skill 6

You may also want to write a program that uses the header file `fitness.h` and two athletes, Sal and Sally. This program should make Sal and Sally perform four jumping jacks and three leftrights.

Integers and Floating Point Numbers

An integer variable can store an integer number ranging from –32,768 to +32,767. Declare these variables by preceding the variable identifier with the keyword `int`. Numbers with a decimal part can be stored in variables of type `float`. Declare these variables by preceding the variable identifier with the keyword `float`. More than one variable of the same type can be declared in a statement. For example:

```
int number, alpha, count;
float x,y,z;
```

It is possible to set an initial value for the variable at the same time you declare it. For example:

```
int one=1,two =2, three=3, other;
float x=3.45,y,z;
```

declares four variables: `one`, `two`, and `three` will be initialized to 1, 2, and 3 respectively, and `other` will not be initialized. Likewise, the floating variable `x` is initialized to the value 3.45. The variables `y` and `z` are declared, but are not initialized to any specific value.

You can change the value of the variable at any point in the program by showing the variable identifier on the left side of an assignment operator (=) and presenting an expression on the right side. In this case, the value of the expression replaces the previous value of the variable. For example:

```
one=54;
two=one+three;
```

The left side of the assignment operator must designate a unique object or variable. It is invalid to have an expression such as

```
one+two = three;
```

It is possible to use a `float` variable to assign a value to an `int` variable and vice versa. When a `float` value is assigned to an integer, the fractional part is lost (it is truncated, not rounded). When an integer value is assigned to a `float` variable, a fractional part consisting of zeros is assumed.

Expressions

Expressions are sequences containing variable identifiers, arithmetic operators, function calls, parentheses, and constants (numbers) arranged according to pre-determined rules. Expressions indicate how to operate with the variables and constants to produce a result.

The arithmetic operators are as follows:

+	addition
–	subtraction
*	multiplication
/	division
%	remainder

In addition, the assignment operator (=) can be used in arithmetic expressions.

Definitions

- Operators can be +, –, *, /, %, and =.
- A term is a variable (or object), a constant, or a function call.

Rules

- Terms must be separated by an operator.
    - The two terms operate according to the rule prescribed by that operator.
- Operations are executed according to their priority. Highest priority operations use *, /, and %. Lowest priority operations use + and –. Operations of the same priority are evaluated in the order they are written (left to right).
- A term may be preceded by the operator –.
    - The negative of the value will be taken. (It is also possible to precede a term by the operator +.)
- Pairs of parentheses may be included anywhere to specify priority.
    - Expressions inside parentheses will be evaluated first. If more than one pair of parentheses is included, the inner parentheses will be evaluated first.

- The increment (++) and decrement (––) operators may be used immediately before or immediately after a variable.

  - The variable will be incremented or decremented.

- A variable (or object) may be used on the left side of an assignment operator (=).

  - The result of the expression is assigned to the variable whose identifier is on the left side of the =.

  - More than one assignment operator may be used in an expression, provided each one is preceded by only a variable.

N NOTE

The value is assigned to each variable from right to left. A legal example is howmany = times = times+1. The value of times+1 will be evaluated, copied into times, and then copied into howmany. An illegal example is howmany = times+1 = 5. The expression times+1 is more than a single variable and, therefore, cannot precede an assignment operator.

Try These for Fun. . .

- Write a function symmetry (athlete he, athlete she); that makes two athletes perform an exercise simultaneously. However, the exercises should be performed symmetrically, in the following manner:

  - he should do the following sequence:

    ready

    up

    left

    up

    right

    up

- she should do the following sequence:

    ready

    up

    right

    up

    left

    up

- Write a program that makes the two athletes exercise six times.

Are You Experienced?

Now you can. . .

☑ **Return values as in functions**

☑ **Use inline functions**

☑ **Use functions to solve your problems**

PART III

Using Repetitions

Computers are great at repetitive work. In fact, their usefulness is so extensive because most problems involve an incredible amount of repetition.

You will now learn how to specify that a piece of program is to be repeated, how to specify how many times it should be repeated, and how to find out the results that will be generated each time.

These pieces of program are called loops. You will learn about how loops work and what the statements are that can be used to build them. You will then learn how to design a loop in order to solve your problems. Finally, you will start working on a down-to-earth application that develops a simplified point-of-sale terminal.

S K I L L

seven

Counting and Repeating

- ❑ Repeating with *while* loops

- ❑ Repeating with *do/while* loops

- ❑ Repeating with *for* loops

- ❑ Using conditional repetitions

- ❑ Nesting loops

In a real fitness class, Sal must perform each exercise several times. For example, he has to repeat the jumping jack a certain number of times. This is the simplest kind of repetition: a given set of instructions is to be repeated a predetermined number of times. If you were Sal's instructor, you would probably instruct him to repeat a jumping jack 15 times.

For a smart guy like Sal, this would probably suffice. He would understand the meaning of the word *repeat,* and he would know what you mean by a jumping jack. Finally, *15 times* complements the order to repeat and, therefore, the jumping jack will be repeated 15 times.

Unfortunately, computers are not as smart as Sal and we must make sure they understand exactly what we want them to do. The process is easy to understand if you think of how a real person executes the instruction to repeat a jumping jack 15 times.

If you want to repeat something, you have to count how many times you have already repeated and stop when you reach the desired count. Very likely, you will see people exercising and shouting, "One! Two! Three!" The process we follow is illustrated in Figure 7.1.

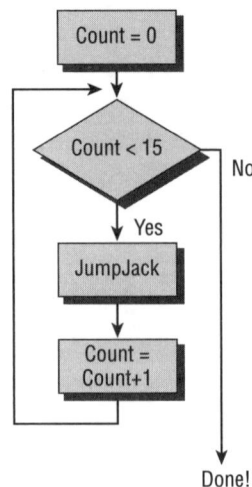

FIGURE 7.1: Counting and repeating

Just like humans, the computer also needs to store a count that will go *one, two, three.* To do this, we can use an integer variable. This Skill will show you how to use integer variables to include counting and repeating in your programs.

Understanding Simple Repetitions

We are now ready to look at simple repetitions that cause a piece of program to repeat a specified number of times. There are three possibilities:

- `while` loops
- `do/while` loops
- `for` loops

Repeating with *while* Loops

The repetition illustrated in Figure 7.1 can be explained as follows:

> Set count to zero.
>
> While count is less than 15, repeat the following:
>
>> JumpJack.
>>
>> Increment count.
>
> You are done!

in which *count* is merely a variable that keeps the count of how many jumping jacks have been completed. At the start, you can make this equal to zero, since you haven't done anything so far.

The next line, *While…*, explains that the indented sequence that follows is to be repeated while the condition *count is less than 15* is true.

Isn't this what you actually do in your mind? And why is the sequence indented? We will find out a little later.

Loops Defined

Figure 7.1 illustrates the sequence in which we want the instructions to be executed. This is called a *flowchart*. If you start at the top (Count=0) and follow the indications in the flowchart, you should observe that the next thing to be done is to compare the count with 15. There are two alternate directions to take, according to the result. Since the count is zero initially, the next steps will be to perform a JumpJack and then increment the count by one.

After that action is completed, the arrows indicate that we should go back to comparing the count with 15. Well, the count is now 1, which is still less than 15, so the same thing is repeated. The path followed in the flowchart each time we repeat this sequence is a closed path that resembles a loop. For this reason, programmers call a piece of program that gets repeated a *loop*.

This loop is executed 15 times (since the count is zero until it hits 14, both inclusive). When the count hits 14, the program performs a JumpJack and then increments the count, resulting in the new value, 15. Now, when the comparison takes place, the count is compared with 15—this time it is no longer less! Finally, the alternate path is taken and we leave the loop.

Infinite Loops

Suppose that we did not include the following statement:

```
Count=Count+1;
```

to update the count in the program. When would we leave the loop? Never!

We would keep comparing the count (which would always be zero) with 15, and the count would always be less than 15 (since the original value wouldn't change). This would result in a well-known bug called an *infinite loop*. This example is very simple and, hopefully, you can see the problem. In other cases, the problem may be more complex, and it may not be so easy to notice that the loop is infinite.

Don't worry, you will eventually make some of your own infinite loops.

TIP   If you suspect you are executing a program that is in an infinite loop, you can cancel the execution by pressing Ctrl+Alt+Delete (at the same time). While you are in Windows, this will bring a message to the screen that allows you to cancel the current program by pressing Enter. The program execution will be canceled, and you will go back to the C++ compiler.

Compound Statements

Take another look at the piece of program we are examining. Why is it that the steps

JumpJack

Increment count

are indented?

You must clearly indicate which set of instructions is going to be repeated. For example, you don't want to repeat *You are done!* every time, do you? As a matter of fact, when you want to group some statements to be treated as a single, big statement, you enclose them in braces to denote that those statements are to be treated as one compound statement.

A *compound statement* is a group of statements (enclosed in braces) that is to be treated as one statement for purposes such as repetitions. (It is also common to refer to compound statements as *blocks*.) When describing the algorithm, you may simply indent this group of statements. In C++, you actually have to use braces.

NOTE   All functions, including `mainprog`, contain a compound statement (which is why a semicolon is not used).

WARNING   Don't place a semicolon between the `while` statement and the compound statement! The semicolon ends a statement right where it is placed.

For example:

```
while (count<15);     // This semicolon is wrong!
{
    JumpJack();
    count=count+1;
}
```

will cause the computer to understand that while `count` is less than 15, you want to repeat *nothing*. Does this look like an infinite loop? Well, it may not look like one, but it certainly is! The empty loop will be repeated forever, because the value of `count` is never incremented.

Also, notice that in the correct program, every time you perform a `JumpJack`, you increment `count`. This means that `count` will equal 1, 2, 3…14. After `count` equals 14, the condition is still good (after all, 14 is less than 15). When we repeat the sequence one more time (the 15th), `count` will be incremented to 15.

At this point, the condition is checked again before the repetition takes place. Since `count` (the number of times we have repeated) is now 15, the condition fails (15 is not less than 15) and the repetition stops! After the loop completes, the program resumes with the next instruction (after the closing brace).

NOTE   You could start with `count=1` and check for a count that is less than or equal to 15, or less than 16. (*Less than or equal to 15* and *less than 16* amount to the same thing.)

Skill 7

In C++, the repetition with which we have been dealing could be written as follows:

```
count=0;            // Set initial count to zero
while (count<15)    // Now repeat the sequence below
{                   //      fifteen times:
    JumpJack(Sal);  //          do a JumpJack
    count++;        //          update count
}                   // Sequence to repeat ends here!
```

The process followed in the while is illustrated in Figure 7.1.

The program above could also be written as follows:

```
count=0;
while (count<15)
{JumpJack(Sal);
count++;}
```

Indentation makes the program more readable.

Using Operators in the *while* Loop

The keyword while indicates that a sequence is to be repeated while the condition is true. The condition is shown inside parentheses and reflects the relationship between two values. In this case, we are interested in a count that is less than 15; therefore, we used the operator < (less than). Other operators are possible:

==	equal to (notice that there are two equal signs)
>	greater than
>=	greater than or equal to
<	less than
<=	less than or equal to
!=	not equal to

Conditions

When you want to repeat a sequence of statements, you must specify when you want the sequence to start repeating and when you want it to stop repeating. To do this, specify the condition for executing the sequence. This condition is usually represented by a relational expression. The relational expression is shown right after the keyword while and is enclosed inside parentheses.

In this example, the relational expression is

```
count<15
```

which means that we want to repeat the sequence as long as the value of `count` is less than 15. The symbol for less than (<) is a relational operator, because it expresses the relationship between objects. Of course, you could use the other operators, as well. There may be times when you have to specify a condition that is much more complex. In Skill 10, we will learn how to combine them into more complex relational expressions.

Try These for Fun. . .

- Write a program to make Sal perform five jumping jacks and five leftrights.

- Write a program to make Sal perform a jumping jack followed by a leftright five times.

- Write a program to make Sal perform a jumping jack five times and to then make Sally perform a jumping jack five times.

- Write a program to make both Sal and Sally perform a jumping jack (simultaneously) five times.

- Write a function, `JmpJack`, that takes two parameters:

  ```
  void JmpJack( athlete somebody, int howmany)
  ```

  - This function should make the athlete `somebody` repeat a jumping jack for the specified number of times.

Repeating with *do/while* Loops

The `do/while` statement is a slightly different variation of the `while` repetition. In the `while` loop, the condition is tested before you start the loop. As a result, if the condition is not true at the beginning, the loop is not executed even once!

`do/while` makes the comparison at the end of the loop, as shown in Figure 7.2. No matter what happens to the condition, the loop is executed at least once. After this first execution, the condition is checked and then the loop may or may not be repeated.

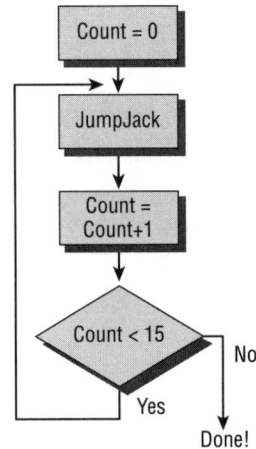

FIGURE 7.2:   The do/while loop

In do/while, the keyword do indicates the beginning of the loop. The keyword while, which is followed by the condition, indicates the end of the loop. Notice the semicolon after the condition!

For example, the same effect could be achieved by the following program:

```
count=0;
do
{
  JumpJack(Sal);
  count++;
}
while (count<15);
```

Notice that the actual loop is enclosed in braces and the while is located after the braces.

Repeating with *for* Loops

You may often find the for statement to be easier and more convenient than while. while requires you to initialize the count and to update its value. If you forget either one of these two things, you will surely end up in trouble.

The following program:

```
count=0;
    while (count<15)
    {
     JumpJack(Sal);
     count++;
    }
```

could also be written as follows:

```
for (count=0;count<15;count++)
    {
     JumpJack(Sal);
    }
```

The two structures are very similar, except that for allows you to specify the initial value, the condition, and the update all in the same place! Inside the parentheses, there are three parts separated by semicolons:

- The first part, count=0, is an expression that will be executed only once before the repetition takes place. This is useful to set the initial value for the count we are using.

- The second part, count<15, specifies the condition that keeps the repetition going. Just like in while, this condition is checked and the repetition takes place if it is true.

- The third part, count++, is an expression that will be executed once at the end of each repetition. It is useful for specifying how we want to update the count.

You might instead use the following statement to achieve the same results:

```
for (count=1; count<=15; count++)
```

It may be more natural to start counting from one and to stop at the desired count than to start counting from zero.

> **NOTE**   Remember, the expressions are separated by semicolons!

It is also possible to declare a new variable inside for. For example:

```
for(int counter=1;counter<=15;counter++);
```

In the example that follows using the program `c3askfor.cpp`, we use `for` to repeat, and we request that the number of times be input through the keyboard using the `ask` function.

```cpp
// Using user input...          // c3askfor.cpp
// This program uses input
// Revised September 7 1994.
#include "franca.h"
void JumpJack(athlete she)
{
   // We make "she" perform a JumpJack
   she.up();
   she.ready();
}
void mainprog()
{
   athlete Kim;
   int howmany,done;
   // Ask how many times you want her to exercise:
   howmany=Kim.ask("How many jumping Jacks?");
   // Now repeat as many as told:
   for(done=1;done<=howmany;done++)
   {
       JumpJack(Kim);          // Do a JumpJack
       Kim.say(done);
   }
       Kim.say("done");        // See the quotes?
}
```

In this program, we don't know how many times the `JumpJack` will be repeated while we write the program. We simply set apart a variable, `howmany`, and tell the computer to execute the loop while `done` is less than or equal to `howmany`.

THE EQUIVALENCE OF *FOR* AND *WHILE*

A piece of program that includes `for` is entirely equivalent to one that includes `while`. The initial expression in `for` is executed before `while`, and the final expression is executed just before the end of the `while` loop.

Thus, a sequence such as

```cpp
for( <exp1> ; <exp2> ; <exp3> )
{
   <statements>
}
```

continued ▶

is the same as

```
<exp1>;
while(<exp2>)
{
    <statements>
    <exp3>;
}
```

Using Conditional Repetitions

In the previous section, we examined the simplest kind of repetition, in which we knew exactly how many times we wanted to repeat the sequence.

We will now examine the other kind of repetition, in which the number of times is not known beforehand. Of course, you may come up with some examples in real life in which you have to repeat something an unknown number of times until, for some reason, you know you are done.

The only difference between these repetitions is the condition that you have to test. Previously, you tested whether the count was still less than or equal to the number of times you wanted to repeat. Now, we aren't going to pay attention to the number of times we want to repeat. Instead, we'll try to check whether we are already done.

Checking Input Values

An interesting and useful application of repetitions is to verify input data. Suppose you want the user to type a value, and you want to make sure it is not negative. This could be solved with the sequence below:

```
float value;
value=ask("Enter a positive value:");
while ( value < 0 )
{
    value=ask("Wrong, enter a POSITIVE value:");
}
```

Skill 7

This piece of program will keep asking the user to reenter the value as long as the input is negative. This kind of data validation is very important, and you should include similar precautions in your programs. You can never trust what the user will input, but you can always trust what your program will do!

Example—At the Store

Suppose we want to compute the change for merchandise sales at a store. The program c3store1.cpp illustrates a solution to this.

```
#include "franca.h"
void mainprog()                    // c3store1.cpp
{
  float price,change,amount,tax=8.25;
  price=ask("Input the price:");
  price=price+price*tax/100;
  Cout<<price;

  amount=ask("Enter the amount:");
  while (amount<price)
  {
     amount=ask("Not enough, re-enter amount:");
  }
  change=amount-price;
  Cout<<change;
}
```

After the amount is first input, a while loop will be repeated as long as the amount is less than the price. If the amount is sufficient, this loop will not be executed (not even once). We may proceed to compute the change. However, if the amount is not sufficient, the loop will be entered to request that a new value be input. It is nice that the program will not go on unless the correct amount is entered, no matter how many times the user makes a mistake!

An equivalent solution to this problem could make use of do/while. Since this kind of loop tests the condition only after the loop has been executed, the resulting program can do without one of the inputs. In this case, the while loop could be replaced with

```
do
{
   amount=ask("Enter amount:");
}
while (amount<price);
```

Notice how do/while served this case better—fewer lines of code were needed. In this case, this solution has the inconvenience of failing to report what is wrong if the user keeps typing an insufficient amount.

Checking the Time

There may be several other reasons that determine the end of the loop besides the number of repetitions. As mentioned, checking the correct value of some input data is one of them. Another interesting case is when we use the time to determine how long a loop should be performed.

As you may have figured out, all you have to do is to write the correct condition in while, do/while, or for.

Example—At the Fitness Class

Let's suppose that Kim wants to exercise for 15 seconds as an example of conditional repetition controlled by time. As you can guess, we cannot tell in advance how many exercises will be done in 15 seconds unless, of course, we know the precise duration of each exercise. This is actually the case in real life. There are many events that you keep doing until the time is up, as in the example program c3dotime.cpp, shown below.

```
// Testing repetitions with time... c3dotime.cpp
// Revised August/8/94
#include "franca.h"
void JumpJack(athlete she)        // Function JumpJack
{
    she.ready();
    she.up();
    she.ready();
}

void mainprog()                   // Main program
{
    athlete Kim;                  // Declare Kim as an athlete
    int howmany=1;                // Declare a counter
    Clock timex;                  // Create a clock
    while (timex.time()<12)       // While time is less than 12
    {
        JumpJack(Kim);            // JumpJack
        Kim.say(howmany++);       // Say how many times
    }
}
```

Skill 7

Execute this program. Notice that the condition in `while` simply checks the time in the clock and keeps repeating while the time is less than 12.

Example—How Fast Is Your Computer?

It is an interesting exercise to see how fast Kim can exercise on your computer. If you modify the program above by inserting a zero as an argument to the messages `ready` and `up`, these movements will be done as fast as possible. See how many exercises can be done in 12 seconds, for example. The result will vary according to the type of computer that you are using. You may try to check your results against your colleagues' results. The faster the computer, the more exercises that can be done.

Using the *yesno* Function

In some situations, you may want your program to ask the user whether a loop is to be repeated. Take the `c3store1.cpp` program, for example. In this program, we requested some input regarding the price and amount tendered to compute the change.

Very likely, this task is going to be repeated many times during the day. We don't want to tell the computer to run our program every time a customer wants to buy something. The appropriate solution is to keep this program running and asking for input. But, when should we stop? Well, we could include a question such as *Do you want to continue? Yes or No?* at the end of the loop. If the user answers *yes*, the loop will be repeated.

How do we know whether the user answers *yes* or *no*?

To make our life simpler, `franca.h` includes a function that displays a dialog box in which the user can click a box marked *Yes* or a box marked *No*. We can pass a sentence as an argument to this function, and this sentence will also be displayed on the screen. Figure 7.3 illustrates the dialog box generated by `yesno`.

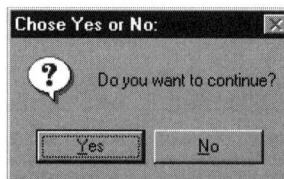

FIGURE 7.3:   The dialog box generated by yesno

The dialog box results from the following call to yesno:

```
yesno("Do you want to continue?");
```

The yesno function also returns a value, which makes it possible to use the function call directly in an expression. If the user clicks Yes, the returned value will be one; otherwise, it will be zero. A revised code for the program is presented below as the program c3store2.cpp.

Essentially, we included the body of the previous program inside a do/while loop. The yesno function is invoked directly as the expression for the loop.

```cpp
#include "franca.h"
void mainprog()                              // c3store2.cpp
{
  float price,change,amount,tax=8.25;
  do
  {
   price=ask("Input the price:");
   price=price+price*tax/100;
   Cout<<price;

   amount=ask("Enter the amount:");
   while (amount<price)
   {
       amount=ask("Not enough, re-enter amount:");
   }
   change=amount-price;
   Cout<<change;
  }
  while (yesno("Do you want to continue?"));
}
```

This function may be used in any expression and is not restricted for use with a do/while.

TIP   Choose your question so that most of the time the answer is *yes*. This is because the default is *yes,* and the user may just hit Enter instead of moving the mouse to click No.

NOTE   The yesno function is not available in standard C++—it is only available with the software developed for this book.

Skill 7

Nesting

You are often faced with the situation in which you have to repeat some directions that include another repetition:

> Take two capsules a day for 10 days.

You have to repeat an action 10 times that is a repetition itself:

> Repeat the following 10 times:
>> Repeat the following 2 times:
>>> Swallow a capsule.
>
>> Wait until the next day.

You will be swallowing a total of 20 capsules.

Notice that one repetition is "nested" inside the other. You have to completely finish the inner repetition to proceed with the outer one. Figure 7.4 shows what we call the *inner* loop—the loop that is repeated every day. Figure 7.5 shows the complete process, in which you can see that there is an *inner* and an *outer* loop.

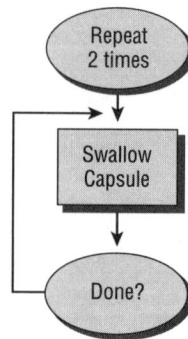

FIGURE 7.4: The inner loop, which you repeat every day

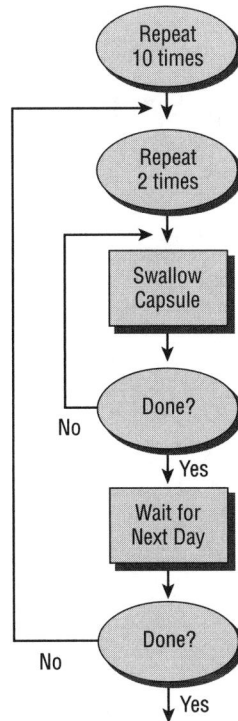

FIGURE 7.5:   The complete loop for 10 days

Another example of nesting appears in the fitness class. Suppose the instructor wants you to do as follows:

Repeat this 5 times:

Repeat this 10 times:

jumping jack.

Repeat this 5 times:

leftright.

Repeat this 3 times:

jumping jack.

You are to do 10 jumping jacks followed by 5 leftrights, and then repeat this sequence 5 times (a total of 50 jumping jacks and 25 leftrights). Then, you do an additional 3 jumping jacks.

The first set of jumping jacks is nested inside another repetition. The second set is not. In C++, this program could be written as follows:

```cpp
#include "franca.h"
void mainprog()
{
  athlete Sal;
  int bigcount,smallcount;        // To keep the count…

  for (bigcount=1;bigcount<=5;bigcount++) // Repeat 5 times
  {
      for (smallcount=1;smallcount<=10;smallcount++)
      {
        JmpJack(Sal);
      }
      for (smallcount=1;smallcount<=5;smallcount++)
      {
        leftright(Sal);
      }
  }                               // End of 5 times
  for (smallcount=1;smallcount<=3;smallcount++)
  {
      JumpJack(Sal);
  }
}
```

Practicing Repetitions with Tracer

The robot operations can now be recoded using repetitions. You can code a function to draw a line of any size specified. Simply include a parameter that lists the number of steps required to draw that line. It is still possible, and desirable, to keep the ability to draw the line in any given color, as dictated by a second parameter.

Specify what the header of this new function will look like:

```cpp
void line (int size, int color = 2)
```

As we have seen before, this function will have to repeat the following statements:

```cpp
mark(color);
step();
```

for as many steps needed. Thus, if the parameter size contains the size of the line in number of steps, this sequence should be repeated exactly that number of steps, minus one (remember the first square?).

You may find it easy to implement this by using for:

```
for ( int howmany=1;howmany<size;howmany++)
```

By specifying the condition howmany<size, you will be executing the sentence *size–1* times.

A complete listing for this function could be as follows:

```
void line (int size,int color=2)
{
  for(int howmany=1;howmany<size;howmany++)
  {
    Tracer.mark(color);
    Tracer.step();
  }
}
```

Before you proceed any further, notice that this function will not require any change to the code no matter how many steps you want. Everything is determined by the parameter size. The program c3square.cpp below contains the complete code, with the other functions modified. This program draws two squares of different sizes and colors.

```
#include "franca.h"    // c3square.cpp
Robot Tracer;
void line (int size,int color=2)
{
  for(int howmany=1;howmany<size;howmany++)
  {
    Tracer.mark(color);
    Tracer.step();
  }
}
```

A repetition could simplify the square function itself :

```
void square(int size,int color=2)
{
  for(int turn=1;turn<=4;turn++)
  {
    line(size,color);
    Tracer.right();
  }
}
```

We could still use the same `mainprog`:

```
void mainprog()
{
  Tracer.face(3);
  square(3);
  Tracer.step(5);
  square(4,5);
}
```

Exploring a Room

Tell Tracer to walk along all the walls of a rectangular room and come back to the original position. How can you solve this problem? Some preliminaries follow.

You can now take advantage of the fact that Tracer can detect whether there is a wall ahead by sending her the following message:

```
Tracer.seewall();
```

Or better still, you can have her keep moving while the following condition:

```
Tracer.seenowall();
```

is true.

This means you can keep her walking until she finds a wall, without actually knowing how many steps are needed! As long as the condition `Tracer.seenowall()` is true, she can keep walking. Do you know how to do this? Try the following listing:

```
for(;Tracer.seenowall();)
{
    // You might also mark:
    Tracer.mark();
    Tracer.step();
}
```

What happened to the other two expressions inside `for`? They vanished! You don't really need the other expressions in this case. There is nothing to initialize and nothing to be done at the end of each iteration.

If you want to count the steps until she reaches the wall, you might then modify the code as follows:

```
for(int howmany=0;Tracer.seenowall;howmany++)
{
    // You might also use mark:
    Tracer.mark();
    Tracer.step();
}
```

A Problem to Solve

Suppose that we have an empty rectangular room and that Tracer is in a corner, facing east. This is illustrated in Figure 7.6.

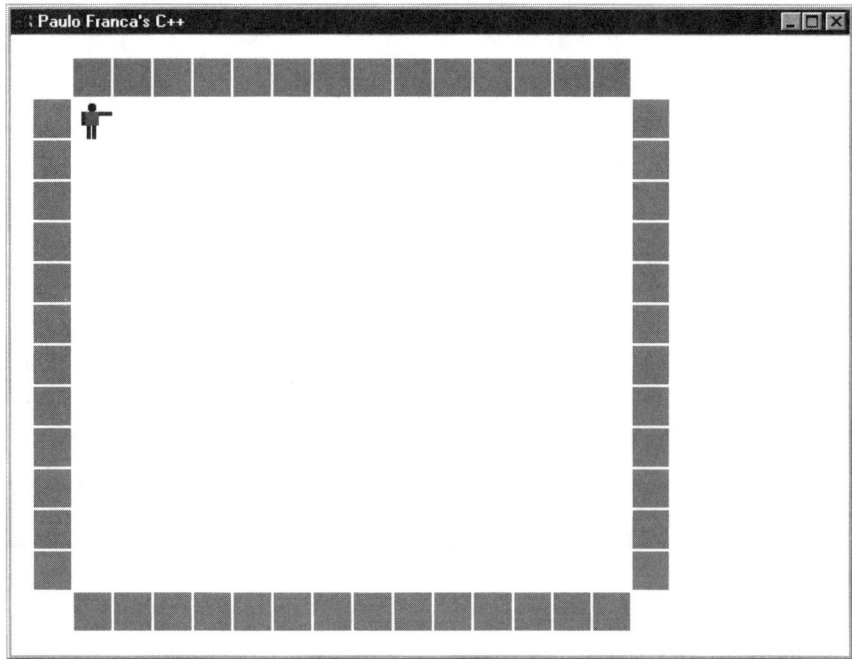

FIGURE 7.6: Tracer in an empty room, facing east

Can you figure out how to have Tracer move around the room? Since you know that the room is rectangular, you may want to tell Tracer to do the following things:

- Step ahead until she finds a wall. Once the first wall is found, there are only three left!

- Have her turn and step ahead until she finds another wall. There are only two left now! What do you do now?

Do you think you can complete this by yourself? Why not try it? After you try, you can check the solutions shown below.

Solution 1: Walk around Four Walls. This program makes Tracer move around, one wall at a time. As you can see, we have her step until she finds a wall, turn right, step until she finds another wall, turn right, etc.

Here is a possible algorithm:

Step ahead until you find a wall;

turn right.

Step ahead until you find a wall;

turn right.

Step ahead until you find a wall;

turn right.

Step ahead until you find a wall;

turn right.

Solution 1 is correct, but, as a programmer, you should not be happy with it. Two statements are written four times in exactly in the same way! This is an obvious repetition.

N NOTE   Thou shalt not write the same line of code twice!

Solution 2: Repeat Four Times. A better solution is to group the actions required to find each wall, and then to repeat them for each wall. The algorithm can be as follows:

Repeat the statements below four times:

Step ahead until you find a wall;

turn right.

This is a good solution to this problem. Solution 3, discussed below, is not necessarily better.

Solution 3: Use a Function. A third possibility would be to use functions. For example:

```
void findwall();
```

makes Tracer move until she finds a wall and then makes her turn right. If this function is made available, the algorithm would become as follows:

Repeat the statement below four times:

findwall.

It is barely justified to use a function in this case, because the procedure is so simple.

Solution 4: Use a Function that Returns a Value.   Finally, let me comment on the possibility of using a function that returns a value—the number of squares in which she stepped until the wall was found.

Here is one implementation of the function:

```
int findwall()
{
   int steps=0;
   while (tracer.seenowall())
   {
      tracer.step();
      steps++;
   }
   tracer.right();
   return steps;
}
```

This function adds the convenience of counting the steps. Although this computation is not necessary at the moment, it may be useful sometime in the future. For example, if we want to move Tracer and keep track of how many steps she takes, we could use

```
int howfar;
howfar=findwall();
```

Although the function returns a value, you don't have to use it. This function could be used just like the previous version was used:

```
for( int i=1;i<4;i++)
findwall();
```

Skill 7

Try These for Fun. . .

- Write a function:

  ```
  int distance()
  ```

  - This function should measure the number of steps needed to reach the wall Tracer is facing. However, Tracer should measure the distance, then come back to the original location and face the same direction.

- Suppose that Tracer is inside a rectangular room. You don't know where she is, nor the direction in which she is facing. Have her measure the room.

- Suppose that Tracer is inside a rectangular room. You don't know where she is, nor the direction in which she is facing. Have her walk in all the locations in the room.

- Draw the picture shown in Figure 7.7

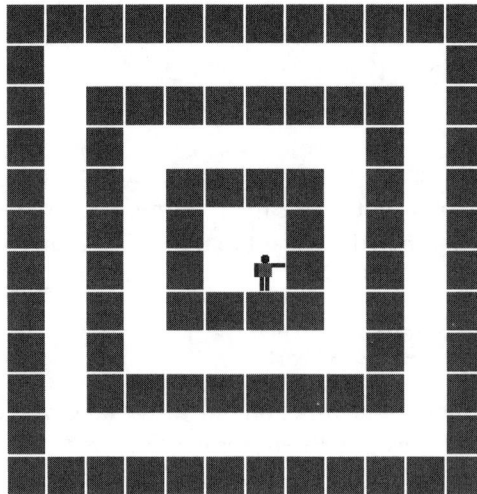

FIGURE 7.7:   Draw this picture.

- Draw the picture shown in Figure 7.8.

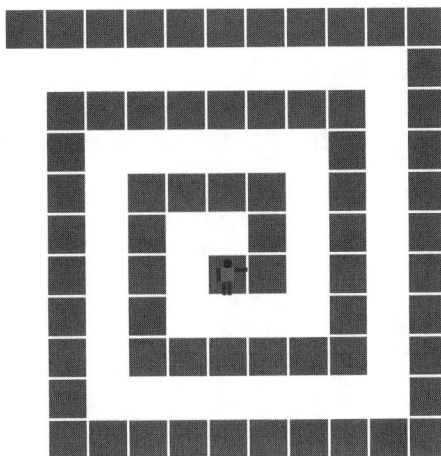

FIGURE 7.8:   Draw this picture.

- Draw the picture shown in Figure 7.9

FIGURE 7.9:   Draw this picture.

- What set of functions could you design to help you draw these pictures (Figure 7.7, 7.8, 7.9)?

Skill 7

Are You Experienced?

Now you can...

- ☑ Write a piece of code that will be repeated
- ☑ Use *while*, *do/while* and *for* loops
- ☑ Specify appropriate conditions for loops
- ☑ Nest one repetition inside another

S K I L L

eight

Designing Basic Loops

❑ Repeating with variations

❑ Designing loops—Part 1

❑ Summarizing rules and regulations

Repetition is not necessarily monotonous. In fact, most of the great harmony of nature is caused by patterns that are repeated, but are slightly different from each other. You may ask, How can something be repeated and yet be different?

Well, you do this all the time. As you go through your daily routine, you wake up, get dressed, eat breakfast…. It's all the same every day, but

- You don't wear the same clothes every day, do you?

- You don't eat exactly the same breakfast every day, do you?

So, although you repeat the major actions, some of the details are changed.

Repeating, but Changing

If you look at Figures 8.1 and 8.2, you will find several sets, each consisting of three squares. In each set, you can see that squares are repeated, but the result is far from being the same!

Squares Can Be Drawn:

Shifted Horizontally

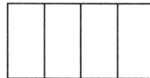

Also Shifted Horizontally

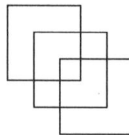

Shifted Horizontally and Vertically

FIGURE 8.1: Three squares of the same size

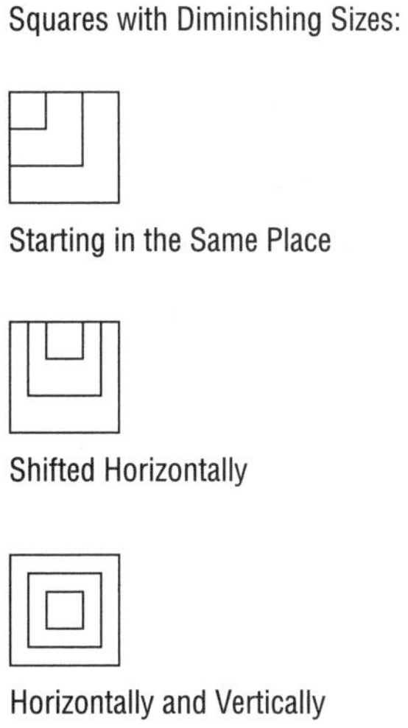

Squares with Diminishing Sizes:

Starting in the Same Place

Shifted Horizontally

Horizontally and Vertically

FIGURE 8.2:   Three squares of diminishing sizes

If you had to give instructions on how to draw these pictures, you would probably notice that you have to repeat the drawing of a square three times. Each time, the square is a different size and is located in a different place.

If you know how to draw a square of a given size at a given location, you should be able to have Tracer draw any of these pictures for you. Let's agree that the largest square will be of size 12, and the others will be of sizes 8 and 4. Why not use your smart robot to draw these squares?

I can give you a hint for one of the pictures:

- Consider the top set of squares shown in Figure 8.2. All the squares start at the same corner, but their sizes decrease—from 12 to 8 to 4! In other words, you start with size 12, but each time you draw the next square, you decrease the size by 4. Get it?

Let's see how we can do this.

Example—Drawing Squares of Diminishing Sizes

The following algorithm is our first attempt in plain English:

Draw a square of size 12.

Draw a square of size 8.

Draw a square of size 4.

By now, you know you can use a function to draw a square. Don't write a new one! Reuse! Once you have this function, you could write the program as follows.

The First Program

Here's what our first attempt would look like:

```
#include "franca.h"
Robot Tracer;
void mainprog()
{
     square(12);
     square(8);
     square(4);
}
```

This program is correct and should work right if you try it—but you can do better.

NOTE   Thou shalt not write the same line of code twice.

Do you see that this program just repeats the drawing of a square? This is repeated three times! A good programmer identifies repeated pieces of code and organizes them, so that they do not have to change if you need to repeat them a different number of times. For example, whether you want to draw 3, 15, or 100 squares, the code will be essentially the same. Ideally, you should obtain something such as the following program.

The Second Program (Incorrect)

Here's what our second attempt might look like:

```
#include "franca.h"
```

```
Robot Tracer;
void mainprog()
{
    int many,size;
    size=12;
    for (many=1; many <=3;many++)
    {
        square (size);
    }
}
```

Well, this would be correct and very easy if all the squares were the same size, but they are not. The squares shrink by 4 units each time. Wait a moment! If you knew how to compute the next size, you could simply compute the new size every time!

The Third Program

Here's what our third attempt might look like:

```
#include "franca.h"    // c3sq3.cpp
Robot Tracer;
void mainprog()
{
    int many,size;
    size=12;
    for (many=1;many <= 3 ;many++)
    {
        square(size);
        size=size-4;
    }
}
```

Can you understand what happens with the size? Initially, there is a value of 12. Then, you start the repetition and draw the first square with this size (12). Next, you compute a new value for the size. What is it? You simply take the old value and decrease it by 4—this becomes the new value. The next time you draw a square, it will be of size 8. This process will be repeated as the squares keep shrinking.

In some of the other pictures, in which each square starts at a different location, all you have to do is to move Tracer to the new starting point. Do you think the directions to move to a new starting point will be very distinct from each other? I don't think so. If you look at most of the pictures, you will find that once you draw a square, you simply move a couple steps horizontally or vertically (or both) and then you are ready for the next square! It's easy, isn't it?

The complete code can be found in c3sq3.cpp.

Skill 8

Repeating the Same Lines of Code

If you compare the first program with the third, you will notice that they both draw the same picture! However, I suggested that you avoid using the first and that you instead use the third. You may be wondering about my opinion. The first program might be easier to understand than the third, yet I argue that the third is preferable. Where is the improvement?

As you compare programs, you may feel tempted to say that the first try is just about as good as the last. Their size isn't much different, and the first one is quite easy to understand. I cannot properly say that you are wrong. In fact, the simple structure of the first program is tempting when it comes to drawing three squares. The problem is that very often you will be faced with larger numbers. If you want to draw 10 squares, you have to add several statements to your first program. How many would you have to add to the last one? None! All you would have to do is modify the initial size and the number of repetitions.

Another valuable benefit of using repetition is when you have to deal with an unknown number of repetitions. The first program will only draw exactly three squares. The last one allows you to draw whatever number is specified in the repetition. If, instead of specifying the number 3, you specified your repetition as follows:

```
for (many=1; many <= total; many++)
```

the sequence would be repeated as many times as the value stored in `total`.

Recognizing Opportunities for Repetition

The role of repetitions should never be underestimated. The more you can identify repetitions in your program, the better. Sometimes the repetition is subtle, making it hard to figure out what changes from one step to the next. As you develop more experience, you will be able to perceive such changes more easily.

The programs to draw three squares could also utilize nested repetitions. For each square, we have to draw four lines. Then, we have to draw three squares, making a total of 12 lines. Therefore, we could also write the program as follows:

Set size=12.

Repeat 3 times:

　　Repeat 4 times:

　　　　Draw a line (size).

Turn right.

Compute new size=size–4.

The Fourth Program

In C++, the program described above would be as follows:

```
#include "franca.h"
    int size,squarecount, linecount;
    size=12;
    for(squarecount=1;squarecount<=3;squarecount++)
    {
        for(linecount=1;linecount<=4;linecount++)
        {
            line(size);
            Tracer.right();
        }
        size=size-4;
    }
```

Again, the result is the same as before. In the previous version of the program, we used the function **square** to make the inner repetition invisible. As a result, I hope you agree that the third program is a little easier to understand. However, you may not find it convenient to create functions for everything, and you should become acquainted with nested repetitions, as well.

Try These for Fun. . .

- Write a program to draw the picture shown in the middle set of squares in Figure 8.2.

- If you'd like to try something more difficult, write a program to draw the picture shown in the bottom set of squares in Figure 8.2.

Designing Your Own Loops—Part 1

Computers are successful only because most problems involve repetition. The procedure to process a customer's check is about the same for all customers and is repeated thousands of times every day. Procedures that compute complex scientific results also involve millions of repetitions of the same piece of program.

NOTE You'll learn more about designing loops in "Designing Your Own Loops—Part 2" in Skill 10.

By now, you possess the means to control the repetition of a piece of a program. The next task is to make sure you know how to use repetitions. There may be situations in which you know something has to be repeated, but you don't know exactly what.

General Guidelines

When a repetition is involved, you have to determine the following items:

- Which task is supposed to be repeated?

- What changes are to be performed after each iteration?

- When do you stop repeating?

- What initial conditions are there for the loop?

Which Task to Repeat

I suggest you start by trying to determine which task must be repeated. It may help if you consider the simplified case in which only one repetition is needed. It is also very helpful to think of which task will be completed after each iteration is completed. You may even try to formulate a sentence that remains true every time a loop iteration is finished.

NOTE A sentence that remains true every time a loop iteration is finished is called a *loop invariant*.

For example, in the program in which we wanted to draw the diminishing squares (`c3sq3.cpp`), we wanted to repeat the drawing of a square:

```
square (12 );
```

This would suffice if we had only one square to draw.

However, the square we want to draw will have a different size each time. Therefore, this size is part of what is changing after each loop, because after each square is drawn, this size is changed for the next drawing. Notice that after each iteration, one square is completely drawn. Therefore, the following assertion:

Square number *n* is drawn.

is true for each iteration.

What to Change

Next, you can try to determine what changes from one iteration to the next.

In the example above, only the size of the square changes. Squares should become 4 units smaller each time. This update can be done inside the loop itself or as part of the third expression of a `for`. Most likely, you will also need to count how many iterations have been completed.

When to Stop

Make sure that your loop stops—either by counting iterations or by some other process. In Skill 10, you will see how to interrupt a loop that is checking some condition. In any event, it is important that you make sure this condition that you are checking to interrupt the loop will happen sometime.

In this example, we want to draw three squares. The loop will stop at the count of three.

How Does the Loop Begin?

Make sure that all the initial values for when the loop begins are correct. You may have to start the count from zero or one, reset a total to zero, or set an initial value for other variables.

Sometimes it is easier to determine the initial conditions after you have designed the loop. In the example, set the initial square size to 12 and the square count to 1.

A Design Example

Suppose that your instructor asks you to assist in computing the average score for all the grades in your class. How would you solve this problem?

Skill 8

You know the average can be obtained by adding all the grades together and dividing the total by the number of students in class. You may have developed the following general explanation for your problem:

> Add all grades together.
>
> Average=total divided by number of students.
>
> Write the average.

How do you add all the grades together?

Clearly, you have to read them so that they can be added. You can do this in the same way that you would if you used a calculator:

> Repeat while there are grades:
>
> > Type a value.
> >
> > Hit the + key.

Since the + key on a calculator adds the current number to the accumulator, this is the same as

> Repeat while there are grades:
>
> > Input grade.
> >
> > Add to total.

If you have any trouble understanding this concept for calculating, you can also try to write a program to compute the average of one, two, or three grades, and transform it into a loop.

At this point, you know what is to be repeated:

> Input a grade.
>
> Add to total.

This becomes the following two lines in C++:

```
grade=ask ("Please enter next grade:");
total=total+grade;
```

You can now check what changes are needed from one iteration to the next. In this case, a new grade is input in each iteration and the total is already updated. No more changes are necessary.

When to Stop the Loop

You have to decide which mechanism to use to stop the loop. The easiest way would be to know in advance how many grades there are in the list and to read exactly that many. For example, if there were 26 grades, just use a loop such as

```
for (int which=0;which<26;which++)
```

Will this work? Sure it will. However, it is not very flexible. Next month, the instructor will come back to you because the class now has only 24 students, which will require program changes.

There are a few alternatives to this structure:

- You can have the program ask for the number of students in the class.

- You can check whether the instructor wants to input more grades after each input.

- You can establish a sentinel value that will signal when no more data are available.

The first alternative is easy to implement—just include some statements before the loop:

```
int class_size;
class_size=ask("enter the number of grades:");
```

and change the for statement as follows:

```
for (int which=0;which<class_size;which++)
```

This is a reasonable solution, but it does require that someone counts how many grades there are before inputting them. The user may not like this if the number is large.

The second alternative can also be easily implemented by means of the yesno function. Remember that you can ask the user to signal *yes* or *no*.

Use yesno in the following condition:

```
for (int which=0;yesno("input another grade?");which++)
```

If you use this before each iteration, the dialog box will come up and the user can decide whether to input another grade. Meanwhile, the user clicks Yes—the loop will go on and request more grades.

Skill 8

In this case, it is not strictly necessary to use the count variable which, since we don't need to count the iterations to stop the loop. However, this variable keeps track of how many grades were input and lets us know the number of students in class. Notice that using a different statement:

```
for(int which=1;which<class_size;which++)
```

would cause the value of the counter which to be one more than the number of grades when the loop finishes. It would then be necessary to decrement it before you use it to compute the average!

> **NOTE** This solution adds inconvenience, because the user has to answer a *yes* or *no* question before each grade is input.

Finally, it is also possible to use a distinctive value to signal the end of the data. In this case, you should use an invalid value for the data to signal that there are no more data available. Since grades cannot be negative in this example, you could use a negative value to explain that all data have been input.

However, this solution will be correctly implemented only after you learn how to break out of the loop. Skill 10 presents these techniques.

Initial Conditions

Once the loop has been essentially designed, check whether all the initial conditions are correct. The total has to be initialized to zero.

Here is a complete implementation:

```
#include "franca.h"
void mainprog()            // c3avgrd.cpp
{
  float grade,total=0;
  float average;
  for (int which=0;yesno("input another grade?"); which++)
  {
    grade=ask("Enter next grade:");
    total=total+grade;
  }
  average=total/which;
  Cout<<average;
}
```

Rules and Regulations

This section summarizes rules for topics covered in the previous Skills.

Compound Statements

A group of statements that starts with { and ends with } is considered a compound statement. For example:

```
for (int times=1;times<=10;times++)
// The lines below form a compound statement
   {
      Kim.JumpJack();
      Kim.say(times);
   }
```

You might have noticed that a function body is also a compound statement. For example:

```
void mainprog() // The lines below form a compound statement
{
   athlete Kim;
    Kim.up();
    Kim.ready();
}
```

Nesting

A compound statement may contain another compound statement. For example:

```
void mainprog()
{
   athlete Kim;
   for (int times=1;times<=10;times++)
   {
      Kim.JumpJack();
      Kim.say(times);
   }
}
```

The closing brace denotes the end of the compound statement. For this reason, no semicolon is needed.

Skill 8

T **TIP**   Although the syntax does not require it, you should always indent inside a compound statement.

Scope

Any variables or objects declared inside the compound statement will be created inside the compound (when the point of declaration is first reached). They will be discarded when the compound statement is terminated. For example:

```
int i,j;
for (i=0;i<3;i++)
{
    int m;
    m=i+3;
}
```

In the sequence above, m is declared inside for. This variable will be created when the loop starts, and it will remain valid until the end of the loop (if the loop is restarted later, the variable will be created again). It is not possible to know the value of m after the loop has ended. Any references to m will cause a syntax error.

N **NOTE**   Even though the declaration of m is inside the loop, the variable is not created again for each iteration. It is created only once.

Simple Conditions

Conditions are expressed by means of relational expressions. As the name implies, the expression explores the relation between two variables or objects. A relational expression causes some kind of comparison to be made between two objects and generates a result.

The result, which we expect to be either true or false, is actually represented in C++ by an integer. A value of zero denotes *false*. Any other value, usually *one*, denotes a true result.

N **NOTE**   The condition is always enclosed in parentheses.

Equality vs. Assignment

Special attention is needed when you compare to determine equality. When you check whether a is equal to b, it is a common mistake to write

```
if (a = b) ... ;
```

In C++, this expression is acceptable in terms of syntax, but it does not compare a with b. In fact, this is an assignment expression, and the value of b will be brought into a (the original contents of a will be lost). The correct comparison should use the following equality operator:

```
if (a==b) ... ;
```

WARNING   The expression if(a=b) ... will be accepted by the compiler and will cause a bug if you use it unintentionally. If the value in b is nonzero, the result will be equivalent to *true*. If the value in b is zero, the result will be equivalent to *false*. Even if you are experienced, you should avoid this type of expression.

Mixing Arithmetic and Relational Operations

Although you are advised against doing so, it is possible to mix arithmetic and relational expressions. For example:

```
k = 1+ a < b;
```

is correct in terms of syntax. If a is indeed less than b, the result of the logical expression will be 1, and the value of k will become 2. On the other hand, if a is not less than b, the value of k will become 1. If you mix expressions, a program may result that is hard to understand.

***while* Loops**   The format of the while statement is as follows:

```
while (  relational expression )  statement
```

in which the statement may be compound. The resulting action is that the relational expression is evaluated and, if the result is true, the statement will be executed. The evaluation of the expression and the execution of the statement will be repeated until the result of the expression is false, in which case the next statement will be executed.

If the statement is not compound, it is not necessary to enclose it in braces, and it may be written on the same line as while.

Skill 8

I strongly encourage you to continue to use braces. A common mistake occurs when you want to include another statement in the loop and forget to include the braces. Also, notice that there is no semicolon after the expression.

***do/while* Loops**   The format of do/while is as follows:

```
do statement while (relational expression);
```
The statement is executed, and then the expression is evaluated. If the result is true, the statement will be repeated, as will the evaluation of the expression. The repetition will end when the expression is evaluated as false.

***for* Loops**   The for statement provides complete control over a repetition and allows initialization, testing, and counting. The general form is as follows:

```
for(initial expression ; condition ; final expression ) statement
```

in which the following items are true:

* The initial expression is executed only once before the loop begins. It is useful for initializing variables.

* The condition is a conditional expression that will be evaluated once before each loop iteration. If the expression is true, the loop will be executed.

* The final expression is executed at the end of each loop iteration. It is useful to increment variables and to keep count of the iterations.

* The statement is any statement (including a compound statement). This statement is what will be executed at a loop iteration.

Absent Expressions

Expressions can be omitted inside the parentheses. It may be easy to see what happens if the initial expression and/or the final expression are missing. However, if you omit the loop condition, it is the same as having always a true condition! The piece of program below is an infinite loop:

```
for (;;)
Sal.say("I am stuck!");
```

Comma Expressions

Whenever an expression can be used, C++ allows you to use more than one expression, separated by commas. For example:

```
for(int done=0,int to_do=10; done<=howmany; done++,to_do-)
```

will cause the variables done and to_do to be created and initialized to 0 and 10 respectively, before the execution of the loop. At the end of each loop iteration, done will be incremented and to_do will be decremented.

If a value that resulted from the evaluation of the expression is to be used, the value of the leftmost expression will be used. For example:

```
howmany= 3,1,2;
```

will assign a value of 3 to the variable howmany.

> **WARNING** Avoid the use of multiple expressions separated by commas. This will result in programs that are hard to understand.

Variable Declarations

It is possible to declare and initialize a variable in the for statement. This may be useful when you need a variable only during the execution of the loop. For example:

```
for (int done=1; done<=howmany; done++)
```

could be used instead of

```
int done;
for (done=1;done<=howmany;done++)
```

Variables declared in the initial expression of for are considered to be declared before the compound statement that defines the loop. Therefore, their scopes remain valid after the loop has been terminated.

> **NOTE** Some compilers consider the declaration to be done inside the loop. In this case, the variables lose their scope when the loop is exited.

Skill 8

Try These for Fun. . .

- In the piece of program below, what is the value displayed on the screen? Why?

```
#include "franca.h"
void mainprog()
{
 athlete Sal;
 int done=5;
 {
  int done;
  for (int done=1; done<=10; done++)
  {

   Sal.ready();
   Sal.up();
  }
 }
 Sal.say(done);
}
```

- Determine the values of *m* and *j*.

    a. for (int m=0,int j=0;m<5;)

    •   ++m++;

    b. for (int m=0,int j=0; m<5;m++);

    •   j++;

    c. for (int j=0,int m=0;m++<5;m++)

    •   j++;

    d. for (int j=0,int m=0;m<5;m=j++)

    •   m++;

- The following exercises are for math-oriented readers:

    - The factorial of a nonnegative integer *N* is defined as the product of all integers from 1 to N. The factorial of zero is defined as 1. Write a program that reads a nonnegative integer from the keyboard, and then computes and displays the value of its factorial. The program should keep looping and asking for new values until you are done.

- Use a function to compute the factorials.

- Even though the factorial is an integer, it is not a good idea to implement a factorial function that returns an `int` as a result. Why is it a better idea to return a `float` or a `long`?

Are You Experienced?

Now you can. . .

☑ **Identify repetitions that change pattern**

☑ **Design loops in your programs**

S K I L L

nine

Developing Basic Applications

- ❑ Implementing a point-of-sale terminal
- ❑ Exploring the design process

You are now going to work on your skill of developing applications by developing a simple point-of-sale terminal (such as what you see in stores and supermarkets). As you improve your skills, more complexity will be added to this terminal, and other applications will be used.

This short project will wrap up some of the skills you have developed so far. We will also discuss some of the issues involved in solving a real-life problem, in which many decisions are left to the designer.

Building a Point-of-Sale Terminal

Suppose that you are hired to develop software to implement a point-of-sale terminal. This software should enable a computer to keep track of sales, compute change, and handle other related issues.

Although your programming abilities are still limited, you can already solve these problems.

Often, in real life the client (the store owner) does not provide a good specification of the product he or she wants. The client knows it is too much trouble to do all this work manually and suspects that a computer can help. It is up to the designer (this means you!) to come up with a reasonable solution.

> **NOTE**   For most point-of-sale terminals, a bar code reader and a small printer are standard equipment. Regrettably, all we have is a standard computer—not even a printer! Your client (the clerk) will have to input the purchase price for each item by typing it from the keyboard.

The software you are about to create should add the prices of all the items in a single sale and write the total to the screen (after including the sales tax). If each customer made only one purchase at a time, you could solve the problem very easily. In fact, you could simply use one of the programs already seen in Skill 7—c3store1.cpp.

However, you will now have to input and add several prices while handling the same customer. Only when all the prices for that sale have been input can you finish the sale by computing the tax, totaling the prices, etc. Besides, your software should enable the computer to handle one customer after another, instead of only one.

Designing Software for Multiple Transactions

Once you understand the basic operation, you may try to write a general algorithmic description of the problem. Here we go!

Clearly, the sales procedure will be repeated for each customer; therefore, you may consider the problem as follows:

> Repeat while there are customers:
>
> > Input and add item prices.
> >
> > Compute and display total with tax.
> >
> > Compute and display change.

This looks like a correct, although still imprecise, description of what you want to do. It is fine as a start, though.

You may notice that inputting and adding item prices will, of course, involve another repetition. You may decide to explain right now how this is done, or you may decide it is a good idea to design a function to read all the items in a sale and to provide you with the total. This will simplify the main program and eliminate the need for an inner loop.

For the time being, we may think of a function that returns a floating point value to contain the total purchase (before tax) for a given customer. It is a good idea to establish a header for this function. For example:

```
float getitems();
```

Another question you may have at this time is, "How should I display these values?"

You could use the standard Cout as a solution. However, everything you write with Cout is erased with the next output. This may prove inconvenient for the store clerk. Another approach is to design a few boxes to display specific information: total price, amount tendered, change, etc.

In fact, we will design how your point-of-sale terminal uses these boxes right now.

Display Boxes

Here are some suggestions for possible display boxes:

- Current total—displays the total price of items entered so far (before tax)

- Sales total—displays the total sales price the customer is supposed to pay (including tax)

- Amount tendered—displays the amount tendered by the customer

- Change—displays the change to be given to the customer

These boxes can be declared as follows:

```
Box Cur_total("Current total:");
Box total("Total Sale:"),Amount("Tendered:");
Box Change("Change due:");
```

The declarations above can be placed at the beginning of the program.

Now, if you look back to the general description, you will have no problem computing the total sales price with tax, inputting the amount, and displaying the change. The general description can be expanded either in algorithmic form or in program form. The complete loop body for each customer could be as follows:

```
// Input and add items for each sale.
// Then include tax:
saletotal=getitems()*salestax;
// Display the sales total:
total.say(saletotal);
// Ask for amount tendered and display it:
amount=ask("Enter amount tendered:");
Amount.say(amount);
// Compute change and display it:
change=amount-saletotal;
Change.say(change);
```

The piece of program above explains what we want to do with each customer. It may be enclosed in a loop. The next question is, How do we determine how many times this loop is repeated?

Remember there are several ways to determine when the loop ended. I hope you realize is it not possible to determine the number of customers in advance. In our case, the most appropriate solution is to ask whether there are more customers. This is very easy:

```
while(yesno("Is there another customer?"))
```

If you think it is useful to keep track of the number of customers, you can increment a variable customer in a for loop:

```
for(;yesno("Is there another customer?");customer++)
```

Initial Conditions

To complete the loop, you should determine the initial conditions. The loop that takes care of each customer does not require a special initialization. However, the processing of each customer sale, as performed by the getitems function, does. Remember that this loop will be executed for each customer. Anything that was computed and/or left displayed on the screen for a previous customer must be cleared. This means that all the boxes should be initialized.

```
saletotal=0;
amount=0;
change=0;
Cur_total=0;
Saletotal.say(saletotal);
Amount.say(amount);
Change.say(change);
Cur_total.say(0.);
```

These statements not only reset the values to zero, but also display these values in the appropriate boxes. You can also clear the boxes instead of writing zeros. For example:

```
Amount.say("");
```

The *getitems()* Function

Essentially, the getitems() function is supposed to keep asking for item prices that belong to the same customer. These item prices should be added up and returned as a result. You can use the same approach to control the loop.

Here is a possible implementation:

```
float getitems()
{
  float total=0;
  for(int item=1;yesno("another item?");item++)
    {
      total=total+ask("Enter item price:");
    }
  return total;
}
```

Don't you think it would be nice if you could display the current total as the item prices are entered? This would look just like a real point-of-sale terminal!

However, this implementation poses a problem. If a box is declared to display this output, a new box will be created each time this function is called. Even though these boxes will be discarded at the end of each function execution, each new box will be assigned to a different location on the screen.

Use a Box Parameter. To solve this problem, you need to use a box that is declared outside the scope of the function. You may declare the box in `mainprog` and pass it as an argument, preferably by reference. Remember that if a box is passed by reference, the function will not create a new (copied) box in a new location. The original box that was declared in the program will be used instead. You may experiment with passing the box by value to see what happens.

The updated code for the function would then be as follows:

```
float getitems(Box &display)
{
  float total=0;
  for(int item=1;yesno("another item?");item++)
    {
      total=total+ask("Enter item price:");
      display.say(total);
    }
  return total;
}
```

The function call must also be updated in `mainprog`:

```
saletotal=getitems(Cur_total)*(1+tax);
```

Finally, you may be wondering how to set up the sales tax information. It is clear that you could define this value in the program as a constant, but then every time the tax percentage changes, you would have to update the program. This is not smart. You may consider asking for the value of the tax percentage at the beginning of the program, and then keep that value throughout the day. This can be easily accomplished.

```
tax=ask("Enter the sales tax %")/100.;
```

The Complete Program Listing

Here is a complete listing of the updated program `c3sale2.cpp` (see also Figure 9.1):

```
#include "franca.h"                    // c3sale2.cpp
// Program to implement a point-of-sale terminal:
```

```
//      Gets tax information for each customer.
//      Reads item prices.
//      Totals each sale.
//      Computes change.
float getitems(Box &display)
{
  float total=0;
  for(int item=1;yesno("another item?");item++)
     {
        total=total+ask("Enter item price:");
        display.say(total);
     }
  return total;
}

void mainprog()
{
  Box Cur_total("Current total:");
  Box total("Total Sale:"),Amount("Tendered:");
  Box Change("Change due:");
  float tax,amount,saletotal,change;
  dailytotal=0;
  tax=ask("Enter the sales tax %")/100.;
  for (int customer=1;
       yesno("Is there another customer?");customer++)
  {
     // Start one sale:
     saletotal=0;
     amount=0;
     change=0;
     Saletotal.say(saletotal);
     Amount.say(amount);
     Change.say(change);
     saletotal=getitems(Cur_total)*(1+tax);
     Saletotal.say(saletotal);
     amount=ask("Enter amount tendered:");
     Amount.say(amount);
     change=amount-saletotal;
     Change.say(change);
  }
}
```

Figure 9.1 shows the result of completing a sale that totaled $12.24 (before the 8.25 percent tax).

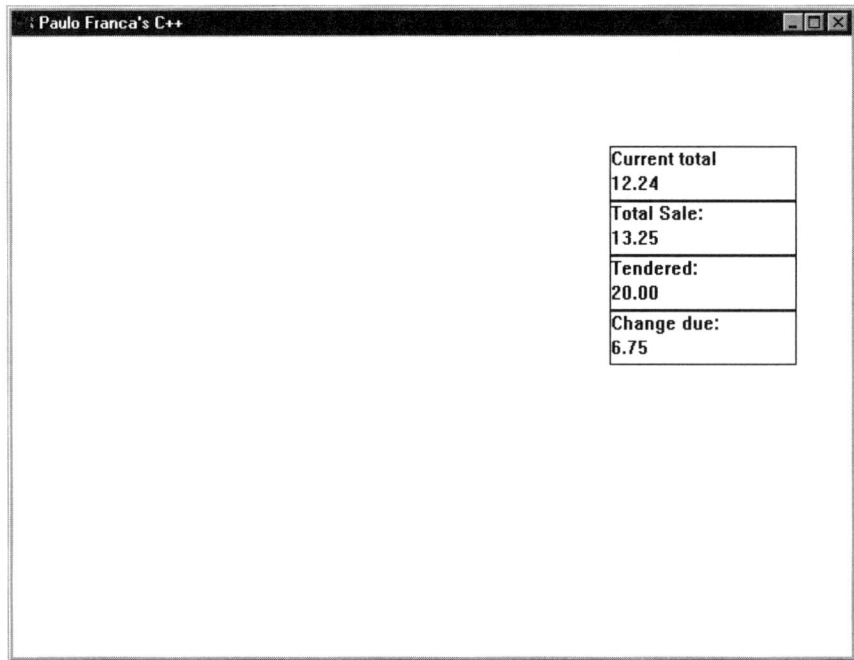

FIGURE 9.1: Your point-of-sale terminal

Exploring the Design Process

The design process is often less structured than you may at first be lead to believe. I could have presented the design steps in a more appropriate sequence. However, the truth is that this is not what will happen when you are creating your designs. For example, when you initially think of using a function (such as `getitems`), you may not have a complete idea of what you need. In this case, I tried to show you that it is only when you write the function code that you notice a parameter is needed. This may happen often in real life. No problem—just go back and revise what is needed.

The more you understand the problem and the available tools, the better you can solve it.

The User Interface

Do not neglect the user interface. The *user interface* is the dialog your program uses to communicate with the user. This dialog may include visual aids, sounds, and text. Keep in mind your average user. Make your interface easy and attractive. This will reduce the risk of input errors, and will keep your user happy with your service.

On the other hand, avoid asking too many questions or offering unnecessary explanations during program execution. This may be extremely annoying to your user.

Improvements and Modifications

After you have solved what you initially proposed, you may still notice several things that you can do to deliver a more useful solution to your user. For example, you could detail the total number of items per sale. You could offer a daily total and the number of customers after the last sale.

Last, but not least, the user will request modifications. No matter how perfect your program is, changes will be needed sooner or later. If you can anticipate some of these changes, go ahead and make them. As you prepare your program, keep in mind that you may have to change it. Make it easy to understand and modify.

Try This for Fun. . .

- Modify the point-of-sale program to
  - Display the number of items in each sale
  - Display the total number of customers and the total value of sales after the final sale

Are You Experienced?

Now you can. . .

☑ **Design a simple application**

☑ **Design a suitable user interface for your applications**

☑ **Understand some of the design trade-offs**

Skill 9

PART IV

Deciding

Often, you will have to check a condition and decide to act one way or another, depending on the result of that condition. In Part IV, you will learn how to incorporate decisions in your programs. You will also learn how to use a technique called *recursion,* in which you essentially work backwards toward the solution of a problem. You will also work on a short project to improve your skills in designing applications.

Incorporating Decisions

- ❏ Deciding *if* you should do something
- ❏ Deciding *if* you should do this or *else* do that
- ❏ Specifying and testing conditions
- ❏ Breaking out of loops
- ❏ Designing loops—Part 2
- ❏ Switching among alternatives

In Skill 10, you will develop your ability to incorporate decisions in your programs. Decisions choose to execute one piece of program or another depending on a condition. You will learn how to specify conditions and how to use conditions in an if statement, so that you can decide the appropriate sequence to execute.

You will also learn how to interrupt a loop if a certain condition arises, and you will improve your skills in designing loops. The Robot objects will assist you with these skills.

Using the *if* Statement: to Do or Not to Do

Most decisions involve a condition, and then an action. For example, if the weather is rainy, take the umbrella. In this case, the condition is *the weather is rainy* and the action is *take the umbrella*. The action is executed only if the condition is satisfied. The condition is the actual basis for the decision. In the example above, all we care to know is whether the weather is rainy.

When you write programs, you use a similar decision process. Most decisions will be based on a condition, and, depending on this condition, you may want to perform some action. The if statement is the most important decision mechanism in programs.

Let's start with the simplest kind of decision. You may simply want to decide whether to do something. You may already be familiar with the following example:

> If you have money:
>
> > Go to the movies.

which means that the action *go to the movies* will only be executed if the condition is true *(you have money)*. Otherwise, nothing will happen, and you will simply execute the next statement, which would probably be *go to sleep*. This process is shown in Figure 10.1.

A more complete description of the problem could be as follows:

> If you have money:
>
> > Go to the movies.
>
> Go to sleep.

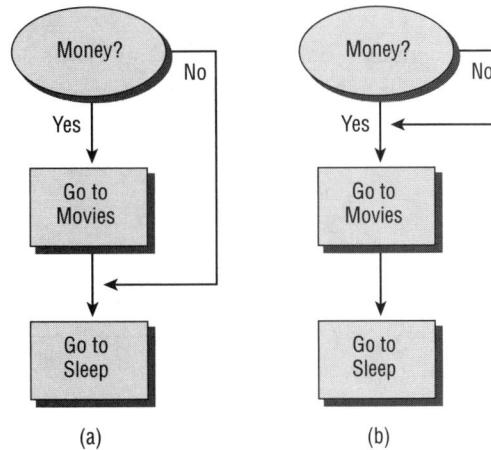

FIGURE 10.1:   Going to the movies

It is important to understand that, in this case, you will go to sleep either way. The difference is that the action *go to the movies* either will be executed or will not be executed. How do we know this? Because of the indentation! If we have the following directions:

> If you have money:
>
> Go the movies.
>
> Go to sleep.

without indentation, you might think that you should check your pocket to see if you have any money, but no matter what the result is, you would go to the movies and then go to sleep. This is because, in our convention, the compound statement affected by the condition should be indented. In a C++ program, you must also include braces.

The kind of decision we are considering is that either you do something or you don't. This is similar to what you've had Tracer do already. You wanted her to step ahead or not, depending on whether she saw a wall. That procedure was enclosed in the following repetition:

```
while (Tracer.seenowall())
{
    Tracer.step();
}
```

The `while` statement decides whether to repeat the loop, depending on the presence of a wall ahead. Did you notice that? What if you want her to take just one step, instead of walking until she finds a wall? Basically, you would explain something like the following instructions:

> If you see no wall:
>
> > Step ahead.

Tracer should check the condition *see no wall*, and, if this is true, she should take the action *step ahead*. What if the condition is not true (if she, indeed, sees a wall)? Well, nothing would happen! She would not step ahead, and the program would just go on to the next statement.

In C++, you use the `if` statement. The action of this statement is shown in Figure 10.2.

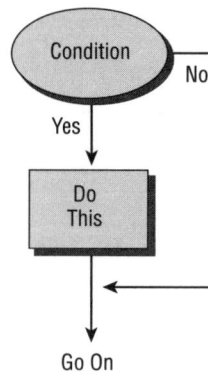

FIGURE 10.2:   Deciding *if* you should do something

The `if` statement looks as follows:

```
if ( condition )
{
     statements   // Do this
}
```

Or, in our example:

```
if(Tracer.seenowall())
{
    Tracer.step();
}
```

Pay attention to the format in which you write the statement:

- Use the keyword `if`.

- Write a condition, which is a relational expression inside parentheses.

- Indent and enclose in braces the sequence of statements that you want executed.

WARNING   There is no semicolon after the condition, nor is there one after the compound statement. This is a common beginner's mistake—if you include a semicolon after the condition, the compiler thinks that you want to do *nothing*. A semicolon after the compound statement is harmless.

TIP   If the sequence to be executed consists of only one statement, you don't need to enclose it in braces. However, I strongly encourage you to develop the habit of using braces.

For example, if you want Tracer to see whether there is a wall ahead and mark that square (and do nothing otherwise), you could write a piece of program such as

```
if (Tracer.seewall())
{
    Tracer.mark();
}
```

As you can see, if there is no wall ahead, no marking will take place.

Example—In the Maze 1

Let's develop a couple of functions that may be used with our robot. One of these functions, **go**, will make the robot step ahead after it checks whether the square is empty. If the square is not empty, no action will be taken. The second function, **crossing**, will examine the squares adjacent to the robot and will compute how many of them are free. In other words, **crossing** will compute how many directions (N, S, E, W) the robot can follow.

The algorithm for **go** is very simple:

If there is no wall ahead:

Step ahead.

Notice that no action is to be taken if there is a wall ahead. Here is one implementation:

```
void go()
  {
     if(Tracer.seenowall())
     {
        // Do this only if the next square is clear:
        Tracer.step();
     }
  }
```

To make this function more interesting, we may include the following items:

- Mark the square with a different color.

- Have Tracer say "OK" to indicate the successful move.

If you use the light-blue color (code=4), the modified function is as follows:

```
  void go()
{
     if(Tracer.seenowall())
     {
        // Do this only if the next square is clear:
        Tracer.mark(4);
        Tracer.step();
        Tracer.say("OK");
     }
}
```

USING INTEGERS AND PARENTHESES

If you declare the Robot object followed by an integer enclosed in parentheses (Robot Tracer (1);), it will place the robot in a maze. The position and direction, as well as the location of the walls, are unknown to you at that time. You may then have fun exploring the maze.

If the Robot object declaration does not include an integer enclosed in parentheses (Robot Tracer;), the robot is placed in an empty room, facing east.

continued

Declare only one Robot object in your programs; also, declare the Robot object globally instead of in a function. This will avoid the need to pass the Robot object as an argument.

The other function, crossing, is also simple. The algorithm consists of using a variable to count the available directions (howmany) and looking at the next square to determine whether it is occupied. If it is not occupied, we add one to howmany. If this procedure is applied to the four available directions, howmany will contain the number of free directions.

Try This for Fun. . .

- Write the function int crossing() to determine how many directions are available to the robot. Test this function with the following program:

```
#include "franca.h"
 Robot Tracer(1);
 void mainprog()
 {
    Tracer.say(crossing());
 }
```

Example—At the Store 1

Let's now consider the problem of computing the change for a merchandise sale. The basic problem is illustrated below.

```
#include "franca.h"
void mainprog()                      // c4change.cpp
{
  float price,amount,change;
  float tax=0.08;
  amount=ask("Enter the amount:");
  price=ask("Enter the price")*(1+tax);
  change=amount-price;
  Cout<<change;
}
```

Skill 10

This program reads an amount and a price, and computes the change after including the sales tax. The program outputs the change to be given to the customer. Notice that the program does not check whether the amount tendered is sufficient to cover the price!

A possible improvement to this program would be to check whether the amount is sufficient, and to warn the clerk when it is not. For example:

```
#include "franca.h"
  void mainprog()
  {
    float price,amount,change;
    float tax=0.08;
    amount=ask("Enter the amount:");
    price=ask("Enter the price")*(1+tax);
    if(amount<price)
    {
       Clock time;
       Cout<<"This is not enough!";
       time.wait(5);
    }
    change=amount-price;
    Cout<<change;
  }
```

The only change is that a message is displayed if the amount is insufficient. A clock was needed to hold the message for 5 seconds, so that it could be read.

Using the *if/else* Statement: to Do This or to Do That

The other kind of decision you may want to use is to choose between two alternatives—to do either this or that.

Take your ATM card.

If the store is open:

Buy a dozen eggs.

Get twenty dollars.

Else:

Get twenty dollars from the ATM.

Fill the gas tank.

Depending on whether the store is open, you will take one of two alternatives:

- Buy a dozen eggs and get twenty dollars (at the store).

or

- Go to a 24-hour ATM to get twenty dollars.

You will not do both things!

No matter which action is taken, you are supposed to fill the gas tank, because this action is not affected by the condition. Essentially, in this case you can specify two alternative actions: either do this or do that, as shown in Figure 10.3.

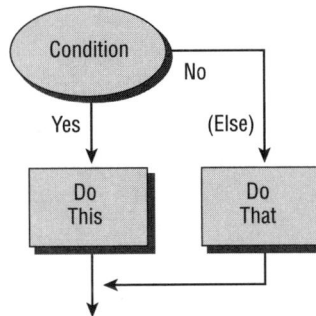

FIGURE 10.3: Deciding *if* you should do this or *else* do that

The syntax is similar to that of the plain `if` statement that we just saw. All you have to do is to append the keyword `else`, followed by the action you want to perform if the condition fails.

```
if ( condition )
{
     statements // Do this
}
else
{
     statements // Do that
}
```

For example, suppose you want Tracer to mark a square in black or green, depending on whether she sees a wall:

```
int black=7,green=2;
```

```
if (Tracer.seewall())        // Check for a wall ahead. If so:
{
    Tracer.mark(black);      // Mark in black
}
else
{
    Tracer.mark(green);      // Else: Mark in green
}
```

Of course, since each alternative action consists of only one statement in this case, you don't really need the braces. You could write this program as follows:

```
if (Tracer.seewall()) Tracer.mark(black);
else Tracer.mark(green);
```

Try This for Fun. . .

- Use Tracer to walk down a corridor and locate the first corridor to the left. Remember that she can only see whether there is a corridor to the left if she turns left to see it! When she finds the corridor, tell her to stay there and report how many steps away the corridor is located.

Example—In the Maze 2

We'll now revise the program c4search.cpp to incorporate a better visual interface. All we need to do is to mark the squares in which a wall was found in a different color. A simple modification of the go() function will do the trick. If you examine the structure of the if/else construct:

```
if ( condition )
{
    // Do this
}
else
{
    // Do that
}
```

you will notice that the *do this* part already exists. We need only to include the *do that* part. Can you do this by yourself? Sure you can! (See the exercise below.)

Or This. . .

- Modify the go() function in c4search.cpp to perform the following actions if the next square contains a wall:

    Mark the next square in black.

    Say "OUCH!"

Example—In the Maze 3

Another interesting example is to have Tracer walk down a corridor and mark the squares that are empty and the ones that are occupied by a wall. To do this, you may tell Tracer to repeat the following sequence in every square:

Turn left and see if there is a wall.

If so:

Mark the square in black.

Else:

Mark it in green.

Face the original direction.

We can describe this problem as follows:

Repeat until you see a wall:

Check your right.

Check your left.

Step ahead.

Of course, we must explain what we mean by *check your right* and *check your left*! Here is how you check your right:

Turn right.

If you see wall:

Mark the square in black.

Else:

Mark the square in green.

Turn left.

You can figure out how to check the left.

Can you see, once again, the role of if/else? Depending on the existence of a wall, Tracer either marks the square in black or marks the square in green. She has to choose one thing or the other. If the condition is true, the action following if is executed and the action following else is skipped. If the condition is not true, the action following if is skipped and the action following else is executed.

The piece of program to check your right could look like as follows:

```
Tracer.right();
if (Tracer.seenowall())
{
    Tracer.mark(green);
}
else
{
    Tracer.mark(black);
}
Tracer.left();
```

You might want to create a function to check:

```
void check()
{
    if (Tracer.seenowall()) Tracer.mark(green);
    else Tracer.mark(black);
}
```

Your program could work as follows:

```
#include "franca.h"
Robot Tracer (1);
void mainprog()
{
    while(Tracer.seenowall)       // Repeat until wall is seen
    {
        Tracer.left();            // Check your left
        check();
        Tracer.right();
        Tracer.right();           // Check your right
        check();
        Tracer.left();
        Tracer.step();            // Step ahead
    }
}
```

Example—At the Store 2

At this point, we may also reexamine the program that computes change, c4change.cpp. This program was presented earlier in the Skill, and was modified to check whether the amount tendered was sufficient to purchase the items.

A better solution to this problem includes a *do this or do that* alternative. In other words, if the amount tendered is insufficient, the sale should not be completed. One possible solution is illustrated below.

```
#include "franca.h"
void mainprog()
{
  float price,amount,change;
  float tax=0.08;
  amount=ask("Enter the amount:");
  price=ask("Enter the price:")*(1+tax);
  if(amount<price)
    {
      Cout<<"This is not enough!";
    }
  else
    {
      change=amount-price;
      Cout<<change;
    }
}
```

In this case, either the message *This is not enough!* will be displayed or the change will be displayed—but not both.

Specifying Conditions

Conditions are used in decision and repetition statements. We have already experimented with simple conditions that compare two numbers. For example:

```
count<=15
```

checks whether the count is less than or equal to 15. Conditions are based on the relationship between values, and are expressed by means of relational expressions.

Relational Expressions

The simplest relational expression consists of two items with a relational operator between them. The items can be

- Variables—for example, the following expression checks whether count is equal to howmany:

    ```
    count==howmany
    ```

- Constants (relational expressions with two constants do not make sense, but they can be used)—for example, the following expression checks whether howmany is *not* equal to zero:

    ```
    howmany!=0
    ```

- Results returned by a function—for example, the following expression checks whether the time in myclock is less than or equal to 20:

    ```
    myclock.time()<=20
    ```

- Arithmetic expressions—for example:

    ```
    how many-steps>10
    ```

> **NOTE**   Objects can also be used in a relational expression, but only if the relational operator is defined for that class of objects.

Unlike the assignment operator, there is no difference whether you use an item to the left or the right of the relational operator. For example, the same results will be achieved if we express the condition count<=15 as follows:

```
15>count
```

Relational Operators

The relational operators, which were seen in Skill 5, are

==	is equal to
!=	is not equal to
<	is less than
<=	is less than or equal to

>	is greater than
>=	is greater than or equal to

Results

The computer evaluates the relational expression and generates a result. For practical purposes, the relation is either true or false. For example, if the current value of count is 13, the following expression:

```
count<=15
```

is true.

> **WARNING**   Once again, remember the most dangerous expression—if (a=b). It is not a condition—it is just an assignment. A condition uses two equal signs (==)!

Compound Expressions

In many cases, we need to base our decision on more than one expression. For example, an athlete may be dismissed if she has performed 50 jumping jacks or if she has exercised for more than 5 minutes. In this case, there are two conditions:

```
count>=50
time>=300
```

When two or more conditions are used, we must explain how they are supposed to be combined. In this case, we want one condition or the other to be satisfied. In other cases, we might want both conditions to be satisfied (one *and* the other).

Logical Operators

Logical operators are used to explain how to combine two or more conditions. The logical operators are

- && — the and operator (one condition and the other must be true)

- || — the or operator (one condition or the other, or both, must be true)

- ! — the not operator (inverts the result of a relational expression)

Skill 10

The not operator is unary; it may precede an expression, and it will invert its value. The other operators are binary; they are placed between two expressions. The expressions must always be enclosed in parentheses.

Here are some examples:

```
(count>=15)||(myclock.time()>300)
```

Either count is greater than or equal to 15 or time is greater than 300.

```
(count>=15)&&(myclock.time()>120)
```

count is greater than or equal to 15 and time is greater than 120.
```
(count>15)&&(!(myclock.time()<240))
```

count is greater than 15 and time is *not* less than 240.

Priority

When more than two expressions are evaluated, it is important to know the operator priority:

- The not operator has the highest priority.

- The and operator has the next priority.

- The or operator has the last priority.

Parentheses can be used to specify or to reinforce priority. For example:

```
(myclock.time()>300)||(myclock.time()>120)&&(count>=50)
```

In this example, the and operation is done first, followed by the or. If this expression is used to dismiss an athlete, the athlete will be dismissed in two cases:

time is greater than 300

or

time is greater than 120 and count is greater than or equal to 50.

Nested Decisions

Some situations require you to check more than one condition, so that some action can be performed. This happens when one of the statements to be executed in an if is another if. Consider the following situation:

```
// Check the right side:
```

```
Tracer.right();
if(Tracer.seewall())
{
    // Check the left side:
    Tracer.left();
    Tracer.left();
    if(Tracer.seewall())
    {
        Tracer.say("corridor");
    }
}
```

In the situation above, we have two levels of nesting. If the first if fails (no wall), the second if is not executed. This piece of program determines whether the squares on both sides of Tracer have walls. Notice that Tracer first turns to the right to check the right side. If there is no wall, there is no need to check the left side, and the test is done. If a wall appears in this right square, Tracer must turn to the left square (two turns will be needed at this point) and check it. If a wall is detected, Tracer can "say" that she is in a corridor in which both left and right squares have walls.

It is a good idea to imagine yourself as the robot and to try to understand exactly how this algorithm works.

The more nested conditions you use in your program, the more complex your program will become. Correct and clean indentation, as well as sufficient comments, will significantly help to keep your programs readable. If complexity persists, you should consider resorting to functions.

A major inconvenience of the C++ programming language is that it makes no provision for the compiler to determine whether an if statement has an else clause.

For example, consider the following listings:

```
k=0;
  if (a<0)
       if (b<0) k=1;
  else k=2;
```

and

```
k=0;
      if (a<0)
          if (b<0) k=1;
          else k=2;
```

Skill 10

Since the computer does not understand indentation, both pieces of program are identical in the eyes of the compiler. However, the indentation leads us to believe that the results would be different. In the first case, if a is greater than or equal to zero, else is executed and k is assigned the value 2. In the second case, the else clause is associated with the inner if, and, therefore, if a is greater than or equal to zero, the inner if is skipped, and the value of k remains zero.

Of course, only one of the alternatives is correct, because, as we mentioned, they appear exactly the same to the compiler. What does the compiler do in this case?

NOTE   The else clause always matches the closest if.

The second alternative is the correct one, because the else clause is closest to the second if.

If you want to make else apply to the first if, you have to include an empty else, as illustrated below.

```
k=0;
 if (a<0)
        if(b<0) k=1;
        else ;
 else k=2;
```

Another, more elegant, approach is to clearly delimit the if without the else.

```
k=0;
 if (a<0)
        {
        if(b<0) k=1;
        }
 else k=2;
```

Breaking Out of Loops

Sometimes you may be repeating a loop, and, for some reason, you decide to interrupt the repetition.

Suppose that our good friend Sal is told to perform 50 jumping jacks in his fitness class. Well, he is happily jumping—1, 2, 3, 4—when all of a sudden the fire alarm sounds! What do you think he should do? Finish the jumping jacks, and then run away? Of course not! Sometimes we want to interrupt a repetition and break out.

The *break* Statement

The break statement serves exactly this purpose. This statement allows you to escape the current loop as if the repetition was finished at that point. Figure 10.4 shows this situation.

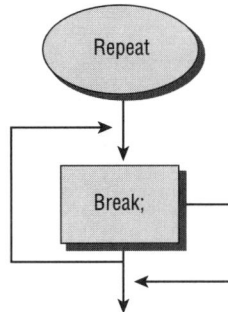

FIGURE 10.4: The break statement

Suppose that you set a loop to repeat a certain number of times. However, in the loop, you test for another condition—*Is it too late? Is the building on fire?*—and then you decide to break the loop. You will not only stop repeating, you will also skip any remaining part of the loop that has not been executed.

To illustrate this, why don't we have Sal do some exercises, and then check the time he has spent. This can be done as follows:

> Repeat 50 times:
>> If time is more than 50 seconds:
>>> Stop.
>>
>> Do a jumping jack.

The following listing could be the program:

```
athlete Sal;
Clock watch;
for (int times=1;times<=50;times++)
{
    if (watch.time()>50.) break;
    JumpJack(Sal);
}
```

Did you miss an `else`? You might have expected the decision to use an `if/else` structure, instead of the plain `if`. After all, `JumpJack` will be executed only if the time is less than 50 seconds. In other words, you might have thought of writing the program as follows:

```
athlete Sal;
Clock watch;
for (int times=1;times<=50;times++)
{
    if (watch.time()>50.) break;
    else JumpJack(Sal);
}
```

This solution is correct. When the `break` occurs, whatever statements are left until the end of the loop (marked by the closing brace) are skipped. The `JumpJack` will be performed only if the `break` is not performed. However, there is no need for the `else` in this case.

An interesting example tells Tracer to step 10 times:

> Repeat 10 times:
>
>> Step.

However, since we don't want her to bump into a wall, we want her to stop this repetition if she happens to see a wall ahead:

> Repeat 10 times:
>
>> If you see a wall:
>>
>>> Stop repeating.
>>
>> Step.
>
> Done!

What do we want her to do? We want her to ignore the condition of the repetition, and to go straight to the next statement after the repetition—*Done!* Use the `break` statement again. The program would look like as follows:

```
int stepcount;
for (stepcount=1;stepcount<=10;stepcount++)
{
    if(Tracer.seewall())
    {
        break;
    }
    Tracer.step();
}
```

The *continue* Statement

In some repetitions, you may decide to suspend the current pass of the loop, but to continue to repeat the next pass. This is the role of the `continue` statement. `continue` is similar to `break`—they both interrupt the repetition. Unlike `break`, `continue` skips only the remaining part of the current loop, but it continues with the next iteration.

> **NOTE**   If you are familiar with board games, you may compare break with being kicked out of the game altogether. `continue` sends you back to the start—go directly to jail, do not pass *Go*, do not collect $200—but you resume play on your next turn.

As an example, suppose that one of our athletes exercises by repeating the following sequence 50 times:

> jumping jack
>
> leftright

If we assume that we have defined the functions as follows:

```
JumpJack(athlete)
leftright(athlete)
```

the program could look like as follows:

```
athlete Kim;
Clock watch;
for (int times=1;times<=50;times++)
{
    JumpJack(Kim);
    leftright(Kim);
}
Kim.say("Done!");
```

Now, suppose that Kim wants to check the time, and, if the time exceeds 15 seconds, to skip the second part of the exercise (the `leftright`). The new listing below includes an `if` that checks the time and skips the remaining part of the loop:

```
athlete Kim;
Clock watch;
for (int times=1;times<=50;times++)
{
    JumpJack(Kim);
    if (watch.time()>15.) continue;
```

```
    leftright(Kim);
  }
  Kim.say("Done!");
```

Each time Kim goes through the loop, she performs a jumping jack and checks the time. If the time is still less than 15, she proceeds to the end of the loop, performing the `leftright`. However, if the time is greater than 15, the `continue` statement is executed. The remaining steps in the loop are skipped, but the variable `times` will be incremented, and the next pass of the loop will take place. Since the time will always be greater than 15 from that point on, Kim will only perform `JumpJacks` and will skip the `leftright`. If a `break` is used instead of a `continue`, the complete repetition will be interrupted and no more `JumpJacks` or `leftrights` will be performed.

Designing Your Own Loops—Part 2

We missed using decisions, and the `break` and `continue` statements, in "Designing Your Own Loops—Part 1" in Skill 8. By using these, you can either skip part of the loop or exit it completely. The loop can be interrupted at any point when you use the `break` statement. The loop does not have to be completed every time.

As an example, let's refer to the program `c3avgrd.cpp`, in which we computed the average grade in a class. The main loop was implemented as follows:

```
for (int which=0;yesno("input another grade?"); which++)
{
  grade=ask("Enter next grade:");
  total=total+grade;
}
```

Suppose that your teacher did not like the idea of having to reply to the question *input another grade?* all the time. After all, if there were 40 students in class, this would represent an extra 40 mouse clicks!

An alternative is to use a sentinel value. For example, since grades are supposed to be all positive, you could reserve a negative value to signal that there are no more grades to be input.

The new loop could then become

```
for (int which=1;; which++)
{
  grade=ask("Enter next grade:");
```

```
    if(grade<0) break;
    total=total+grade;
}
```

This causes immediate interruption of the loop when a negative grade is input. This negative grade is read, but it will not be added to the total (break occurs before addition). The variable which will not be incremented either. Notice that I changed the initial value to 1, instead of zero. I did this because once break is executed, the counter will no longer be incremented. If you set the initial value to 1, it will result in correct values for total and which.

Notice that no condition is necessary in the for statement. However, make sure that at some point, some statement causes the loop to end!

You may feel tempted to use the sentinel value in the for statement. For example:

```
for (which=1;grade>=0; which++)
{
    grade=ask("Enter next grade:");
    total=total+grade;
}
```

may seem right, because the loop will be executed as long as the grade is not negative. However, this is not true. Remember that the condition is tested before the loop is executed. The negative grade will be read and added to the total, and the control variable (which) will be incremented. Only then will the condition be checked for the next iteration and the loop be stopped! Furthermore, when you execute the loop for the first time, you don't know whether grade has any valid contents.

Switching among Several Alternatives

In certain situations, instead of having to choose between two alternatives, we have to choose one among several. For example, if we want an athlete to assume a different position according to the value contained in a variable code, we could use

```
if(code==1) Kim.ready();
if(code==2) Kim.up();
if(code==3) Kim.left();
if(code==4) Kim.right();
```

The switch statement uses one variable to decide which action to take (see Figure 10.5).

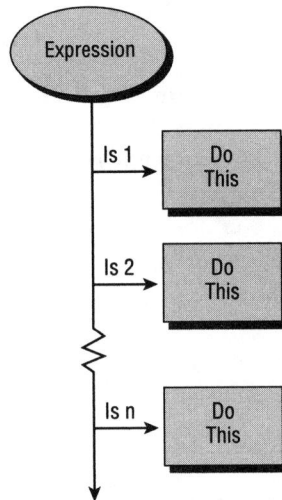

FIGURE 10.5:   The general procedure of switch

It works as follows:

Use the value to choose one case from the list below:

Case—the value is 1:

ready!

End of this case.

Case—the value is 2:

up!

End of this case.

Case—the value is 3:

left!

End of this case.

Case—the value is 4:

right!

End of this case.

End of the list of cases.

switch includes a header and a list of cases. (Figure 10.5 illustrated the procedure.) The general form of switch is as follows:

```
switch ( expression )
{
    list of cases
}
```

in which *expression* is any expression that returns an integer value (int, long, or char) and the *list of cases* (enclosed in braces) consists of any number of cases that have the following form:

```
case integer value:
    statements
break;
```

The effect of the switch statement is as follows:

- The expression is evaluated, and the resulting value (which must be an integer) is checked for a match with the integer values listed in the case labels.

- If a match is found, the sequence of statements that follows the label is executed until a break is found.

Example—Thank You for Calling!

To illustrate the use of switch, let's consider the problem of an international communications carrier that wants to write a message—*Thank you*—in the language that is spoken in the country they are calling.

You can write a program that requests the country code (for international direct dialing). Since there are many alternatives, it is impractical to use if. On the other hand, switch is very convenient. Once you have the country code, use it to switch:

```
switch (country_code):
{
    case    1:
        message.say("Thank you");
    break;
    case    34:
        message.say("Gracias");
    break;
...
```

To make the problem even more interesting, consider the case of Switzerland. Each of its regions typically uses a different language. No problem! Just use the area code, as well. The complete program is shown below.

```cpp
#include "franca.h"          // c4switch.cpp
  void mainprog()
  {
    Box display;
    int country,area;
    while(yesno("Shall we continue?"))
    {
        country=ask("Enter the country code:");
        area=ask("Enter the area code:");
        switch (country)
        {
            case 55:          // Brazil
            case 351:         // Portugal
                display.say("Obrigado");
            break;
            case 81:          // Japan
                display.say("Arigato");
            break;
            case 82:          // Korea
                display.say("Gamzahamnidah!");
            break;

            case 52:          // Mexico
            case 34:          // Spain
            case 54:          // Argentina
                    display.say("Gracias!");
            break;
            case 41:          // Switzerland
                switch (area)
                {
                    case 21: // Lausanne
                    case 41: // Lucerne
                    case 22: // Geneva
                      display.say("Merci");
                      break;
                    default:
                      display.say("Danke");
                }
            break;

            case 49:          // Germany
            case 43:          // Austria
                display.say("Danke!");
```

```
            break;
            default:
                display.say("Thank you!");
        }
    }
}
```

It is important that you note the following items:

- The statement begins with the keyword `switch`, followed by an integer variable (or any expression that results in an integer value) in parentheses. This is the value that determines which action will be executed.

- The set of cases is enclosed in braces ({}).

- Each case is labeled with one possible value (expressed by a constant) and ends with a `break` statement. If you omit (or forget) a `break` statement between two cases, the *breakless* case will proceed until a `break` is found. In our particular problem, this comes in handy. We may group all countries that use the same language and end them with the same `break`.

- The label consists of the keyword `case`, a constant that expresses the selected value, and a colon. The label can be written in the same line as the first statement in the case. For example, the following statement is also correct:

```
    case 51: message.say("obrigado");
```

- If the value that is used for switching does not match any of the listed cases, no action will be taken.

- It is possible to specify a default case, which will be executed if the value does not match any of those listed. The default case is labeled with the keyword `default`, as in the following example:

```
    default:
        message.say("Thank you");
```

WARNING   Make sure that you include a break at the end of each alternative. Unlike other structures that use a compound statement to locate the beginning and the end, `switch` requires you to use break to locate the end of a case. Until a break is found, the program continues to execute the next statements, which may belong to the next alternative.

Skill 10

Are You Experienced?

Now you can...

- ☑ Use *if* to decide on the right piece of program to execute
- ☑ Use *if/else* to decide between two alternatives
- ☑ Build a condition on which you can base your decisions
- ☑ Break out of loops
- ☑ Design more complex loops
- ☑ Use a *switch* statement to choose one among several alternatives

S K I L L

eleven

Using Recursive Functions

- ❑ Understanding recursive algorithms
- ❑ Creating recursive functions

Recursion is a technique that solves a problem by working as if a simpler, similar problem has already been solved (although it has not). The question then becomes, Who is going to solve the simpler problem? This is where recursion really takes over—it calls the same function (itself), but now it requests the solution to the simpler problem. What happens if the simpler problem is still not easy to solve? No problem, it just keeps calling itself!

As you use the same technique to solve the simpler problem, you will postpone the solution of an even simpler problem again and again. The simple problem becomes simpler each time—until it becomes trivial. What do you do then? You go back and solve each of the other problems whose solution was postponed.

This skill will be developed with the aid of the `Robot` object.

Understanding Recursive Algorithms

Recursive algorithms use themselves to reach an answer. Consider the problem in which you want to measure how many steps the robot has to take to reach a wall. A recursive answer to this problem would be as follows:

> This is how you compute *distance:*
>
> > If you see the wall, the answer is zero.
> >
> > Otherwise:
> >
> > > Step ahead.
> > >
> > > The answer is 1+*distance.*

TIP   "Master, how many steps to the top of the mountain?" "Take one step now—you will be one step closer."

When the expression *1+distance* is reached, the result cannot proceed until *distance* is known. The computation is then suspended, so you can compute the new distance. When this value is found, you add one to it to find your answer. Let's try to understand how this algorithm works.

When you are told to compute the distance, the first thing you do is to check whether you are already facing a wall, in which case the distance is zero. However, if you are not facing a wall, you have to step ahead—your answer will be one plus the new distance. You could say that this is pretty obvious. But how do you compute the new distance? Just interrupt your computation and look in the algorithm again to check whether you are facing a wall—but remember to proceed when you obtain the result!

At some point, the wall will be reached, and the result *zero* will be returned. You then resume the computation that was interrupted and add one to the distance from the next square (which was found to be zero). The new result (one) will be returned, and the previous computation, which was interrupted, can now resume. Several algorithms can be best expressed by means of recursion.

> **NOTE** The distance from a given square equals the distance from the next square plus one.

Creating Recursive Functions

C++ supports recursive functions—functions that can call themselves. Here is one example:

```
int distance()
  {
    if(Tracer.seewall())return 0;
    Tracer.step();
    return 1+distance();
  }
```

This example is an implementation of the recursive algorithm to compute the distance to a wall, as discussed above. The last statement returns the value of the expression 1+distance(). However, distance() is a function call to the same function (the function calls itself!). The only difference is that now the robot is one step closer than it was before.

At this point, you are strongly encouraged to visualize yourself as the robot and follow this algorithm to compute the distance, in steps, to the nearest wall. It would also be useful to have a function that shows the actual step count while the computation proceeds. The following listing is a possibility:

```
int distance()
  {
    if(Tracer.seewall())return 0;
    Tracer.step();
    Tracer.say(1+distance());
    return 1+distance();
  }
```

The function above seems to do the job, but it is inconvenient. Notice that we are invoking `distance()` twice. Suppose that you are the robot. Would you walk to the wall to compute the distance, say it, then walk back to return the result? If the `distance()` function leaves the robot next to the wall, this function will not work correctly, because the second time you call `distance()`, the result will be one. Try it! You may check this with the program `c4dist1.cpp`.

It is a good idea to store the result in a variable, so we do not have to invoke the function twice.

```
int findwall()
{
  int steps;
  if(Tracer.seewall())return 0;
  Tracer.step();
  steps= 1+findwall();
  Tracer.say(steps);
  return steps;
}
```

If you execute this function, you will notice the following things:

- The values of the steps are "said," *1, 2, 3....*

- The values of the steps are "said" only after the robot reaches the wall. Why?

How Does a Recursive Function Work?

Every time a function is called, the computer keeps track of where it is in the program's execution, and then it starts to execute the function. Any variables that were declared in the function are then created, and the arguments are copied to the parameters (unless they are passed by reference). When a function calls itself, it is as if the function is frozen at that time, and a new copy of the same function starts to execute.

The `findwall` function illustrates this process. Let's suppose that Tracer is located three squares away from the wall when the function is first called. Since there will be further calls, let's denote this as the first instance.

First instance: When the function is first invoked (by another program), the variable `steps` is created, and Tracer is in square number 1. Since she is still away from the wall, the function instructs her to step ahead. Tracer is now in square number 2.

Next, the function computes the value of `steps` as `1+findwall`. The recursion starts here. The remaining statements in the function are not executed. The function will be frozen with all the current variables until this result can be computed. The variable `steps` still does not have a value assigned to it. The function is called again (the second instance starts).

> *Second instance:* A new instance of the function is started. Another variable `steps` is created, and Tracer is in square number 2. Since she is still away from the wall, the function instructs her to step ahead. Tracer is now in square number 3.
>
> Next, the function computes the value of `steps` as `1+findwall`. The recursion takes place again. The remaining statements in the function are not executed. (Wow! Do you remember doing the same thing in the previous issue of the function?) This issue of the function will now be frozen until this result is available. The second version of the variable `steps` also does not have a value assigned to it. The function is called once more (the third instance starts).

> > *Third instance:* A new instance of the function is started. Another variable `steps` (this is the third version) is created, and Tracer is in square number 3.
> >
> > Since she is now next to the wall, the function terminates, and then returns the value *0* as a result. This terminates this instance of the function and yields a result, so the previous version can continue. Nothing is assigned to the variable `steps` (the computer now returns to the second instance).

> *Second instance:* The computer continues the computation. The second version of the variable `steps` is now assigned a value of 1+0. Tracer sends this value to the screen, and the function returns this value (which happens to be 1). This instance of the function terminates and yields a result, so the previous version can continue (the computer finally returns to the first instance).

First instance: The computer continues the computation. The original version of the variable `steps` is now assigned a value of 1+1. Tracer sends this value to the screen, and the function returns this value (which happens to be 2). The first instance of the function terminates, and this result is passed to the original calling program.

Improving the Algorithm

Something still makes me unhappy about this function. Every time we tell the robot to take a measurement, she walks to the wall and stays there! Couldn't she come back to the original place?

The crucial elements of this function are when we compute the value of `steps` and then invoke the function `findwall`, because the computer must do the following things:

- Suspend the work and remember where to resume.

- Restart the function to compute the distance.

- Resume where work was suspended when the result is available.

Well, one thing is certain—if we want her to come back to the place where she started, we better tell her to step back again after the measurement. It is as if we undo the steps after we find the result.

At this point, we could have a function that looks as follows:

```
int distance()
{
  int steps;
  if(Tracer.seewall())return 0;
  Tracer.step();        // Move forward
  steps= 1+distance();  // Compute distance
  Tracer.say(steps);    // Display current distance
  Tracer.step();        // Step back!
  return steps;
}
```

Did we forget to tell her to turn back? After all, she is moving toward the wall. Yes, we have to tell her to turn back. When shall we tell her?

WARNING You may think it is a good idea to tell her to turn back before she steps back—it is not! Notice that she only has to turn back once. If she turns back before she has taken the step back, she will end up turning several times. (Try it! It's fun!)

The appropriate thing to do is to have her turn back when she finds the wall. From then on, every time she has a measurement, she is already facing the return direction.

A final version of this function could then be as follows:

```
int distance()
{
```

```
int steps;
if(Tracer.seewall())
{
    Tracer.right();
    Tracer.right();
    return 0;
}
Tracer.step();        // Move forward
steps= 1+distance();  // Compute distance
Tracer.say(steps);    // Display current distance
Tracer.step();        // Step back!
return steps;
}
```

A version of this function that is slightly more elaborate can be found in the program `c4dist2.cpp`.

Recursive Function Calls Use Memory

A recursive function "remembers" all the values as they were before the recursive call. All variables that were declared in the function are re-created in a new version, leaving the previous version intact. The same thing is true of any parameters passed by value, which are like new variables that are re-created every time the function is called. In addition, the function remembers exactly what it was doing, so it can later resume.

Trade-Offs in Recursion

Recursive algorithms are good because they may express a simpler way to solve a problem. However, there are some inconveniences of which you should be aware.
Every time a function is called:

- Memory space is allocated to accommodate any variables or objects that were declared in that function.

- Arguments and returned values also need memory space. In the `findwall()` example, a variable `steps` is declared in the function.

- The computer has to keep track of the place in the program where operation should resume after it executes the function.

Every time the function is invoked, some memory locations will be set apart. If the distance is 1,000 steps, the function will be called 1,000 times; each time, 1,000 locations will be reserved.

Besides consuming storage space, you should know that each function call consumes some time, utilizing the microprocessor and other overhead, as well.

Ending Recursive Algorithms

Once you grasp the concept, recursive algorithms and recursive function calls are very easy to use. The most important thing to keep in mind when you use a recursive solution is to make sure that the recursion ends at some point. You can proceed with the computation only when a recursive function returns.

In our examples, it was easy to see when the recursion ends. The recursion ends when the robot reaches a wall. But what if there is no wall? We could use this program only because we were guaranteed to find a wall. Likewise, while we explore the maze, either we ask for user input or we use the timer to limit our search.

In any event, make sure you clearly know the condition that signals the end of the recursion, and make sure that it will be reached. Observe also that any variables or objects that are passed by reference or defined globally are not re-created!

The Great Escape—Part 3

Since we can use a recursive function to compute the distance to the next wall, it seems perfectly possible that we can use a recursive function with the c4search.cpp program to keep track of how Tracer moves around the maze.

When you compute the distance to the next wall, use a simple recursive algorithm to make sure that Tracer can come back to the original location. If we keep moving left and right to explore the maze, can we still use a recursive function to make Tracer come back? Yes, indeed! All we have to do is to undo the turns and steps.

Let's start with a small modification to c4search.cpp. In this new program, instead of using a loop to ask whether she may come back, we use a recursive function to do the same thing. Here is the program c4back1.cpp:

```
#include "franca.h"
// Recursive maze exploration
Robot Tracer(1);        // c4back1.cpp
void explore1()
{
  int direction;        // The direction she will face
  if(yesno("Should I go on?"))
```

```
{                          // As long as you answer
  do                       //      yes, this will be done
  {
      direction=ask("which way should I go?");
      Tracer.face(direction);
      Tracer.mark(7);
  }                        // Repeat until the direction
                           //      leads to a free square
  while (Tracer.seewall());
// Once the square ahead is clear:
Tracer.mark();             // Mark it green
Tracer.step();             // Step forward
explore1();                // Continue
                           // This part will only be executed after
                           //      exploration is done!

  }
}

  void mainprog()
  {
    explore1();
  }
```

This program is very similar to the original program. Besides a few minor changes, the essential difference is that `c4search.cpp` had a loop that was terminated by your answer to the `yesno` function—this program does not seem to have a loop. Does it? Well, it does have a recursive loop!

As long as you reply *yes* to the question, the robot will move into a new square, and then a call to `explore1` will be made. But a call to `explore1` will simply start this function all over again! Isn't this just like a loop? After all, if we reply *yes* 15 times, we invoke `explore1` 15 times. A new variable `distance` is created every time, and a new value is stored in it. Then, the robot marks the next square and moves into it. What is the difference?

The difference is that each time the function is called, a new set of information, including `direction`, is used. The old `direction` is preserved. When you finally reply *no*, the 15th issue of this function will be done, and it will be able to proceed past the `explore1` function call (for the first time). The function will terminate, the content of `distance` will be discarded, and the 14th issue of the function then resumes right after the `explore1` function call. This sequence of events will be repeated until the original issue of the function is also terminated.

Can we use this to make Tracer come back to the original position? Aren't we in the same situation the recursive function was in to measure the distance to the wall?

Indeed, we are. All we have to do is to undo the step taken in the current issue of the function—as in the `findwall` functions. Remember that, this time, we are facing a different direction. But we know the direction that Tracer was facing when we last told her to explore, don't we? It is stored in the variable `direction`. So, if the direction was north, we have to make Tracer face south and then step. Can you figure out the rest? Please do!

Are You Experienced?

Now you can. . .

☑ **Identify problems that can use recursive solutions**

☑ **Understand how a recursive algorithm works**

☑ **Use recursive functions**

Completing a Short Project

- ❏ Creating a user interface
- ❏ Moving a robot
- ❏ Choosing functions
- ❏ Implementing a simple application

In Skill 12, you will continue to develop your skills in solving problems and developing applications. You will work on a short project that requires you to design and build software. This project will use Robot objects.

Creating the User Interface

In this short project, you will develop a program that can place the robot in any location in an empty room. The location will be determined by specifying the following coordinates:

- Distance, in steps (or squares), from the left wall (horizontal coordinate)
- Distance, in steps (or squares), from the upper wall (vertical coordinate)

The purpose of this software is to keep asking the user for the desired location, and then to move the robot to this location. Since the room has no inside walls, you can rest assured that the robot will not crash, as long as the coordinates remain in the valid range.

For the user interface, use the robot itself and a pair of boxes that indicate the current coordinates (horizontal and vertical). You may consider using the following declarations for these boxes:

```
Box X("Horizontal:"),Y("Vertical:");
```

Moving the Robot—A General Description

The robot always starts in the upper-left square. Since this square is one step from the left wall and one step from the upper wall, it is correct to consider this square to have the coordinates (1,1).

It is important to keep track of the robot's coordinates at all times. If the robot moves one step to the right (east), the horizontal coordinate increases by one. You can determine what happens when the robot moves in other directions.

The software essentially will consist of the following steps:

Repeat:

Get new horizontal and vertical coordinates.

Move robot to new coordinates.

Update current coordinates.

What else do we need to explain? You know how to make a loop, and you will probably have no problem asking for new coordinates to be input. The really interesting problems, then, are to move the robot and to update the coordinates.

What Is Each Move?

Moving from one location to another is really simple. Suppose that the robot is in location (1,1) and that you are requested to move it to (4,9). What do you have to do? Nothing could be easier:

- Horizontally, you have to move from square 1 to square 4—a total of 3 steps.

- Vertically, you have to move from square 1 to square 9—a total of 8 steps.

So, if the robot is in position (x,y), and you want to move it to $(newx,newy)$:

- Horizontally, you have to move $newx–x$ steps.

- Vertically, you have to move $newy–y$ steps.

Is there any problem with this? No, not really—unless you have to move a negative number of steps, which means moving west (horizontally) or moving north (vertically).

Choosing Functions That Help

At this point, it may be a good idea to design a function to deal with this problem. Suppose that we have a function that tells Tracer how many steps to move horizontally and vertically. This function will check whether the number of steps is positive or negative, and move in the appropriate direction.

```
void move( int xsteps, int ysteps)
```

To make our design simple, we may think of another function that actually moves the robot from a given coordinate to another:

```
void moveto(int &currentx,int &currenty,int newx,int newy)
```

Since we may want this function to automatically update the coordinates, we can pass by reference. If these functions are available, the description of the main body of the loop can be expanded either in algorithmic or program form:

```
// Input new horizontal coordinate:
    horiz=ask("horizontal:");
```

```
// Input new vertical coordinate:
    vert=ask("vertical:");
// Move to new location:
    moveto(currentx,currenty,horiz,vert);
// Display coordinates:
    X.say(currentx);
    Y.say(currenty);
```

The loop itself can be controlled very easily:

```
while(yesno("Want to move?"))
```

At this point, your `mainprog` is just about complete. All you need to do is to declare and initialize the variables.

The *moveto()* Function

The code for the two functions, `moveto` and `move`, is interesting. The following function:

```
void moveto(int &currentx,int &currenty,int newx,int newy)
```

is supposed to move the robot from the current coordinates to the new coordinates and to update the current ones. As we know, this function can use the `move()` function. How can you do this?

As we have seen before, all we have to do is to move the robot *newx–currentx* steps horizontally and *newy–currenty* steps vertically. Or, use the `move()` function as follows:

```
move(newx-currentx,newy-currenty);
currentx=newx;
currenty=newy;
```

It's still easy, isn't it? We left all the trouble for the next function!

The *move()* Function Refined

The `move()` function was mentioned above, but it was not completely explained. Now, we can completely define the following function:

```
void move( int xsteps, int ysteps)
```

This function should verify whether `xsteps` is positive or negative, and then move in the appropriate direction. The same procedure is then applied to `ysteps`.

All you have to do is to turn the robot to face either east (positive *x*) or west (negative *x*), and then step the number of steps that has been specified. Here is how you can do it in the horizontal:

```
void move(int x,int y)
{
  if(x>0)              // Check horizontal direction
  {
     Tracer.face(3);
     Tracer.step(x);
  }
  else
  {
     Tracer.face(1); // If x is negative,
     x=-x;           //      make it positive
     if(x!=0) Tracer.step(x);
  }
  if(y>0)              // Now do the same for y
  {
     Tracer.face(2);
     Tracer.step(y);
  }
  else
  {
     Tracer.face(0);
     y=-y;
     if(y!=0) Tracer.step(y);
  }
  Tracer.face(3);
}
```

Notice that you have to step a positive number, and you cannot step *zero*.

Checking Errors

It is a good idea to avoid, when possible, erroneous user input that causes your program to misbehave. In this case, a range of coordinates is allowed, but the robot must remain in the room. You can restrict the user input of the coordinates to be greater than zero and less than 13.

You can either send an error message or keep asking for the correct input. The latter solution could be as follows:

```
do
   {
       horiz=ask("horizontal (between 1 and 13):");
   }
while ((horiz<1) || (horiz>13 ));
```

The Complete Robot Project

Here is a complete listing of the modified c4move2.cpp program:

```cpp
#include "franca.h"      // c4move2.cpp
#include "robot.h"
Robot Tracer;
void move(int x,int y)
{
  if(x>0)                  // Check horizontal direction
  {
    Tracer.face(3);
    Tracer.step(x);
  }
  else
  {
    Tracer.face(1);    // If x is negative,
    x=-x;              //      make it positive
    if(x!=0) Tracer.step(x);
  }
  if(y>0)
  {
    Tracer.face(2);
    Tracer.step(y);
  }
  else
  {
    Tracer.face(0);
    y=-y;
    if(y!=0) Tracer.step(y);
  }
  Tracer.face(3);
}

void moveto(int &currentx,int &currenty,int x,int y)
{
  int stepx,stepy;
  // How many steps in the horizontal?
  stepx=x-currentx;
  // How many steps in the vertical?
  stepy=y-currenty;
  move(stepx,stepy);
  // What are the new coordinates?
  currentx=currentx+stepx;
  currenty=currenty+stepy;
}
```

```
void mainprog()
{
  int currentx=1,currenty=1;
  Box X("Horizontal:"),Y("Vertical:");
  int horiz,vert;
  for(;yesno("Want to move?");)
  {
     do
     {
        horiz=ask("horizontal (between 1 and 13):");
     }
     while ((horiz<1)||(horiz>13));
     do
     {
        vert=ask("vertical (between 1 and 13):");
     }
     while ((vert<1)||(vert>13));
     moveto(currentx,currenty,horiz,vert);
     X.say(currentx);
     Y.say(currenty);
  }
}
```

Try These for Fun. . .

- Modify the point-of-sale terminal software to count the following items:

  1. The number of sales that had a total value under $10.00.

  2. The number of sales that had a total value between $10.00 and $50.00.

  3. The number of sales that had a total value between $50.00 and $100.00.

  4. The number of sales that had a total value over $100.00.

     - This information is to be displayed only after the last customer has checked out.

- Write a program to input grades from the keyboard and to compute the average of all the students who scored 50 or more.

NOTE   The next three exercises are for readers who are more mathematically inclined.

- The factorial function for a nonnegative integer n can also be defined recursively:

  - If n is zero, the factorial is 1.

  - If n is greater than zero, the factorial is n multiplied by the factorial $n–1$.

- Write a function to compute the factorial that uses this recursive definition. Test your function.

- Write a function to compute and return the absolute value of a floating point number. Test your function.

TIP   If y is positive, the result is y. If y is negative, the result is $–y$.

- Write a program to request that grades (between zero and 100) are input from the keyboard. This program should compute how many of these grades are between 0 and 25, how many of these grades are between 26 and 50, how many of these grades are between 51 and 75, and how many of these grades are between 76 and 100. Display the results.

Are You Experienced?

Now you can. . .

☑ **Analyze and decide on a user interface**

☑ **Write a general description of an application**

☑ **Choose functions and program pieces that can be useful in your application**

☑ **Implement a simple application**

PART V

PROGRAMMERS
C, C, VB, Cobol, exp.
Call 534-555-6543
or fax 534-555-6544.

PROGRAMMING
MRFS Inc. is looking for a Sr. Windows NT developer. Reqs. 3-5 yrs. Exp. In C under Windows, Win95 & NT, using Visual C, Excl. OO design & implementation skills a must. OLE2 & ODBC are a plus. Excl. Salary & bnfts. Resume & salary history to HR, 8779 HighTech Way, Computer City, AR

PROGRAMMERS/ Contractors
Wanted for short & long term assignments: Visual C, MFC Unix C/C, SQL Oracle Developers PC Help Desk Support Windows NT & NetWareTelecommunications Visual Basic, Access, HTML, CGL Perl MMI & Co. 885-555-9933

COMPUTER PROGRAMMER

Dealing with Numbers

In Part V, you will further develop your skills in handling numeric data. Thanks to the special software designed for this book, you will be able to learn numeric manipulation by producing graphics and animations. You will learn how to program relatively complex numeric expressions before moving on to manipulating Screen Objects and animations. A limited knowledge of geometry will come in handy.

Manipulating Numeric Expressions

- ❑ Identifying the numeric types used in C++

- ❑ Writing and evaluating expressions

- ❑ Using math functions

In Skill 13, we will expand your knowledge of using numbers. You will learn how to determine what types of variables to use for your data, how to manipulate values in variables by using expressions, and how to use the math function library. Many applications require extensive numeric manipulation. In Skills 14 and 15, you will be provided with interesting and relevant opportunities to practice your new-found skills in manipulating numeric expressions.

Expanding the Discussion of Numbers

Very often, you will need to manipulate numbers with your computer. In fact, when computers were first put into use, all their work related to numeric computation. Computers were used to compute trajectories and integrals, to solve equations, and so on. Computers represent information in numeric form, but numbers can represent colors, shapes, sounds, and nearly anything else you can imagine.

Since many applications require extensive use of numeric data, we will spend some time in this Skill exploring numeric manipulation. To make the subject more interesting, our applications in Skills 14 and 15 will involve graphics and animations.

Identifying Numeric Types

Numeric types and expressions were introduced briefly in Skill 5. In the following sections, we shall expand the discussion.

You don't usually manipulate numbers that are represented by an arbitrary number of digits in a computer. It is much simpler for the computer to set apart some space in its memory for numbers of a fixed size, according to the *type* of number with which you want to work. This process is similar to how some hand calculators work. If the calculator has an eight-digit display, you cannot operate with numbers that are longer than eight digits.

Storing Integer Numbers

As you know, computers can operate with integers and floating point numbers. To store integers, there are the types `int` and `long`. Here is a summary of how they work:

- We have already used the type `int` in previous Skills. To store an integer number (of type `int`), the computer sets aside a space in which you can store an integer number.

- Check your particular compiler for the range of numbers you can store. Most compilers use 16 bits to represent `int`s, which results in a range of numbers from –32,768 to +32,767. Other compilers may be able to accommodate larger ranges of numbers.

- The type `long` stands for *long int*, and tells the compiler that you want to deal with an integer that has a wider range. In that case, twice the space will be used to store this kind of number, and then you may deal with a wider range of numbers.

  - Check your particular compiler for the range of numbers you can store. Most compilers use 32 bits to represent `long` integers, which results in a range of numbers from –2,147,483,648 to +2,147,483,647. In any event, `long` integers take up twice the space in memory, and can accommodate a much larger range of numbers than an `int`.

TIP   Don't try to memorize these numbers—just remember that you can go to approximately two billion each way.

Unsigned Integers   If you are dealing with a variable that takes only positive values (for example, the number of students in a class), you can stretch the range of an `int` (or `long` integer) by prefixing the declaration with the keyword `unsigned`. For example:

```
unsigned int number_of_students;
```

Since you don't need to accommodate the negative values, the computer will be able to accommodate a positive number that is twice as large as the largest number that you could accommodate previously. If your compiler has an `int` range from –32,768 to +32,767, the unsigned `int` can range from 0 to +65,535.

NOTE   You don't have to use unsigned integers if you don't need the extra values. If you are dealing with the number of students in a class, it is likely that 32,767 integers will be enough.

Short Integers   If you really want to be savvy about memory, you can declare variables that are expected to accommodate very small integer values by prefixing the declaration with the keyword `short`. For example:

```
short int color;
```

Storing Floating Point Numbers

Some problems arise in which integer numbers are not appropriate. Often, you may need to use a decimal point and/or an exponent. In these cases, you have to resort to floating point numbers.

- The standard type in which to store floating point numbers is `float`. The type `float` takes up a little more space in the computer memory than `int` does, and, since it is a bit more complicated, more time is consumed to perform operations with floating point numbers than with integers. Again, there are some limitations. The regular floating point numbers may range from 3.4×10^{-38} to 3.4×10^{38}, may be either positive or negative, and may hold up to seven digits of precision. If you need more than that, do not despair....

WHAT DO YOU MEAN—SEVEN DIGITS?

If you try to store the number 1.0000001, the computer will not store the complete number. Only the seven most significant digits (1.000000) will be stored. However, it has nothing to do with the position of the decimal point; the same thing would happen with the number 234.56789, which would end up being 234.5678.

- Another type that is useful for dealing with large floating point numbers is the type `double`. It works just like the type `float`, but it is able to store numbers that have more significant digits and, depending on the compiler, a wider range of exponents.

- If you have to manipulate numbers with even more digits, you can prefix `double` with the keyword `long`. Again, check your compiler for the actual range.

Using Constants

Since you can refer to integer and floating point numbers, you may also need to use integer and floating point constants.

Constants are values that cannot change during the program execution. You will learn three ways to manipulate constant values in your programs:

- *Literal* constants literally write the value.

- *Labeled* constants are exactly like variables to which you give a name and assign a value, but you instruct the compiler to prevent any change to their value.

- *Enumerated* constants are a set of labeled constants to which you can assign a specific type and which use a list of names to denote the value.

Integer Constants   You write an integer constant pretty much like you write an integer number in everyday math. Observe the following items:

- You can precede the number with a + sign or a – sign.

- You cannot use commas or decimal points.

- You cannot leave spaces between the digits.

- You should avoid preceding the number with irrelevant zeros, which may cause confusion.

WARNING   Be aware of leading zeros! Leading zeros are used in C++ to identify integer constants that are expressed in octal notation. A value expressed in this notation is different from everyday decimal notation. For example, a constant expressed as *010* in C++ will be assumed to be in octal notation, resulting in the value *8* in decimal notation.

Floating Point Constants   You can write a floating point constant in C++ in two forms. The first form is similar to our everyday notation:

- You can precede the number with a + sign or a – sign.

- You can include one (and only one) decimal point.
- You cannot use commas or spaces between the digits.

Here are some examples of floating point constants:

35.

73.12

0.001

+54.3

−0.2

The second form is exponential notation, which is similar to how we represent large numbers in physics. This notation consists of two parts: the mantissa, which is represented by a floating point number, as in the examples above, and the exponent, which consists of the letter *E* followed by an integer number that represents the exponent.

For example, the following number:

6.02×10^{23}

can be written in C++ as 6.02 E23 or 6.02E+23. Both parts—the mantissa and the exponent—can have a sign.

Labeled Constants   It is possible to use an identifier to denote a constant value. If you need to use the value *3.1416* many times in your program, you may be better off declaring as follows:

```
float pi=3.1416;
```

and using `pi` instead of `3.1416` throughout your program. This idea is pretty cool! The only problem you may have is if this value of `pi` is erroneously altered in the program. You can avoid having a value altered by including the keyword `const` in the variable declaration. If you declare as follows:

```
const float pi=3.1416;
```

the compiler will not allow changes to this value. Any statement that attempts to alter the value of `pi` will cause an error.

Another convenience of `const` is that sometimes you may want to use a different value for a particular quantity. For example, you may decide to use the more precise value *3.14159*, instead of using *3.1416*. It is much simpler to change just the declaration than to look through the entire program and change the values! `const` lets you use a variable whose value is fixed during program execution.

Enumerated Constants   Enumerated constants are especially useful when a set of integers is used as a code. Take the example of the directions north, east, south, and west, which may be assigned the codes *0, 1, 2,* and *3.* To avoid dealing with the numbers in the program, we could declare as follows:

```
int N=0,E=1,S=2,W=3;
```

Or, better still:

```
const int N=0,E=1,S=2,W=3;
```

In either case, we could use the identifiers *N, E, S,* and *W* instead of the codes in the program. For example:

```
if(direction==N) ...
```

A simpler way to achieve the same result, with a few extra benefits, is to use the enum constant declaration:

```
enum  type  { identifiers list };
```

Or, in our case:

```
enum directions {N,E,S,W};
```

This declares the identifiers that are contained in the list to be constants of type int, and automatically initializes them to 0, 1, 2, and 3. Unless otherwise specified, the first identifier is initialized to 0, and each other identifier is initialized to the next integer.

The *type* is optional. In our example, directions could be omitted. The advantage of using the type is that you may declare a variable in the program that has this new type. For example:

```
directions  comingfrom,goingto;
```

allows you to assign any direction to these new variables. Therefore, if your program has assignments of the following form:

```
comingfrom=N;
goingto=S;
```

these statements will be considered correct. However, if you try to assign anything different (including an integer), the compiler will issue a warning. In the following example:

```
comingfrom=8;
goingto=2;
```

the compiler may suspect that you are doing something wrong.

Finally, it is possible to overrule the default sequence by specifying which value should be assigned to each identifier. For example:

```
enum colors (red=1,green,pink=5,yellow);
```

assigns value 1 to red, value 2 to green (previous value plus 1), value 5 to pink (as specified), and value 6 to yellow.

Reviewing Expressions

The rules for performing arithmetic operations and assigning values are reviewed here with some examples. For the examples in this section, let's assume that we have declared as follows:

```
int i, j, k;
float x,y,z;
```

Mixing Types, Variables, and Constants

You can combine variables and constants of either type in expressions. For example:

```
float x=0.5,y;
int i=5;
y=x-i+1;
```

takes the value of x, subtracts from it the value of i, and adds 1. The result will be stored as the new value of y.

So far, this is very close to what you would expect. In fact, the way we represent arithmetic expressions in C++ (as well as in most other computer languages) similar to the way we do it in math. There are a few things that you must know before we examine any rules:

- In math, you can omit the multiplication operator: 3xy means 3 times x times y.

  - In C++, we cannot do this. There is no way for a compiler to tell whether you have an object xy or x times y. Therefore, we must explicitly use the multiplication operator. Which symbol should we use? We cannot use x, because it could signify an object called x. Therefore, the multiplication operator is represented by *.

- In math, you can write values above and below a bar to indicate divisions.

- In a program, this is inconvenient, because we type from a keyboard. Instead, we use the slash symbol (/) to denote division. However, dividend and divisor are supposed to be in the same line. For example, x/y means that you should take the value of x and divide it by the value of y.
- In math, you don't usually differentiate between an integer and a floating point number when you compute an expression.

  - In most programming languages, integers and floating point numbers are treated quite differently. The result of an arithmetic operation that involves two integers is always an integer! Does this make any difference? Of course it does! If you divide 3./2. (notice that both are floating point numbers), the result is 1.5. If you divide 3/2 (notice that both are now integers of type int), the result is 1, because only the integer part is considered. Similar problems may happen in other operations.

For example:

```
int i,j;
i=30000;
j=i+i;
```

results in a value of 60,000, which most likely exceeds the range of an int.

Since you are now aware of these differences, we can actually move on to our rules.

Using Arithmetic Operators

The following arithmetic operators can be used in expressions:

+	addition
–	subtraction
*	multiplication
/	division
%	remainder of division

In addition, the assignment operator (=) can be used to assign the result of an expression to the variable on its left side. Here are some examples:

```
x=3*a+1; // Multiply a by 3, add 1, and store result in x
y=a+1*3; // Multiply 1 by 3, add to a, and store result in y
```

The second example illustrates that in expressions in C++, just like in expressions in math, multiplication takes priority over addition. Therefore, multiplication is done first. You may remember that an expression such as x+3a means that you should multiply *a* by 3, then add the result to *x*.

The rules for precedence are as follows:

- Higher priority operators are *, /, and %.

- Lower priority operators are + and –.

- Higher priority operations are executed first.

- If more than one operation has the same priority, execute from left to right.

You can explicitly specify the priority by using parentheses:

```
3*(x+1); // Add x to 1, then multiply by 3
3*x+1;   // Multiply x by 3, then add 1
```

If you need to, you can also nest parentheses in parentheses. In this case, the operation in the inner parentheses is solved first. For example:

```
3*(x/(y+1) + 4);
```

adds 1 to *y*, then divides *x* by this result. Then, it adds 4. Finally, this result is multiplied by 3. Notice that *x* is divided by *y+1* and not by *y+1+4*, as you might think if you were distracted.

Assigning Results

Use the assignment operator (=) in an expression to take the result (shown on the right side of the =) and assign it to the variable on the left side. Remember that the meaning of the operator is not the same as its meaning in a mathematical equation! For example:

```
s=s+3;
```

is correct. But the following expression:

```
s+3=s;
```

is not acceptable in C++!

Generating Results   Besides moving a value from one place to another, the assignment operator also generates a result that has the value of the value that was moved. In other words, the following statement:

```
s=3;
```

besides storing the value 3 in the variable s, will generate a result of 3. This is why the compiler considers the following statement to be correct in terms of syntax:

```
if(s=3) ...
```

Instead of comparing s to 3, this statement will move 3 to s, and generate 3 as a result. Since 3 is nonzero, it gives a *true* result inside the if.

Multiple Assignments   Since each assignment generates a result, it is possible to write the following statement:

```
x=y=1;
```

because the assignment operation:

```
y=1;
```

generates a result of 1. This result will be used by the next assignment operator.

> **NOTE**   Multiple assignments are executed from right to left.

Conversions   If an assignment operation involves operands of different types, the result will be converted to assume the type of the variable on the left side of the assignment operator. For example, suppose that we have the following expressions:

```
int  m=1,j=2,k;
float x=0.5,y;
```

An expression such as

```
m=x;
```

will have a result of 0.5, which will be converted to int so it can be stored in m. The new value of m will then be zero. Now, consider the following expression:

```
x=m=x;
```

which will result in a value of 0 for both m and x.

Finally, how about the following expression:

```
m=x=x;
```

What do you think will be the result?

Mixing Types

Expressions may contain objects of different types. When an operation involves operands of different types, the compiler tries to "promote" one of them. For example, if a float is to be added to an int, the int is promoted to float, and then the operation takes place.

PROMOTIONS AND DEMOTIONS

Although it may not seem important to you, the compiler automatically converts one of the operands so the operation can take place. When an expression calls for an operation between an integer and a floating point number, the integer is first converted to the floating point equivalent, and then the operation takes place (we say that the int was "promoted" to float, in this case). Similarly, if a float result is to be assigned to an int, the compiler "demotes" the float result by truncating its decimal part and converting it to an integer.

You can control the conversions yourself by using typecasting. To convert a variable or an expression to another type, write the type into which you want the variable or the expression to be cast in parentheses immediately before the variable or the expression.

For example, x=(float)m/(float)j; guarantees that both m and j will be converted to float before they are divided.

Returning Values in Functions

Expressions can also use functions. Any function can generate a result of any type, and that result can be used as part of an expression. For a function to generate a result, you must do the following things:

- Specify the type of the result. For example, the type may be int, float, long, etc. void means that nothing will be returned as a result.

- Use a return statement to indicate the result you are returning.

The *return* Statement

The `return` statement simply consists of the keyword `return` followed by an expression. The value of the expression is returned as a result. After executing the `return`, the function ends—the next statement in the sequence (if there is one) will not be executed.

For example, suppose that you want to create a function to compute the position of a body in free fall. The formula in physics is as follows:

$$h = \tfrac{1}{2}gt^2$$

in which *h* is the height, *g* is the gravity, and *t* is the time. Since *g* can be assumed to be constant near the earth's surface (32 feet per second squared or 9.81 meters per second squared), for any given time *t*, you can compute a value for *h*. In this case, you want *h* to be the result of this function. What is the type of this result? You probably want it to be a `float`, since the height may be measured in feet or meters, and it may have a fractional part.

If you call this function `height`, the actual code could be as follows:

```
float height (float t)
{
   return 0.5*g* t * t;
}
```

Instead of ½, I chose to use 0.5, which is the same. Beware! If you write ½, which implies the division of one `int` (1) by another (2), it will generate an `int` result equal to zero. This is not what you want! You can avoid this problem by making one or both of the operands a `float`. For example, 1./2 will work. However, every time the computer evaluates the formula, it will divide 1 by 2 again. It may be a little better to use 0.5.

C++ offers no operator for computing the square of a value. The simple solution is to recall that squaring *t* is the same as *t* times *t*. You may also use the function `sqr(t)`, as seen in the next section.

Using the *math.h* Library

Several of the mathematical functions that are used most are included in the header file `math.h`. Some of the most important functions are summarized below.

These functions take a double floating point argument (represented by *x*) and return a double floating point result. Since the conversion is automatic, you can supply arguments such as `float` and assign results to `float`, as well.

Skill 13

There are trigonometric functions to compute the sine, cosine, and tangent, as well as the arc sine, arc cosine, and arc tangent of a given argument. Be aware that the arcs must be specified in radians. Table 13.1 shows all the functions.

T A B L E 1 3 . 1 :   Functions in `math.h`

Function	Its Purpose
`sin(x)`	Returns the sine of x
`cos(x)`	Returns the cosine of x
`tan(x)`	Returns the tangent of x
`asin(x)`	Returns the arc sine of x
`acos(x)`	Returns the arc cosine of x
`atan(x)`	Returns the arc tangent of x
`exp(x)`	Returns the exponential of x
`log(x)`	Returns the natural (base e) logarithm of x
`log10(x)`	Returns the decimal logarithm of x
`sqrt(x)`	Returns the square root of x
`sqr(x)`	Returns the square of x
`fabs(x)`	Returns the absolute value of floating point x
`ceil(x)`	Returns the round-up value of x
`floor(x)`	Returns the round-down value of x
`rand()`	Returns a random integer (the range of the integer will vary with the compiler)

You may be interested in other mathematical functions that are included in `math.h`. However, we will not discuss them here.

An Example

You can use the program below to compute the square root of a value that is input from the keyboard:

```
#include "franca.h"
#include <math.h>
void mainprog()
{
    float value,root;
```

```
value=ask("Enter a positive value:");
if (value>=0)
{
   root=sqrt(value);
   Cout<<root;
}
else
{
   Cout<<"Sorry, negative value!";
}
}
```

Are You Experienced?

Now you can. . .

☑ Choose the appropriate types of variables to handle your data

☑ Use expressions to compute results

☑ Use functions from the *math.h* library in your programs

Working with Graphics

- ❑ Specifying coordinates to locate points on the computer screen

- ❑ Drawing and showing Screen Objects

- ❑ Moving Screen Objects

- ❑ Changing coordinate systems

In Skill 14, we will work with graphics, because they are an interesting application of numeric manipulation, and because they are a subject of growing importance in the computer field.

Novices usually cannot afford to learn how to use graphics because of the complexities involved. However, thanks to our special software, it is very easy to show and manipulate objects such as circles, squares, and boxes. A special class of objects—Screen Objects—will be used to help you improve your skills with graphics and numeric manipulation.

> **NOTE** Objects of class Circle, Square, Stage, and others are not available in standard C++. They are only available with the special software developed for this book.

Dealing with Graphics

One of the most interesting applications of numeric computation is the manipulation of graphics on the computer screen. Graphics manipulation will serve two purposes:

- You will learn (and practice) how to deal with graphics, which is a very interesting thing in itself.

- You will learn (and practice) several aspects of numeric computation.

Locating Points on the Screen

To understand how graphics objects work, we must first understand how to locate points on the computer screen. Since the screen is a two-dimensional object, coordinates to locate a point on it must include two numbers, the x coordinate and the y coordinate.

This coordinate system is essentially the same one that was used in the short project in Skill 12 to place and locate the robot in a room.

On the computer screen, the point of origin is the upper-left corner—by definition, the point (0,0). The x coordinate increases from left to right (just like the convention used in geometry), but the y coordinate increases from top to bottom (unlike the convention used in geometry).

Coordinate Units

Only a finite number of points can be represented on the computer screen. Not only is the size of the screen finite, but there is a minimum distance between points. The actual number of points may vary according to the computer display adapter that you are using. For example, if you are using a computer with a screen resolution of 1,024×768, your screen can accommodate 1,024 points in a horizontal line and 768 points in a vertical line. Regardless of the size of your monitor's screen, your computer will work with one given resolution. Figure 14.1 shows the most common resolutions available.

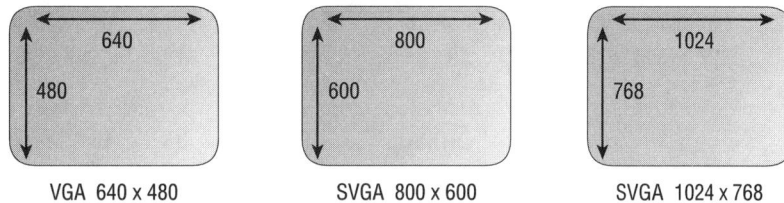

VGA 640 x 480   SVGA 800 x 600   SVGA 1024 x 768

FIGURE 14.1: Common screen resolutions

Since the number of points that can be represented in each line is finite, it is logical to use the actual number of points that can be drawn between two points as the distance between them. This is called the *pixel* coordinate system.

> **NOTE**   Pixel stands for *picture element*—a point that can be represented on the screen in a given color.

It is clear that it is possible to transform coordinates so you can work with inches or centimeters, instead of pixels. We will learn how to change coordinate systems later in this Skill.

In this pixel coordinate system, the coordinates of a given point are determined by the horizontal and vertical distances, measured in the number of points (pixels), from the point of origin in the upper-left corner of the screen to the given point.

Remember that, contrary to the usual geometric notation, the vertical coordinates increase from top to bottom.

Drawing Screen Objects

To explore graphics applications, I have prepared a class of Screen Objects. This class is also included in the header file `franca.h`. Some of the interesting Screen Objects that we will use are as follows:

- Boxes (you used these in Skill 2)
- Squares
- Circles

If the object is a square or a circle, it is located on the screen by the coordinates of its center. If it is a box, it is located by the coordinates of its upper-left corner. There are a few things that you can do with Screen Objects:

- You can place them anywhere on the screen. `place(x,y)` places an object's center at coordinates *(x,y)*. For example, `ball.place(20,20);`.

- You can show them on the screen (objects are not automatically shown). The `show()` function draws the object at its current location. For example, `ball.show();`.

- You can erase them from the screen. `erase()` erases the object by painting it white in its current location. For example, `ball.erase();`. Be sure not to erase the object before moving it.

- You can resize them. Screen Objects are created with a default size of 20. You may specify one or two arguments when resizing. If only one argument is specified—for example, `ball.resize(40)`—both dimensions (width and height) change to the same value. Otherwise, width and height will both be changed. For example, `ball.resize(40,30)` will transform the object into an ellipse with a height of 40 and a width of 30. There are two functions to resize, `resize` and `absize`. The function `resize` is affected by any scales that you may have set up; `absize` is not affected by scales.

- You can change their color. By default, Screen Objects are created with a white fill color and a black contour color. You can specify one color to change the fill and the contour to the same color—for example, `ball.color(2)`—or you can specify two colors to change each to a different color—for example, `ball.color(2,4)`.

In addition, there are specific things you can do with a Box object:

- You can "say" something inside the box. For example, if `message` is declared to be a `Box`, `message.say("Here!");` displays the string `Here!` in the box. You may also use an integer or floating point number as an argument.

- You can provide a "label" for the box. Labels identify the kind of messages for which the box is used. The labels are written above the message in the box. The statement `message.label("Your change:");` followed by `message.say(change);` displays a box with a label and a message.

For example, if the value of `change` is 12.45, the box above would look as follows:

```
Your change:
12.45
```

Boxes behave somewhat differently, because the box is automatically drawn when you want to say something. In other words, you don't have to show a box. Remember that box coordinates refer to the upper-left corner of the box, and not to the center.

It is also possible to change the point of origin and the scale. We will study these shortly.

Tables 14.1 and 14.2 summarize the orders you can give to Screen Objects.

TABLE 14.1: Orders You Can Give to a Screen Object

Message	Its Purpose	Arguments
place(*float*,*float*)	Places object	*x,y* coordinates
show()	Shows object on screen	None
erase()	Erases object from screen	None
resize(*float*)	Resizes object	New size
absize(*float*)	Resizes without scaling	New size
color(*int*,*int*)	Changes object's color	Colors
scale(*float*,*float*)	Changes scales	New scales
origin(*float*,*float*)	Changes point of origin	*x,y* coordinates

TABLE 14.2: Orders You Can Give to a Box Object in Particular

Message	Its Purpose	Arguments
label("*Label*")	Writes a label	A string of characters, an identifier representing a string of characters or an int
say("*Sentence*")	Writes a sentence	A string of characters, an identifier representing a string of characters, or an int or a float
resize(*float*)	Changes object's length	New length

Since boxes are Screen Objects, you can also place(), show(), and erase() them.

When you declare a Circle, it is assumed by default that the diameter is 20 pixels. If you want a circle with a different size, you can resize it.

```
Circle mycircle;
mycircle.resize(10);
```

creates a circle with a diameter of 10 pixels.

In a similar way, a Square is assumed to have a default side of 20 pixels (notice that this is the same as the circle's default diameter).

Adding Color

Screen Objects can be drawn using different colors. There may be two colors in an object, the fill color and the contour color. For example, the object may be a circle of red delimited by a black line. The colors are denoted by the following codes:

0	White
1	Red
2	Lime green
3	Blue
4	Light blue
5	Pink
6	Yellow
7	Black

It may be a good idea to use the following statement in your programs:

```
enum (white,red,green,blue,lightblue,pink,yellow,black);
```

If you use a number greater than seven, the remainder of the division by seven is used as the code.

Defaults

Here are some default assumptions when Screen Objects are created:

- Boxes are stacked vertically on the right side of the screen; other objects are positioned at (0,0).

- All objects are created with a white fill color and a black contour color.

Using Integer Values

Even though we are now dealing with coordinates in pixels, Screen Objects support coordinates and sizes with fractional parts—float values. If you use integer values, the compiler automatically converts them to floating point values. It is important to learn how to use float, because we will use it later to make scale conversions.

The piece of program below creates a circle, places it at (50,50), and shows it on the screen.

```
#include "franca.h"
void mainprog()
{
    int x,y;
    x=50;
    y=50;
    Circle mycircle;
    mycircle.place(x,y);
    mycircle.show()
}
```

Remember that you have to declare the objects you want to use. You do this in the same way that you have already done it with other classes of objects.

As an improvement to this program, you can ask for the circle coordinates and show them in boxes. This is shown in the program c5circl.cpp. If you execute this program and enter the coordinates (50,100), your computer screen should look like Figure 14.2.

```
#include "franca.h"
//                                    c5circl.cpp

//  This program draws circles on the screen
//      at locations specified by the user.
void mainprog()
```

```
{
  Box coordx("X:"),coordy("Y:");      // Use boxes for
                                      //     x and y coordinates
  int x,y;                            // Declare coordinates
  Circle mycircle;                    // Declare a circle
  do
  {
    x=ask("Enter x coordinate:");
    y=ask("Enter y coordinate:");
    mycircle.place(x,y);              // Put the circle in place
    mycircle.show();                  // Show the circle
    coordx.say(x);                    // Write coordinates
                                      //     in boxes

    coordy.say(y);
  }
  while (yesno("Wanna try again?"));
}
```

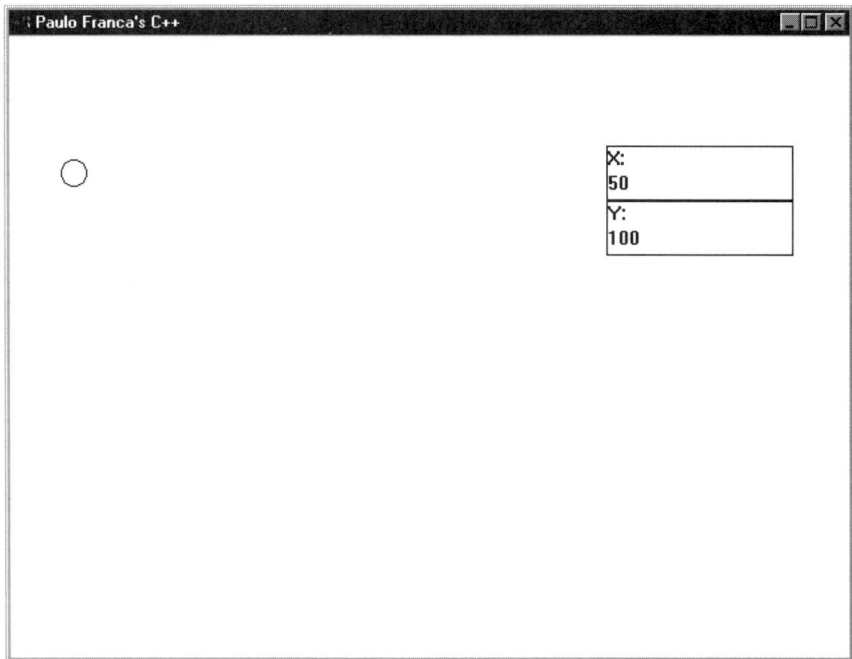

FIGURE 14.2: The result of executing c5circl.cpp

Notice that two new objects are declared, `coordx` and `coordy`. Both objects are of type `Box`, as indicated in their declaration. The box `coordx` will be used to display the x coordinate of the circle, and the box `coordy` will be used to display the y coordinate of the circle. The boxes could be placed anywhere on the screen; they are automatically positioned by default.

The following lines:

```
x=ask("Enter x coordinate:");
y=ask("Enter y coordinate:");
```

request that you provide values for x and y. This lets you place the circle anywhere on the screen, instead of at (50,50), as before. The main piece of code is surrounded by the `do/while` repetition:

```
do
{
...
}
while(yesno("Wanna try again?"));
```

What does this repetition do? The loop repeats as long as the condition is true. Thus, as long as you choose *yes*, the program will keep asking for new coordinates and drawing circles. If, instead, you choose *no*, the loop will end.

Erasing

Each time we draw a new circle, the old drawing remains. What should we do if we don't want to see it anymore? How about using the `erase` function? Can you try it? It is quite simple! All you have to do is to include the following statement:

```
mycircle.erase();
```

in a convenient place in the program.

What do I mean by *convenient place*?

- You cannot erase the circle immediately after showing it. If you do so, you will not have enough time to see it. You could declare a `Clock` and tell the clock to wait a few seconds (objects of class `Clock` were introduced in Skill 2).

- You cannot erase the circle after placing it at the new coordinates. The `erase` function works by drawing a white circle on top of the old one to erase it. If you move the circle to a new place, the white circle will be drawn in the new place.

Besides using a Clock object, you may consider two alternatives:

- You can erase the circle immediately before changing its place. The first time that the program goes through the loop, you will erase the circle before actually drawing it or even giving coordinates to it. There is nothing wrong with erasing before showing. However, erasing before placing the circle is the same as erasing in the wrong place!

WARNING

Oops! If the circle is at the default (0,0) location and you try to erase it, you will get an *Object out of range* error message. This is because part of the circle will be off the screen.

- You can erase the circle after asking the *yes or no* question, but before restarting the loop! How? In this case, you would pose the question before you end the loop, and then save the answer. As a matter of fact, the yes function returns an integer value (1 means *yes*, 0 means *no*). You may use an additional variable to save this answer:

```
int answer;
   ...
   do
   {
   ...
      answer=yes("Wanna try again?");
      mycircle.erase();
   }
   while (answer);
```

Error Messages

Any attempt to draw a point outside the valid screen region will generate an error message in a dialog box. The *Object out of range* error message is shown in Figure 14.3. The wrong coordinate (*x* or *y*) will be displayed in the upper-left corner of the screen, and you will be requested to check the object that is out of range.

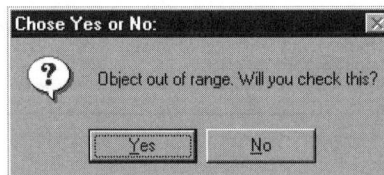

FIGURE 14.3: The dialog box telling you that your object is out of range

Try These for Fun. . .

- Modify the program `c5circ1.cpp` to erase each circle before drawing the next one.

- Modify the program `c5circ1.cpp` to draw two circles (using two sets of coordinates), instead of drawing one circle. Both circles should be erased before drawing the next two circles.

- Write a program (or modify the program `c5circ1.cpp`) to draw several circles in a horizontal line. You should request the coordinates (*x*,*y*) of the first circle, the number of circles to draw, and the distance between them. (Hint: you can declare only one circle in this case.)

- Include a `Clock` object in `c5circ1.cpp` in the exercise above to draw circles at 2-second intervals.

Moving Screen Objects

By now, you should know how to draw and erase Screen Objects. The next thing we want to do is to move them around. Just like in movies or in cartoons, the illusion of movement is caused by drawing several images very quickly. This was already done with the athletes in Skill 1.

You can achieve a high-quality animation by displaying 30 frames per second. What does *30 frames per second* mean? In one second, you change your drawing 30 times. In other words, each drawing should last 1/30 of a second! If you have a very complex picture, you need a very fast computer to draw the next picture in less than 1/30 of a second. Since our pictures are simple, I don't expect you to run into this kind of problem.

To get started, look at the program `c5circ2.cpp`, which implements a very simple animation. If you run this program, you should see a circle moving on the screen.

Try running this program using the coordinates x=100 and y=100 and using 300 circles. Experiment with other values, as well.

```
#include "franca.h" // c5circ2.cpp

// This program moves a circle on the screen.
void drawing(Circle &mycircle,int x,int y,Box &coordx,Box &coordy)
{
 // This function draws one frame:
 mycircle.place(x,y);                 // Put the circle in place
 mycircle.show();                     // Show the circle
```

```
  coordx.say(x);                    // Write coordinates in boxes
  coordy.say(y);
}

void mainprog()
{
// Declaration of objects and variables:
Box coordx("X:"),coordy("Y:");     // Use boxes for x and y
int x,y;                           // Declare coordinates
Circle mycircle;                   // Declare a circle
Clock mytimer;                     // And a clock
int howmany;

do
{
  x=ask("Enter x coordinate:");
  y=ask("Enter y coordinate:");
  howmany=ask("How many circles?");
  for(int k=1;k<=howmany;k++)
  {
    drawing(mycircle,x,y,coordx,coordy);
    mytimer.wait(0.033);
    mycircle.erase();
    x++;
  }
}
while (yesno("Wanna try again?"));
}
```

How Does This Program Work?

The program above uses three Screen Objects:

- coordx

- coordy

- mycircle

The objects coordx and coordy are boxes that display the current coordinates of the circle. The object mycircle is a circle that is moved on the screen.

A drawing() function produces a frame. This function does as follows:

- Receives the circle, the coordinates, and the boxes as parameters

- Places the circle at coordinates (x,y)

- Shows the circle

- Writes the coordinates in the appropriate boxes

The main program consists of two essential parts:

- Initialization

- Loop

The initialization declares the objects and labels the boxes.

The loop is repeated as long as the user replies *yes* to the *yes or no* question at the end. This loop requests that the user provide the *x* and *y* coordinates, as well as a number to specify how many circles (each circle corresponds to a frame) will be drawn. An inner loop calls the drawing() function several times to produce the frames.

Another alternative would be to declare and use a Clock inside the drawing() function. In this case, the function could have the following code:

```
void drawing(Circle &mycircle,int x,int y,
                 Box &coordx,Box &coordy)
{
  Clock mytimer;
  // This function draws one frame:
  mycircle.place(x,y); // Put the circle in place
  mycircle.show();     // Show the circle
  coordx.say(x);       // Write the coordinates in boxes
  coordy.say(y);
  mytimer.watch(.033);
  mycircle.erase();
}
```

The drawing() function displays the circle for .033 seconds, and erases it afterward. The wait() and the erase() could then be removed from the main function. As you can see, there are many ways to design and implement your functions.

TIP   To achieve a successful animation, keep the time that elapses between erasing an object and showing it again to the minimum duration possible.

Try These for Fun. . .

- Modify the program c5circ2.cpp to make the circle move vertically, instead of horizontally.

- Modify the program c5circ2.cpp to start with a circle of diameter 2 and increase the diameter at each iteration.

- Modify the program c5circ2.cpp to draw the circle with a different color.

Changing Coordinate Systems

It may not be convenient all the time to deal with coordinates in pixels. You may want to use your knowledge of geometry to work with a different system of coordinates.

Changing the Point of Origin

The simplest thing to do is to change the point of origin. If you don't wish to refer all the points to the upper-left corner, you can redefine the point of origin for your coordinate system.

Suppose that you want your new point of origin to be 100 pixels horizontally and 150 pixels vertically from the upper-left corner. This is the same as saying that the coordinates of your new point of origin are (100,150). If you want to place an object at the coordinates (x,y) using your new point of origin, the only thing you have to do is to perform a simple operation on (x,y) before you place the object on the screen.

In this case, the transformations are very simple. You can obtain a new set of coordinates $(x1,y1)$ as follows:

```
x1=x+100;
y1=y+150;
```

In more general terms, if the coordinate of your new origin is $(x0,y0)$, you can use the following expressions:

```
x1=x+x0;
y1=y+y0;
```

Notice that every time you want to draw an object in the position (*x,y*), you actually have to draw it in the position (*x+x0,y+y0*).

Changing Scale

You may want to work with distances in centimeters, inches, or anything besides pixels. In other words, you may want to change the scale.

This is also a simple operation. Suppose that in a space of 100 pixels, you want to represent 1,000 of your new units (for example, if you want to represent 1,000 feet in a space of 100 pixels). What do you do? Since your scale is now 1,000 units per 100 pixels—or 10 units per pixel—all you have to do is to divide your new coordinate by 10 to obtain the pixel coordinate. Therefore, if your horizontal scale is *scalex* and your vertical scale is *scaley*, you can obtain new coordinates by using the following expressions:

```
x2=x/scalex;
y2=y/scaley;
```

NOTE You cannot represent anything that is smaller than 1 pixel on the screen. In the example above, 10 feet will be represented by 1 pixel, which means that the 10-foot mark, the 12-foot mark, and the 18-foot mark will all be placed at the same location.

If you want to combine the change of the point of origin with the change of the scale, you can use the following expressions:

```
x3=(x+x0)/scalex;
y3=(y+y0)/scaley;
```

TIP The factor for your new scale is obtained by dividing the number of units in your new coordinate system by the equivalent number of units in the original coordinate system.

Changing Orientation

Finally, how can we make the vertical coordinate increase upward, instead of downward? This is particularly relevant because most mathematical formulas use this notation.

What we want to do in this case is to simply change the sign of the vertical coordinate. This can easily be done by multiplying it by a negative number. Why not use a negative scale then?

A value of –1 for *scaley* would be enough to invert the orientation of the vertical axis.

As an example, let's use a different coordinate system that is located closer to the bottom of the screen and that has a vertical-axis orientation from bottom to top.

Here is what we have to do:

- Determine the coordinates of our new origin. Suppose that we decide to use the point (50,400) as the new origin.

- Determine the scale and use a negative value for the vertical scale. Suppose that we want each unit to be 60 pixels. We may then use *scalex=1/60.* and *scaley=–1/60.*

- Translate our coordinate to the computer coordinate by using the expressions above every time an object is to be placed on the screen.

If we want to modify the program `c5circl.cpp` to handle our new coordinates, the solution is quite easy. Since we must make sure that the object is placed at the transformed coordinates, we may simply correct the following statement:

```
mycircle.place(x,y);  // Put the circle in place
```

This statement should now be as follows:

```
mycircle.place((x+50)/60.,(y+400)/(-60).);
```

> **WARNING** Do not forget to use both of the decimal points in the fraction! If the fraction has no floating point numbers, the result will be only the integer part, which in this case is zero!

This solution would work fine. However, it is a very simple program that places only one object in only one spot. If many other statements placed objects on the screen, you would have to include this new expression in all of them.

Also, if you decide later that either the point of origin or the scale was not well chosen, you will again have to go through all those statements to use the new values. A better idea would be to use functions to transform the coordinates. If you assume that you declare the following variables globally:

```
float scalex=1./60.,scaley=-1/60.;
float x0=50.,y0=150.;
```

the functions could be as follows:

```
float newx(float oldx)
{
    return (oldx+x0)/scalex;
}
float newy(float oldy)
{
    return (oldy+y0)/scaley;
}
```

and the circle could be placed using the following statement:

```
mycircle.place(newx(x),newy(y));
```

Try These for Fun. . .

- Modify the program c5circl.cpp, which draws circles at given coordinates, to use a new coordinate system with a point of origin at (50,400) and to scale 0.01 in each direction. The vertical axis should increase upward.

- Modify the program c5circl.cpp to request that you input the new point of origin and scales.

No Need for New Functions

The good news is that you do not need to write functions or to modify your programs to use a different coordinate system. A mechanism for changing the coordinate system is already embedded in the Screen Objects.

By telling a Screen Object to scale(), you can change the scales for the horizontal and vertical axes. Of course, if you supply a negative scale for the vertical axis, you will also change the orientation of y. Notice that you will change the scale for all objects, not only for the object to which you sent the message! Any drawings that are already on the screen will remain unaffected, but any other object that you move, erase, or show will be subject to the new scale.

Similarly, you can change the point of origin of your coordinate system by telling any Screen Object to `origin()`. For example:

```
Circle ball;
ball.scale(1.,-1.);
ball.origin(20,400);
```

causes the new origin to be located at (20,400), and causes the orientation of the vertical axis to increase upward. The new coordinates are always expressed in pixels, using the original scale and orientation. If an object is invoked to change either scale or origin, the new change will again affect all objects.

WARNING If you set different values for the horizontal and vertical scales, squares and circles will be distorted! Also, you should place boxes in their appropriate locations when you redefine scales. Otherwise, the mechanism that automatically creates one box under another may assign a location that is off the screen to your boxes.

The *Grid* Object

`Grid` is an object that can represent the horizontal and vertical axes. Declare `Grid` like you declare any other Screen Object. When the grid is shown, the horizontal and vertical axes will be drawn to intersect at the point of origin (0,0).

Try This for Fun. . .

- Modify the program `c5circl.cpp` to accept a given point of origin and scale, as well as to display the *x-y* axis.

Using Polar Coordinates

Another coordinate system that we may be interested in using is the polar-coordinate system. In this system, instead of expressing coordinates by the distances to the *x* and *y* axes, the coordinates are expressed by the distance to the point of origin (called the *radius*) and by the angle made with the horizontal axis.

Figure 14.4 shows both coordinate systems. Point *A* can be located by giving the (*x,y*) coordinates, or by giving the distance from the origin *O* to *A* and the angle that the segment *OA* forms with the horizontal axis.

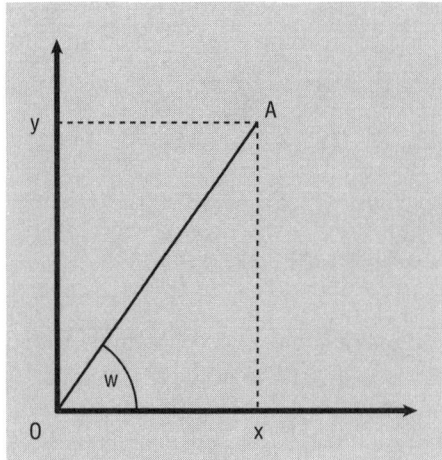

FIGURE 14.4: Polar and screen coordinates

Polar coordinates are very useful and easy to deal with when describing circular motions. On the other hand, it is easier to manipulate objects on the computer screen using screen coordinates. Since the screen coordinates are expressed in (x,y) form, it is interesting to learn how to transform polar coordinates into (x,y) coordinates.

Given a point A, defined by the following polar coordinates:

Distance to origin: r=OA

Angle: w=xOA

we may compute as follows:

```
x = r* cos (w);
y = r* sin (w);
```

It is common to have the angle denoted by θ (the Greek letter *theta*).

If point O (the origin of the polar coordinate) is located at the coordinates $(x0,y0)$ in the (x,y) system, the expressions above can be modified as follows:

```
x = r* cos (w) + x0;
y = r* sin (w) + y0;
```

It is then possible to write a C++ function to transform a point from polar coordinates to screen (x,y) coordinates. You may choose to write one function to obtain the x coordinate and another function to obtain the y coordinate:

```
float coordx(float r,float theta, float x0)
{
    return r*cos(theta)+x0;
}
float coordy(float r,float theta,float y0)
{
    return r*sin(theta)+y0;
}
```

Or, you may choose to write a single function that computes the two values and returns them in one of the arguments:

```
void polarxy (float r, float theta, float x0,float y0,
              float &x, float &y)
{
  x=r*cos(theta)+x0;
  y=r*sin(theta)+y0;
}
```

Either solution will work fine.

NOTE   The last two parameters, x and y, are passed by reference (they are preceded by &). If this is not done, the function will not be able to alter the values of the real arguments!

Are You Experienced?

Now you can. . .

- ☑ **Locate a point on the screen by using coordinates**
- ☑ **Use Screen Objects such as Circles, Squares, and Boxes**
- ☑ **Place, show, move, and erase Screen Objects anywhere on the screen**
- ☑ **Change coordinate systems**

S K I L L

fifteen

15

Creating Animations

- ❑ Drawing function graphs
- ❑ Simulating movements on the computer screen
- ❑ Handling several Screen Objects at one time
- ❑ Completing a short project—Sun, Earth, Moon

Now that you know how to manipulate numbers to compute the coordinates of objects, you can move them to produce an animation. The Screen Objects that you learned to use in Skill 14 can be moved according to your instructions to produce an animation.

While you learn how to create animations, you will also learn how to use Screen Objects to draw the graph of a mathematical function. This is a very simplified application of animation. You don't really have to be concerned with the speed at which you are moving, and the vertical coordinate y is given by a mathematical function that depends on the value of the horizontal coordinate x. While you learn how to draw functions, you will also learn how to pass a function name as a parameter to another function.

The process of animation is very simple. It essentially consists of repeating the following steps:

1. Place the objects that you want on the screen in the desired location.

2. Show them for an appropriate amount of time.

3. Erase them.

When you have to deal with several Screen Objects that move together, the program may become lengthy and repetitive. A new kind of Screen Object—the Stage object—will help you to manipulate several objects as if they are only one object.

Drawing Mathematical Functions

Since you now know how to place and to move objects on the screen, and you also know how to change coordinates and scales, it will be very easy to draw the graph of a function. Given a mathematical function $y=f(x)$, we can display the graph of this function by moving a dot (a small circle) along the coordinates $(x,f(x))$.

Suppose that our function is $y=x^2-x+1$, and that we want to view the graph between the points $x=-5$ and $x=20$. It is a good idea to define the mathematical function as a C++ function:

```
float f(float x)
{
    return x*x-x+1;
}
```

This is a good solution, because if we want to compute the function somewhere else in the program, we may simply refer to $f(x)$, instead of writing the complete expression. Also, it will make it much easier to draw the graph of a different function, as we will see later.

We must now place the dot at the initial point, and then move it to the final point. Of course, we should not erase the points that we draw!

Moving a Dot

The procedure for drawing the function is very easy:

- Declare dot as a small circle.

- Repeat the steps below for different values of x, ranging from an initial value to a final value, at small intervals (such as 0.01).

    - Place dot at new coordinates.

    - Show dot on screen.

In C++, this could be written as follows:

```
Circle dot;                       // Declare dot a circle
dot.color(7,7);                   // Use the color
dot.resize(2);                    // Make dot small
for (x=xstart;x<=xend;x=x+0.01)   // Loop from xstart to xend
{
    dot.place(x,f(x));            // Place dot at x,y
    dot.show();                   // Show dot
}
```

You must make sure that you do not attempt to draw an object outside the boundaries of your screen. Always transform your expressions or use scales to make sure that the ranges for x and y are respected:

- x must be between 0 and 640 (both inclusive).

- y must be between 0 and 480 (both inclusive).

Of course, if you want to use scales and to draw the x and y axes, it has to be done before the function is drawn. It may also be a good idea to transform the piece of program above into a function. Why? Functions are easier to reuse at a later time. If you want to write another program to draw a mathematical function, you can reuse the same function and save time. Shall we explore some alternatives?

Skill 15

The *draw()* Function

One possible idea is to take the code above and transform it into a C++ function. Initial and final values for *x* can be specified as arguments, and we may assume that the coordinate system is already set. This would result in the following code:

```
void draw(float xstart,float xend,int dotcolor=7)
{
  Circle dot;                          // Declare dot a circle
  dot.color(dotcolor);                 // Use appropriate color
  dot.absize(4);                       // Make dot small
  for (x=xstart;x<=xend;x=x+0.01)      // Loop
  {
    dot.place(x,f(x));                 // Place dot at x,y
    dot.show();                        // Show dot
  }
}
```

In this case, the main program could be as follows:

```
void mainprog()
{
  ...
    draw(-5.,20.);
}
```

A complete program is supplied to draw the sine function. The resulting screen is shown in Figure 15.1.

Here is the program c5sin.cpp:

```
#include "franca.h"
#include <math.h>
            // c5sin.cpp
            // Program to draw graph of sin(x).
float f(float x)
{
  return sin(x);
}

void draw (float firstx,float lastx,int color=7)
{
 float x;
 Circle dot;                          // Declare dot a circle
 dot.color(color,color);              // Use a colored dot
 dot.absize(4);                       // Make dot small
 for (x=firstx;x<=lastx;x=x+0.1)      // Loop
 {
```

```
      dot.place(x,f(x));            // Place dot at x,y
      dot.show();                   // Show dot
   }
}

void mainprog()
{
   // Use a grid, set scales and origin:
   Grid mygrid;
   mygrid.scale(20.,-20);
   mygrid.origin(50.,300.);
   mygrid.resize(10.);
   mygrid.show();
   const float pi=3.14159;
   float xstart=0.;
   float xlimit=8.*pi;
   draw(xstart,xlimit);
}
```

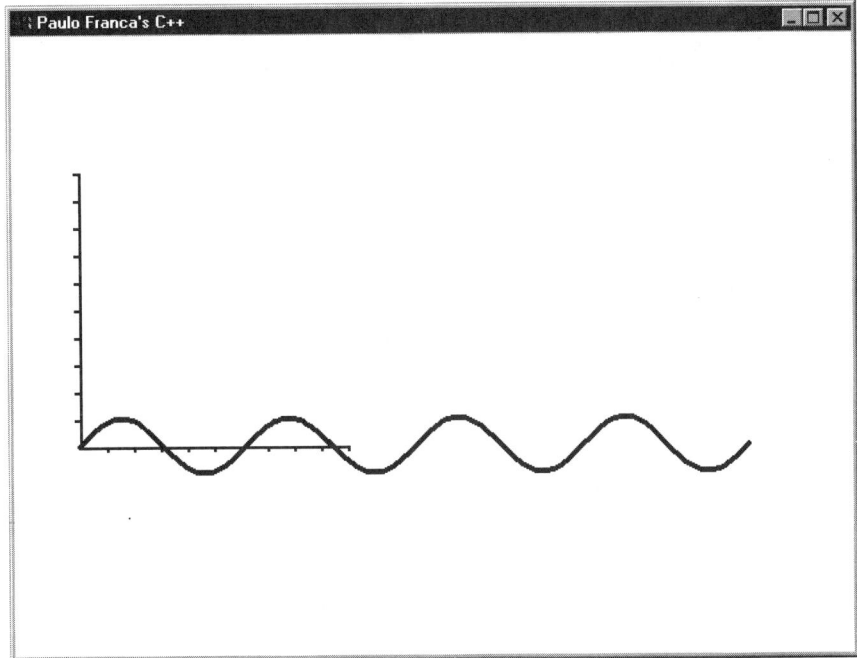

FIGURE 15.1: The result of executing c5sin.cpp

Using the draw() function is a reasonable solution to this problem. However, you must always ask yourself whether there is anything you can do to make your solution more general and more reusable. In this case, if you want to reuse the draw() function in the future, what kind of obstacles might you face?

Two issues may arise:

- Scale—couldn't the draw() function include a scale and axis definition?

- Function name—what if you want to draw a function that has a different name?

The scale problem is relatively easy to fix. You can request the data of the new coordinate system as arguments to the draw() function, and declare your own Grid object in the function. You may want to think twice before doing this. It would be a better idea to request that the coordinate system is established before the function call.

The function-name problem is more interesting. At first, you may not think it is very relevant. After all, you could simply change the name of the function and reuse exactly the same code. However, this is not true. There may be cases in which you want to draw the graphs of more than one function in the same program. How would you do it?

It is simple—pass the function name as an argument to the draw() function.

Passing Functions as Arguments

C++ allows you to pass a function as an argument to another function. In other words, if you have two functions, f1(x) and f2(x), that you want to use to draw a graph, it is possible to redesign the draw() function to accept three arguments, instead of two. The new argument is the name of the function. When you call the new drawf() function, you would use statements such as the following statements:

```
drawf(f1,xstart,xend);
drawf(f2,xstart,xend);
```

This is not very different from the usual function call. We are providing three arguments: the function to be used (f1 or f2), the starting value of x (xstart), and the ending value of x (xend). The only thing that will be different is the declaration of the function drawf(). The original draw() function was declared as follows:

```
void draw(float xstart,float xend)
```

The new `drawf()` function must have another parameter that specifies the function—but the question is, What is the argument type? We know it is neither an `int` nor a `float`. What could it be? This parameter is a function.

Functions as Parameters

Function types are declared by summarizing the appearance of the function. To do this, you must include the following items:

- The return type (for example, `float`, `void`, etc.)
- A symbolic name with which to refer to the function (for example, `func`)
- The list of argument types inside parentheses (for example, `(float)`)

In our example, the description of the `drawf()` function could be as follows:

```
void drawf ( float func(float),float firstx,float lastx)
```

Notice that this function has three parameters:

- A function that takes a floating point variable as an argument and that returns `float`. This function is denoted by the symbolic name `func`.
- Two floating point variables. These variables are denoted by the symbolic names `firstx` and `firsty`.

The complete function listing is shown below.

```
void drawf (float func (float), float firstx,float lastx)
{
  float x;
  Circle dot;                    // Declare dot a circle
  dot.color(7,7);                // Use a black dot
  dot.resize(2);                 // Make dot small
  for (x=firstx;x<=lastx;x=x+0.01) // Loop
  {
     dot.place(x,func(x));       // Place dot at x,y
     dot.show();                 // Show dot
  }
}
```

When we place the dot using arguments x and `func(x)`, the function whose nickname is `func` will be called with x as an argument. The result will then be used as the vertical coordinate to place the dot.

Try This for Fun...

- Develop a program to draw the graph of the sine and cosine functions. The sine should be drawn in red, and the cosine should be drawn in blue. Hint: The sine and cosine functions are available if you include the header file `math.h`. The resulting screen should look like Figure 15.2.

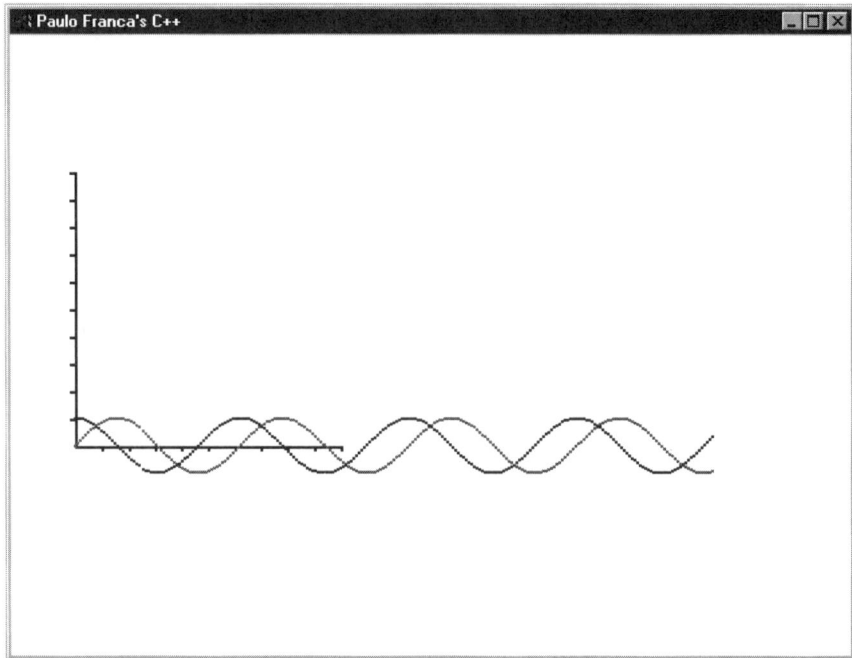

FIGURE 15.2: Sine and cosine functions

Producing Animations

We will now use Screen Objects to produce an animation. A simple animation was already introduced with the program `c5circ2.cpp`. This section shows you how to use Screen Objects to illustrate some of the movement equations you may know from physics.

Creating the Illusion of Movement

It is possible to simulate movement on the computer screen in the same way it is done in motion pictures—by providing different images at small intervals of time. This approach enables you to produce several kinds of animations.

One of the easiest animations is to express all movements by a mathematical formula. This is the case in many physical phenomena. Several of the phenomena studied in physics have equations that can determine the position of a given body.

Simulating Composite Movements

Suppose that there is a body in movement and that you know the equations x=dist(t) and y=height(t) that specify the horizontal distance to the origin (x) and the height above the ground (y).

As they usually do in physics, these equations express x and y as functions of the time (t).

Some examples follow.

Uniform Horizontal Movement   Here is an example of uniform horizontal movement:

```
x=speedx*t+x0;
y=y0;
```

in which speedx is a constant horizontal speed and y0 is any constant value. A constant x0 is included to set an initial horizontal position for the body.

Uniform Horizontal and Vertical Movement   Here is an example of uniform horizontal and vertical movement:

```
x=speedx*t+x0;
y=speedy*t+h0;
```

in which speedx and speedy are constant speeds in the horizontal and vertical directions, respectively.

Uniformly Accelerated Movement   If the body is subject to a constant acceleration, the following lines may also be included in the equations:

```
x=accx*t*t/2+speedx*t+x0;
y=accy*t*t/2+speedy*t+y0;
```

If you look carefully, you might notice that as long as you provide the functions dist(t) and height(t), the movement simulation will be exactly the same no matter what kind of movement you are trying to simulate.

If the functions are properly written, we can develop a program to produce an animation using the following strategy:

- Declare a Screen Object to represent the moving body (a circle, for example).

- Declare a Clock object to keep track of the time.

- Perform a loop causing a standard interval of time to elapse from one frame drawing to the next (for a smooth animation, use 1/30 of a second). This loop will consist of the following items:

    1. Compute the new coordinates as functions of *time*.

    2. Move the body to the new position.

    3. Show the body.

    4. Wait for the time interval to exhibit the next frame (1/30 of a second).

    5. Erase the body from the screen.

Our next piece of program will do all of the above.

A Body in Free Fall   The program c5body.cpp assumes two functions dist(t) and height(t) to compute the *x* and *y* coordinates of a moving body. The current coordinates of the moving body and the current value of time are displayed in appropriate boxes.

```
#include "franca.h"              // c5body.cpp
#include "math.h"
Grid mygrid;
// Use standard coordinates:
const float v0x=10.,v0y=20.;
float dist (float t)            // Function to determine
{                               //      the x coordinate
   return v0x*t+10.;
}

float height (float t)          // Function to determine
{                               //      the y coordinate
   return v0y*t+50.;
}

void mainprog()
{
  // Declare and label boxes for displaying
  //     x, y, and time:
  Box boxx("x:"),boxy("y:"),boxt("Time:");
  mygrid.show();                 // Show axis
```

```
float t;                    // t is the time
Circle body;                // Declare the body
body.resize(12);            // Size it at 12
body.color(3,3);            // Color it
Clock timer;                // Declare a timer clock
Clock mywatch;              // Declare another clock
// The loop below will be repeated
//      as long as the time is less than 15 seconds.
//      Note that the current time is copied into
//      the variable t:
while ((t=mywatch.time())<15.)
{
    boxx.say(dist(t));                  // Update value of x, y,
    boxy.say(height(t));                //      and time in the
    boxt.say(t);                        //      appropriate boxes
    body.place(dist(t),height(t)); // Place the body in
                                        //      current location
    body.show();                        // Show the body
    timer.watch(.033);                  // Wait until timer reaches
    timer.reset();                      //      .033 seconds and reset
    body.erase();                       // Erase the body
}
}
```

The program simply follows the general strategy mentioned above, and, by now, you should be able to understand how it works. However, it may be worthwhile to explore a few items.

Using Two Clocks

There are two objects of type Clock declared, mywatch and timer. We use one as a regular watch (such as your wristwatch) and the other as a stopwatch (a timer). The stopwatch is really handy because it will make it easier for us to draw a new frame every .033 seconds.

The *while* Expression

There is a very tricky expression used in the while statement. We want to keep looping while time is less than 15, but we also want to copy the value of time into the t variable. We could solve this problem by using two separate steps:

```
while(mywatch.time()<15)
{
    t=mywatch.time();
    ...
```

In this case, this would work fine. However, you may notice that the value assigned to t is a little greater than the value tested in the while expression. You might be tempted to use an expression as follows:

```
while (t=mywatch.time()<15)
```

instead of using

```
while ((t=mywatch.time())<15.)
```

Unfortunately, the first expression will produce an incorrect result! Expressions are evaluated in C++, and then the value is assigned to the variable on the left side of the equal sign. First, time is compared with 15, and this comparison produces a result—the integer *1*, which stands for *true*. Then, this result is assigned to t. As you can see, as long as time is less than 15, the value of t will be 1.

Using the watch member function is more convenient for simulating than using the wait member function, because you can make the frames appear at more precise intervals. The time that it takes for the computer to prepare the next frame is implicitly added when you wait, but not when you watch.

Handling More Generic Movements

The example above uses functions that represent the equations of uniform movement in both coordinates. As a result, you will see the circle move in a straight line at a constant speed when you run the program. However, the same program can be used for any kind of movement. All we have to do is to change the function definitions!

As an example, let's simulate a body that is dropping while moving horizontally at a constant speed. In this case, the equations for the x coordinate will still be the same as above, but the equations for the y coordinate will be as follows:

$$y = h_0 + v_{0y}\, t - \tfrac{1}{2}\, g\, t^2$$

or, in C++:

```
y=h0+v0y+0.5*g*t*t ;
```

The following items are assumed:

- h0 is the initial height at time t=0.

- v0y is the initial vertical speed at time t=0.

- g is the gravity acceleration (9.81 m/s^2 or 32.18 ft/s^2).

- The body is dropped with no vertical speed—v0y=0.

The function `height(t)` could then be defined as follows:

```
float height(float t)
{
    const float h0=200.,g=32.18;
    return h0+0.5*g*t*t;
}
```

Skill 15

ON GLOBALLY DEFINED CONSTANTS AND VARIABLES...

The functions we are using in this section can have variables other than the time (for example, h0, V0, and g). If so, try to use these variables as arguments to the function, as well. A previous example used V0x and V0y as globally defined constants to avoid passing them as arguments. Although the practice of using global constants may not be harmful to your programming habits, the practice of using global variables should be avoided.

Substitute the definition above for the function `height(t)` in the program `c5body.cpp`, and then run it to see the results. But wait—if you do only this, your body will drop until it falls off the screen. After all, there is no floor to hold it! It may be a good idea to check the height, and to stop the program when the height becomes negative. There are two alternatives:

- You can expand the condition in the `while` statement so the loop is repeated while the time is less than 15 *and* while the height is greater than or equal to zero. For example:

  ```
  while (((t=mywatch.time(t))<15.)&&(height(t)>=0))
  ```

NOTE Notice the parentheses in the statement above!

- You can test `height(t)` in the loop, and then break out of the loop if the result is negative. For example:

  ```
  if (height(t)<=0) break;
  ```

Try This for Fun. . .

- Modify the program c5body.cpp to simulate a body in free fall. Stop the simulation when the body reaches the height of zero.

Efficiency Matters

It is a well-known fact that computers are very fast at their work. However, it is up to the programmer to avoid unnecessary work for the computer, so all the computations can be done in the appropriate amount of time. If you look in the program c5body.cpp, you may notice that the functions dist(t) and height(t) are called twice in the loop. There is nothing wrong with that, except that both times the functions are called with the same value of t—both calls will result in the same value!

Is that a smart way to use the computer? Not really. If you compute a value and expect to use it several times in the program, you may be better off to keep this value in a variable, and then to avoid computing it over and over again. In this case, you could declare two additional variables:

```
float x,y;
```

and then modify the loop as follows:

```
while ((t=mywatch.time())<15.)
  {
    x=dist(t);
    y=height(t);
    boxx.say(x);      // Update value of x, y,
    boxy.say(y);      //     and time in the
    boxt.say(t);      //       appropriate boxes
    body.place(x,y);  // Place body in
                      //       current location
  {
```

If you want to be really fancy, you can assign the values to x and y, and tell the boxes to say:

```
boxx.say(x=dist(t));
boxy.say(y=height(t));
```

NOTE   This second alternative does not bring significant savings, and it may make your program less legible.

Another issue is the use of expressions that use constants, such as 1./2. The computer will actually divide 1 by 2 every time this expression is found in the program. You can save time by using the equivalent value of 0.5. You can also define a constant or a variable that has the value you want to use. For example:

```
const float pi2=3.14159/2;
```

Then, use pi2 in the program.

Simulating a Cannonball

Our next simulation deals with a cannon firing at different angles. As the cannon-ball starts to move, it has a velocity in the direction that the cannon is firing. This direction is given by an angle *theta*. As you may know from physics, you can deconstruct this velocity into components:

velocx=veloc*cos(theta)

velocy=veloc*sin(theta)

The movement of the cannonball can then be expressed by the functions dist(t) and height(t). Horizontally, the cannonball moves at a constant speed (uniform movement), whereas vertically, its movement is subject to the accelera-tion of gravity.

The functions could be defined as follows:

```
const float g=32.18;            // Gravity
// Functions to compute coordinates:
float dist(float velocx,float t)
{
    return velocx*t;
}
float height(float velocy,float t)
{
    return velocy*t - 0.5 * g * t * t;
}
```

You can define g as a global constant.

The main program should request that you give the angle *theta* and the initial velocity *veloc*. The program then computes the values of velocx and velocy. After doing this, the program can simulate the movement as seen in previous programs.

N NOTE   Remember that trigonometric functions require that angles are expressed in radians, so we should convert them before we use them.

Computing the Cannonball's Coordinates

The program c5cannon.cpp implements the simulation of the cannonball being fired. The program is straightforward, and it includes the following items:

- Functions that determine distance and height
- Setting of initial conditions
- Simulation loop

The functions have already been explained. The setting of initial conditions determines scales, draws the x-y axis, creates the circle that represents the cannonball, and initializes the clocks needed for the simulation. Only one of these issues may confuse you—the setting of scales.

The scales should be set to accommodate all the objects we want to draw on the screen. It is necessary to look at the height() and dist() functions to determine the maximum values that will be used for x and y. Unfortunately, these values depend on the values that are input for the velocity and the angle. One thing that makes computer programming difficult is that you don't always know how your programs will be used!

The best we can do is to make a reasonable guess. If we assume a speed such as 1,000 feet per second, we may find that the horizontal distance can reach a little less than 30,000 feet, with a 45-degree angle (which gives the maximum range). If the cannon is fired at a 90-degree angle (gosh—who is in charge of this cannon?), the maximum height will be a little more than 15,000 feet.

It is a good idea to use the same scale for both axes, because both axes represent distances. Therefore, we can assume a maximum of 30,000 feet for both height and distance.

Calculating for VGA   On the other hand, even though our screen can usually accommodate 640×480 pixels, it may be a good idea to restrict the pictures to a smaller area—for example, 400×400. This means that the 30,000 feet we will show in the simulation should fit in 400 dots on the screen. As a result, our scale, which expresses how many dots there are per foot, will be 400/30,000.

TIP   If you ever become confused while computing scales, it will help you to consider the units. In the case above, we had 30,000 feet to correspond to 400 dots. At first, you may be confused: should you use 400/30,000 or 30,000/400? If you include the units, which would be dots per foot in the first case and feet per dot in the second, you will notice that the second alternative gives you square feet per dot as a result when you multiply the distance (in feet) by your scale. Of course, this is wrong!

The Simulation Loop

The most interesting part of the program appears in its second part—the simulation loop. The loop is repeated while the time, as reported by the sidereal clock, is less than 50 seconds. In the loop, new coordinates are computed for the new value of *time.* The circle is then erased from the old position, placed in the new position, and then shown. The stopwatch is then instructed to wait for .033 seconds, so we can see the frame on the screen. After this, the stopwatch is reset, and the loop resumes.

Figures 15.3, 15.4, and 15.5 show the results of executing the cannonball simulation program at different times.

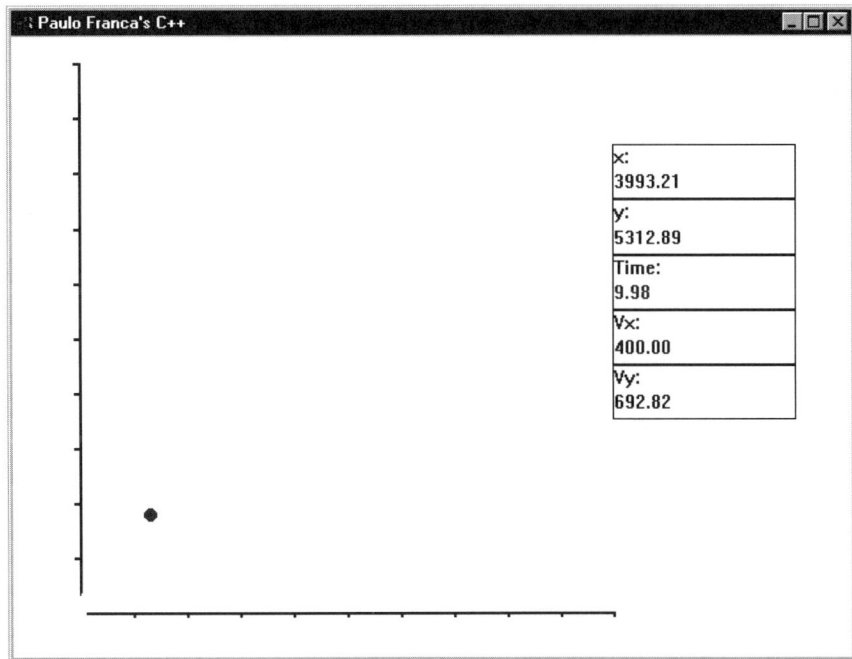

FIGURE 15.3:   The rest of executing c5cannon.cpp at a certain point in time.

The listing for the c5cannon.cpp program is shown below.

```
void mainprog()              // Part 1
{

   Grid mygrid;
```

```
mygrid.origin(50.,420);
mygrid.scale(400./30000,-400./30000);
// Declare and label boxes for displaying
//       x, y, and time:
Box boxx("x:"),boxy("y:"),boxt("Time:");
Box vx("Vx:"),vy("Vy:");
mygrid.resize(30000.);
mygrid.show();             // Show axes
float t;                   // t is the time
Circle body;               // Declare the body
body.absize(10.);          // Size it
body.color(3,3);           // Color it
Clock timer;               // Declare a timer clock
Clock watch;               // Declare another clock
float theta,veloc,velx,vely;
// Request data:
theta=ask("Enter angle of firing:");
theta=theta*3.14159/180.;// Convert to radians
veloc=ask("Enter initial velocity:");
velx=veloc*cos(theta);     // Deconstruct into x and y
vely=veloc*sin(theta);
vx.say(velx);
vy.say(vely);
float x,y;                 // c5cannon.cpp-Part 2
// The loop below will be repeated
//       as long as the time is less than 15 seconds.
//       Note that current time is copied into
//       the variable "t":
timer.reset();
watch.reset();
while ((t=watch.time())<50.)
{
  y=height(vely,t);
  if (y<0) break;
  x=dist(velx,t);
  boxx.say(x);             // Update values of x, y,
  boxy.say(y);             //       and time in the
  boxt.say(t);             //       appropriate boxes
  body.erase();
  body.place(x,y);         // Place the body in current location
  body.show();             // Show the body
  timer.watch(.033);       // Wait until timer reaches
  timer.reset();           //       .033 secs and reset
}
}
```

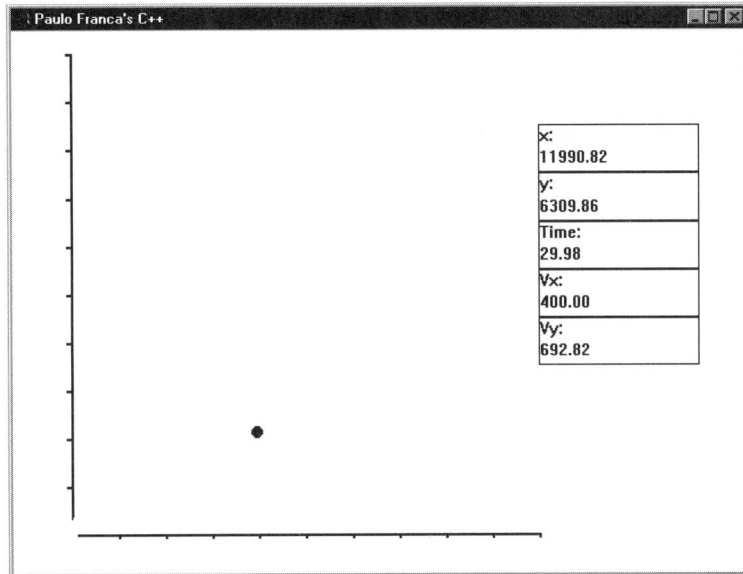

FIGURE 15.4:   The result of executing c5cannon.cpp at another point in time

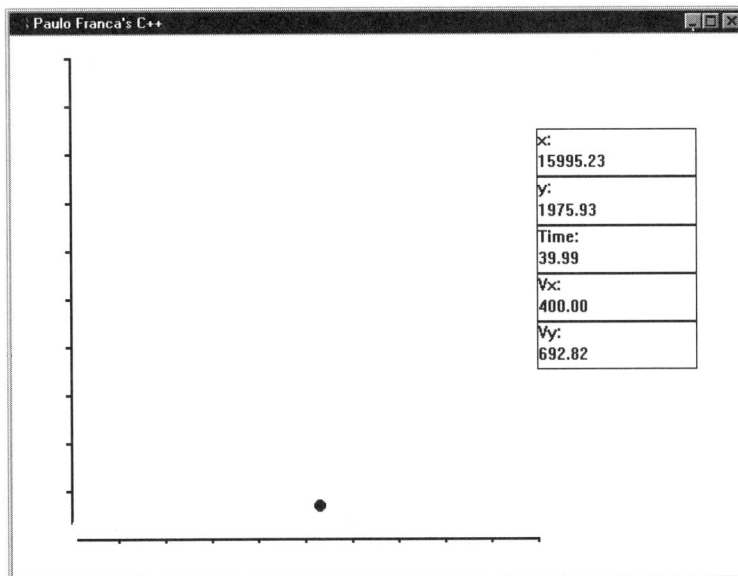

FIGURE 15.5:   The result of executing c5cannon.cpp at a third point in time

Try These for Fun. . .

- Use the `dist(t)` and `height(t)` functions to write a program that finds the maximum value of height for given values of velocity and angle. Use boxes to display the current values of distance, height, and time, and to display the maximum value that was observed of height. You can use the general structure of the cannonball program.

- Modify the `c5cannon.cpp` program to find the maximum distance reached by the cannonball, which is the value of x when height drops to zero.

Handling Multiple Screen Objects— the *Stage* Class

There are cases in which you have an object that can be drawn as a set of other Screen Objects. Remember the athletes? How can you draw one of them?

The athlete figure, like the figure of most real people, is represented by the following parts:

- Head—represented by a circle

- Trunk—represented by a square

- Left and right arms—represented by rectangles

- Left and right legs—represented by rectangles

For the sake of simplicity, we use only two values for sizing the body parts. We can call these values L and W, as shown in Figure 15.6. The head is a circle whose radius is given by the value of L. The arms and the legs are rectangles whose width is given by the value of W, and whose length is given by the value of L. The trunk is a square whose sides are each given by the value of L.

Building an Athlete Piece by Piece

Can you draw an athlete? There's the hard way, and there's the easy way. You may start by declaring the objects that represent the body parts (the hard way!). A little later, you will learn how to use the `Stage` class (the easy way!).

```
Circle head;
Square trunk;
Square leftleg,rightleg;
Square leftarm,rightarm;
```

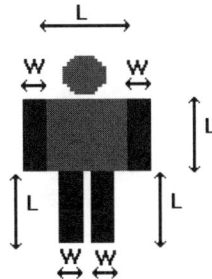

FIGURE 15.6:   Drawing an athlete

Since we know how to deal with circles and squares, all we have to do now is to position these objects in the right places and to assign them the appropriate colors and sizes.

Assume that the athlete is enclosed by a square whose center has the coordinates x and y. Furthermore, let's declare some constants to hold the values of W and L, using the names armwidth for W and armsize for L.

```
const int armsize=20;
const int armwidth=6;
```

Coloring Your Athlete

The following statements can be used to color the objects:

```
head.color(5,5);
trunk.color(5,5);
leftarm.color(3,3);
rightarm.color(3,3);
leftleg.color(3,3);
rightleg.color(3,3);
```

Scaling Your Athlete

Next, you can make all the objects assume the appropriate sizes:

```
head.resize(2*armwidth);
trunk.resize(armsize);
leftarm.resize(armsize,armwidth);
rightarm.resize(armsize,armwidth);
leftleg.resize(armsize,armwidth);
rightleg.resize(armsize,armwidth);
```

Placing Your Athlete

Then, you can place all the objects:

```
head.place(x,y-armsize/2.-armwidth);
trunk.place(x,y);
leftarm.place((x-(armsize+armwidth)/2.),y);
rightarm.place((x+(armsize+armwidth)/2.),y);
leftleg.place(x-(armsize/2.-armwidth),y+armsize);
rightleg.place(x+(armsize/2.-armwidth),y+armsize);
```

Showing Your Athlete

Finally, you can now show all the objects:

```
head.show();
trunk.show();
leftarm.show();
rightarm.show();
leftleg.show();
rightleg.show();
```

You are welcome to try these statements to draw an athlete. However, you may want to be patient and learn how to use the Stage class in the next section.

Using the *Stage* Class

The Stage class handles a group of Screen Objects as if they are all bonded together.

Objects of class Stage are also of class ScreenObj. Therefore, Stage has coordinates, and can be shown and erased. However, Stage objects do not have a shape. Instead, you can insert several other Screen Objects in the Stage object, and when you instruct the Stage object with show(), all the objects that were inserted will be shown.

In addition to the usual operations you can perform with a Screen Object, you can perform an operation called insert in a Stage object. By using insert, you can insert any Screen Object into the Stage object.

NOTE You can also insert a Stage object into another Stage object.

As you know by now, an athlete is composed of several objects. If you want to move the athlete on the screen, you will have to perform the following operations on each object that makes up the athlete:

- Erase the object from the old location.
- Move the object to the new location.
- Show the object in the new location.

Stage Saves Time and Trouble

If we use a `Stage` class, we can perform the same operations with all the objects in the `Stage` object by sending the appropriate message only once to the `Stage` object! In other words, instead of showing the head, left arm, right arm, etc., all we have to do is to show the athlete.

```
Stage body;
body.place(x,y);
```

It is important to place the `Stage` object appropriately, because when the `Stage` object is placed somewhere else, all the objects in the `Stage` object will also be moved!

All we have to do now is to insert each object in the `Stage` object (just once):

```
body.insert(trunk);
body.insert(leftarm);
body.insert(rightarm);
body.insert(leftleg);
body.insert(rightleg);
```

If we want to move the whole `Stage` object to a new location *x1,y1*, we can use the following statements:

```
body.erase();
body.place(x,y);
body.show();
```

Of course, this is much simpler than having to erase, place, and show each part individually.

A Short Project—Sun, Earth, Moon

This short project for Skill 15 simulates a simplified planetary system. Suppose that you were hired by your physics instructor to develop a visual animation of Earth revolving around the Sun, while the Moon revolves around Earth.

This software should represent the movement of these bodies on the computer screen. It makes no sense to try to keep the planet sizes and the distances between them proportional, because Earth and the Moon would not be visible on the screen!

Instead, you can choose an arbitrary size (diameter) for each body, as well as an arbitrary distance from one body to another body. We will also represent these movements as circular, instead of as elliptical as in real life.

However, it is important to keep the time in proportion. For example, 1 second in the simulation could correspond to 1 day in real life. This may still be too slow for our purposes—a complete simulation involving a 365-day year would take 365 seconds to complete. Your fellow students may be too impatient to sit and watch for that long! You may try to simulate each 10th of a second as a day in real life.

NOTE While you work through this project, remember that Earth takes 365.25 days to complete a revolution around the Sun, and that the Moon takes 28 days to complete a revolution around Earth.

Once you have declared and initialized the Sun, Earth, and the Moon as objects of class `Circle`, the simulation itself is relatively easy to carry out.

The position of each body is merely a function of time. Each body can be erased from its position, placed in the new position, and then redrawn. Polar coordinates come in really handy in this case. Since the angular speed is known for Earth and the Moon, the angle can be determined as a function of time.

Useful Objects for Your Planetary Project

It is easy to imagine that we can use objects of class `Circle` to represent the Sun, Earth, and the Moon. You can declare these objects as follows:

```
Circle Sun, Earth, Moon;
```

These objects must be initialized with an appropriate size, color, and initial position.

Figure 15.7 displays a convenient initial position. In this case, all the bodies are horizontally aligned when the simulation starts. As stated before, the distances between them are arbitrary, and it is a good idea to use a named constant to experiment with these distances and sizes.

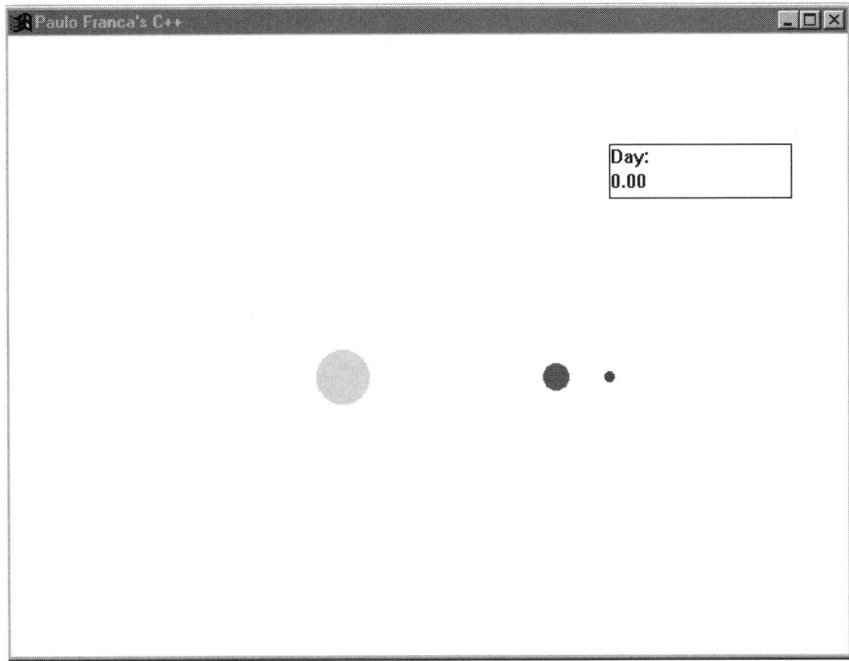

FIGURE 15.7: Initial positions for the Sun, Earth, and the Moon

You may try the following statements:

```
const float earthradius=160.,moonradius=40.;
const float earthsize= 20., moonsize=8., sunsize = 40.;
```

Don't Forget the *Stage* Class!

It may not be obvious at first, but you may also consider using an object of class Stage. During the simulation, you will have to erase and redraw Earth and the

Moon. If you include all the objects that are to be erased and redrawn in a Stage object, you can save yourself some lines of code. Here is what I suggest:

```
Stage universe;
universe.insert(Sun);
universe.insert(Earth);
universe.insert(Moon);
```

You will also need a Clock object to keep track of time. In fact, it would be convenient to use two clocks. One clock can be used to keep track of the simulated time and can be continuously displayed, so the users know the day of the year. Another clock can be used just to pace the frames at 30th-of-a-second intervals.

```
Clock universal, clock stopwatch;
```

Initialization

To get started, we have to declare, size, place, and color our planets. In other words, these Screen Objects have to be initialized.

Scaling   Since all the distances were arbitrarily chosen, there is no need for a specific scale. It may be convenient to use a negative vertical scale, so you can work with the convention that is used in geometry. It may also be a good idea to set the point of origin near the center of the screen, and to locate the Sun in that position.

Any object can be used to set up the scale and the point of origin. For example:

```
universe.scale(1.,-1.);
universe.origin(250.,250.);
```

Positions   The initial cartesian coordinates could be set as follows:

```
Sun:   x=0;                       y=0;
Earth: x=earthradius;             y=0;
Moon:  x=earthradius+moonradius;  y=0;
```

The complete initialization is implemented below.

```
const float earthradius=160.,moonradius=40.;
const float earthsize=20., moonsize=8., sunsize=40.;
Stage universe;
universe.origin(250.,250.);
universe.scale(1.,-1.);
// Set Sun's data:
Circle sun;                    // Declare the Sun's shape
float xsun=0,ysun=0;           // Initial coordinates
sun.resize(sunsize);
```

```
sun.color(6,6);
sun.place(xsun,ysun);
universe.insert(sun);

// Set Earth's data:
Circle earth;                              // Declare Earth's shape
float xearth=earthradius,yearth=0.;  // Initial coordinates
float wearth=(2*pi)/365.25;           // Angular speed in radians per day
earth.resize(earthsize);
earth.color(5,5);
earth.place(xsun+earthradius,ysun);
universe.insert(earth);

// Set Moon's data:
Circle moon;
float xmoon=moonradius,ymoon=0;
float wmoon=(2*pi)/27.;                 // Angular speed
moon.resize(moonsize);
moon.color(1,1);
moon.place(xsun+earthradius+moonradius,ysun);
universe.insert(moon);
```

The Simulation Loop

As usual, the simulation loop consists of producing frames at regular intervals. Earth and the Moon have to be moved to their new locations before they are redrawn.

Here is the general procedure in the simulation loop:

1. Erase the universe.
2. Compute Earth's new location.
3. Place Earth in new location.
4. Compute the Moon's new location.
5. Place the Moon in new location.
6. Show the universe.
7. Display the time.
8. Wait for the time to show the next frame.

Where Is Earth?

Can you figure out where Earth is at any given time t? Remember that Earth takes 365.25 days to complete its revolution around the Sun.

You can compute the angular speed either in degrees:

w = 365.25 / 360 degrees per day;

or in radians:

w = 365.25 / (2*pi) radians per day;

The angular speed `wearth` can be used to compute the angular position of Earth on any given day, represented by `time`:

```
thetaearth= wearth * time;
```

Now, since the Sun is at the point of origin, you can use `earthradius` (distance from the sun) and this angle as polar coordinates to compute the cartesian coordinates.

If you simply issue a call to the `polarxy` function:

```
polarxy(earthradius,wearth*time,xsun,ysun,xearth,yearth);
```

you will return the cartesian coordinates in `xearth` and `yearth`.

Where Is the Moon?

In a similar way, you can determine the cartesian coordinates of the Moon. Remember that all that is needed is to find out the angle. When you call the `polarxy` function, consider your point of origin to be Earth:

```
polarxy(moonradius,wmoon*time,xearth,yearth,xmoon,ymoon);
```

The piece of program below implements the simulation loop.

```
for (;time<365.25;)
  {
    universe.erase();
    polarxy(earthradius,wearth*time,
            xsun,ysun,xearth,yearth);
    earth.place(xearth,yearth);
    polarxy(moonradius,wmoon*time,
            xearth,yearth,xmoon,ymoon);
    moon.place(xmoon,ymoon);
    day.say(time);
```

```
    universe.show();
    stopwatch.watch(.033);
    stopwatch.reset();
    time=sidereal.time()*timescale;
}
```

For this simulation loop, there is a variable `timescale` that can make the simulation run faster or slower. `timescale` is defined as 10, which means that each day in the simulation lasts a 10th of a second. This loop only checks whether the simulation time is greater than 365.25 (the end of the year).

The complete implementation can be found in the program `c5stars.cpp`.

Try These for Fun...

- Modify the `c5stars.cpp` program so the Moon's orbit is shown. To do this, simply avoid erasing the Moon in the loop.

- Modify the `c5stars.cpp` program so the background is shown in blue instead of in white.

Are You Experienced?

Now you can...

☑ **Use a moving object to draw a function graph**

☑ **Move an object with appropriate timing to simulate a real-life movement**

☑ **Use *Stage* objects to manipulate several Screen Objects at one time**

☑ **Develop a simulation of Earth and the Moon revolving around the Sun**

PART VI

Getting Smarter

Since Part I, you have been able to use objects. However, you have been able to use only readily available objects, because you do not know how to make your own class of objects. In Part VI, you will learn how to create your own classes of objects, and, even smarter, you will learn how to derive your classes from existing classes to *inherit* everything that interests you. Screen Objects will be used again to help you. Finally, your skill in developing applications will be improved.

Making and Modifying Classes

- ❏ Declaring and defining classes

- ❏ Making members public, private, or protected

- ❏ Isolating information with encapsulation

- ❏ Building constructors

- ❏ Using objects

- ❏ Creating a new class of objects

- ❏ Accessing class members

Objects and classes—you have been using these since Skill 1. It is now time to get to know a little more about them.

You already know that each class of objects knows how to respond to a specific set of messages. For example, `athlete` knows up, ready, etc. `Clock` knows `reset`, `time`, `wait`, etc. This is because each class of objects has a set of functions that is tied to these objects. They are part (or members) of that class of objects. Figure 16.1 shows an object containing member functions. The program sends *messages* to this object that invoke the object's member functions. The member functions then manipulate the object accordingly.

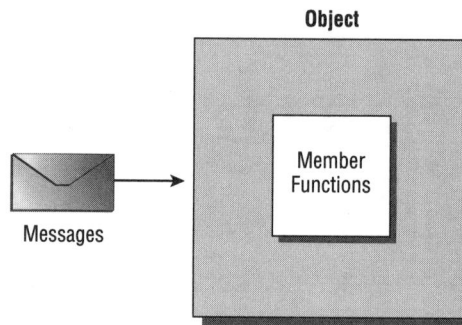

FIGURE 16.1: Messages to an object containing member functions

These functions are called *member functions* because they belong to and are *members* of the class. Member functions are programmed in the same way that ordinary, *nonmember* functions are programmed. However, as we shall see, member functions are declared to be members of the class, and can only be used with an object of that class.

By now, you are ready to better understand the relationship between a class and an object. *Class* refers to all objects that behave similarly. For example, all circles have a particular shape, a location, a color, and a diameter. *Object* refers to specific instances of that class. For example, Earth has a different size, color, and location than the Moon and the Sun. The relationship between classes and objects is essentially the same as the relationship between types and variables.

Skill 16 will teach you how to make your own classes and how to understand how classes work. Most examples will use Screen Objects, so that you can make classes with interesting applications.

Making Your Own Classes

The athletes you have created and worked with throughout this book have the following member functions, which can be used only with an athlete:

- ready()
- up()
- left()
- right()

which means you can use

```
Sal.ready();
```

but not

```
ready();
```

unless you have a nonmember function named ready(), too.

Also, you cannot use

```
myclock.ready();
```

because Clock does not have a ready() member function.

Since you have been using objects mainly by invoking their member functions, I hope you have a good idea by now of what member functions are. Figure 16.2 shows athlete and its member functions.

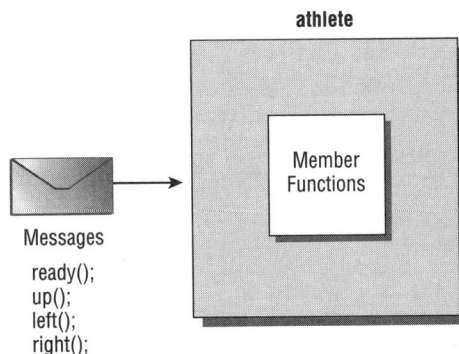

FIGURE 16.2: Member functions in athlete objects

Another very important aspect of objects may have passed unnoticed until now. Most likely, each object also has some data that determine the status of the object. This is not restricted to our book's objects. Any class can determine that objects belonging to the class have data as well as functions.

For example, athletes are shown in a position on the screen. Each athlete has an *x* and a *y* coordinate to identify this position. This is done by keeping two variables (for each object) to hold the coordinates. Similarly, the shape of the athlete is determined by a set of rectangles and a circle. Each rectangle is an object of class Square (distorted to appear as a rectangle), and the circle is an object of class Circle. So, in addition to the variables *x* and *y*, each object also has a Circle and five Squares as data members, conveniently sized and located.

In another, simpler example, clocks have only one variable as a data member, as we shall see in detail. Since Clock objects are supposed to know the elapsed time, there must be a way to know the time when the object was created or reset. This is done by a variable timestarted that holds the value of the computer clock (the *hardware* clock) when the object was created or last reset. The member function time() simply subtracts timestarted from the current time held in the hardware clock to determine the elapsed time. The member function reset() just copies the value in the hardware clock to the timestarted variable.

Data members can be of any type. They may be int, float, long, or other common types, and they may also be athletes, Squares, Clocks, or any other available class of objects.

Each object of a given class possesses the complete set of member functions and data members defined for that particular class. For example, it is not possible for a circle (such as Earth) to have a color, while another circle (such as the Sun) does not have a color. However, the data members most likely will hold a different value for each object (each athlete has his or her own coordinates). This means that each object will have its own data. However, unlike the data members, all the member functions are exactly alike, and the same function can be used with every object of that class. This means that only one copy of the member functions for a given class is included in your program.

For example, if you declare two Clocks, clock1 and clock2, each one will need to store a different value for timestarted, since they were created at different times and may be reset at different times, too. If you declare one thousand objects of class Clock, there will be one thousand variables timestarted—one for each object—but only one copy of the functions reset(), time(), and wait().

Building a Class of Objects

You are probably anxious to learn how to build a class of objects. To do this, you will learn how the Clock class was built.

Real-life clocks have a dial where the time is shown. All you have to do is to look at the dial to know the time. The Clock objects used in our programs work a little differently because of the following reasons:

- They can tell the time elapsed since the clock was created or reset (not since midnight).

- They keep the time in seconds (not in hours, minutes, and seconds).

- They can perform the operations reset(), time(), wait(), and watch().

It is not possible to set our Clocks to a given value. They can only be reset.

Skill 16

NOTE   The clock you have been using in your examples and exercises uses the hardware clock in your computer to keep track of the time.

Building the *Clock* Code

There is a way to find out the time elapsed since your computer was turned on— it is a function offered by Windows:

```
timeGetTime();
```

If you want to use this function directly, you must include the header file mmsystem.h.

This function returns a long integer containing the number of milliseconds elapsed since the system was started. If we keep a variable timestarted, we can implement our functions as follows:

```
void reset()
{
    timestarted=timeGetTime();
}
float time()
{
    // Divide result by 1000 because we want
    //      result in seconds, not in 1/1000ths:
    return (timeGetTime()-timestarted)*.001;
}
```

The wait() function is somewhat trivial. If we need to wait for a given number of seconds (tsec), we can determine the time of the computer clock by adding the current time to tsec. We can call this result willbe. All we have to do now is to keep looping until the computer clock reaches the same value as willbe.

```
void wait(float tsec)
{                            // If we want to wait for tsec
   float willbe;             //     seconds, we have to wait until
   willbe=time()+tsec;       //     the time becomes current time
   while (time()<willbe);//     plus tsec
}
```

Notice that we are using the member function time() inside another member function wait(). This is perfectly OK. However, you may be confused, because a member function is always supposed to be used in conjunction with an object—here, we are using the time() function by itself as if it is a nonmember function.

Implicit References to Objects

It just so happens that the wait() function is used with a Clock object while the program is running. The Clock that was used to wait() will be the same clock used with the time() function.

> **NOTE** Member functions are assumed to operate with the object that is being used.

For example, if you have an object BigBen that is declared to be an instance of class Clock:

```
Clock BigBen;
```

and you tell BigBen to wait() in your program:

```
BigBen.wait(10);
```

the wait() function automatically assumes that BigBen is to be used in conjunction with the time() member function when the wait() function invokes time().

In fact, it could not work any other way. When you write the code for a member function (such as wait() and time()), you don't really know which object you will have to use. Will it be mywatch? Will it be timer? Will it be BigBen? You are not able to use an object name, because you don't know what it is.

All you know is that it will be an object that is an instance of the class Clock. It will have a value in the long integer timestarted, and it will have the member functions wait(), time(), and reset(). When your member function is invoked, the compiler will remember which object was used, and it will use the data pertaining to that object in all the member function calls that omit the object name.

The implementation of the wait() member function restricts the maximum waiting time to 60 seconds. Here is the code:

```
void wait(float tsec)
{
    float willbe;
    if (tsec>60) tsec=60;// Will not wait more than
                         //     1 minute!
    willbe=time()+tsec;
    while (time()<willbe);
}
```

WARNING Notice that while only compares the value of the current time with the variable willbe. It keeps comparing until, eventually, the time() function replies with a value that is greater than willbe, and then the loop ends. The computer does nothing else in the meantime, because it is busy waiting for the correct time. In a multitasking computer, this is not a good idea.

Declaring a Class of Objects

Well, so far we've done nothing new. You already know how to write functions, so you could write the code to reset(), time(), and wait(). We still do not know how to incorporate these functions in a class. Actually, we are very close to implementing classes.

A class is implemented in two steps:

- The *class declaration* gives a name to the class, and explains which variables or objects are contained in the class (data members) and which functions belong to the class (member functions). The class declaration does not include the actual code for the member functions.

- The *class definition* includes the code for all the member functions.

The class declaration has the following general format:

```
class classname
{
    declaration of data members
    declaration of member functions
};  // Don't forget the semicolon!
```

Using and Avoiding *struct*

Classes can also be declared as a structure using the keyword `struct`. This technique will be presented in Skill 20, but it is not encouraged—there is nothing to be gained by it.

The declaration of data members and member functions must be enclosed in braces, and there must be a semicolon following the closing brace! It is a common mistake to omit this semicolon. The compiler messages that result are very misleading and may not help you locate this error.

You need the following items in the class declaration presented in the general format above:

- The *classname* is any valid identifier of your choice. This will be the name you give to your new class of objects.

- The *declaration of data members* is just the declaration of all the variables or objects that will belong to each object of the class.

- The *declaration of member functions* lists what we call the *function prototypes* of the member functions. A prototype identifies a function, its result type, and the number and the types of arguments. The prototype is followed by a semicolon. You can mix declarations of data members and member functions in any order.

One Example of a *Clock* Class

As an example, let's examine one possible declaration of class `Clock`.

```
class Clock //*************************  Clock
{
    long timestarted;
    public:
    float time();          // Returns the time elapsed
    void wait(float tsec); // Waits tsec seconds
    void reset();          // Resets
};
```

The first line presents the keyword `class` and the identifier (name) of the new class we are creating. Next, a set of braces (followed by a semicolon) encloses the declarations.

The `Clock` class has only one data member—the long integer `timestarted`. This is declared right after the opening braces, but could be declared anywhere inside the braces.

Then, the prototypes for the member functions appear: `time()`, `wait()`, and `reset()`. Notice that each prototype is essentially the same as the first line in the function itself. Each prototype contains the result type, the function identifier (name), and the types of arguments inside parentheses. You don't have to include an identifier for the arguments in the prototype (`tsec` could be omitted in the declaration for `wait()`).

The only thing unexplained in this declaration is the purpose of the word `public`? Hold on!

Class Definition

As we said before, the class definition contains the actual code for all the member functions in the class. This code is included in the program, essentially, in the same way the code is included for a nonmember function.

How do you specify that these functions are the member functions of your class? After all, C++ allows you to have a nonmember function `wait()` in addition to a member function `wait()` of class `Clock`.

Due to function overloading, several functions may have the same name. You must clearly state that the code you are providing refers to a member function of a given class.

You must attach each function you define to its class. This is done by preceding the function identifier by a qualification. The *qualification* is the class name followed by two colons, such as

```
class name :: function name (argument list)
```

or, in our clock example:

```
Clock::wait()
```

Thus, the actual class definition for the class `Clock` could be as follows:

```
void Clock::reset()
{
    timestarted=timeGetTime();
}
```

```
float Clock::time()
{
   // Divide result by 1000 because we want
   //       result in seconds, not in 1/1000ths:
   return (timeGetTime()-timestarted)*.001;
}
void Clock::wait(float tsec)
{
   float willbe;
   if (tsec>60) tsec=60;      // Will not wait more than
                              //       1 minute!
   willbe=time()+tsec;
   while (time()<willbe);
}
```

TIP   You may try to type this class and use it. However, since there is already a class Clock in the software, the compiler will issue an error message. You can overcome this by using the name clock instead of Clock. You must also include the mmsystem.h header file.

Making Members Public, Private, or Protected

When you design a class, you may want the class members (data or functions) to be either visible or not visible to other parts of the software. There are three possibilities.

Public

Public members can be accessed not only by your member functions, but also by any piece of program that can access the object. This is the case for the reset(), time(), and wait() member functions of class Clock. If an object of class Clock is declared, we want to be able to perform these functions with it.

Private

Private members can be accessed only by the member functions of the same class. It is not possible for other pieces of program to access a private member of an object. *Private* is the default. If nothing is declared about a member, it is assumed to be private. The `timestarted` variable is private—only the member functions of class `Clock` (`reset()`, `wait()`, `time()`) can use this variable.

Protected

Protected members can be accessed by member functions, but they can also be accessed by member functions of derived classes. We will see how to use these later.

The `public`, `private`, and `protected` keywords are enforced until another one of these keywords occurs in the listing. In other words, when a class declaration is started, it is assumed to be private. All members are assumed to be private until either `public` or `protected` is found. From then on, this new option is valid until another option is set. In the example of the `Clock` class, all the member functions are public, because the first one is preceded by `public`, and neither `private` nor `protected` can be found in the declaration.

ENCAPSULATION

The ability to isolate information from unauthorized interference is called *encapsulation* in object-oriented programming. By making sure that data can only be manipulated by member functions that are associated with it, we can build more reliable and more maintainable software.

The software is more reliable because you can be assured that data is manipulated only as expected. It is more maintainable because, when modifications are needed, they are usually isolated to the object itself and are not scattered throughout the code.

Building Constructors

How can we be sure the clock will always be reset? The `Clock` class is still missing something. As you know, once a `Clock` is declared, it is automatically reset. This means that when a new `Clock` is created, the value of `timestarted` is set to the current time in the computer clock.

It must be possible for us to specify a special function that is automatically invoked every time an object is created. C++ allows us to do this by means of *constructor* functions.

The constructor function is very similar to other member functions, except for the following items:

- Its name is the same as the class name. For example, the constructor for class Clock is :Clock().

- It is automatically invoked when a new object is created. For example, when you have Clock mine, yours;, the constructor function Clock::Clock will be invoked twice—once to create mine and another time to create yours.

- It cannot be explicitly invoked in the program. For example, you cannot say mine.Clock();. The constructor is supposed to be invoked only once when an object is created.

- It does not have a return type (not even void). It is possible to have more than one constructor if the argument lists are different. For example, class Box has one constructor without arguments and one with an argument: box x, y("Y:"); invokes the constructor without arguments for object x and invokes the constructor with one argument for object y. In this case, the box for y will automatically have a label that reads Y:.

> **NOTE** Constructors must be public. They must be visible from any piece of program that can declare an object of that class, otherwise construction of the object will be impossible.

Initializing Objects with Constructors

Constructors are extremely useful for initializing objects. They provide us with an opportunity to prepare each object before it is put into use. Most classes of objects that you have used so far have a constructor. The clocks are reset, and the athletes are positioned one after the other. Other screen objects are assigned default coordinates and other attributes.

The complete declaration of class Clock is as follows:

```
class Clock //*************************  Clock
{
```

```
      protected:
       long timestarted;
      public:
       Clock();
       float time();          // Returns the time elapsed
       void wait(float tsec); // Waits tsec seconds
       void watch(float set); // Waits until time=set
       void reset();          // Resets
    };
```

and the class definition should include the code for the constructor:

```
Clock::Clock()
{
    timestarted=timeGetTime();
}
```

Using Objects

When you build a class, you do not build one object of that class. You give an explanation of how all the objects of that class behave. Even if you are interested in using only one clock, you have to submit an explanation of the behavior of all possible clocks. Once the class Clock is built, you can use Clock objects in your program.

To use an object, all you have to do is to declare it. This is done in the same way you have been declaring athletes and clocks. The declaration consists of the class name, followed by spaces and the identifiers (names) of the objects that you want to use. If you want to use more than one object, their identifiers should be separated by commas:

```
class name,   object identifier;
```

or, in our examples:

```
Clock timer,mywatch;
athlete Sal;
```

The object declaration tells the compiler that you will be using in your program one (or more) object(s) of that particular class, and that you will be referring to that object by the identifier you provided. The compiler then sets apart some space in the computer memory, and makes sure that when the program execution reaches that stage, a call to the appropriate constructor is made to initialize the object.

Skill 16

Notice how similar the declaration for variables is:

```
type    variable identifier;
```

For example:

```
float   x,y;
```

This reinforces the fact that there is a very strong resemblance between variables and objects, and also that there is an equivalent resemblance between types and classes. In this Skill, you will learn why we say that variables are just a limited form of objects, and for this reason, why we have referred to objects many times when we were referring to either objects or variables.

Accessing Object Members

Public members (functions and data) may be accessed by other parts of your program. To access a member, it is imperative that the object name precedes the member name as a qualifier. This is the way we have been accessing member functions of class `athlete`, in which the athlete's name is followed by a dot and then the member function name. For example:

```
sal.ready();
```

invokes the member function `ready()`, which belongs to the object `sal`.

You can do the same thing with data members. For example, `Clock` objects have the data member `timestarted`, which can be accessed by preceding the data member name with the object name:

```
bigben.timestarted=mine.timestarted;
```

However, since `timestarted` is not public, it cannot be accessed by other parts of the program. It can only be accessed by member functions of class `Clock`.

Accessing Members in Member Functions

When you code member functions, the compiler understands that you are explaining how to manipulate each object of the class you are implementing. Since member functions can be invoked only for a particular object of that class, the compiler automatically understands that any reference, either to a member function or to a data member, is supposed to be tied to that particular object. This is why it is not necessary to qualify data members or member functions in member functions.

Creating a New Class of Objects

We are now ready to experiment with a new class—one that we will build our-selves. We will create a class of wagon objects. Wagons can be drawn on the screen and can move horizontally. Our wagon is built with a rectangle and two circles. Figure 16.3 shows our concept of a wagon.

FIGURE 16.3: A wagon

The wagon class will have a constructor and a move() member function. The move() member function should make the wagon move on the screen. Obviously, we need a couple of variables to keep track of the coordinates on the screen, since the wagon will be moving.

One possible declaration for class wagon is as follows:

```
class wagon
{
   Circle frontwheel,rearwheel;
   Square body;
   float x,y; // Coordinates
   public:
   wagon();
   void move();
};              // Never forget the semicolon!
```

There are three objects that function as data members: frontwheel and rear-wheel (which are circles), and body (which is a square). There are also two float-ing point variables, x and y. There was no specification of whether these members are public. Therefore, they are assumed to be private. This is convenient, because only the move() member function and the constructor can access them.

Building a Wagon with Constructors

As we already know, the constructor will be invoked for each object created. The constructor assigns convenient sizes, colors, and locations for the objects that compose the wagon, and it sets initial coordinate values for x and y.

```
const int red=1,green=2;
wagon::wagon()
{
    x=60;                          // Initial coordinates
    y=200;
    frontwheel.resize(20);         // Assign size to wheels
    rearwheel.resize(20);
    body.resize(20,80);            // Make the body a rectangle
    frontwheel.color(red);         // Assign colors
    rearwheel.color(red);
    body.color(green);
    body.place(x,y);               // Place all parts
    rearwheel.place(x-25,y+10);
    frontwheel.place(x+25,y+10);
    body.show();                   // Show the wagon
    rearwheel.show();
    frontwheel.show();
}

void wagon::move()
{
    body.erase();                  // Erase from previous location
    rearwheel.erase();
    frontwheel.erase();
    x++;                           // Increment x
    body.place(x,y);               // Place parts in new location
    rearwheel.place(x-25,y+10);
    frontwheel.place(x+25,y+10);
    body.show();                   // Show
    rearwheel.show();
    frontwheel.show();
}
```

The class above works, and you may try it as is. You may be wondering whether it is a good idea to define functions to erase(), place(), and show(). Yes, it is a good idea—but there is a better one!

Building a Wagon with the *Stage* Class

If we use one object of class Stage, we can insert the body and the wheels in the Stage object—we will have a much simpler program. This is shown in the program c6train.cpp:

```cpp
#include "franca.h"
// Implementation of class wagon              c6train.cpp
// Part 6
// Version 2.0—uses a Stage
//
int const red=1,green=2;
class wagon
{
   Stage railroad;             // Stage included
   Circle frontwheel,rearwheel; // Declare wheels and body
   Square body;
   float x,y;                  // Coordinates
 public:
   wagon();
   void move();
};                            // Never forget the semicolon!

wagon::wagon()
{
   x=60;                      // Initial coordinates
   y=200;
   railroad.place(x,y);
   frontwheel.resize(20);     // Size the objects
   rearwheel.resize(20);
   body.resize(20,80);
   frontwheel.color(red);     // Color the objects
   rearwheel.color(red);
   body.color(green);
   body.place(x,y);           // Place the objects
   rearwheel.place(x-25,y+10);
   frontwheel.place(x+25,y+10);
   railroad.insert(rearwheel);  // Insert the objects in Stage
   railroad.insert(frontwheel);
   railroad.insert(body);
}
void wagon::move()
{
   railroad.erase();          // Erase previous
   x++;                       // Move forward
   railroad.place(x,y);
   railroad.show();           // Show current position
}
```

This new version alters the class declaration to include only an object of class Stage. The constructor did not change much, except that, instead of showing the body and wheels, it simply inserts them in the Stage object.

Making the *move()* Function Easier to Use

The move() function was simplified, because all the operations can be done with the Stage object, instead of each being repeated.

You can try our new class with the program below.

```
void mainprog()
{
   int i;
   wagon front;              // Declare front wagon
                             // Wagon constructor is invoked
   Clock station;           // And a clock
   for ( i=1;i<=80; i++)    // Loop
   {
     front.move();          // Move the wagon
     station.wait(.03);
   }
   wagon caboose;            // Declare one more wagon
                             // Wagon constructor is invoked
                             // Caboose is constructed only
                             //     after the previous loop
   for ( i=1;i<=200;i++)    // Loop
   {
     front.move();          // Move both wagons
     caboose.move();
     station.wait(.06);
   }
}
```

Accessing Class Members

Since the beginning of this book, we have been accessing member functions of the class athlete. To access a member function, qualify the function name with the object name followed by a dot. For example:

```
Sal.ready();
```

invokes the ready() member function of the object Sal, which belongs to class athlete. It is also possible to access data members in the same way. The data member must be preceded by the object name and a dot. For example, the program c6train.cpp, using the wagon class, can access the data members of this class. For example:

```
front.x=0.;                    // Sets x coordinate to zero
                               //      for first wagon
front.rearwheel.resize(15);    // Changes size of rearwheel
caboose.y=10;                  // Sets y coordinate to 10
                               //      for second wagon
```

However, if you try to do this, the compiler will issue an error message saying that these data members are not accessible. Why? Well, all the data members in class wagon are assumed to be private. If you insert the keyword public (followed by a colon) before the data members are declared, you may try again and see the results.

In this example, a wagon is always created at the coordinates (60,200). It may be a good idea either to allow the wagon to be placed somewhere else or to allow it to be created at a specified coordinate. Let's study some alternatives to this problem:

- Make the wagon's coordinates publicly accessible.

- Use arguments in the constructor.

- Have a member function change the coordinates.

Making the *x* and *y* Coordinates Public

If the coordinates are made public, you will be able to modify them after the object is created. By changing the coordinates, the wagon will be shown at a different location next time it is drawn. This seems like a pretty cool idea, doesn't it? Well, you will see that it is not!

This alternative is easy to implement—just include the following statement:

```
public:
```

before the declaration of x and y in the wagon class declaration. Then, you can change the wagon's position in the program by directly modifying the values of the coordinates of each wagon. For example:

```
front.x= 120;
front.y= 100;
caboose.x= 60;
caboose.y= 100;
```

will work if you change each coordinate before the wagon is moved. For example, we could have

```
front.x=180;
front.move();
```

However, if you modify the coordinates after you have started moving the wagon (it is already drawn on the screen), you may have strange results. For example:

```
front.move();
front.x=200;
front.move();
```

Think about what could happen in this case—then go ahead and change the program to see the result. Do you like the result? Do you know why it happened?

Worse yet, these coordinates could be set to wrong values somewhere in the program:

```
caboose.x=z1;
caboose.y=z2;
```

You may ask, What would be wrong with this? Nothing, really—except that z1 and z2 could hold results of some strange computations, whose values could be –432 and 221,345, for example. How could you tell?

In any event, the result is undesirable. In the first case, the move member function erases the wagon from its current location, moves it one step along the horizontal, and then redraws it. If you change the coordinates, the old drawing of the wagon will not be erased properly. The erase function will erase the object using its current coordinate!

This is the reason for using private or protected in your class. You can make sure that only the member functions use these data members, and, since you are coding and testing them, you can guarantee they will work.

You could still argue that you are also coding the program, and, therefore, you know what you are doing to these data members. Don't do this. Never underestimate your ability to mess up software!

TIP   A bit of prevention is worth a megabyte of cure....

Finally, the most important argument in favor of keeping most data members nonpublic is that you should never build your software thinking you will be the only one to use it. Worse than this, never assume that you will make a program, use it, and then throw it away. The current trend is to reuse software. If you become a professional programmer, you will be building software for others to use. Software may be built in teams, and what you build will be used by somebody else to build something bigger. Every opportunity to avoid errors should be taken.

Using Arguments in the Constructor

The next alternative is to allow the constructor function to receive the coordinates as arguments. For example:

```
wagon::wagon ( int x0, int y0)
{
      x=x0;
      y=y0:
      . . .
```

If the constructor is modified in this way (oops—don't forget to modify the constructor declaration in the class declaration, too), wagons can be placed anywhere when they are declared:

```
wagon  front (120,220);
. . .
wagon caboose(60,220);
```

The constructor without parameters is also known as the *default constructor*. It is always a good idea to include the default constructor in your class, even when you also provide a constructor with parameters.

Using a Member Function

You could consider yet another alternative—including a member function to place the wagon at a given location. This is reasonable and is much better than making the coordinates public. This member function can check the given coordinates to make sure they are valid.

> **TIP** This third alternative for implementing the class wagon has some advantages over the second one. However, I am still not happy with it! After studying inheritance in Skill 17, try to solve the same problem by deriving wagon from the class Stage, and see how much better you can do.

Try These for Fun. . .

- Modify the class wagon to show a picture resembling a locomotive. Include a couple of extra rectangles to represent the cabin and the chimney.

- Modify the class Clock into a new class (for example, Clock1), so that the member function mark() automatically resets the clock. In other words, if you want to wait for periods of 5 seconds, you could use

```
Clock1 mytimer;
for (int i=1;i<=20; i++)
{
    mytimer.mark(5.);
}
```

- Create a class pair to consist of two athletes. pair should have the member functions ready, up, left, and right. Use this class to write a program that makes the pair perform a jumping jack.

- In implementing the Clock::wait(float) member function, I used the variable willbe to hold the current time. Try using Clock::time() to get the time.

- Remove the semicolon after the closing brace in the wagon class declaration. Observe the error messages that result.

Are You Experienced?

Now you can. . .

- ☑ **Make a new class by declaring it and defining it**

- ☑ **Choose which members are public, private, or protected**

- ☑ **Build constructor functions to initialize your objects**

- ☑ **Create a new class of objects**

- ☑ **Access data members and member functions in your objects**

S K I L L

seventeen

Deriving Classes
from Existing Classes

- ❏ Declaring and defining derived classes

- ❏ Inheriting members

- ❏ Understanding polymorphism

Making your own class of objects is not the most interesting application of classes. When it is possible, deriving a new class from an existing one is the real deal—you don't have to redo what you inherit, and you can modify whatever does not suit your taste.

We say that objects are smart because objects know how to do things that you tell them. For example, objects of class `athlete` know how to assume the positions `ready`, `up`, `left`, and `right`. They also know how to "say" something. In this Skill, you will learn how to create objects that are smarter than the ones you had before.

In the previous Skill, you were asked to modify the `wagon` class in a few exercises in the "Try These for Fun..." section. To work through these exercises successfully, you have to do one of the following things:

- Take the old code, remove parts that are no longer needed, and insert new parts that are needed. In this case, you have only one piece of code implementing the new class. There is no way to use the old class.

- Copy the old code, and then make alterations as needed. In this case, you have two versions of the same class. You may even consider using a different name for the new class. You are able to use objects of both classes in the same program.

The second alternative is slightly more convenient, because the old class remains usable and unaltered. If it remains unaltered, you are sure that no new errors were inserted in the code. But now you have two pieces of code to fix when you have a problem! Another concern is that if you use the two classes in the same program, the common code (the unaltered part) will be duplicated.

If you have available two (or more) pieces of code that do essentially the same thing, it is a real pain in the neck for software management. It may not seem so to you at this time, but since software has to be updated—not only to be corrected, but in response to external factors—it will be necessary to perform the same maintenance in all pieces of software. It is definitely preferable to use, or better yet, to reuse a unique piece of code.

Deriving Classes

Object-oriented programming has a special feature to help you reuse software. When you want to use a class of objects that is very similar to an existing one, yet you want it to operate slightly differently, you can *derive* a new class from the existing one. In C++, the original class is called the *base class;* the one you derive from it is called the *derived class*.

A special kind of wagon that looks like a locomotive and a special kind of Clock that resets itself after each waiting period are good possibilities for using derived classes. This would lead us to new classes: locomotive, which is a special kind of wagon, and timer, which is a special kind of Clock.

Each object of the derived class can still be regarded as an object of the base class from which it was derived. A locomotive can still be regarded as a wagon, and a timer can still be regarded as a clock. In fact, a locomotive is just another wagon in the whole train.

The good thing about deriving classes is that anything that already works in the base class will be automatically *inherited* by the derived class. You never need to duplicate anything that previously existed! You only have to worry about the special features you want implemented in your new, derived class.

For example, to implement a locomotive class, you don't have to specify how to draw the wheels or the wagon itself. There is also no need to explain how to move it. All you have to specify is how to draw the cabin and the chimney, which were not present in the base wagon class.

Similarly, for the timer class, all you have to do is to write the mark member function, so that it will reset the clock every time.

Creating Derived Classes

To derive a class from another, the steps are similar to the ones you took to create a new class:

1. Declare the class—declare all the members that do not exist in the base class (you must also declare member functions that will replace existing member functions in the base class). When you declare a derived class, explicitly mention that this class is derived from a given base class.

2. Define the class—write the code for the new member functions.

Declaring the Derived Class

When you declare a derived class, you must state that it is a derived class, and you must identify the base class from which it is derived. This is done right after we give the name of this new, derived class. The syntax is as follows:

```
class derived class name : public base class name
{
    member declaration
}; // Never forget the semicolon!
```

Notice the addition of the colon, the keyword `public`, and the base class name that identifies the base class from which we are deriving.

The following listing could be the declaration for the `timer` class:

```
class timer: public Clock
{
    void mark (float time);
};
```

Defining the Derived Class

The definition of the new member function could be as follows:

```
void timer::mark(float time)
{
    watch(time);
    reset();
}
```

The new class `timer` will still be able to perform all the member functions that already existed in the base class. The functions `reset()`, `time()`, `watch()`, and `wait()` are inherited from the base class. You don't have to specify anything more about these functions. Actually, you may not even know how they work! This is the wonder of inheritance—you get something without having to work for it.

Classes and Objects in the Real World

The classes and objects that are used in object-oriented programming are concepts borrowed from the real world. Objects are the things we see around us.

What things? Well, anything that exists—any of your colleagues, a piece of furniture, a car driving down the street, the stoplight at the intersection, even the birds flying overhead! These are all examples of objects (and don't forget the objects you see on your computer screen).

Of course, you may have realized that some of these objects are similar. They may look alike, or they may have similar characteristics. Take your colleagues, for example. Although each colleague is an individual, each person shares common characteristics with every other person that distinguish them from stoplights, furniture, or birds.

We may say that objects that have the same characteristics belong to the same class. We can readily identify some classes:

- The class of colleague objects

- The class of stoplight objects

- The class of furniture objects

- The class of bird objects

- The class of Screen Objects

The class is the set of all objects, not one object in particular. So, there is a class of stoplight objects, but the stoplight down the street is one object. Each colleague is one object, as is the desk you use.

Furthermore, classes can be subdivided to help you understand the world better. For example:

- You can split the class *furniture* into desks, chairs, lamps, beds, etc.

- You can classify birds into many species.

- You can classify your colleagues.

Parent Classes and Child Classes

Figure 17.1 shows the class *person,* which has the descendents *male person* and *female person.* It then shows a few objects of these classes in the bottom row.

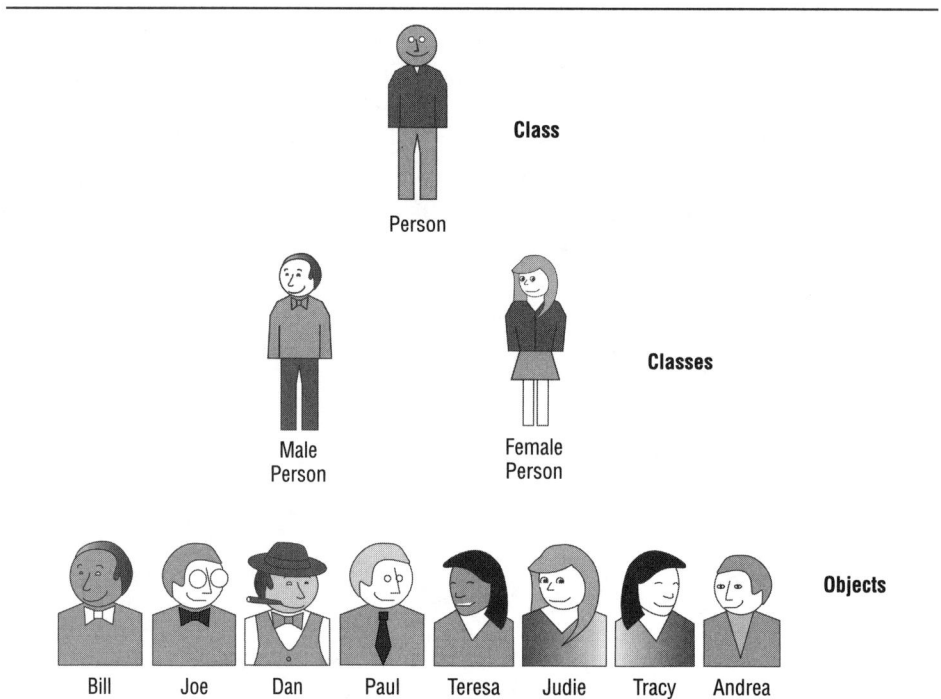

FIGURE 17.1: Classes and objects

There is more to this simple picture than what meets the eye at first. If you look carefully, you will notice that all the pictures "descend" from the one at the top. The picture illustrating the class *person* defines the basic body used in the next classes.

From the class *person* we derived two other classes, *male person* and *female person.* Keep in mind that both *male* and *female* are also *person.* Both classes have all the basic attributes of a *person,* except that when you designate a person as *male* or *female,* you give them additional attributes that are undetermined in the class *person.* In our overly simplified world, the *male* has pants, and the *female* has skirts and longer hair.

Remember that a derived (or descendent) class has all the attributes of the base (or parent) class. Therefore, a *male person* is also a *person.*

Notice also that a derived class designates a *special kind* of class within the existing base class. *Male person* is a special kind of *person. Female person* is another special kind of *person.* Similarly, a `Circle` is a special kind of `ScreenObj`.

Objects—Particular Instances of Classes

Person, male person, and *female person* are still vague. There are many people who can be denoted by those class names. If you want to refer to a specific individual, you have to point out one particular *person*—a particular *instance* of that class.

Again, our simplified example (shown in Figure 17.1) shows a group of individuals at the bottom. They are specific. We are now talking about Bill, Joe, Dan, and Paul, as well as about Teresa, Judie, Tracy, and Andrea. Bill is not a class! Bill is one specific guy who happens to be a *male person.* Bill is an object that belongs to the class *male person.* Joe, Dan, and Paul are also objects that belong to the class *male person.* Similarly, Teresa, Judie, Tracy, and Andrea are objects that belong to the class *female person.* All these objects also belong to the class *person.*

In your programs, you can also use objects to represent the real world. You have used objects of class `athlete`, Sal and Sally. You have used an object of class `Robot`, Tracer. You have used circles, squares, boxes, and clocks.

Special Kinds of Screen Objects

The idea of deriving a class from another one was exploited extensively with Screen Objects. `ScreenObj` was a class that allowed you to place, resize, erase, show, and color objects on the screen. The class `Box` is derived from `ScreenObj`. In other words, `Box` is a special kind of `ScreenObj`. You can do anything with a `Box` that you can do with a `ScreenObj`. However, you can also label and "say" something with a `Box`. The idea is very simple: if you want to create a *special class* that is derived from an existing class, you have to do the following things:

- Give a name to the new class, and indicate the existing class from which it is derived. For example, the new class could be `Box`, and we would indicate that it is derived from `ScreenObj`. The class could also be `athlete`, and we would indicate that it is derived from `Stage`.

- Declare any variables or objects that will exist in the new class that did not exist in the base class. Each object of the class `Box` may have data, such as the label and the message to be printed. These data did not exist in a plain `ScreenObj`. Each object of class `athlete` will have several objects: head, trunk, left arm, right arm, left leg, and right leg. These objects did not exist in a plain Stage.

• Declare and write the code for any functions that will exist in the new class that did not exist in the base class. Each object of the class Box must know how to label and say. Each object of the class athlete must know how to assume ready, up, left, right, etc.

Objects of the new derived class possess all the data and functionality of the base class, as well as the new data and functions that were specifically added when the derived class was created. We only have to write programs for the functions that we are adding. We can completely reuse all the software that existed.

Figure 17.2 shows the relationship between a base class ScreenObj and the derived classes Circle and Box. An object of the class ScreenObj contains the data and functions listed in the inner *ScreenObj* rectangles. An object of the class Box contains the data and functions listed in the outer *Box* rectangle.

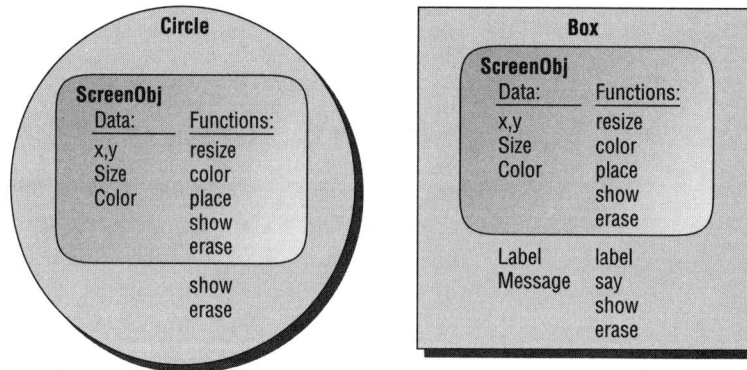

FIGURE 17.2: ScreenObj and its derived classes Circle and Box

Notice that the *Box* rectangle contains the *ScreenObj* rectangle. Therefore, a Box contains its own data and function members, as well as those inherited from the ScreenObj class. Similarly, objects of class Circle contain all the members enclosed in the *Circle* circle, which, of course, also includes the *ScreenObj* rectangle.

Inheriting Characteristics from Base Classes

Another way to represent the relationship between classes is to use a hierarchical diagram, as shown in Figure 17.3. In this diagram, each box represents a class of objects. The classes that are used as bases from which to derive new classes are shown above, and are linked to the derived classes below. For example, the class ScreenObj is a base for the classes Circle, Square, Box, and Stage. The class Stage is a base for the class athlete. Also, it is not shown, but the class athlete is a base for the class Robot (no wonder they look so much alike).

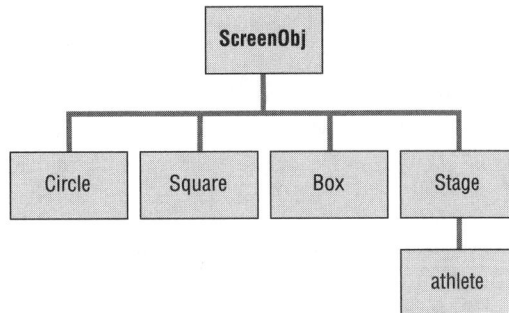

FIGURE 17.3: Base and derived classes

C++ nomenclature includes base and derived classes. It is also common to refer to parent and child classes, or to refer to ancestor and descendent classes (instead of base and derived classes).

A derived class maintains all the characteristics of the base class. This is called *inheritance.* The derived class has either additional data or additional functions (or both).

An object belonging to a derived class may still be considered as an object of the base class: a Circle is a ScreenObj, because you can use a Circle anywhere you can use a ScreenObj. The opposite is not true, however.

NOTE   Although every Circle is a ScreenObj, a ScreenObj is not necessarily a Circle.

Replacing Inappropriate Inherited Functions

Compared to ScreenObj, Circle does not have any additional data members. However, you may wonder why we repeat the member functions show and erase in each class. After all, don't circles and boxes inherit these member functions from the base class ScreenObj?

They do, but isn't the procedure for drawing a circle different from that of drawing a box? What kind of shape will be drawn if we use the show function of a Screen Object? There may be cases in which the inherited function is not appropriate. You must supply another function to perform the equivalent action.

In this example, although a Screen Object has coordinates, size, and color, it does not have a defined shape. Therefore, the show function cannot show anything! Boxes, circles, and squares have a shape and can be drawn, but the procedure that draws a box is not the same as the one that draws the circle or the square. Each of these classes will have a different show function.

But what happens to the inherited show function? It *is* inherited, isn't it?

Yes, it is. However, it is automatically understood that if you use an object of class Circle and you issue show, the show that is used is the one defined for the class Circle. This is the essence of *polymorphism,* which we will discuss later.

> **NOTE** Even though the show function for ScreenObj is fake, it must exist. If a function prototype is not included in the class declaration, the compiler does not allow any objects of that class to use that member function.

The *athlete* Class

The class athlete descends from Stage, which, in turn, descends from ScreenObj. All objects of class ScreenObj have a set of variables *x, y,* and *z* that represents the screen coordinates of the center of the object. Although there are only two dimensions to the screen, the *z* coordinate may be used to place an object behind another. Here is the declaration of data members for class ScreenObj.

```
protected:
    float x,y,z;              // Screen coordinates of object
    int colorbrush,colorpen;  // Inside color and contour
    float size,length;
```

Since all these data members are *protected*, they are not only inherited, but also accessible from the descendent classes, such as Stage and athlete.

Deriving More Classes

In our next example, we will derive two new classes from athlete:

- runner will contain objects similar to athletes, but it will have the ability to "run." Runners will move their legs and arms while stepping to a neighboring location on the screen.

- skater will also have the ability to "run." However, since it will run while wearing skates, the skater will slide over a few neighboring locations before switching from one leg to the other.

The most tedious task in this implementation is the simulation of the arm and leg movements. You could do this by studying how the athlete is built, but I will save you some time and give you a couple of functions, stepleft and stepright that will do the trick.

Figure 17.4 shows athletes stepping right and stepping left. The animated sequence—ready, stepright, ready, stepleft—as shown in Figure 17.5, will create the illusion that the athlete is actually moving their arms and legs.

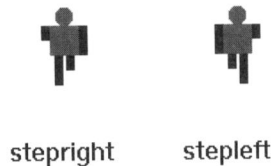

stepright   stepleft

FIGURE 17.4: An athlete stepping right and stepping left

FIGURE 17.5: An animated sequence for running

The function `stepright` draws the athlete with the right leg and the left arm raised (from the viewer's vantage point). The function `stepleft` does the same with the left leg and the right arm. Both functions can receive a floating point argument that expresses the time, in seconds, that we want to hold the picture in the given position. Here are the functions that can be found in `c6run.h` (the values of `armsize` and `armwidth` are already defined in `franca.h`. They are included in the initial comment so you remember what they are):

```
// const int armsize=20,armwidth=6;
void runner::stepright(float time)      // c6run.h
{
    Clock any;
    erase();
    leftarm.resize(armsize/2,armwidth);
    leftarm.place((x-(armsize+armwidth)/2.),y-armsize/4);
    rightleg.resize(armsize/2,armwidth);
    rightleg.place(x+(armsize/2.-armwidth),y+3*armsize/4);
    show();
    any.wait(time);
}
void runner::stepleft(float time)
{
    Clock any;
    erase();
    rightarm.resize(armsize/2,armwidth);
    rightarm.place(x+(armsize+armwidth)/2,y-armsize/4);
    leftleg.resize(armsize/2,armwidth);
    leftleg.place(x-(armsize/2-armwidth),y+3*armsize/4);
    show();
    any.wait(time);
}
```

Athletes That Run and Skate

Since we know how to draw the athlete in these new positions, the `run()` function essentially consists of the following steps:

- Step left
- Ready
- Move one position
- Step right

- Ready

- Move one position

TIP

Remember to erase the pictures immediately before you move them, because the erase function simply redraws the picture in white at the current location. If you move the picture and then erase it, a piece of the picture that was drawn in the old location will not be erased.

It is very simple to move the runner. Since the runner is an athlete (and, consequently, a `Stage` object), we can use the `place()` member function to place the runner anywhere we want. Moreover, since we already know the x and y coordinates, we can easily figure out where the next location will be.

In this implementation, we are making the runner go only from the left to the right of the screen, which means that the x coordinate will increase with each movement.

Here is one implementation of the `run()` member function:

```
void runner::run()
{
    stepleft(.1);
    erase();
    ready(.1);
    stepright(.1);
    erase();
    ready(.1);
    erase();
    place(x+1,y);
    ready(0.);
}
```

Make sure you do not update the value of the screen coordinates yourself. The `place()` member function will update the coordinates of all the objects contained in that `Stage` object by computing the difference between the new coordinates (given as arguments to `place()`) and the previous coordinates (the values of x and y).

NOTE

If you update the value of x, or use x++ as the parameter, the new and old coordinates will be the same, and no movement will take place.

The declaration of the class `runner` is as follows:

```
class runner: public athlete
{
  protected:
   void stepleft(float);
   void stepright(float);
  public:
   void run();
}; // Never forget the semicolon!
```

It is useful to keep the `stepleft` and `stepright` member functions `protected`, because it will make it impossible for a common piece of program to use these functions, but it will allow member functions of descendent classes (such as `skater`) to use them.

The declaration of the class `skater` can be as follows:

```
class skater:public runner
{
 public:
   void run();
};
```

Overriding an Inherited Function: Polymorphism

Notice that `stepleft` and `stepright` are not declared again in the example above. They are inherited from the base class `runner`. You may think it is odd that we are declaring a member function with the same name as one that is already inherited! What will happen in this case? When you tell a skater to run, the object will use the `run` member function that was specifically declared for the class `skater`, and will not use the inherited one. Essentially, this is what we call *polymorphism* in object-oriented programming. You can specify a different way of handling a given request (`run()`), according to the object class that you are using.

The `run()` function for the skater simulates the skater sliding for a distance while alternately standing on each foot. Here is one implementation:

```
void skater::run()
{
  for(int i=1;i<=5;i++)// Move 5 steps
  { // Standing on left foot:
    stepleft(.1);
    erase();
```

```
      place(x+1,y);
      ready(0.);
  }

  for(i=1;i<=5;i++)     // Move 5 steps
  { // Standing on right foot:
    stepright(.1);
    erase();
    place(x+1,y);
  }
  ready(0.);
}
```

You can make both athletes run by using a program such as the following one:

```
void mainprog()
{
  runner jane;
  jane.place(20,80);
  skater julia;
  int k;
  for (k=1;k<=10;k++)
  julia.run();
  for (k=1;k<=10;k++)
  jane.run();
}
```

What if you want to make the skater run like a runner? She should be able to do this, since the skater is still a runner, after all. All you have to do is to use the `run()` member function that the skater is entitled to as a member of the class `runner`, instead of using the standard member function belonging to the class `skater`. To do this, qualify the `run()` function with the class name `runner`. In this example, it would suffice to include the following statements:

```
    for (k=1;k<=10;k++)
    julia.runner::run();
```

to have Julia run as a runner.

Polymorphism Defined

Polymorphism is a term originating from Greek. It means "many shapes." Objects that share common ancestry can assume many shapes, and still be treated the same. Notice that both the runner and the skater can `run`. Yet, the way a skater runs is not the same as the way a runner does. The nice thing is that you don't have to constantly worry about this. You can just tell either one of them to run, and they will rush off in whichever way they know.

This concept was already explored with the Screen Objects. All of them could be shown, erased, and placed anywhere. Nevertheless, the way we show a square is not the same way we show a circle, an athlete, a robot, a stage, etc. Objects of the class ScreenObj have many shapes indeed!

The *Stage* Class and Polymorphism

Stage objects are a particularly interesting case, since a Stage object may contain several other Screen Objects, including other Stage objects. For example, you can insert an athlete (whose attributes are inherited from the Stage class) and a runner (whose attributes are also inherited from the Stage class). When the Stage object is told to show itself, it will know precisely how to show each part of itself. However, we have not yet explored fully the polymorphism capability.

For example, suppose that you have a function that takes a runner as an argument.

```
void march(runner volunteer)
{
    volunteer.run();
}
```

If you have the following program:

```
runner smith;
skater yamaguchi;
march (smith);
march (yamaguchi);
```

you might expect that it will cause smith to run like a runner and yamaguchi to run like a skater. This will not happen, though. The function march() knows only that a runner will be used. When this function is compiled (translated into machine language), there is no information specifying which runner will be used.

It is only when the program is executed that the function will receive either smith or yamaguchi. However, at that point it is a bit too late! The function is already translated into machine language, and it thought that using the run() function that was defined for a runner was the appropriate thing to do.

To postpone the decision to choose the kind of run() function to use, we can specify that the runner's run() function is a virtual function. This is done by simply including, in the declaration of the runner class, the keyword virtual in the run() function prototype. For example:

```
virtual void run();
```

instructs the compiler to avoid sticking to the runner class's run() function, allowing it to be replaced later by any other version. Of course, this makes your program a little larger and slower.

Try These for Fun. . .

- Modify the skater::run() member function so that the skater has to take some steps (running as a runner) before being able to actually skate.

- Since both skaters and runners are athletes, they should be able to behave like athletes, as well. Write a program that declares a runner and a skater, and have them perform a jumping jack, then run, and then do another jumping jack.

- Although a runner is an athlete, an athlete is not a runner. If you declare an athlete and order the athlete to run(), what will happen?

- The function jumpjack you developed that takes an argument of class athlete can also take runner and skater as arguments. Try this and see how it works. C++ is severe about making a correspondence of type between the parameters defined in the function and the actual arguments used in the function call. Why is it that you can use the jumpjack function with a runner, while it was designed to be used with an athlete?

- Write a function goaway(runner someone). This function should make the runner that was passed as an argument run 10 steps. Use this function with an object of class runner, and with an object of class skater. Notice the results.

- Include a constructor function for the class skater that includes a skateboard at the skater's feet. You can easily construct the skateboard with a rectangle and two circles.

> **TIP** Since the skater descends from Stage, you can simply insert() the rectangle and the two wheels.

- The wagon class as implemented does not allow the user to place, erase, and show a wagon. This is because wagon is not a descendent of ScreenObj. Implement another version of the wagon class by deriving it from Stage. In this case, you don't have to declare a Stage object—the class is already a Stage object.

Are You Experienced?

Now you can. . .

☑ **Derive a new class from an existing class**

☑ **Inherit data and functions from a base class**

☑ **Manipulate objects in the same class hierarchy as if they are alike**

356-555-3398.

PROGRAMMERS
C, C, VB, Cobol, exp. Call 534-555-6543 or fax 534-555-6544.

PROGRAMMING
MRFS Inc. is looking for a Sr. Windows, NT developer. Reqs. 3-5 yrs. Exp. In C under Windows, Win95 & NT, using Visual C, Excl. OO design & implementation skills a must. OLE2 & ODBC are a plus. Exd. Salary & bnfts. Resume & salary history to HR. 8779 HighTech Way, Computer City, AR

PROGRAMMERS
Contractors Wanted for short & long term assignments: Visual C, MFC Unix C/C, SQL Oracle Dev elop ers PC Help Desk Support Windows NT & NetWareTelecommunications Visual Basic, Access, HTMT, CGI, Perl MMI & Co., 885-555-9933

PROGRAMMER World Wide Web Links wants your HTML & Photoshop skills. Develop great WWW sites. Local & global customers. Send samples & resume to WWWL 2000 Apple Road, Santa Rosa, CA.

TECHNICAL WRITER Software firm seeks writer/editor for manuals, research notes, project mgmt. Min 2 years tech. writing, DTP & programming experience. Send resume & writing samples to: Software Systems, Dallas, TX.

TECHNICAL Software development firm looking for Tech Trainers. Ideal candidates have programming experience in Visual C, HTML & JAVA. Need quick self starter. Call (443) 555-6868 for interview.

TECHNICAL WRITER/ Premier Computer Corp is seeking a combination of technical skills, knowledge and experience in the following areas: UNIX, Windows 95/NT, Visual Basic, on-line help & documentation, and the Internet. Candidates must possess excellent writing skills, and be comfortable working in a quality vs. deadline driven environment. Competitive salary. Fax resume & samples to Karen Fields, Premier Computer Corp., 444 Industrial Blvd. Concord, CA. Or send to our website at www.premier.com.

WEB DESIGNER
BA/BS or equivalent programming/multimedia production. 3 years of experience in use and design of WWW services streaming audio and video HTML, PERL, CGI, GIF, JPEG. Demonstrated interpersonal, organization, communication, multi-tasking skills. Send resume to The Learning People at www.learning.com.

WEBMASTER-TECHNICAL
BSCS or equivalent, 2 years of experience in CGI, Windows 95/NT, UNIX, C, Java, Perl. Demonstrated ability to design, code, debug and test on-line services. Send resume to The Learning People at www.learning.com.

PROGRAMMER World Wide Web Links wants your HTML & Photoshop skills. Develop great WWW sites. Local & global customers. Send sam-

PROGRAMMERS Multiple short term assignments available: Visual C, 3 positions SQL ServerNT Server, 2 positions JAVA & HTML, long term NetWare Various locations. Call for more info. 356-555-3398.

PROGRAMMERS
C, C, VB, Cobol, exp.
Call 534-555-6543
or fax 534-555-6544.

PROGRAMMING
MRFS Inc. is looking for a Sr. Windows NT developer. Reqs. 3-5 yrs. Exp. In C under Windows, Win95 & NT, using Visual C, Excl. OO design & implementation skills a must. OLE2 & ODBC are a plus. Excl. Salary & bnfts. Resume & salary history to HR. 8779 HighTech Way, Computer City, AR

PROGRAMMERS/ Contractors Wanted for short & long term assignments: Visual C, MFC Unix C/C, SQL Oracle Developers PC Help Desk Support Windows NT & NetWareTelecommunications Visual Basic, Access, HTMT, CGI, Perl MMI & Co., 885-555-9933

PROGRAMMER World Wide Web Links wants your HTML & Photoshop skills. Develop great WWW sites. Local & global customers. Send samples & resume to WWWL 2000 Apple Road, Santa Rosa, CA.

TECHNICAL WRITER Software firm seeks writer/editor for manuals, research notes, project mgmt. Min 2 years tech. writing, DTP & programming experience. Send resume & writing samples to: Software Systems, Dallas, TX.

COMPUTER PROGRAMMER
Ad agency seeks programmer w/exp. in UNIX/NT Platforms, Web Server, CGI/Perl. Programmer Position avail. on a project basis with the possibility to move into F/T. Fax resume & salary req. to R. Jones 334-555-8332

TECHNICAL WRITER Premier Computer Corp is seeking a combination of technical skills, knowledge and experience in the following areas: UNIX, Windows 95/NT, Visual Basic, on-line help & documentation, and the Internet. Candidates must possess excellent writing skills, and be comfortable working in a quality vs. deadline driven environment. Competitive salary. Fax resume & samples to Karen Fields, Premier Computer Corp., 444 Industrial Blvd. Concord, CA. Or send to our website at www.premier.com.

WEB DESIGNER
BA/BS or equivalent programming/multimedia production. 3 years of experience in use and design of WWW services streaming audio and video HTML, PERL, CGI, GIF, JPEG. Demonstrated interpersonal, organization, communication, multi-tasking skills. Send resume to The Learning People at www.learning.com.

WEBMASTER-TECHNICAL
BSCS or equivalent, 2 years of experience in CGI, Windows 95/NT,

COMPUTERS Small Web Design Firm seeks indiv w/NT, Webserver & Database management exp. Fax resume to 556-555-4221.

COMPUTER Visual C/C, Visual Basic Exp'd Systems Analysts/ Programmers for growing software dev. team in Roseburg. Computer Science or related degree preferred. Develop adv. Engineering applications for engineering firm. Fax resume to 707-555-8744.

COMPUTER Web Master for dynamic SF internet co. Site, Dev, test, coord, train, 2 yrs prog. Exp. C C Web C, FTP. Fax resume to Best Staffing 845-555-7722.

COMPUTERS/ QA SOFTWARE TESTERS Qualified candidates should have 2 yrs exp. performing integration & system testing using automated testing tools. Experienced in documentation preparation & programming languages (Access, C, FoxPro) are a plus. Financial or banking customer service support is required along with excellent verbal & written communication skills with multi levels of end-users. Send resume to KKUP Enterprises, 45 Orange Blvd Orange, CA.

COMPUTERS Programmer/Analyst Design and maintain C based SQL database applications. Required skills: Visual Basic, C, SQL, ODBC. Document existing and new applications. Novell or NT exp. a plus. Fax resume & salary history to 235-555-9935.

GRAPHIC DESIGNER
Webmaster's Weekly is seeking a creative Graphic Designer to design high impact marketing collateral, including direct mail promo's, CD-ROM packages, ads and WWW pages. Must be able to juggle multiple projects and learn new skills on the job very rapidly. Web design experience a big plus, technical troubleshooting also a plus. Call 435-555-1235.

GRAPHICS - ART DIRECTOR - WEB-MULTIMEDIA
Leading internet development company has an outstanding opportunity for a talented, high-end Web Experienced Art Director. In addition to a great portfolio and fresh ideas, the ideal candidate has excellent communication and presentation skills. Working as a team with innovative producers and programmers, you will create dynamic, interactive web sites and application interfaces. Some programming experience required. Send samples and resume to: SuperSites, 333 Main, Seattle, WA.

COMPUTER PROGRAMMER
Ad agency seeks programmer w/exp. in UNIX/NT Platforms, Web Server, CGI/Perl. Programmer Position avail. on a project basis with the possibility to move into F/T. Fax resume & salary req. to R. Jones 334-555-8332

PROGRAMMERS / Established software company seeks program-

ment. Must be a self-starter, energetic, organized. Must have 2 yrs web experience. Programming plus. Call 985-555-9854.

PROGRAMMERS Multiple short term assignments available: Visual C, 3 positions SQL ServerNT Server, 2 positions JAVA & HTML, long term NetWare Various locations. Call more info. 356-555-3398.

PROGRAMMERS
C, C, VB, Cobol, exp. Call 534-555-6543 or fax 534-555-6544.

PROGRAMMING
MRFS Inc. is looking for a Windows NT developer. Reqs. yrs. Exp. In C under Windows Win95 & NT using Visual C, E OO design & implementation s a must. OLE2 & ODBC are a p Excl. Salary & bnfts. Resume salary history to HR. 8779 HighT Way, Computer City, AR

PROGRAMMERS/ Contract Wanted for short & long term ass ments: Visual C, MFCUnix C/C, Oracle Developers PC Help D Support Windows NT & NetW Telecommunications Visual Ba Access, HTMT, CGI, Perl MMI & 885-555-9933

PROGRAMMER World Wide Links wants your HTML & Photos skills. Develop great WWW si Local & global customers. Send s ples & resume to WWWL, 2 Apple Road, Santa Rosa, CA.

TECHNICAL WRITER Software seeks writer/editor for manu research notes, project mgmt. M years tech. writing, DTP & progr ming experience. Send resum writing samples to: Softw Systems, Dallas, TX.

TECHNICAL Software develope firm looking for Tech Trainers. I candidates have programming e rience in Visual C, HTML & J Need quick self starter. Call (4 555-6868 for interview.

TECHNICAL WRITER Pre Computer Corp is seeking a co nation of technical skills, knowle and experience in the follow areas: UNIX, Windows 95/NT, V Basic, on-line help & documenta and the internet. Candidates possess excellent writing skills, be comfortable working in a qu vs. deadline driven environm Competitive salary. Fax resum samples to Karen Fields, Pre Computer Corp., 444 Industrial Concord, CA. Or send to our w at www.premier.com.

WEB DESIGNER
BA/BS or equivalent prog ming/multimedia production years of experience in use design of WWW services strea audio and video HTML, PERL, GIF, JPEG. Demonstrated inte sonal, organization, communica multi-tasking skills. Send resum The Learning People at www.le ing.com.

WEBMASTER-TECHNIC

Developing More Advanced Applications

- ❑ Completing a short project—an improved point-of-sale terminal
- ❑ Choosing a programmer-user interface
- ❑ Choosing an end-user interface
- ❑ Choosing and implementing classes
- ❑ Completing another short project—a satellite simulation

The ability to develop applications is the essence of the programmer's profession. This ability has been continuously developed in most Skills in this book. In Skill 18, you will continue to improve it by completing two short projects:

- Developing an improved point-of-sale terminal using classes

- Developing a satellite simulation using classes

Short Project 1—an Improved Point-of-Sale Terminal

You will now learn how to transform the point-of-sale terminal you developed in Skill 9 into an object. The goal is to use as many of the features as possible that were discussed in Skill 9 (using the c3sale2.cpp program).

The functionality of the terminal will be the same as the previous terminal's functionality. All I want to do now is to show you how to transform the terminal into an object. This will allow you to work on interesting expansions in the next Skills. You may benefit from looking back to Skill 9, and from running the c3sale2.cpp program once more.

Choosing the Programmer-User Interface

As you progress in your programming career, more people will use the programs that you develop. Some people may use your software as end users. For example, a clerk at a store using your terminal program is an end user. This person does not know how your program was built. All he or she cares to know is how to hit the right keys to do his or her job. However, there is another kind of user of whom you must be aware.

The Programmer User

In a world in which software is extremely complex, programmers use programs that were developed by other programmers to produce better software. You have been using the programs in franca.h, which I developed. You are a programmer user of my software. However, you use this software to help produce your own software, which may have an end user who knows nothing about programming.

When you design software for programmer users, you must also exercise care to make it simple to use.

The current project consists of creating a class of point-of-sale terminals, so an object of this class can be used in a program to generate a final product—the terminal.

In this case, you will implement the class, and you will be the one to use it. You will be your own programmer user. However, this may not always be the case!

Interfacing

There may be many ways to implement the terminal as a class. One possibility is to have a terminal that is only created and told to operate. This means that the main program, besides creating the terminal, only has to issue a call to one function to put it to work.

The main function could look as follows:

```
void mainprog()
{
  terminal cashregister;
  cashregister.operate();
}
```

This will indeed be a very simple interface for the programmer who uses your class.

A class that does everything by itself, like this one, may not be the best idea. You may consider including some operations that allow the programmer to manipulate the object with greater flexibility. For example, you could provide member functions that allow the programmer to write to the boxes or to process one customer at a time.

Choosing the End-User Interface

The end-user interface will be the same one used in c3sale2.cpp. It is a good idea to keep the user interface as long as the clients are happy with it. Anytime you change the user interface—move a box from one place to another, ask a question in a different way, etc.—the user will spend some time to get used to the changes. Sometimes the user will not like the changes!

Declaring and Defining Classes

The terminal class should contain most of the variables and objects that were present in the previous program. This could lead to the following declaration:

```
class terminal
{
 protected:
  float tax,amount,price,saletotal,change;
  Box Price,Cur_Total;
  Box Saletotal,Amount,Change;
  void items(); // Process items in a sale
 public:
  terminal();
  void operate();
};
```

Notice that in the c3sale2.cpp program, you could initialize the boxes. In this case, you cannot initialize the boxes in the class declaration. This task has to be left to the constructor.

NOTE   No initial values can be set in a class declaration.

The Constructor Code

The constructor code is relatively simple. The only reason it looks a little long is that the boxes have to be positioned and provided with labels.

```
terminal::terminal()
{
  tax=ask("Enter the sale tax %")/100.;
  Price.place(450,100);
  Price.label("Price:");
  Cur_Total.place(450,140);
  Cur_Total.label("Subtotal:");
  Saletotal.place(450,180);
  Saletotal.label("Total Sale:");
  Amount.place(450,220);
  Amount.label("Amount Tendered");
  Change.place(450,260);
  Change.label("Change:");
}
```

Figure 18.1 shows these boxes after processing a sale.

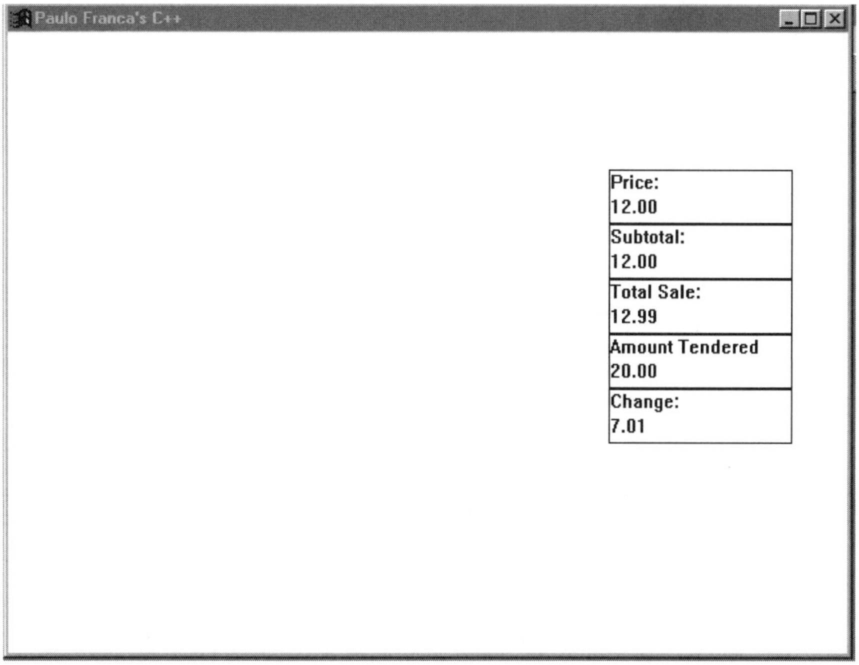

FIGURE 18.1: Boxes after a sale has been processed

The *operate()* Member Function

The operate() member function actually makes the terminal work. You may notice that this function closely resembles what was done
in the previous program. A loop handles the sale to each customer. After each sale, the total is displayed and the change is computed.

To simplify the code, the loop that handles each item in a sale is handled by another function, items(). Still, this is just like the c3sale2.cpp program. However, notice that the programmer user is not supposed to invoke the items() member function. This function was designed to be used internally only. For this reason, this member function is not public.

Here is the code for the `operate()` function:

```
void terminal::operate()
{
    float tendered,change;
    for(;;)
    {
        saletotal=0.;
        Price.say(" ");
        Cur_Total.say(" ");
        Saletotal.say(" ");
        Amount.say(" ");
        Change.say(" ");
        items();
        Saletotal.say(saletotal);
        amount=ask("Enter amount tendered:");
        Amount.say(amount);
        change=amount-saletotal;
        Change.say(change);
        if(!yesno("Another customer?"))break;
    }
}
```

Notice that all the values and the boxes displaying them are cleared at the beginning of each sale. Then, the `items()` member function handles all the items in the sale. After doing this, all the boxes are updated with the pertinent information.

> **WARNING** The program above uses two very similar names for different things: there is a box named Change (capitalized) and a variable named change (lowercased).

The *items()* Member Function

The `items()` function serves a purpose similar to that of the `getitems()` function used in `c3sale2.cpp`. It adds all the items purchased by the same customer.

The code for the `items()` function is as follows:

```
void terminal::items()
{
    for(;;)
    {
        price=ask("enter the price:");
        saletotal=saletotal+price;
        Price.say(price);
        Cur_Total.say(saletotal);
```

```
        if(!yesno("Another item?")) break;
      }
      saletotal=saletotal*(1+tax);
      Saletotal.say(saletotal);
    }
```

IMPROVEMENTS

The most relevant improvement to this terminal would be to replace input from a price with input from a code. This is what most present-day point-of-sale terminals do. Currently, you don't have the means to make this improvement. Further versions of this project will be presented in upcoming Skills.

Skill 18

The Complete Program Listings

The complete code for this project can be found in c6term.cpp and c6term.h.

The Main Program *c6term.cpp*

Here is the code for c6term.cpp:

```
#include "franca.h"
#include "c6term.h"
void mainprog()
{
  terminal cashregister;
  cashregister.operate();
}
```

The Header File *c6term.h*

Here is the code for c6term.h:

```
#ifndef C6TERM_H
#define C6TERM_H
#include "franca.h"
class terminal
{
```

```
protected:
 float tax,amount,price,saletotal,change;
 Box Price,Cur_Total;
 Box Saletotal,Amount,Change;
 void items(); // Process items in a sale
public:
 terminal();
 void operate();
};
terminal::terminal()
{
  tax=ask("Enter the sale tax %")/100.;
  Price.place(450,100);
  Price.label("Price:");
  Cur_Total.place(450,140);
  Cur_Total.label("Subtotal:");
  Saletotal.place(450,180);
  Saletotal.label("Total Sale:");
  Amount.place(450,220);
  Amount.label("Amount Tendered");
  Change.place(450,260);
  Change.label("Change:");
}
void terminal::items()
{
  for(;;)
  {
    price=ask("enter the price:");
    saletotal=saletotal+price;
    Price.say(price);
    Cur_Total.say(saletotal);
    if(!yesno("Another item?")) break;
  }
  saletotal=saletotal*(1+tax);
  Saletotal.say(saletotal);
}
void terminal::operate()
{
    float tendered,change;
    for(;;)
    {
      saletotal=0.;
      Price.say(" ");
      Cur_Total.say(" ");
      Saletotal.say(" ");
```

```
        Amount.say(" ");
        Change.say(" ");
        items();
        Saletotal.say(saletotal);
        amount=ask("Enter amount tendered:");
        Amount.say(amount);
        change=amount-saletotal;
        Change.say(change);
        if(!yesno("Another customer?"))break;
    }
}
#endif
```

Short Project 2—Satellites

The program c5stars.cpp, developed as a project in Skill 15, will now be reviewed and improved with the use of objects. Indeed, the circles were used to represent a star (the Sun), a planet (Earth), and a satellite (the Moon).

Generally speaking, these objects orbit other objects at a particular distance and angular velocity. If you think abstractly instead of using the usual nomenclature that differentiates between stars, planets, and satellites, you may realize that all of them can be treated like satellites.

Indeed, Earth, as well as the other planets in our solar system, is a satellite orbiting the Sun. You can consider that the Sun itself is orbiting any distant body at speed zero, or that it is orbiting itself. This abstract thinking leads to the idea of creating a new class of objects—satellites.

Satellites can be used to simplify the c5stars.cpp program, and can also be used in other applications.

A satellite can be represented by a circle that moves in a circular pattern around a specific point or, to be more interesting, around another satellite (including itself). Besides all the usual features of a circle, satellites have the following features:

- A planet to orbit. This planet gives the coordinates of the point they are orbiting.

- A distance from that planet. This is the radius of the orbit.

- An angular velocity for the movement.

- A current angle in the orbit. This angle and the radius constitute the polar coordinates of the satellite, relative to the planet.

In addition, satellites should know how to move from one place to the next place as time passes. However, instead of using a time-dependent equation to compute the position, you can define a function move that will be invoked for each drawing frame (every 30th of a second). This function computes the coordinates of the satellite after each time frame elapses.

Designing the *satellite* Class

Here is the declaration of the satellite class:

```
class satellite: public Circle
{
  protected:
   float xplanet,yplanet;
   float radius,omega,wspeed;
  public:
   satellite();
   move();
};
```

Data members include the planet's coordinates (notice that you don't need the planet—you only need to know where it is), the orbit's radius (radius), the current angle (omega), and the angular velocity per unit of time (wspeed).

There are a few design choices concerning the angular velocity. Ultimately, you need to know how many radians the satellite moves per time frame (a 30th of a second). However, you may choose to allow a user of your class (including yourself) to specify it as degrees per second, even though you convert this value and store it as radians per time frame.

Using a Constructor

A constructor function is always desirable, so we can color, size, place, and perform other initialization tasks with the object. The move function, discussed in an earlier Skill, should be called to move the satellite to a new location in the orbit after the time frame has elapsed.

It is clear that you could use a function such as move(t) to determine the current time and to compute the position at this time.

Unfortunately, the class declaration above is not appropriate, yet. How will we set values for the data members?

One alternative is to allow the constructor to take these values as parameters. This would work, but once a value is set, it cannot be changed unless one of the following items is true:

- The data member is public.

- There is a member function that allows you to change the values.

Even though you may think that some of the data members, such as the radius, the coordinates of the planet, or the angular velocity, will never change, you may be amazed by what you can accomplish with a little flexibility.

Member functions can be included to change the following items:

- The coordinates of the planet

- The radius

- The angular velocity

Specifying a Coordinate System for the Satellites

Finally, as you may have noticed in `c5stars.cpp`, it will come in very handy to convert from polar coordinates to cartesian coordinates. Include a `polarxy()` function in the class. Here is the declaration proposed for this design:

```
class satellite: public Circle
{
  protected:
    float xplanet,yplanet;
    float radius,omega,wspeed;
    void polarxy(float r,float theta,float x0,
                 float y0,float &x,float &y);
  public:
    satellite();
    void center(float x,float y);
    void dist(float rad);
    void angle(float ang);
    void speed(float ws);
    void move();
    void center(satellite &another);
};
```

There are two `center()` functions that allow you to change the planet's coordinates. These functions allow you to specify that a planet revolves around a given point (x,y) or around another planet.

In this case, the `polarxy()` function can be modified so that no arguments are needed. This may be a good idea, but it is left unmodified, so we can reuse the same code.

Implementing the Class

Once the class declaration is ready, the code for the functions can be developed.

The Constructor Code

Here is the constructor code:

```
satellite::satellite()
{
    color(2);
    xplanet=yplanet=0;
    radius=0;
    omega=wspeed=0;
}
```

There is nothing special about this constructor. Notice that the satellite's color can be modified at any point, since the `color()` function is public for the circles.

Changing the Center

The functions to change the planet's coordinates are as follows:

```
void satellite::center(float xc,float yc)
{
    xplanet=xc;
    yplanet=yc;
}
void satellite::center(satellite &another)
{
    center(another.x,another.y);
}
```

Do you see anything interesting in this code? Why does the second function use the *x* and *y* coordinates of the other planet? Aren't these coordinates protected?

Indeed, they are! However, protected members can be used by member functions of the same or derived class. Since the second function is a member function for `satellite`, which is derived from `Circle`, it is possible to access the coordinates. Not only the coordinates of this satellite are accessible, but the coordinates of any other satellite that is used inside the member function are accessible.

It makes the use of satellites much more convenient to include the second version of the center() function. It is definitely easier to say

```
Moon.center(Earth);
```

than it is to determine Earth's coordinates to include in the function call.

Updating the Radius, Angle, and Angular Velocity

The functions to update the radius, the current angle, and the angular velocity are simple.

```
void satellite::dist(float rad)
{
    radius=rad;
}
void satellite::angle(float ang)
{
    omega=ang;
}
void satellite::speed(float ws)
{
    wspeed=ws;
}
```

Moving Around

Finally, the function to move the satellite from one position to the next is as follows:

```
void satellite::move()
{
    omega=omega+wspeed;
    polarxy(radius,omega,xplanet,yplanet,x,y);
}
```

It is very simple, isn't it? All you do is increment the current angle, and then compute the new cartesian coordinates. There is no need to invoke the place(x,y) function. The cartesian coordinates are directly updated with this function call.

The New Stars Program

Once the satellite class is available (c6satell.h), you can write a new version of the c5stars.cpp program (c6sat.cpp).

You can declare objects and initialize them as follows:

```
const float pi2=2*3.14159;
```

```
Stage universe;
Clock timer,sidereal;
satellite Sun,Earth,Moon;
Sun.resize(40);
Sun.origin(320,240);
Sun.scale(1.,-1.);
Earth.dist(120);
Earth.speed(pi2/36.5/30.);// In a 30th of a second
Earth.center(Sun);
Moon.resize(12);
Moon.dist(80);
Moon.color(3);
Earth.color(4);
Moon.speed(pi2/2.8/30.);   // In a 30th of a second
universe.insert(Earth);
universe.insert(Moon);
Sun.show();
```

The animation loop is simple.

```
for(;sidereal.time()<36.5;)
  {
    Earth.move();
    Moon.center(Earth);
    Moon.move();
    universe.show();
    timer.watch(.033);
    timer.reset();
    universe.erase();
  }
```

Why is the Moon told to center using Earth inside the loop? Couldn't this be done only once before the loop, as it was done with the Sun? No, it could not!

The problem is that Earth's coordinates are changing, and what we actually give the Moon are the new coordinates of Earth. This procedure is not needed for the Sun, because it does not move. Now do you see why it was useful to be able to change the center coordinates?

From Outer Space to Inner Space

What else can you do with satellites? Electrons are also satellites of the nucleus of an atom.

You can write a program to simulate electrons orbiting a nucleus just as easily as you wrote the previous program. If you want 10 electrons orbiting the nucleus, declare 10 satellites, initialize them, move them…. Wow—it may become an extensive program! Well, not really—wait until you learn about arrays!

Are You Experienced?

Now you can. . .

- ☑ Choose appropriate classes to implement your applications
- ☑ Evaluate possible improvements to your designs

PART VII

Using Arrays and Structures

When you need to handle several objects of the same type, arrays come in very handy, because they eliminate the need to designate each object by a different name. This tremendously simplifies your programs, because the code is essentially the same no matter which object in the array you manipulate.

In Part VII, you will learn how to manipulate arrays of any class of objects, including arrays of numeric variables. Words, sentences, and text in general can also be manipulated by using arrays of characters. Finally, to further improve your skills in application development, you will make additional improvements to the point-of-sale terminal and to the satellite simulation.

S K I L L

nineteen

19

Using Arrays

- ❑ Declaring and using arrays
- ❑ Using arrays of arrays
- ❑ Using numeric arrays
- ❑ Sorting arrays

In this Skill, you will use athletes to illustrate the purpose of arrays and the use of arrays to denote collections of identical objects of any type. After you grasp the initial concepts using arrays of athletes, you will study and use the more common-place arrays of numeric data.

You will learn how to declare arrays, how to access elements of arrays, how to use arrays in expressions, how to pass arrays as arguments, and how to receive arrays as parameters in functions.

Understanding and Working with Arrays

An *array* is a collection of objects of the same class in which you can designate one of the objects by its position in line. For example, if the athletes in a fitness class are aligned and you do not know their names, the easiest thing for you to do would be to refer to each one of them by their relative position in line—the first, the second, the third….

It is important that you understand the convenience of using arrays. Let's take a very simple example: Suppose that you want to write a program to tell five athletes, such as the ones shown in Figure 19.1, to exercise.

You would probably consider creating five athletes and giving each one a name:

```
athlete Julia, Andrea, Ricardo, Andy, Michael;
```

Then, you would have to tell each one of them to exercise:

```
JumpJack(Julia);
JumpJack(Andrea);
JumpJack(Ricardo);
JumpJack(Andy);
JumpJack(Michael);
```

Well, maybe you can do this so far, but what if there are one hundred athletes? What if there are one thousand?

A convenient way to deal with this problem is to give a name to a collection of athletes, and then to refer to each individual athlete as the first, the second, the third….

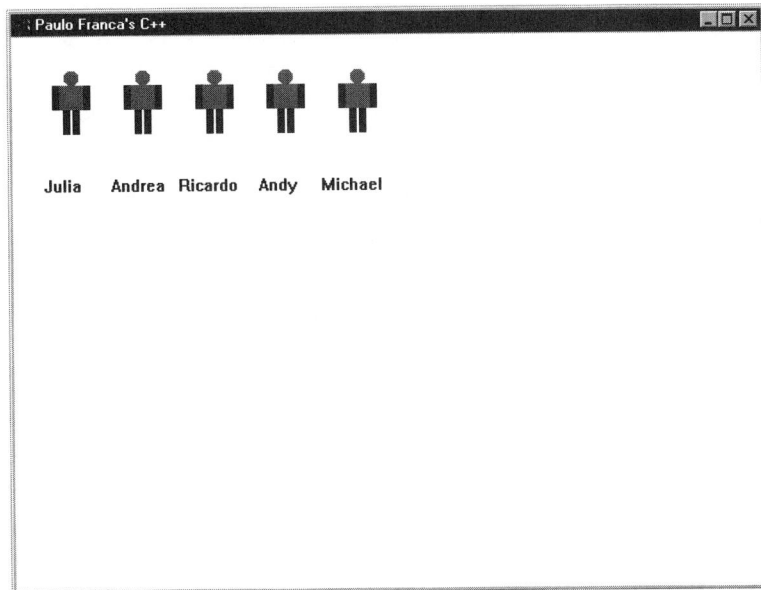

FIGURE 19.1: Five individual athletes

The process would be something like the following process:

>Let Guy be a collection of five athletes.

>Repeat for each value of *index* from 1 to 5:

>>Take the *Guy* in position *index* and make him do a jumping jack.

As it has been with all the repetitions we have studied, the computer will make sure that all the *Guys* exercise, but you, the almighty programmer, do not have to write one thousand lines of code—no matter how many *Guys* you want to deal with! Figure 19.2 shows this array of athletes.

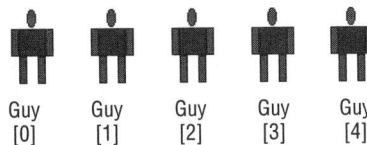

FIGURE 19.2: Guy is an array of athletes.

Now, compare a program that deals with each athlete individually:

```
void mainprog()
{
    athlete Julia, Andrea, Ricardo, Andy, Michael;
    JumpJack(Julia);
    JumpJack(Andrea);
    JumpJack(Ricardo);
    JumpJack(Andy);
    JumpJack(Michael);
}
```

with a program that uses an array of five athletes:

```
void mainprog()
{
    athlete Guy[5];              // Declares an array of five athletes
    for (int which=0; which<=4; which++)
    {
        JumpJack(Guy[which]);// Each athlete does a jumping jack
    }
}
```

The last program will be essentially the same whether you want to deal with 5, 10, or 100 athletes. The first program would have to be modified according to how many athletes you use.

Do you remember that we said an array is composed of elements of the same class? Very well, you can also use objects of the class runner if you'd like:

```
void mainprog()
{
    runner Guy[5];         // Declares an array of five runners
    for (int which=0;which<=4;which++)
    {
        Guy[which].run();// Each runner runs
    }
}
```

Ways to Use Arrays

You can have arrays of all kinds of objects: athletes, runners, robots, and circles—even the most modest int and float can be elements of an array. In C++, the elements of an array are designated by an index value, which is an integer (int). The first element of an array is designated by the index value *0*, the second element by the index value *1*, and so on.

In the previous program, the array Guy had five elements:

Guy[0] was the first.

Guy[1] was the second.

Guy[2] was the third.

Guy[3] was the fourth.

Guy[4] was the fifth.

Guy[5] did not exist, since there were only five elements!

> **WARNING** It is a common bug to declare an array with *N* elements, and to then try to use element *N*, which, of course, does not exist. The element indexes start with zero, and go to *N-1*. Don't forget to use element zero.

Using Arrays in Functions

If you want to use an array in a function, you must declare it, so the compiler knows that you are using an array. You declare an array much like you declare any other object, but you follow the array name with brackets enclosing the number of elements in the array. For example:

```
int  points[10];
```

declares an array named points with 10 elements (numbered 0 through 9), in which each element is an int.

```
float  measurements[12];
```

declares an array named measurements with 12 elements (numbered 0 through 11), in which each element is a float.

The array name denotes the whole collection of elements. The array name followed by an index value inside brackets denotes one particular element. For example, in the first example in this section:

```
points
```

is a collection of 10 elements.

```
points[1]
```

is one particular element (the second) in points.

Skill 19

As long as the index value is an `int`, you can use any expression in the brackets:

- `Guy[which]` ... denotes one particular *Guy*. If you know the value of `which`, you can determine which element that particular *Guy* is.

- `Guy[which-1]` ... denotes another particular *Guy*.

However, the index value should not denote a nonexistent element in the array. In the case of `Guy[which]`, `which` should have values between 0 and 4. Any other value will be outside the bounds of the array. It is your responsibility, as a programmer, to make sure that this does not happen.

ASSIGNING THE WRONG INDEX VALUE

A major cause of errors in programs is to assign an index value that denotes an invalid entry. You may often need to use an expression in brackets to denote the index value, and you can never be sure what values the expression will take during the program execution. For example, suppose that you declare an array `List` with 10 elements (numbered 0 through 9). Suppose that you use an array such as:

```
List[ (k-3)*j]=0;
```

The values of `k` and `j` determine the index value (which should be between 0 and 9). However, it is unlikely that you will watch everything that happens to `k` and `j` in the program, and you may eventually have a value like *–13* as your result.

In a case like this one, the computer will usually go to the wrong place in the memory and place the *zero* where it thinks the `List[-13]` should be. The consequences will be unpredictable!

Using Arrays in Expressions

You can use arrays in expressions—they will usually be arrays that have numeric elements, such as `int` and `float`. Since each element is usually a number, the value of that element will be used when you use that element in an expression.

For example, consider the following piece of program:

```
void mainprog()
{
    int  value[10];                      // Declares an array of 10 integers
        for (int  index=0;index<=9; index++)
        {
            value [index]=9-index;// Computes the value for each element
        }
...
```

Can you determine the value of each element of the array after this piece of program is executed? What will be the value of element *0*? What about element *1*?

Notice that in the loop, we compute an expression 9-index, and we store the result in value[index].

Therefore, after the piece of program above, the array value will have a number stored in it. We can use this number for anything.

For example, we can use a box to "say" the value of each element:

```
void mainprog()
{
    int  value[10];                      // Declares an array of 10 integers
        for (int  index=0;index<=9; index++)
        {
            value [index]=9-index;// Computes the value for each element
        }
    Box Sal;
    for (which=0;which<=9;which++)
    {
        Sal.say(value[which]);
    }
}
```

Skill 19

Can you see that we can use the array element as an argument? I suggest that you try this to determine whether you guessed correctly the values in the array.

Using Arrays as Arguments

Arrays and array elements can also be used as arguments in functions. It is important that you know exactly which type of object you are using. For example, if you declare

```
athlete Guy[10];
```

there is a big difference between using

```
JumpJack(Guy);
```

and using

```
JumpJack(Guy[1]);
```

The first form is wrong! Can you understand why? The `JumpJack` function requires one parameter of the type `athlete`. Indeed, `Guy[1]` is an athlete, but `Guy` is not. `Guy` is an array of athletes!

It is possible to use each athlete as an argument to the `JumpJack` function and to have each one of them do the jumping jacks. However, it is impossible to use the whole array as an argument, since the function expects to deal with only one object. We can define a different version of the `JumpJack` function that takes an array of athletes as an argument. In this case, the following statement:

```
JumpJack(Guy);
```

would be correct.

Using Arrays in Parameter Lists

When a function receives an array as a parameter, the function header must indicate this fact. For example:

```
void jumpjack(athlete eachone[10], int howmany_athletes)
{
    for (int i=0;i<howmany_athletes;i++)
    {
        eachone[i].ready();
        eachone[i].up();
        eachone[i].ready(0.);
    }
}
```

You can call this function with an array of athletes as an argument. If you expect to always have 10 athletes, you may want to omit the `howmany_athletes` argument.

In this case, the function header specifies clearly that `eachone` is an array. It tells the compiler to expect that indexes will be associated with it. Another interesting fact is that you don't really need to specify the size of the array. Since the array was declared somewhere else in the program, memory space will not be allocated again in the function, because arrays are passed by reference in C++. All the function needs to know is that `eachone` may be followed by an index.

The function header could then be as follows:

```
void jumpjack (athlete eachone[], int howmany_athletes)
```

> **NOTE** If you have a multidimensional array (you will learn about these arrays later in this Skill), only the last bracket can be left blank.

The *c7jack.cpp* Program

The c7jack.cpp program demonstrates how to use an array of athletes and how to have each athlete perform a jumping jack.

```
//                              c7jack.cpp
// This program illustrates use of arrays.
//                    July 31, 1994
//
#include"franca.h";
athlete Guy[7];
void JmpJack(athlete somebody)
{
     somebody.up();
     somebody.ready();
}
void mainprog()
{
  for (int i=0;i<7;i++)
  {
    JmpJack(Guy[i]);
    Guy[i].say("Done!");
  }
}
```

This program will remain essentially unchanged whether you have only one athlete or several athletes. The difference would be as follows:

- The array should be declared with as many elements as needed.

- The loop should go from *zero* to the number denoting the last athlete.

The Number of Elements in an Array

If you declare an array with seven elements and use only three elements, the program should run correctly. The only problem is that you will leave unused space in the computer memory. On the other hand, if you want to use more elements than you have declared, you may cause an error in the program.

In many situations, you may have to deal with an array in which you don't know exactly the number of elements that will be used. For example, suppose that you have to deal with the ages of students in a classroom. You may have 28 students in your classroom, but if you make a program that deals with 28 students, you will not be able to use the same program with another class. When you develop programs, you should try to make them as useful as possible.

One solution would be to declare the array as follows:

```
int student_age[28];
```

Then, you could exchange the number *28* for another number—for example, 32—to deal with a larger class. This is not a good solution, because other places in the program may also use the number of students. For example, if you compute the average age of the students, you will certainly have a piece of program like the following one:

```
sum=0;
for (int i=0; i<28; i++)
    {
        sum=sum+student_age[i];
    }
average=sum/28;
```

Did you notice that there are two other places that you may have to change the value *28*, and use 32 instead? It may look easy to do this in the example, but if you have a very long program, it will not be so easy to locate all the values!

A more important case is the case in which you want to use this piece of program with different classes in a school, in which each class is likely to have a different number of students. As a novice, you may think that all you have to do is to change the number of students in the program for each new class you want to process. This method is extremely unprofessional!

TIP

Keep in mind that you, the professional programmer, are not expected to be present while the program runs.

A good solution for this problem is to keep the number of students separately and to give it a name:

```
int number_of_students;
```

This variable could either be read from the keyboard or be passed as an argument to a function. The array would have been declared with enough elements to accommodate all the students. For example:

```
int student_age[100];
```

Then, the part that computes the average could be as follows:

```
sum=0;
for (int i=0; i<number_of_students; i++)
    {
        sum=sum+student_age[i];
    }
average=sum/number_of_students;
```

Constants and Array Sizes

It is illegal to use a variable to indicate the array size in a declaration. We must use a constant. Why? It is not possible to use a variable in the array declaration. You must use an integer. For example:

```
athlete Guy[n];
```

is incorrect, unless n is a constant.

WHY DOES THE ARRAY SIZE NEED TO BE A CONSTANT?

The value of a variable will only be known during program execution. Also, as the name implies, a variable may have its value changed as the program executes. Long before the program is able to execute, the compiler needs to set apart memory space to accommodate all the variables the program will need (including the arrays). This is why the number of elements must be known—the compiler must reserve memory space for all elements. By the time the program starts executing and the variables start having values assigned to them, all the memory has already been allocated. For this reason, the size of the array must be specified as a constant. It is possible to define a named constant and to use it as the array size. For example:

```
const int arraysize;
float prices[arraysize];
```

However, remember that since arraysize was defined as a constant, you cannot change its value during program execution.

Skill 19

Try This for Fun...

- Change the program `c7jack.cpp` so you can give the number of athletes that you want to see. Have each athlete do as follows:

  - Say "Hi."

  - Perform a jumping jack.

  - Say its index value ("0, 1, 2...").

Numeric Arrays

In many situations, we use arrays containing numeric values. For example, we use arrays of the types `int`, `long`, `float`, or `double`.

An Array of Arrays

You can have arrays of several types of elements. Here's a brain teaser: Can you have an array in which each element is an array?

Suppose that we have a group of athletes that have shown up for the eight o'clock class. If we treat them as an array, we can denote them by their index values—0, 1, 2.... Now, suppose that another group comes in for the nine o'clock class. They can also be treated as an array, can't they?

In that case, we could designate that each group is an array, and then we could have the following groups:

- group 0 (the eight o'clockers)

- group 1 (the nine o'clockers)

- group 2 (the ten o'clockers)

You can now understand that what we call *group* is actually an element of an array. For example, suppose that the array we are talking about consists of three groups of four athletes each. This situation is shown in Figure 19.3.

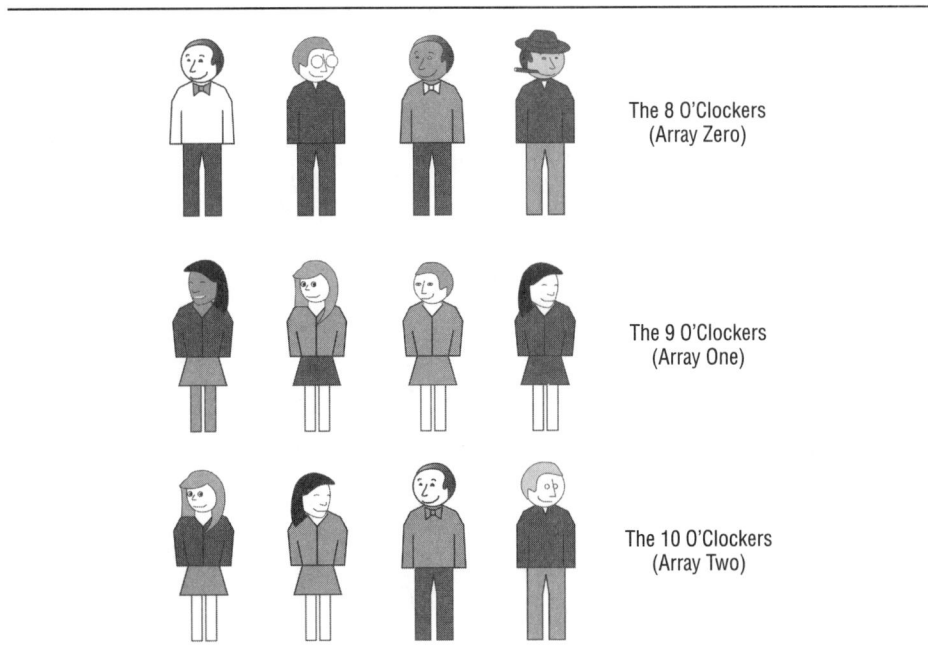

FIGURE 19.3: Arrays of arrays

We could declare this situation as follows:

```
athlete Guy[3][4];
```

in which Guy is an array of three elements, in which each element is an array of four athletes.

Arrays, Rows, and Columns

If you look at Figure 19.3, you may notice that the athletes are arranged in three rows of four athletes each. You may also notice that each row contains athletes of the same group; therefore, when we refer to *group zero*, we actually refer to *row zero*—each row corresponds to one group.

When elements are arranged in tabular form, such as the athletes in Figure 19.3, you can designate one element by the row and the column where the element is located. Therefore, Guy[2][3] denotes the athlete in row 2, column 3. Figure 19.4 shows the rows and columns in the array of athletes.

FIGURE 19.4: Rows and columns in an array of athletes

Initialization

In the same way that you are responsible for any object or variable in the program, you, as a programmer, are responsible for setting the appropriate values for the elements of the array. When an array is created, its elements contain any garbage that was in the computer's memory. You should not assume that the values of the elements are zero or any other value.

You can assign a value to each element of an array during the execution of the program, or you can assign an initial value as soon as you declare your array. In the case of an array that holds numeric values, you can set an initial value for each element at the declaration. Simply follow the declaration with an equal sign and a set of braces that enclose the initial value for each element separated by commas. The first value corresponds to the first element (numbered zero), the second value to the second element (numbered 1), and so on.

```
int values[10] = {9,8,7,6,5,4,3,2,1,0};
```

The declaration above assigns the value 9 to element [0], the value 8 to element [1], the value 7 to element[2], and so on.

Here are some notes on the syntax:

- There is an equal sign after the brackets.

- The values of each element are separated from each other by commas.

- All the values are enclosed in braces.

When you initialize a two-dimensional array as follows:

```
int matrix[2][3] = { {0,0,1},{2,3,4} };
```

the last index value is changed first. In this case, the initialization will have the same effect as the following statements:

```
matrix[0][0] =0;
matrix[0][1] =0;
matrix[0][2] =1;
matrix[1][0] =2;
matrix[1][1] =3;
matrix[1][2] =4;
```

In the sequence of statements above, notice that, initially, the first index value was kept at 0, while the second index value was changed to become 0, 1, and then 2. Then, the first index value was changed to 1, while the second index value again was changed to become 0, 1, and then 2.

Using Arrays

Suppose that you want to keep track of the ages of five athletes in a group in an array. You can declare an array as follows:

```
athlete guy[5];
int age[5];
```

You can have each athlete "say" his or her number, ask you for his or her age, and, finally, "say" his or her age.

Skill 19

The *c7age.cpp* Program

The procedure above can be accomplished by the c7age.cpp program, shown below.

```
//                              c7age.cpp
// This program illustrates use of integer arrays.
//                      July 31, 1994
//
#include"franca.h"
athlete Guy[5];
void mainprog()
{
 int age[5];
 for (int i=0;i<=4;i++)
 {
   Guy[i].ready();
   Guy[i].say(i);
   age[i]=Guy[i].ask("What is my age?");
 }
}
```

Using Numeric Arrays

You may have noticed in the examples above that we did not use the athlete array too often. Most of the work was done by the age array. As a matter of fact, we deal very often with simple numeric arrays in real life. For example, you may have to deal with an array that contains the grades of students in a class, or that contains the balances in customer accounts. If we have only the age array, instead of having an array of athletes and the age array, the program will not be too different.

Try This for Fun. . .

- Write another program that contains only an age array to find out the value and location of the greatest age. Use the ask function to request the values of the ages and to tell you the greatest one after the comparisons are made. Use a box to display your result.

Avoiding the Use of Unnecessary Arrays

Arrays are needed only when you are required to keep all the values at hand for later use. Unless other requirements demand the use of an array, you should

decide whether you even need an array. For example, if you want to input several values and to compute their average, there is no need to use an array. You
can add the numbers as you read them, and divide the total by the number of
elements:

```
Box result ("Average:");
int n; // The number of elements
float value, total;
n = ask ("Input number of elements");
total = 0;
for (int i=1;i<=n;i++)
{
    total=total+ask("Input a number");
}
total = total / n;
result.say(total);
```

In the example above, the numbers are added as they are typed. There is no
need to use an array to store all the numbers. If you use unnecessary arrays, they
may consume computer memory and make your program harder to understand.

Defining a Type with *typedef*

If you are using several arrays that have the same declaration—for example:

```
float  matrix[5][3], prices[5][3], cost[5][3];
```

you may consider creating a new type:

```
typedef float theusual[5][3];
```

and then declaring the arrays that you are going to use:

```
theusual matrix,prices,cost;
```

In this case, you simply create a new type of variable. From this point on, the
compiler will recognize `theusual` as a type that represents a floating point array
of five by three elements. `typedef` can be used in any situation, not only with
arrays.

Here is the syntax:

```
typedef  type declaration    identifier ;
```

in which the identifier of the new type may be followed by an array size.

Try These for Fun. . .

- Modify the c7age.cpp program so the oldest athlete presents him- or her-self. You need to include more code that determines who is the oldest athlete. Then, make the athlete say "Here!" Notice that you have to determine whether the oldest athlete is Guy[0], Guy[1].... You will need to find the index value of the *Guy* who is the oldest athlete. Notice that the solution to this problem is an algorithm to find the largest element in an array.

> **TIP**
>
> Use an integer—for example, oldest—to examine one athlete at a time, and make the integer equal to zero (to point to the first athlete). Then, compare the age of the athlete examined by oldest with the age of every other athlete. Every time you find an age that is greater than the one you are examining, make oldest point to this new athlete. This way, oldest always indicates the oldest athlete that you have examined. After you have examined all the athletes, oldest will point out the oldest athlete.

- The problem of finding the smallest element in an array is very similar to the problem above. Try to find the youngest athlete.

- Write the code of a function float average(int array[], int from, int to); to compute and return as a result the average value of the array elements, starting from the position from and ending at the position to.

- Write the code of a function int less (int array[], int from, int to, int value); to compute and return as a value the number of elements whose values are less than the argument value, starting from the position from and ending at the position to. For example, if the array contains the values 21, 32, 15, 80, 75, and 43, and the function call is x = less (array, 1, 4, 50), the result should be 2.

Example—Handling a Numeric Array

In this example, we will read a set of numbers and store them in an array. Some operations are performed, such as searching for the largest number and sorting numbers. The numbers in the array are displayed in a list of boxes, which, in turn, illustrates how to deal with an array of objects. This example deals with an integer array of 10 numbers.

Getting and Showing the Array

In the simplest version of this program, we will read and show the array in boxes on the screen. The steps involved in this program are as follows:

- Declare the objects and the variables that are needed.

- Get the values for the array.

- Show the values for the array.

This simple list of steps suggests that we develop a function to get the values for the array and another function to show the values for the array. We may have a program like the following program:

```
void mainprog()
{
  int values[10];       // Array of numbers
  getarray(values,0,9);
  showarray(values,0,9);
}
```

The program simply consists of two function calls—a call to a function `getarray` (to get the values for the array from the keyboard) and a call to a function `showarray` (to display the array on the screen). Both functions will have to be programmed.

There are several ways to conceive of these two functions—the main concern is to determine what kind of arguments should be passed to them.

The *getarray* function   The `getarray` function needs to know how many elements to get from the keyboard and where to store them. We may consider building a function with no arguments that would be called as follows:

```
getarray();
```

This function would work OK. In this case, you may have to declare the array `number` outside the `mainprog` function to make it global, so the other functions can use it. You also may assume that 10 elements are to be read, and that they will always be read from element 0 to element 9. The disadvantage of this approach is that your functions will not be reusable. You may want to read and show several arrays, but if you restrict yourself to always reading the same array name, the following difficulties arise:

- You cannot use this function if you want to get values for two different arrays. (If you are not convinced, go ahead and try it!)

- If you want to use this function in another program, you must also name the array in the other program `number`. You can give up all hope of selling software with this kind of restriction!

On the other hand, if you include arguments, it will make your functions a little more general and more reusable. A similar reasoning applies to the function `showarray`. The main program is now very simple and complete. All we have to do now is to code the two functions.

Reading the Array

The `getarray` function requests numbers from the keyboard and stores them in the array. Since several elements are to be read, this process has to be done in a loop. A possible solution to this problem could be as follows:

```
void getarray(int number[],int from,int to)
{
  for (int i=from;i<=to;i++)
  {
    number[i]=ask("Input a number");
  }
}
```

This function is also a very simple function.

> **NOTE**   In C++, arrays are always passed by reference to functions, whether you precede the parameter name with the ampersand (&) or not. Therefore, the values read from the keyboard will be available to the main program.

Showing the Array

The `showarray` function displays each value of the numeric array in a separate box. Here is a possible implementation:

```
void showarray(int number[],int from,int to)
{
  Box list[10];
  for (int i=from;i<=to;i++)
  {
```

```
        list[i%10].place(400,50+(i%10)*40);
        list[i%10].label(i);
        list[i%10].say(number[i]);
    }
}
```

Since the range of array indexes is beyond our control, this function displays up to 10 boxes and places the array elements in the boxes according to the last digit of the array index. For example, if the user requests the display of elements 31 to 40, element 31 is displayed in box 1, element 32 is displayed in box 2…. Element 40 is displayed in box 0, because the index of the array of boxes is the remainder of division by 10. Figure 19.5 shows how this function displays array elements 15 to 24.

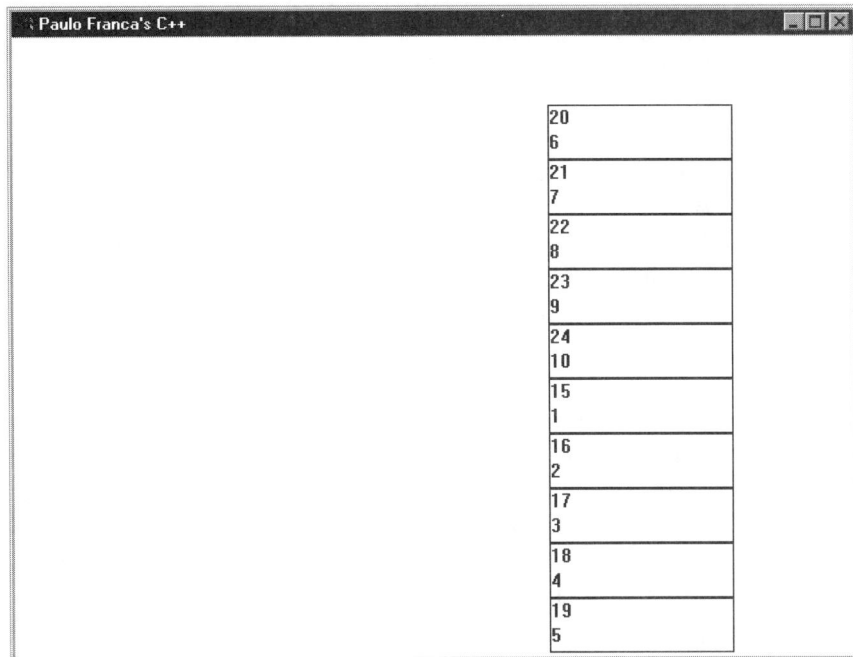

FIGURE 19.5: Displaying 10 elements of an array

This function does not use the feature that automatically places boxes on the screen. Instead, each box is individually placed at given coordinates, so each new box will be automatically placed in a new location, and a new set of boxes is created every time the function is called. After a few calls to this function, the boxes will be placed off the screen.

At this point, you should try to run this program.

NOTE   The functions used in this section can be found in the header file c7intfun.h.

Finding the Largest Element

The next step in this array manipulation is to search the array to find the largest value. We will use the same functions as above to get and to show the array, and essentially the same program. Instead of including the search in the program, we can conceive of another function to find the largest element in the array. This function call could be as follows:

```
findlargest(values,from, to);
```

It is especially useful to include arguments that let us search from a given start to a given limit, as we shall see shortly. This function must, somehow, identify the *largest value found* or *where it was found*! Do you understand clearly the two options?

Suppose that we have the following numbers in the array:

23, 12, 45, 11, 89, 21, 32, 55, 81, 32

If you examine the values, you will determine that the largest value is 89. But you may also say that the largest value is in position 4 (remember to start counting from 0, as is the case in C++). If the result is known by the index position where the largest number was found, you can easily learn its value. But if you know the largest value, it is not easy to find the index position. For this reason, you should return the index position as a result.

Comparing Two Numbers at a Time

How do you find the largest value in an array?

As you know very well by now, the computer can compare two numbers at a time. It cannot look at a whole set, and then find the largest. You must tell the computer to examine each number. A simple solution to this problem is to have the computer remember the largest value that has been found as each value is examined in the array.

In the beginning, you can safely assume that the first value in the array is the largest one found so far (since you have not examined any other value). Then, as you loop through all the elements, check whether the value you think is the largest is still the largest. If it is, fine. If it is not, just dispose of it and keep the new value that is the largest.

An implementation could be as follows:

```
int findlargest(int number[],int from,int to)
{
 int index;
 int guess;
 guess=from;                // Take the first as a guess
 for (index=from;index<=to;index++)
   {
     if(number[found]<number[index])
     {
            guess=index; // Change the guess
     }
   }
   return guess;
}
```

Can you follow the idea? The variable `guess` keeps the position of the largest number found so far. In the beginning, since no numbers have been examined, use the first position (`from`) as your guess. Now, since you guess that this position holds the largest number so far, you assume that `number[guess]` is the largest number.

Next, start looping through the array. Use the integer variable `index` to denote the current position you are examining. The index starts with `from`, which is the first position to examine, and ends with `to`, which is the last position.

> **TIP**
>
> You may also consider looping from `from+1` onward, because we are already holding the first element, and it is no help to compare `number[found]` with `number[index]` when both `found` and `index` are equal. It is a good idea, but it may fail in the extreme case in which `from` and `to` have the same value.

As you compare the number you think is the largest (`number[guess]`) with the current element (`number[index]`), you correct the position of the largest number. If the current number is larger, you forget the old position and copy the current position (`index`) to `guess`. When you do so, you remain sure that `guess` always designates the element containing the largest value. As you reach the end of the loop, you can be sure that `guess` designates the position of the largest value found in the array.

You can include a call `findlargest` in the main program to find the largest element. Of course, once this value is found, it is a good idea to display it. The program below includes a couple extra boxes to display the largest value, as well as its position in the array.

```
void mainprog()
{
  Box largest(50,350,"Largest:");
  Box index(50,400,"Position:");
  int values[10];
  int k;
  getarray(values,0,9);
  showarray(values,0,9);
  k=findlargest(values,0,9);
  largest.say(values[k]);
  index.say(k);
}
```

Sorting Arrays

Since you have functions to help you easily get, show, and find the largest element in an array, you can also sort the array. In other words, you can rearrange it so all the elements appear in ascending order, for example. Sorting is a very common and useful procedure that deserves a lot more study than we present here. We do present a very simple sorting algorithm.

Again, instead of adding more statements to our program, we can build a `sort` function and call it from the main program. It could be as follows:

```
sort(values,from,to);
```

This function keeps the main program simple, and, in addition, provides a `sort` function that may be useful another time!

The idea of the `sort` function is simple. Since you can easily find the largest element, why not move it to the end of the array, where it belongs? If you know that the largest element is in position `larger`, and that the last element is in position `last`, all you have to do is to exchange `number[larger]` for `number[last]`. At least you can be sure that the last element is in its correct place. How does this help, though? You are still left with elements 0 to 8, which are not sorted. But wait! Can't we now tell the `findlargest` function to search for the largest number from 0 to 8? Of course, we can!

EXCHANGING VALUES

It can be tricky for beginning programmers to exchange values in two variables. To exchange the values in variables a and b, some beginners are tempted to do as follows:

```
a=b;
b=a;
```

Of course, this will not work. As b is copied into a, the old value of a is lost. Therefore, when a is copied into b, the new value of a, which is the same as the value of b, is copied. To solve this problem, we must use a third variable; for example, temp.

```
temp=a;
a=b;
b=temp;
```

This problem is similar to the problem of exchanging the contents of two glasses—one containing wine, another containing milk. You need to use a third glass to hold the wine, and then you pour the milk into the glass that contained the wine. It is only after you do this that you can pour the wine into the glass that contained the milk.

As we keep selecting the largest element and moving it to the end, we are left each time with a smaller unsorted array. At some point, we are left with an unsorted array of only one element, and, at this point, we know that the array is sorted!

Here is an implementation:

```
void sort (int array[],int fromwhere,int towhere)
{
  int largest,temp;
  // Loop decreasing "last" each time:
  for (int last=towhere;last>fromwhere;last-)
  {
```

Skill 19

```
    // Find largest from beginning to "last":
    largest=findlargest(array,fromwhere,last);
    // Switch largest with "last":
    temp=array[largest];
    array[largest]=array[last];
    array[last]=temp;
  }
}
```

The main program to sort the array would then be as follows:

```
void mainprog()
{
  int values[10];
  getarray(values,0,9);
  showarray(values,0,9);
  sort(values,0,9);
  showarray(values,0,9);
}
```

Recursive Sorting

A variation of the sort function uses the following idea: You can check whether there is only one element to be sorted. In that case, you are done. Otherwise, you can find the largest element, exchange it with the element in the last position, and then sort the remaining elements.

When I say *sort the remaining elements,* what do I mean? Well, I mean to call the sort function again. This is a recursive solution, since the sort function includes a call to itself.

An implementation of this variation could be as follows:

```
void recsort(int array[],int fromwhere,int towhere)
{
  // This is a recursive version of sort:
  int largest,temp;
  int last;
    last=towhere;
    // Check whether sort is not complete:
    if(fromwhere<=towhere)
    {
    // Find largest from beginning to "last":
    largest=findlargest(array,fromwhere,last);
    // Switch largest with "last":
    temp=array[largest];
```

```
array[largest]=array[last];
array[last]=temp;
// Sort the remaining array:
recsort(array,fromwhere,last-1);
}
}
```

Are You Experienced?

Now you can...

- ☑ Manipulate several objects of identical types by using arrays
- ☑ Use arrays of objects or numbers
- ☑ Use arrays of arrays
- ☑ Sort an array

S K I L L

20

twenty

Working with Text and Practicing with Arrays

- ❑ Using character arrays
- ❑ Manipulating strings with the functions in *string.h*
- ❑ Converting between numbers and characters
- ❑ Understanding and using structures
- ❑ Searching arrays

You can manipulate text in C++ by using character arrays, in which each element of the array contains one character. Most of the usual operations with character arrays can be performed using available functions. You don't have to write programs to copy one string to another or to compare strings.

You may also have to deal with information that is organized in several pieces, such as an account number, a customer name, or a current balance. This problem can be solved with objects, but it can also be solved with structures.

Finally, when you have data stored in an array, you may have to search the array to locate a specific element. You will learn how to search at the end of this Skill.

Using Text in Your C++ Programs

Another important application of computers is to manipulate text. Even though the computer stores everything in its memory as a number, characters can be stored and manipulated by using numeric codes. The code the computer uses to store the characters is irrelevant in most cases. You will be able to manipulate characters without knowing their codes.

Using *char* in Your Code

The type char can be used for variables that are supposed to store characters. For example:

```
char initial;
```

establishes that the variable initial will be used to store a character. Each char variable can store only one character. For this reason, it is very likely that handling characters will require the use of arrays. You can use a character variable in an expression, and you can assign a value corresponding to a character by enclosing the character in single quotes. For example:

```
initial = 'A';
```

assigns the value corresponding to the character A (uppercase) to the variable initial. We could have also set an initial value at the time that we declared the variable. For example:

```
char choice='y';
```

Notice that codes are not the same for upper- and lowercase letters. The program can differentiate between *a* and *A*.

Comparing by Using *char* Codes

Of course, character variables can also be compared, just like any other variable:

```
char choice;
...
...
if (choice=='N') break;
```

In the example above, the character variable choice is compared with the character N (uppercase). If choice contains the code representing the character N, a break occurs.

Adding a Blank Space   It is possible to use a blank space in the quotes to indicate a blank space. A blank space has a code just like any other character:

```
char blank=' ';
```

The statement above will declare a variable blank of type char, with an initial value of a blank space.

Characters and Character Codes

It is legal to assign a numeric value (int, long, float, etc.) to a character variable. Since the character is represented by a code that is an integer ranging from 0 to 255, it is legal in C++ to assign an integer value. In fact, a character enclosed in single quotes signifies the numeric code of the character. In other words, 'N' is the same as 78, 'A' is the same as 65, 'a' is the same as 97, and so on. Don't worry about the numeric codes—they were established as standard codes for communicating characters in electronic form. You will find more information on this topic in an exercise later in this Skill. If the numeric value is not in the range of 0 to 255, the computer will truncate the number, and the result may not be what you expected.

It is also legal to assign a character to an integer variable. However, it is illegal to assign more than one character (a character array, as we will see in the next section) to a character variable.

Each character position in the computer's memory can hold a numeric code ranging from 0 to 255, which means that a total of 256 characters can be represented. This total is enough to represent the letters of the Roman alphabet in

Skill 20

lower- and uppercase, special signs, and control characters. All we have to do is to associate each code with a character. Most computers use the correspondence known as the American Standard Code for Information Interchange (ASCII).

Try This for Fun. . .

- Assume the following declarations in a program:

```
int i,j,k;
float x,y;
char a,b;
```

- Indicate which of the following statements are correct in terms of syntax:

  a. `i=j;`

  b. `a=j;`

  c. `x=a;`

  d. `for (a='a';a<='z';a++)`

  e. `b=b+3;`

Using Character Arrays

Since each variable can hold only one character, the obvious choice to handle words and phrases is an array of characters. Some programming languages have a type to handle *strings,* which are sequences of characters. C++ does not have a built-in string type, so it uses arrays. However, keep in mind that C++ allows classes. Therefore, you can either build a class to handle strings or buy one!

Character arrays are declared in the same way that you declare other arrays. For example:

```
char first_name[20];
```

Each element of the array can be used. For example:

```
first_name[0]='a';
first_name[1]='n';
first_name[2]=first_name[0];
```

The example above results in the name ana being stored in the first three positions of the array first_name.

It is also possible to initialize the array as you declare it:

```
char last_name[20]= { 'f','r','a','n','c','a'};
```

Keeping Track of Word Length

Since words and names have varying lengths, and since every memory position either is initialized with a value or contains some trash, how will we know that a particular last name contains six characters? Obviously, if this variable was created to hold only that name, we could remember the size—this is not usually the case, though. It is useful to be able to tell where the string ends.

Although there is no string type, C++ offers some functions to manipulate strings and some amenities for programmers. By convention, strings in C++ are marked with a special code that follows the last position. This code is referred to as null. It is not a keyword, but it is defined in almost every header file used in C++. In fact, null is defined as the value *zero* (not the character *0*).

To correctly initialize last_name in the example above, we should have done as follows:

```
char last_name[20]= { 'f','r','a','n','c','a',null};
```

or:

```
char last_name[20]= { 'f','r','a','n','c','a',0};
```

> **NOTE**   The zero is not enclosed in quotes, because we mean to use the value *zero,* not the character *0.*

We are lucky that C++ offers another way to initialize character arrays:

```
char last_name[20] = "franca";
```

This statement works the same as the previous statement worked. When you enclose a sequence of characters in double quotes, you indicate to the compiler that you are representing a string. The compiler automatically inserts null after your string, provided you have one array element available to accommodate the null. Sequences of characters terminated with null are called *null-terminated strings.*

Skill 20

As you may remember, athletes can "say" something that is enclosed in double quotes. Why? A sequence of characters that is enclosed in double quotes is a null-terminated string. In general, you can replace any message that is enclosed in double quotes with any null-terminated string.

For example, you could use:

```
Sal.say(last_name);
```

Similarly, null-terminated strings can be used as labels in boxes and as messages that ask for data from the keyboard.

String Arrays

It is possible to manipulate an array in which each element is a character array. This process is a simple use of arrays of arrays. For example:

```
char name [5][20];
```

declares an array of five elements, in which each element is an array of 20 characters. This kind of array is useful to store a list of names, for example. Notice that name[0] is an array of characters, and so are name[1], name[2], name[3], and name[4]. We can store a null-terminated string in each of these arrays. For example, the following loop:

```
for (int i=0;i<=4;i++)
  askwords(name[i],20,"Enter a name");
```

reads a name for each of the five arrays of 20 characters.

A more readable version of the same program could be as follows:

```
typedef char onename[20];   // Creates a type
onename  namelist[5];       // namelist has five names
for (int i=0;i<=4;i++)
    askwords(namelist[i],20,"Enter a name");
```

Suppose that you want to store the names of a few athletes: you could have an array of five athletes and an array name as declared above. You could store the name of the first athlete in name[0], the name of the second athlete in name[1], and so on.

It is also possible to initialize a string without specifying the length. For example:

```
char first_name []="Mitiko";
```

You must include the brackets, even if they are empty.

In this case, the character array `first_name` will be declared with a size of 6 (the five letters plus the `null` terminator). This feature is convenient because it saves you the time you would have to spend counting how many spaces you need to store a given string. However, keep in mind that in this case, the array will not be able to accommodate a first name that has more than five characters.

Inputting a String with _askwords_ You can use the function `askwords`, which is included in `franca.h`, to input a string from the keyboard into a character array. This function:

```
askwords(char inputstring[],int maxsize,char message[])
```

displays a dialog box showing the message string that was provided as the third argument, as well as the `inputstring` that was supplied as the first argument. The user may type any string to replace `inputstring`, up to the maximum number of characters specified in `maxsize`.

For example, the program below reads a list of names and displays each name under each athlete.

```
#include "franca.h"
void mainprog()                    // c7names.cpp
{
    athlete player[5];
    char name [5][20];
    for (int i=0;i<=4;i++)
      askwords(name[i],20,"Enter a name");
    for (i=0;i<=4;i++)
    {
      player[i].ready(0.);
      player[i].say(name[i]);
    }
}
```

Using String Functions

It is regrettable that you cannot compare strings the same way you compare numeric variables. You also cannot copy a string to another string by using the assignment operator as you do with numeric variables.

For example, if a program has the following declarations:

```
char agent[]="Bond",client[]="Flint";
```

the following statements will not work:

```
if (agent=="Bond") ...
        client=agent;
```

However, you don't have to compare or copy, one by one, all the elements in a character array to accomplish your task. The header file `string.h` has a few functions that come in handy for this job. It is a standard header file that is available with almost every C++ compiler. Use the `#include` directive shown below to access the string functions:

```
#include <string.h>
```

We will not study in detail all the functions provided in `string.h`, only the functions that you will most likely need. Refer to the compiler's Help menu topics on `string.h` to learn more about the other functions. The following functions will be discussed:

strcmp	compares two strings (alphabetically)
stricmp	compares two strings (alphabetically), disregarding case
strcpy	copies a string to another string
strcat	appends a string to another string
strlen	computes the length of a string

Comparing Strings with *strcmp*

The following function:

```
int strcmp (char s1[],char s2[]);
```

compares the character arrays s1 and s2. If s1 comes before s2 in alphabetical order, the function returns a negative integer. If both strings are equal in alphabetical order, the function returns a zero. If s1 comes after s2 in alphabetical order, the function returns a positive integer.

For example:

```
char city[20];
Cin>>city;
if(strcmp(city,"Cupertino")==0)
    Cout<<"You live in a good town!";
```

In the example above, a string (city) is read from the keyboard, and then compared with Cupertino. If the string exactly matches Cupertino, the message *You live in a good town!* is displayed. However, if the typed string is cupertino, there will be no match, since its case is different from the previous string's case. For this kind of problem, use the function stricmp, as described below.

Comparing Strings while Ignoring Cases with *stricmp*

The following function:

```
int stricmp(char s1[],char s2[]);
```

compares the character arrays s1 and s2. This function works the same as the strcmp function, with the exception that case is ignored.

Copying Strings with *strcpy*

The following function:

```
strcpy (char dest[], char source[]);
```

copies the contents of the source string (source) into the destination string (dest). The original contents of the destination string are lost. It is the programmer's responsibility to make sure that the source string can be accommodated in the space available in the destination string.

For example;

```
char name1[]="Brandon",name2[]="Daisy";
strcpy(name1,name2);
...
```

In the example above, the array name1 will contain Daisy after the function is invoked. If you copy name1 into name2, it could lead to an erroneous result, because the string name2 is not large enough to accommodate the contents of name1.

Concatenating Strings with *strcat*

The following function:

```
strcat (char dest[],char source[]);
```

appends the contents of the source string to the end of the destination string (dest).

Skill 20

For example:

```
char message[20]="The exit ";
strcpy( message, "is near!");
...
```

causes the character array to become *The exit is near!*

Returning String Length with *strlen*

The following function:

```
int strlen(char string[]);
```

returns the length of the string. The length does not include the `null` terminator character.

For example:

```
char sentence[80]="He that shall persevere to the end ...";
Cout<< strlen(sentence);
...
```

The sequence above causes the number *38* to be displayed, since this is the number of characters contained in the array `sentence`. The string length and the array size are not usually the same! The string length is the number of characters from the beginning position to the `null` terminator. This length is very likely to change during program execution, since you may copy different characters into the same string. On the other hand, the array size is usually set when you declare the array. The string length should never exceed the array size.

Determining Declared Size with *sizeof*

Although the array size may be constant throughout program execution, C++ offers an operator to determine the size of any array, object, or structure that you declare in your program—the `sizeof` operator.

The `sizeof` operator returns an integer representing the size of any variable, object, array, or structure that you declared in your program. It is obvious that since you declared the variable, you should be able to determine the size . Why use this operator?

There may be several reasons to use it, including the fact that computations may sometimes become a little tedious. For example, what is the size of the array declared as follows:

```
char listen[]="He that shall persevere to the end, he shall be saved.";
```

This computation presents absolutely no problem. Just count all the letters, the blank spaces, and the period; then, add one for the `null` terminator to compute the size. However, you may not only find this tedious, you may also make a mistake somewhere.

Another, and more important, reason stems from the fact that you often have to modify programs, and an array that was originally declared with 40 elements may, in a later version of your program, be changed to accommodate 50 elements. If you have loops that go from 0 to 39 to handle the array, you will have to inspect the program completely to determine which of these constants needs to be changed. You can easily avoid this hassle if, instead of using the following code:

```
char array[40];
...
for ( int i=0; i<=39;i++)
```

you use

```
char array[40];
...
for (int i=0; i<sizeof(array) ; i++)
```

Converting between Numbers and Characters

Each numeric digit—0, 1, 2, 3, 4, 5, 6, 7, 8, and 9—can be represented as a character, and, therefore, any number stored in the computer can also be written if each of its digits is converted to the character representation. C++ offers functions to assist you in doing this kind of type conversion:

atoi	converts from alphanumeric array (character) to integer
atof	converts from alphanumeric array (character) to floating point number
itoa	converts from integer to alphanumeric array (character)

These functions are included in the header file `stdlib.h`, which must be included in your program with the following directive:

```
#include <stdlib.h>
```

Converting from Character Array to Integer with *atoi*

The following function:

```
int atoi( char number[])
```

returns an integer, which is represented by the character array (string) number. If the array cannot be converted, or if it contains invalid characters, a zero is returned.

For example:

```
char number[20];
int k;
askwords(number,20,"Enter the value");
k=atoi(number);
Cout<<k;
```

Converting from Character Array to Floating Point Number with *atof*

The following function:

```
float atof(char number[])
```

returns a floating point number represented by the string number. If this string cannot be converted, a zero is returned.

Converting from Integer to Character Array with *itoa*

The following function:

```
itoa (int value, char number[], int radix)
```

converts the integer value value, and stores the result in the string number. radix is an integer value that specifies the radix of the numbering system to be used. In most cases, we are interested in decimal representation, so the number 10 can be used.

For example:

```
int k=25;
char number[20];
itoa(k, number, 10);
```

Try These for Fun...

- Write a program to read a first name, a middle name, and a last name. Then, have it write the last name, a comma, and then the first name and the middle initial.

- Write a function to compare positions i through j of a character array with positions of another character array starting at position k. Return 1 if the strings match, and zero otherwise.

- Write a program to read an integer N, and then to read N names while storing them in an array of character arrays.

- Expand the program above to read an integer m, and then to display the mth name in the array.

Understanding and Using Structures

A *structure* is a set of data of varying types and/or meanings that are all related to the same item. For example, to describe a customer, you may use the following information:

- Name

- Address

- Zip code

- Phone number

- Account number

Each piece of data, called a *field*, has a different meaning. One field keeps the name of a person, another field keeps the name of a street, another field keeps a phone number, etc. However, these fields are related because they describe a single customer. The address reflects the street address of the customer whose name is the *name* field, the telephone number reflects his or her telephone number, etc.

Since objects also have data that belong to the same object, it may be said that objects also contain a structure. For example, athletes have coordinates, a head, a trunk, a left arm, a right arm, a left leg, a right leg, and other data, as well. Indeed,

Skill 20

there is a strong resemblance between structures and classes. In fact, it is also possible to include member functions in a structure, and then to declare objects. The only difference is that there are no private or protected members in a structure. They are all public.

N **NOTE**   Although it is possible to use structures to work as classes, I strongly suggest that you use structures only in the cases for which you do not need member functions.

A structure is declared in a similar way that a class is declared. Use the keyword `struct`, followed by an identifier that will name the structure; then, include the declaration of the data that compose the structure in braces.

```
struct    identifier
{
     data or object declarations ;
};    // Don't forget the semicolon!
```

For example:

```
struct student
{
   char lastname[20];
   char firstname[20];
   long enrollment_number;
};
```

Just like it is with a class, a structure does not imply the creation of an object or a variable—it simply describes what a student looks like. To use an object of a class, you have to declare an object of that class. To use a variable of a given type, you have to declare a variable of that type. To use a structured variable, you must declare a variable that has that structure. For example:

```
student customer;
```

creates a variable `customer` that has a structure such as that defined in `student`.

You can access fields in the structure by qualifying the field with the structured variable name. For example:

```
customer.enrollment_number=924054;
```

Again, this is the same way that we access data in objects.

Structures and Arrays

A field in a structure may be an array. Actually, the *student* example uses character arrays for `firstname` and `lastname`. A field itself may also be a structure.
Consider the following structure:

```
struct address
{
    char street[40];
    char city [20];
    char zipcode[10];
};
```

Once this address structure is declared, we can declare a structure that describes
an employee to include a field that happens to be an address—in other words, it's
another structure. For example:

```
struct employee
{
    char lastname[20];
    char firstname[20];
    long salary;
    address home;
}
```

If you wonder how to access the address field, here is how to do it:

```
employee person;
...
strcpy(person.home.street,"221 Baker St.");
strcpy(person.home.city,"London");
...
```

Inheritance in Structures

Another alternative you can use to implement the `employee` structure above is
to use inheritance to make the `employee` structure a descendent of the `address`
structure. In other words, you can think of an employee as an address that has
first and last names, as well as a salary.

```
struct employee: address
{
    char lastname[20];
    char firstname[20];
    long salary;
};
```

Arrays of Structures

It is also possible to have arrays in which each element is a structure. For example:

```
employee  staff[100];
student group[30];
```

The first statement creates an array of 100 elements, in which each element is an employee with all the fields described for this structure. The second statement creates an array of 30 students.

To access the city field of a given staff member, you will also have to specify an index, so the computer can understand which staff member you are talking about. For example:

```
staff[10].home.city
```

Copying Structures

You can copy a variable to another variable that has the same structure by using the assignment operator. For example, if you have the following declarations:

```
employee worker1,worker2, staff[100];
```

the following statements are correct:

```
worker1=worker2;
staff[5]=worker1;
worker1.home=staff[1].home;
```

because the compiler can copy variables that have the same structure.

Searching Character Arrays

An interesting searching situation is when you have to locate a given element in a character array. For example, you may have to determine which element in an array has the value *zero*.

This situation can be illustrated with a null-terminated string. Do you remember that a string is terminated by the character null, whose value is zero? How do you suppose the strlen function computes the size of a string? Can you do it?

All you have to do is to search all the elements of the string to determine where the null character is. In fact, it is easier to do this than it is to search for the largest element, because, from the beginning, you know the element for which you are looking.

Go ahead—compare the value you are looking for with the first value, with the second value, with the third value….

If you have the following string:

```
char name[50];
```

and, at some point in the program, if you want to determine the size of the string without using the strlen function, you can do as follows:

```
for(int position=0;position<50;position++)
{
   if (name[position]==0) break;
}
```

After this piece of program executes, the variable position should contain the number of characters before null. However, if there is no terminator, the answer will be 50.

> **NOTE**   Since you know how to find a null, do you think you can find any other character? What if you want to look for a *t*?

Searching with More Arrays

A more interesting situation of array searching is when you use a structure or multidimensional array. For example, consider the following structure:

```
struct student
{
   int idnumber
   char lastname[30];
}
student myclass[50];
```

In this case, there is an array myclass with 50 elements. Each element is a structure consisting of an ID number and a last name.

Position	ID#	Last Name
00	5002	Rogers
01	6754	Smith
02	6003	Adams
03	6532	Rodriguez
...		
19	6021	Arentz

Suppose that all the elements in the array contain valid data. How could you find the last name of the student whose ID number is 6021?

The problem is essentially the same as the problem of searching in an array for a given value. All you have to do is to search the field idnumber for a match. While you do this, keep track of the position in the array where you are working.

```
for (int position=0;position<50;position++)
{
    if(myclass[position].idnumber==6021) break; // Found it!
}
```

If a match is found—for example, in position 19—the last name you want is the field lastname in position 19 of the array. In this case, you want the following name:

```
myclass[position].lastname
```

What If the Student Is Not Found?

What if there are no students with the ID number you found in the example above? In this case, the loop will check all the elements in the array, and will not execute a break. You may be able to avert this situation by checking the value of position—valid values are only between 0 and 49. A complete loop will leave position with the value *50*.

TIP   It is a good idea to leave searching tasks for specialized functions. You may consider returning the index value where the match was found, or a negative number to inform you that there was no match.

Try These for Fun. . .

- Write the code for a function to examine a string `inputstring` and return as a result the position where a character `thischaracter` was found. If the character was not found, the result should be zero. The string and the character are passed as arguments.

- Write a program to read an array of 10 integers and locate the position of a given value. The value is also supplied from the keyboard. Try to use a function to search the array.

Are You Experienced?

Now you can. . .

- ☑ Use character arrays to store text data
- ☑ Use string-manipulation functions to operate on character arrays
- ☑ Convert between numeric and character format
- ☑ Use structures
- ☑ Search for specific values in an array

Skill 20

Developing Applications—
Short Projects

❏ Improving the point-of-sale terminal

❏ Improving the satellite simulation

To further develop your skills in developing applications, you will now make a few changes to two applications you created earlier—the point-of-sale terminal (originally created in Skill 9) and the satellite simulation (created in Skill 18). Here's how you'll improve the code for each of these programs:

- You will incorporate arrays and text manipulation into your point-of-sale terminal.

- You will incorporate arrays into the satellite project to handle a collection of satellites.

Short Project 1—Point-of-Sale Terminal

When you go to the supermarket or to any other store, you hardly ever see a cash register that makes the clerk type in the price. It is most likely that the product code is input using a bar code reader. How does this kind of terminal work?

The computer has a list of all the products that are on sale. In this list, there must be a code, a price, and, possibly, a description of the product. As the clerk inputs the code, the computer searches the list for a product with that particular code. Does this remind you of the searching operation? Well, it should!

In this version of the point-of-sale terminal, a list of items is kept in the computer's memory. Each sale is transacted by entering a product code (or part number) from the keyboard (regrettably, there is no bar code reader available to you). The list is then searched for this particular item, and the price and the product description will be obtained. This new version of the terminal also displays the product description on the screen.

The end-user interface should remain as similar to the previous terminal's interface as possible.

Implementing New Features

The list will be kept in the computer's memory. The following information must be known for each product:

- The product code
- The product description
- The product price

Since several products will be on sale, you may consider declaring an array of structures:

```
struct product
{
  int code;
  char description[20];
  float price;
};
product list[20];
```

Use this array to locate the information for the items that you need. Since the computer's memory cannot hold information while the power is off, you will need to input information every time your program starts. You can think of this array as a *parts catalog* that is checked for every purchase. In the old days, when you wanted to buy parts for your car, the clerk had to look for the part number in a big catalog to find out the price and other information.

Should we consider having the program also use a `catalog` class to look for the product information? Actually, this is a great idea! You can design an additional class of objects that acts like a catalog, allowing you to look up information as long as you know the product code. If a catalog is available, the remaining operation is very similar to the old terminal's operation. In fact, why build another class? We can inherit several things from the old one!

The *catalog* Class

The `catalog` class can implement all the operations needed to handle the parts catalog. Although this particular implementation solves only the problem we have at hand, you may find out later that it is a very useful piece of code. Here is one possible declaration:

```
struct product
{
  int code;
  char description[20];
  float price;
};

class catalog
{
 protected:
  product list[20];
  int listsize;
```

Skill 21

```
public:
  catalog();
  virtual product find(int part_number);
};
```

This class has an array and an integer as data members to hold the number of products present in the array. The array itself consists of elements that are structures, as previously described. Since this is not a commercial product, the array uses only 20 elements.

As far as member functions are concerned, there is a constructor and a find function. The constructor automatically asks you to input the array elements, so you don't use an empty list. The find function searches the catalog for the given part number. Notice that this function returns, as a result, a structure of type product. You enter a part number, and the function returns a complete structure with all the information (code, description, price) that is associated with the given part number.

NOTE   The find function may need to be replaced by other find functions in derived classes. It should be a virtual function.

Here is the code for the constructor:

```
catalog::catalog()
{

  listsize=0;
  for (listsize=0;yesno("Another item?")&&(listsize<20)
              ;listsize++)
  {
    list[listsize].code=ask("Enter product code:");
    strcpy(list[listsize].description,
          "Product description");
    askwords(list[listsize].description,20,
          "Description:");
    list[listsize].price=ask("Enter the price:");
  }
}
```

The find function is very similar to what you have already seen while searching an array:

```
product catalog::find(int part_number)
{
  for(int item=0;item<listsize;item++)
```

```
    {
        if(part_number==list[item].code) return list[item];
    }
    product nonexistent;
    nonexistent.code=0;
    return nonexistent;
}
```

If there is no match for the requested code, even in this case, a structure is returned, but the field `code` is zero. This is how you can find out whether the item was found. On the other hand, if the match was found in position `item`, the returned structure is the array element indexed by `item`.

NOTE   The code for the `catalog` class is included in `c7catalo.h`.

The New *terminal* Class

The new `terminal` class is an expansion of the old one. You can inherit what was available, and just add the expansions. The new class `saleterm` can be declared as follows:

```
class saleterm: public terminal
{
  protected:
    catalog parts;
    product sale;
    Box Part_Number,Part_Description;
    void items();
  public:
    saleterm();
};
```

By deriving this new class from the `terminal` class, you inherit everything that exists in `terminal`. You only have to declare the new items. The new terminal consists of a catalog, a structure to describe one product (the product currently being sold), a couple of new boxes to display the product code (`Part_Number`), and the product description.

The `items` function is inherited, too. However, since this terminal requests codes instead of prices, you cannot use the same function. You have to provide a new function to handle the items.

You *can* keep the `operate` member function intact and use it as inherited, because this function only catches up after the price has been obtained.

Constructors

An interesting thing happens with the constructors when an object of a derived class is created. (Pay attention—this is new!) The constructor for an object of the base class is invoked, and then the constructor for the derived class is invoked. When the constructor for the derived class is invoked, an object of the base class already exists. This new constructor only has to add the features that are particular to the derived class to finish the construction.

In this example, the constructor only needs to position and to label two additional boxes.

Here is the code for the constructor:

```
saleterm::saleterm()
{
  Part_Number.place(450,300);
  Part_Description.place(450,340);
  Part_Number.label("Part Number:");
  Part_Description.label("Description:");
}
```

Here is the code for the new items function:

```
void saleterm::items()
{
  int somecode;
  for(;;)
  {
    do
    {
      somecode=ask("Enter part number:");
      sale=parts.find(somecode);
      if(sale.code==0)
          yesno("Wrong part number, please check");
    }
    while (sale.code==0);
    Part_Number.say(sale.code);
    Part_Description.say(sale.description);
    saletotal=saletotal+sale.price;
    Price.say(sale.price);
    Cur_Total.say(saletotal);
    if(!yesno("Another item?")) break;
  }
    saletotal=saletotal*(1+tax);
    Saletotal.say(saletotal);
}
```

You will find the complete code for this project in `c7term.h` and `c7term.cpp`, shown below.

```
#ifndef C7TERM_H         // c7term.h
#define C7TERM_H
#include "franca.h"
#include "c6term.h"
#include "c7catalo.h"
#include <string.h>
class saleterm: public terminal
{
  protected:
   catalog parts;
   product sale;
   Box Part_Number,Part_Description;
   void items();
  public:
   saleterm();
};
saleterm::saleterm()
{
  Part_Number.place(450,300);
  Part_Description.place(450,340);
  Part_Number.label("Part Number:");
  Part_Description.label("Description:");
}
void saleterm::items()
{
  int somecode;
  for(;;)
  {
    do
    {
      somecode=ask("Enter part number:");
      sale=parts.find(somecode);
      if(sale.code==0) yesno("Wrong part number, please check");
    }
    while (sale.code==0);
    Part_Number.say(sale.code);
    Part_Description.say(sale.description);
    saletotal=saletotal+sale.price;
    Price.say(sale.price);
    Cur_Total.say(saletotal);
    if(!yesno("Another item?")) break;
  }
    saletotal=saletotal*(1+tax);
    Saletotal.say(saletotal);
}
```

```
#endif

// End

#include "franca.h"    // c7term.cpp
#include "c7term.h"
#include <string.h>
void mainprog()
{
    saleterm cashregister;
    cashregister.operate();
}
```

IMPROVEMENTS

Can you save the product information so you don't have to retype it every time your program starts? It will definitely be difficult to sell your terminal otherwise, don't you think?

You can store this information in a disk file, which we will learn about in the next Skill.

Short Project 2—Satellites

Arrays make it easy for you to manipulate a collection of objects. If you want to simulate electrons orbiting around a nucleus, as suggested in Skill 18, without using arrays, you will end up with a large, repetitive program that handles each electron individually.

Because arrays allow you to deal with all elements using the same name (for example, electron) and designate each element by a variable index (for example, electron [n]), you have to write only one loop to explain what you want done with any element. Not only will you save work, but the program does not have to change if you ever need to change the number of elements in the array.

As an example, we will use the satellite class to simulate an atom with two electrons in the first orbit and eight electrons in the second orbit. We will use an array `electron`, consisting of 10 objects of type `satellite`. Of course, the nucleus can also be a satellite.

Enhancing Capabilities with Arrays

To make things more interesting, you can make the nucleus perform a circular movement, as well. In the example below (`c7atom.cpp`), a special satellite `ether` is used as the center for the nucleus's orbit.

The declaration and the initialization are as follows:

```
const float pi2=2*3.14159;
Box clock("Time: ");
Clock timer,sidereal;
satellite electron[10];
satellite nucleus,ether;
nucleus.resize(40);
ether.place(320,200);
nucleus.center(ether);
nucleus.dist(80);
nucleus.speed(pi2/800.);
nucleus.move();
```

Initializing Electrons

You have to initialize each electron, as well. Electrons in the first orbit are initialized as follows:

```
for (int i=0;i<2;i++)
{
  electron[i].center(nucleus);
  electron[i].dist(80);
  electron[i].speed(pi2/300.);
  electron[i].resize(12);
  electron[i].color(5,5);
  electron[i].angle(i*pi2/2.+pi2/4.);
  electron[i].move();
}
```

Electrons in the second orbit are initialized as follows:

```
for (int i=2;i<10;i++)
{
  electron[i].center(nucleus);
  electron[i].dist(120);
  electron[i].speed(pi2/600.);
  electron[i].resize(12);
```

```
        electron[i].color(5,5);
        electron[i].angle(i*pi2/8.);
        electron[i].move();
    }
```

When all the objects have been initialized, the actual simulation can take place:

```
nucleus.show();
for(;sidereal.time()<20.;)
{
  nucleus.erase();
  nucleus.move();
  nucleus.show();
  for(int i=0;i<10;i++)
  {
    electron[i].erase();
    electron[i].center(nucleus);
    electron[i].move();
    electron[i].show();
  }
  clock.say(sidereal.time()*10);
  timer.watch(.033);
  timer.reset();
}
```

In this case, the nucleus was represented as a separate satellite, but it is not necessary to represent it this way. You can choose electron[10] to represent it if you add one more electron to your array.

Try This for Fun. . .

- The program c7pool.cpp (listed below) implements and uses a class pool, which simulates a ball rolling on a pool table and bouncing against the walls.

    - Derive a class that simulates a pool table by including six black circles, as shown in Figure 21.1. When the ball drops into a pocket (reaches a black circle), you score a point. To determine whether the ball has dropped into a pocket, check whether the ball's coordinates (x,y) are at a distance that is less than the pocket's radius. In this program, the pocket's radius is 15 and the ball's radius is 10.

FIGURE 21.1: The pool table

- Here is the listing of c7pool.cpp:

```cpp
#include "franca.h"
#include <math.h>
#include <stdlib.h>
  const int ballradius=10,poolradius=15;
  const int poolx=400,pooly=200;
class pool:public Stage
{
 protected:
  Square table;
  Circle ball;
  float xb,yb;      // The ball's coordinates
  float incx,incy; // Incremental movements
  float speed;
 public:
  pool();
  void shoot(float angle);
};

pool::pool()
{
  float angle;
  speed=1.5;
  table.resize(pooly,poolx);
  table.place(320,240);
  table.color(2);
  ball.color(0,0);
  ball.resize(ballradius*2);
  table.show();
  insert(table);
  insert(ball);
```

```
    xb=rand()%(poolx-ballradius)+320-poolx/2.+ballradius;
    yb=rand()%(pooly-ballradius)+240-pooly/2.+ballradius;
    ball.place(xb,yb);
    ball.show();
}

void pool::shoot(float angle)
{
  angle=3.14159*angle/180.;
  incx=cos(angle)*speed;
  incy=-sin(angle)*speed;
  Clock cuckoo,timer;
  for (;cuckoo.time()<30;)
  {
    if((xb<=(320-poolx/2.+ballradius))||
       (xb>=(320+poolx/2.-ballradius))) incx=-incx;
    if((yb<=(240-pooly/2.+ballradius))||
       (yb>=(240.+pooly/2.-ballradius))) incy=-incy;
    xb=xb+incx;
    yb=yb+incy;
    ball.place(xb,yb);
    table.show();
    ball.show();
    timer.watch(.033);
    timer.reset();
  }
}

void mainprog()
{
  pool billiard;
  float angle;
  for(;yesno("Take a shot?");)
  {
    angle=ask("input the angle:");
    billiard.shoot(angle);
  }
}
```

Are You Experienced?

Now you can. . .

- ☑ Use character arrays in a point-of-sale or similar application to display product information

- ☑ Use an array of Screen Objects, such as satellites, to manipulate several objects

PART VIII

Getting Real

In real-life programming, you will not be able to use the Screen Objects that were available with our special software. You will have to deal with standard text input and output (i/o) using the keyboard and the display. In Part VIII, you will develop your ability to perform i/o operations using the standard C++ i/o streams. You will also learn how to format input and output.

Also, in real-life programming, you don't want to type data all the time. It is most likely that you will have your data stored in a disk file, so you can read them and update them at will. In Part VIII, you will develop your ability to use files.

Finally, to keep improving your skills in developing applications, you will work on further improvements to the point-of-sale terminal. The most remarkable improvement this time is that you will store your product catalog in a disk file.

PROGRAMMERS
C, C, VB, Cobol, exp. Call 534-555-6543 or fax 534-555-6544.

PROGRAMMING
MRFS Inc. is looking for a Sr. Windows NT developer. Reqs. 3-5 yrs. Exp. In C under Windows, Win95 & NT. using Visual C. Excl. OO design & implementation a must. OLE2 & ODBC are a plus. Excl. Salary & bnfts. Resume & salary history to HR, 8779 HighTech Way, Computer City, AR

PROGRAMMERS
Contractors Wanted for short & long term assignments: Visual C, MFC Unix C/C, SQL Oracle Developers PC Help Desk Support Windows NT & NetWare Telecommunications Visual Basic, Access, HTML, CGI, Perl MMI & Co. 885-555-9933

PROGRAMMER World Wide Web Links wants your HTML & Photoshop skills. Develop great WWW sites. Local & global customers. Send samples & resume to WWWL, 2000 Apple Road, Santa Rosa, CA.

TECHNICAL WRITER Software firm seeks writer/editor for manuals, research notes, project mgmt. Min 2 years tech. writing, DTP & programming experience. Send resume & writing samples to: Software Systems, Dallas, TX.

TECHNICAL Software development firm looking for Tech Trainers. Ideal candidates have programming experience in Visual C, HTML & JAVA. Need quick self starter. Call (443) 555-6868 for interview.

TECHNICAL WRITER/ Premier Computer Corp is seeking a combination of technical skills, knowledge and experience in the following areas: UNIX, Windows 95/NT, Visual Basic, on-line help & documentation, and the internet. Candidates must possess excellent writing skills, and be comfortable working in a quality vs. deadline driven environment. Competitive salary. Fax resume & samples to Karen Fields. Premier Computer Corp. 444 Industrial Blvd. Concord, CA. Or send to our website at www.premier.com.

WEB DESIGNER
BA/BS or equivalent programming/multimedia production. 3 years of experience in use and design of WWW services streaming audio and video HTML, PERL, CGI, GIF, JPEG. Demonstrated interpersonal, organization, communication, multi-tasking skills. Send resume to The Learning People at www.learning.com.

WEBMASTER-TECHNICAL
BSCS or equivalent. 2 years of experience in CGI, Windows 95/NT, UNIX, C, Java, Perl. Demonstrated ability to design, code, debug and test on-line services. Send resume to The Learning People at www.learning.com.

PROGRAMMER World Wide Web Links wants your HTML & Photoshop skills. Develop great WWW sites.

---

system testing using automated testing tools. Experienced in documentation preparation & programming languages (Access, C, FoxPro) are a plus. Financial or banking customer service support is required along with excellent verbal & written communication skills with multi levels of end-users. Send resume to KKUP Enterprises, 45 Orange Blvd. Orange, CA.

COMPUTERS Small Web Design firm seeks indiv. w/NT, Webserver & Database management exp. Fax resume to 556-555-4221.

COMPUTER/ Visual C/C, Visual Basic Exp'd Systems Analysts/ Programmers for growing software dev. team in Roseburg. Computer Science or related degree preferred. Develop adv. Engineering applications for engineering firm. Fax resume to 707-555-8744.

COMPUTER Web Master for dynamic SF Internet co. Site, Dev. test, coord., train. 2 yrs prog. Exp. C C Web C, FTP. Fax resume to Best Staffing 845-555-7722.

COMPUTER PROGRAMMER
Ad agency seeks programmer w/exp. in UNIX/NT Platforms, Web Server, CGI/Perl. Programmer Position avail. on a project basis with the possibility to move into F/T. Fax resume & salary req. to R. Jones 334-555-8332.

COMPUTERS Programmer/Analyst Design and maintain C based SQL database applications. Required skills: Visual Basic, C, SQL, ODBC. Document existing and new applications. Novell or NT exp. a plus. Fax resume & salary history to 235-555-9935.

GRAPHIC DESIGNER
Webmaster's Weekly is seeking a creative Graphic Designer to design high impact marketing collateral, including direct mail promos. CD-ROM packages, ads and WWW pages. Must be able to juggle multiple projects and learn new skills on the job very rapidly. Web design experience a big plus, technical troubleshooting also a plus. Call 435-555-1235.

GRAPHICS - ART DIRECTOR - WEB-MULTIMEDIA
Leading internet development company has an outstanding opportunity for a talented, high-end Web Experienced Art Director. In addition to a great portfolio and fresh ideas, the ideal candidate has excellent communication and presentation skills. Working as a team with innovative producers and programmers, you will create dynamic, interactive web sites and application interfaces. Some programming experience required. Send samples and resume to: SuperSites, 333 Main, Seattle, WA.

MARKETING
Fast paced software and services provider looking for MARKETING COMMUNICATIONS SPECIALIST to be responsible for its webpage

---

PROGRAMMERS Multiple short term assignments available: Visual C, 3 positions SQL ServerNT Server, 2 positions JAVA & HTML, long term NetWare. Various locations. Call for more info. 356-555-3398.

PROGRAMMERS
C, C, VB, Cobol, exp. Call 534-555-6543 or fax 534-555-6544.

PROGRAMMING
MRFS Inc. is looking for a Sr. Windows NT developer. Reqs. 3-5 yrs. Exp. In C under Windows, Win95 & NT. using Visual C. Excl. OO design & implementation skills a must. OLE2 & ODBC are a plus. Resume & salary history to HR, 8779 HighTech Way, Computer City, AR

PROGRAMMERS/ Contractors Wanted for short & long term assignments: Visual C, MFC Unix C/C, SQL Oracle Developers PC Help Desk Support Windows NT & NetWare Telecommunications Visual Basic, Access, HTML, CGI, Perl MMI & Co. 885-555-9933

PROGRAMMER World Wide Web Links wants your HTML & Photoshop skills. Develop great WWW sites. Local & global customers. Send samples & resume to WWWL, 2000 Apple Road, Santa Rosa, CA.

TECHNICAL WRITER Software firm seeks writer/editor for manuals, research notes, project mgmt. Min 2 years tech. writing, DTP & programming experience. Send resume & writing samples to: Software Systems, Dallas, TX.

COMPUTER PROGRAMMER
Ad agency seeks programmer w/exp. in UNIX/NT Platforms, Web Server, CGI/Perl. Programmer Position avail. on a project basis with the possibility to move into F/T. Fax resume & salary req. to R. Jones 334-555-8332.

TECHNICAL WRITER Premier Computer Corp is seeking a combination of technical skills, knowledge and experience in the following areas: UNIX, Windows 95/NT, Visual Basic, on-line help & documentation, and the internet. Candidates must possess excellent writing skills, and be comfortable working in a quality vs. deadline driven environment. Competitive salary. Fax resume & samples to Karen Fields. Premier Computer Corp., 444 Industrial Blvd, Concord, CA. Or send to our website at www.premier.com.

WEB DESIGNER
BA/BS or equivalent programming/multimedia production. 3 years of experience in use and design of WWW services streaming audio and video HTML, PERL, CGI, GIF, JPEG. Demonstrated interpersonal, organization, communication, multi-tasking skills. Send resume to The Learning People at www.learning.com.

WEBMASTER-TECHNICAL
BSCS or equivalent, 2 years of

COMPUTERS Small Web Design Firm seeks indiv. w/NT, Webserver & Database management exp. Fax resume to 556-555-4221.

COMPUTER Visual C/C, Visual Basic Exp'd Systems Analysts/ Programmers for growing software dev. team in Roseburg. Computer Science or related degree preferred. Develop adv. Engineering applications for engineering firm. Fax resume to 707-555-8744.

COMPUTER Web Master for dynamic SF Internet co. Site, Dev. test, coord., train. 2 yrs prog. Exp. C C Web C, FTP. Fax resume to Best Staffing 845-555-7722.

COMPUTERS/ QA SOFTWARE TESTERS Qualified candidates should have 2 yrs exp. performing integration & system testing using automated testing tools. Experienced in documentation preparation & programming languages (Access, C, FoxPro) are a plus. Financial or banking customer service support is required along with excellent verbal & written communication skills with multi levels of end-users. Send resume to KKUP Enterprises, 45 Orange Blvd. Orange, CA.

COMPUTERS Programmer/Analyst Design and maintain C based SQL database applications. Required skills: Visual Basic, C, SQL, ODBC. Document existing and new applications. Novell or NT exp. a plus. Fax resume & salary history to 235-555-9935.

GRAPHIC DESIGNER
Webmaster's Weekly is seeking a creative Graphic Designer to design high impact marketing collateral, including direct mail promo's. CD-ROM packages, ads and WWW pages. Must be able to juggle multiple projects and learn new skills on the job very rapidly. Web design experience a big plus, technical troubleshooting also a plus. Call 435-555-1235.

GRAPHICS - ART DIRECTOR - WEB-MULTIMEDIA
Leading internet development company has an outstanding opportunity for a talented, high-end Web Experienced Art Director. In addition to a great portfolio and fresh ideas, the ideal candidate has excellent communication and presentation skills. Working as a team with innovative producers and programmers, you will create dynamic, interactive web sites and application interfaces. Some programming experience required. Send samples and resume to: SuperSites, 333 Main, Seattle, WA.

COMPUTER PROGRAMMER
Ad agency seeks programmer w/exp. in UNIX/NT Platforms, Web Server, CGI/Perl. Programmer Position avail. on a project basis with the possibility to move into F/T. Fax resume & salary req. to R. Jones 334-555-8332.

PROGRAMMERS / Established software company seeks program

---

seminar coordination, and ad placement. Must be a self-starter, energetic, organized. Must have 2 web experience. Programming a plus. Call 985-555-9854.

PROGRAMMERS Multiple short term assignments available: Visual C, 3 positions SQL ServerNT Server, 2 positions JAVA & HTML, long term NetWare. Various locations. Call for more info. 356-555-3398.

PROGRAMMERS
C, C, VB, Cobol, exp. Call 534-555-6543 or fax 534-555-6544.

PROGRAMMING
MRFS Inc. is looking for a S... Windows NT developer. Reqs. 3... yrs. Exp. In C under Windows, Win95 & NT. using Visual C. Ex... OO design & implementation ski... a must. OLE2 & ODBC are a pl... Excl. Salary & bnfts. Resume... salary history to HR, 8779 HighT... Way, Computer City, AR

PROGRAMMERS/ Contracto... Wanted for short & long term assignments; Visual C, MFCUnix C/C, S... Oracle Developers PC Help De... Support Windows NT & NetWa... Telecommunications Visual Bas... Access, HTML, CGI, Perl MMI & C... 885-555-9933

PROGRAMMER World Wide W... Links wants your HTML & Photosh... skills. Develop great WWW sit... Local & global customers. Send sa... ples & resume to WWWL, 20... Apple Road, Santa Rosa, CA.

TECHNICAL WRITER Software fi... seeks writer/editor for manua... research notes, project mgmt. Mi... years tech. writing, DTP & progra... ming experience. Send resume... writing samples to: Softw... Systems, Dallas, TX.

TECHNICAL Software developm... firm looking for Tech Trainers. Id... candidates have programming ex... rience in Visual C, HTML & JA... Need quick self starter. Call (4... 555-6868 for interview.

TECHNICAL WRITER Prem... Computer Corp is seeking a com... nation of technical skills, knowle... and experience in the follow... areas: UNIX, Windows 95/NT, Vi... Basic, on-line help & documentat... and the internet. Candidates n... possess excellent writing skills, ... be comfortable working in a qu... vs. deadline driven environme... Competitive salary. Fax resume... samples to Karen Fields. Pre... Computer Corp. 444 Industrial B... Concord, CA. Or send to our web... at www.premier.com.

WEB DESIGNER
BA/BS or equivalent progr... ming/multimedia production. ... years of experience in use... design of WWW services strea... audio and video HTML, PERL... GIF, JPEG. Demonstrated inter... sonal, organization, communica... multi-tasking skills. Send resum... The Learning People at www.le... ing.com.

S K I L L

twenty-two

22

Living without *franca.h*

- ❑ Inputting with streams
- ❑ Outputting with streams
- ❑ Formatting

In the real world, there are no franca.h header files or ScreenObj, athlete, Clock, or most of the other object types we have used to learn C++. Now that you are a programmer, you must learn to live on your own, without the help of the class libraries that were developed to help you take your initial programming steps.

It is regrettable that it is still too hard for a beginning programmer to use a graphic interface in Windows. In this Skill, we will resort to the more modest text interface to enable you to face the real world without fear. In fact, the main difference between what we have been using so far and what is available in the real world is the way that you interact with your computer.

Our predefined classes made it easy for you to develop programs that could produce pictures and animations on the screen. Our communication with the user was a bit more attractive due to the graphic interface. When you use every-day C++, you will be restricted to writing data to the screen and reading data from the keyboard.

In this Skill, we will concentrate on reading textual data from the keyboard, on displaying textual data on the screen, and on using files—with no help from pre-built libraries.

> **NOTE**   Of course, you are always welcome to use the classes declared in franca.h. You may also continue to study C++ and, more specifically, Windows programming, so you may learn how to communicate with users of your programs through a graphic interface.

LIVING WITHOUT I/O STATEMENTS

It is amazing that C++ does not have special statements to deal with inputting and outputting data. Essentially, data to be output are sent to special objects in charge of output, and data to be input are retrieved from other special objects.

The Real World of C++ Programming

The best way to learn what "real" C++ programming is like is to study examples. The following example is a very simple program that runs in C++ using only standard header files. This program asks you for your first name, and writes a message back to you. When you execute this program, notice the first difference between what you have done so far and what you can do now—there are no more projects!

> **NOTE**   You do not have to use projects anymore. Instead of opening a project, removing the previous `.cpp` file, and including the new one, all you have to do is to open your program file and then run it.

You can type or load a program, and then just run it!

```
#include <iostream.h>
#include <iomanip.h>
void main()                  // c8cngrat.cpp
{
  char yourname[30];
  cout<<"Hello!"<<endl<<"What is your name?";
  cin>yourname;
  cout<<endl;
  cout<<"Congratulations, "<<yourname;
  cout<<", you are now a programmer!";
}
```

The code snippet above shows clearly a few differences from the exercises you've been working with throughout this book:

- There is no `franca.h`, so there are no athletes, runners, Screen Objects, Clocks, etc. There are also no functions such as `ask`, `yesno`, etc.

- It is most likely that you will use the header files `iostream.h` and `iomanip.h`. You may also have to use other header files.

> **WARNING**   Do not use `franca.h` with `iostream.h`—it may cause unpredictable problems!

- There is no `void mainprog`. Instead, your main function is called `main`.
- You don't have to use a project—just type or load your program, and then run it.

- As you run the program, no graphic interfaces will be available. (Well, you are not a kid anymore....)

Execute this program and see how it works. Experiment with typing your full name instead of your first name only. What happens?

LIVING WITHOUT PROJECTS

The following hints may help you run your first few programs that are not part of a project:

- Make sure there are no projects or workspaces open. If there are, close them.
- In the main menu, choose File ➤ Open to open the program that you want.
- Run the program using the same procedure you used to run a project.
- Microsoft compilers will create a standard project to run your program. Make sure to close the project or workspace after you run your program.

Using C++ Streams

Two alternatives govern input and output in C++. It is possible to use a set of functions to perform these operations or a set of objects to perform them. In fact, the use of functions was created with the C programming language, the ancestor of C++.

The use of objects to perform input and output was specifically developed for C++, and is simpler and more powerful. Your program generates data that flow to an output. This is the concept of C++ output streams. You take all the data that you want to output and "move" them to a special object (cout) that forwards your data to the screen.

Actually, it is very simple—if you have an integer variable number, you can write this variable to the screen with the following statement:

```
cout<< number;
```

which means *put the variable* number *in the C output.*

Similarly, you request another kind of object to provide you with data collected from the keyboard. You "retrieve" the data from this input object (cin) and bring them to variables in your program. Using the same example, you can input a value to the variable number with the following statement:

```
cin>> number;
```

which means *extract data from the C input and bring it into the variable* number.

NOTE   The names *cin* and *cout* are derived from *C input* and *C output.*

As you may notice, the input and output operations use special operators, << and >>. These operators remind you that the data flow from data to output (cout<<number) and from input to data (cin>>number).

This syntax is very similar to what you used with Cin and Cout in franca.h.

INPUT AND OUTPUT

Novice programmers are often confused by the terms *input* and *output*. Keep in mind that these terms refer to the computer. What you type from the keyboard is *input to* the computer; values that you display on the screen are *output from* the computer.

The *iostream.h* Header File

To use stream input and output (stream i/o), you must include a new header file in your programs. Do not use franca.h with stream i/o. Instead, type the following line at the beginning of your program file:

```
#include <iostream.h>
```

Now, the header file is enclosed by < and >, instead of by double quotes (""). When you use header files that are in the compiler directories, you should use this new form.

The iostream.h file contains the class declarations and definitions that allow you to use the objects cin and cout.

Stream i/o handles all the fundamental data types of C++. The following data types may be directly used:

- int
- char
- float
- double

You cannot use arrays. You can only input and output an element of an array that happens to be of a fundamental data type. You also cannot use a structure. You can only input and output a field in a structure that happens to be of a fundamental data type.

However, there is a notable exception: null-terminated strings, although a special case of arrays, can be used, too! For example:

```
char name[] = "Alfred E. Newman";
...
cout<<name;
```

> **NOTE**   Once you have included iostream.h in your program, the objects cin and cout are automatically declared and usable.

Outputting with Streams

Stream output consists of the object cout, followed by the operator << and the variable (or constant) to be output:

```
cout <<    variable identifier  ;
```

For example:

```
cout<< number;
```

If several variables are to be output, each one has to be preceded by another operator (<<):

```
cout<<"The result is:"<<number<<" and that is final";
```

The output is displayed on the screen with no spaces between the values. For example:

```
int number=32;
char name[]="Sonny Bonds";
cout<<name<<number;
```

results in the following output:

```
Sonny Bonds32
```

Two output statements do not cause two lines. In other words, in the example above, if the output was split into two statements:

```
cout<<name;
cout<<number;
```

the result would be the same.

Spacing

If you desire a space between values, an easy solution is to insert a blank string between them:

```
cout<<name<<"   "<<number;
```

Or, a more detailed explanation could also be used:

```
cout<<"Customer Name:   " << name << "   code is: "<<number;
```

Starting on a New Line

It is also possible to instruct the output to start on a new line. There are two ways to do this: you can write the control character \n (new line) to the output, or you can include the i/o manipulator endl in the output. For example:

```
cout<<"Customer Name:"<<name<<'\n'<<" code is:    "<<number;
```

or:

```
cout<<"Customer Name:"<<name<<endl<<" code is:    "<<number;
```

Either one will cause the same output:

```
Customer Name:Sonny Bonds
  code is:    32
```

Inputting with Streams

Stream input consists of the object cin, followed by the operator >> and the variable to which the input value should be assigned:

```
cin >>     variable identifier     ;
```

For example:

```
cin>>i;
```

fetches a value from the keyboard and assigns it to the variable i. It is possible to assign values to more than one variable with a single input:

```
cin>>i>>j>>k;
```

In this case, the first value will be assigned to i, the second value to j, and the third value to k. To make the computer separate one input from another input, use a blank space or hit Enter after each value when you type the values. If you choose to separate them with blank spaces, you still have to hit Enter after the last value.

You can experiment with the following program, which requests three integer values to be input and then displays them:

```
#include <iostream.h>
#include <iomanip.h>
void main()
{
  int i,j,k;
  cout<<"Enter three values:\n";
  cin>>i>>j>>k;
  cout<<endl<<"Your values are:"<<'\n';
  cout<<i<<" "<<j<<" "<<k;
}
```

Run this program to make sure that the numbers that you input are correctly displayed.

You can move to a new line on the screen either by including the i/o manipulator `endl` in the stream, or by including the control character for a new line, which is represented in C++ by a backslash followed by the character n. Wherever this control character is found in a literal string or in the output stream, it is interpreted as an instruction to move to the next line. A new line control character can be inserted in the output stream either by including it in another string (`Enter three values: \n`), or by including it by itself (as in the second `cout` in the program above). Whether you use single quotes or double quotes to enclose the character, they will achieve the same effect. However, double quotes generate a null-terminated string, instead of a single character.

When you run the program, observe the following points:

- You can type one or more blank spaces between each number.

- You can press Enter between each number.

- You cannot use blank spaces in a number.

- You cannot use other characters (such as a comma) between numbers.

Example—Using Streams to Input and Output Arrays

Suppose that we want to work with some numeric arrays. It is very likely that we will want to list the whole array to determine the values. We can use a function `show` to do this:

```
void show (int array[], int from, int to)
{
    cout<<endl<<"Contents of array:"<<endl<<"Index"
        <<"  Value";
    for (int k=from;k<=to;k++)
      cout<<endl<<k<<"        "<<array[k];
}
```

This function takes three parameters: the array itself and the index positions that denote where to start and stop the listing. Remember that you do not have to specify the size of the array.

Similarly, we can also use a `readarray` function to input the values:

```
void readarray(int array[],int from,int to)
{
    for (int i=from;i<=to;i++)
```

```
        {
         cout<<endl<<"Please input element index "<<i<<':';
         cin>>array[i];
        }
    }
```

This function illustrates the good practice of keeping the user informed of what the computer is expecting them to type. Remember that it is very likely that you will make programs for other people to use. The more they know what the computer wants them to do, the fewer mistakes they will make. On the other hand, be careful to avoid including unnecessary messages in your functions. If your software is going to be embedded in other pieces of software, it may jam the user screen with useless information.

You can test the functions above with the program c8show.cpp:

```
void main()          // c8show.cpp
{
    int number[10];
    readarray(number,0,9);
    show(number,0,9);
}
```

Formatting

A large amount of a professional programmer's time is spent getting data and producing reports. Professional reports have to look good. Names and numbers must be displayed in convenient places in the report, and numbers must be well aligned.

This is what we call *formatting*. Both input data and output data must be well formatted, so people can readily understand the information.

Elementary formatting was achieved by moving to a new line and inserting blanks, but this is not enough. You still need to know a few more items to conveniently format your reports.

Assuring Floating Point Precision

If you print floating point values, you may not like the way they appear. For example:

```
#include<iomanip.h>
void main()
```

```
{
 float price,tax=6.75,total;
 cout<<"Enter the price:";
 cin>>price;
 total=price+tax*price/100;
 cout<<endl<<"Please pay: $"<<total;
}
```

Although this example is a very simple program to compute the price after sales tax, you may not be very happy with the results. If you enter the price as 10, you will see the following result:

```
Please pay: $10.675
```

There is no such thing as a half cent—you really expected the result to come out with only two decimal places. How can you ensure this? You will learn how to implement floating point precision a little later in this Skill.

Aligning Fields

Another important issue is to make sure that all fields are aligned. Consider the program that reads and shows an array. If you execute it using numbers with varying lengths, you may end up with the following screen:

```
Contents of the array:
Index    Value
0        1
1        23456
2        23
3        -4567
4        3
5        23
6        -21005
7        32
8        21
9        6789
```

This is not desirable because the array elements have an unusual alignment. They should all finish, not start, in the same vertical line. To avoid this problem, specify that all these numbers occupy a given width, in columns, in the output.

Skill 22

Using I/O Manipulators

The header file `iomanip.h` defines several manipulators that can be included in the i/o stream to format the data to be input or output. So far, we have seen `endl`, but there are others (see Table 22.1).

TABLE 22.1: Manipulators in `iomanip.h`

Manipulator	Its Purpose
`endl`	Start on new line
`ends`	Insert null in output
`flush`	Flush stream
`setiosflags(long flag)`	Set i/o flag bits
`resetiosflags(long flag)`	Clear i/o flag bits
`setfill(char fillchar)`	Set fill character to `fillchar`
`setprecision(int places)`	Set precision to `places`
`setw(int width)`	Set total field width

The manipulators `setiosflags`, `resetiosflags`, `setfill`, and `setprecision` remain effective until you specify otherwise. For example, once the fill character is set to a dot, it will remain a dot until another fill character is specified. However, the manipulator `setw` is only effective once.

COMPILER DIFFERENCES

Microsoft compilers do not allow you to alternate the alignment by setting the flags to `ios::left` or `ios::right`. Once you have set the alignment to left:

        setiosflags(ios::left)

you have to reset it:

        resetiosflags(ios::left)

Borland compilers allow you to set the alignment without resetting.

Manipulators are inserted in the stream in the same way that you insert a variable that you want to read or write. Do you remember how `endl` was used? For example, if you want to make sure that all the numbers in the array are displayed correctly, you can modify the `show` function:

```
void show (int array[], int from, int to)
{
    cout<<endl<<"Contents of array:"<<endl<<"Index"
        <<"  Value";
    for (int k=from;k<=to;k++)
      cout<<endl<<setw(3)<<k<<"        "<<setw(8)<<array[k];
}
```

Manipulating Field Width with *setw*

The change that we just made to the `show` function illustrates the use of the manipulator `setw`. In this case, each index value k will occupy exactly three spaces, no matter how many spaces are actually needed to write k. Similarly, each value in the array will occupy exactly eight columns. You should specify a width that is wide enough to accommodate the value you expect to show. If you specify a width that is not sufficient, the computer uses more columns so the number can be correctly written (which ruins your format). The default is `setw(0)`, which means that the minimum number of columns that are needed to represent the value will be used.

Manipulating Decimal Digits with *setprecision*

When you display floating point numbers, you may want to limit the number of decimal places shown. For example, if you are dealing with money, you probably want your results to contain up to two decimal places only. The `setprecision` manipulator can be used for this purpose. Once you have specified the number of decimal places to be displayed, this specification remains in effect until you change your settings with another `setprecision` manipulator. For example, to avoid displaying a price with more than two decimal places, you could do as follows:

```
float price;
cout<<setprecision(2);
...
cout<<price;
```

Any floating point variable that you forward to `cout` is displayed with only two decimal places until you use the manipulator again. Unfortunately, you may be left with other problems that will not be solved completely by this manipulator.

Skill 22

If your floating point variable needs fewer than two decimal places, it prints with fewer than two decimal places, and the decimal point may even be omitted. For example:

```
float x[3]={12.35,10.,5.};
cout<<setprecision(2);
for(int i=0;i<3;i++)
cout<<endl<<setw(8)<<x[i];
```

will display results as follows:

```
12.35
   10
    5
```

which may not be appropriate in a report. To align the decimal point, you will need to use the `setiosflags` manipulator.

The other problem you face is that, due to your settings of width and/or precision, the computer may choose to display the value in exponential (scientific) notation. If this does not suit you, you will have to resort to `setiosflags` to change it.

Manipulating Fill Characters with *setfill*

When you specify the width for a field (by using `setw`), and when the value to be displayed requires fewer columns than are available, the remaining columns are filled with blank spaces. In this case, we say that the fill character is *blank*. It is possible to use any other character as a fill character, instead of using a blank. This is done by the `setfill` manipulator. Once a fill character is specified, it remains in use until you use `setfill` again. If you want to go back to using a blank as the fill character, all you have to do is to use `setfill(' ')`.

For example, it is common to fill dollar values with a nonblank character such as * when printing checks. This is easy to implement:

```
cout<<"US$"<<setfill('*')<<value;
```

There may be other situations in which you want to include leading zeros, dots, or other characters, as well.

Manipulating I/O Controls with *setiosflags* and *resetiosflags*

The `setiosflags` and `resetiosflags` manipulators can be used to change the controls of a set of flags that affect the input/output operations. The flags are shown in Table 22.2.

TABLE 22.2: Flags in `iomanip.h`

Flag	Its Purpose
skipws	Ignore white spaces in input
left	Left align
right	Right align
showpoint	Show decimal places and point
scientific	Use scientific (exponential) notation
fixed	Use fixed floating point notation

To set a flag, use the `setiosflags` manipulator with an argument that consists of the sequence `ios::` followed by the flag you want to set. To reset the flag, use `resetiosflags` with the same argument. For example:

```
cin>>resetiosflags(ios::skipws);
```

resets the `skipws` flag and allows you to read blank (white) spaces in the input.

Reading White Spaces with *skipws*

The `skipws` flag is set as the default. Blank spaces are used as separators between values, and you cannot read them. If you read a string to an array of characters, the input stream assumes that the string is terminated when the first blank space is reached.

You may try to run the following program:

```
#include <iomanip.h>
void main()
{
    char mark[]="-----+";
    char name[30];
    cin>>name;
    cout<<name;
}
```

If you input a string such as Sonny Bonds as data, you will see the result Sonny, because the first blank space indicates the end of the string.

If you reset the skipws flag by including the following statement:

```
cin>>resetiosflags(ios::skipws);
```

you will get the same result! How can you read the blank spaces?

The only way you can read the blank spaces is to undo the automatic feature of C++ that reads character arrays as strings. You have to read the characters one at a time. Consider the following program:

```
#include <iomanip.h>
void main()
{                                    // c8skipws.cpp
    const char enter=10;
    char mark[]="-----+";
    char name[30];
    cin>>resetiosflags(ios::skipws);
    cout<<mark<<mark<<mark<<endl;
    for (int i=0;i<29;i++)
    {
      cin>>name[i];
      if(name[i]==enter) break;
    }
    name[i]=0;]
    cout<<endl<<setw(5)<<i<<" characters read";
    cout<<endl<<name;

}
```

This program resets the skipws flag and reads the input string one character at a time. To avoid reading all 30 characters, this program also tests whether the user has hit Enter. This is done by comparing the input with the code for Enter, as defined in the constant (the code for Enter is equal to the numeric value *10).*

If you remove resetiosflags, the whole string will still be read, but all the blank spaces will be ignored. Worse than this, the code for Enter will not be detected, and you will have to actually complete the typing of 30 nonblank characters (which means that control characters such as Enter are also skipped).

The character array mark is used merely to help you keep track of how many characters you have typed.

Aligning Values with Left and Right I/O Flags

When a value needs fewer columns than there are available, you can align it to the left or to the right by setting either the left or the right flag. The default is to align to the right, which is probably what you want to do when displaying numeric quantities, but is less acceptable when displaying character strings.

Consider the following program:

```
#include <iomanip.h>
void main()
{
    char name[5][20];
    int code[5];
    for (int i=0;i<=4;i++)
    {
      cout<<endl<<"Enter a name:";
      cin>>name[i];
      cout<<endl<<"Enter a code:";
      cin>>code[i];
    }
    for (i=0;i<=4;i++)
    {
      cout<<endl<<setw(20)<<name[i]<<setw(6)<<code[i];
    }
}
```

This program reads a sequence of names and numbers from the keyboard, and then displays them on the screen. Your results may look as follows:

```
Clarice             12
    Liz           4532
  Lucia            435
 Marcos             21
Claudio             43
```

Text on the Left, Numbers on the Right

The formatting above may not be your idea of good formatting—you may want to make sure that the names are left aligned and that the numbers are right aligned. The new listing would be as follows:

```
#include <iomanip.h>
void main()
```

```
{                                              // c8align.cpp
  char name[5][20];
  int code[5];
  for (int i=0;i<=4;i++)
  {
    cout<<endl<<"Enter a name:";
    cin>>name[i];
    cout<<endl<<"Enter a code:";
    cin>>code[i];
  }
  for (i=0;i<=4;i++)
  {
   cout<<endl<<setiosflags(ios::left)<<setw(20)<<name[i]
   <<setiosflags(ios::right)
   <<setiosflags(ios::right)<<setw(6)<<code[i];
  }
}
```

The new output would then look as follows:

```
Clarice                    12
Liz                      4532
Lucia                     435
Marcos                     21
Claudio                    43
```

NOTE   The left-alignment flag was reset so that you could use this program with Microsoft compilers.

Including the Decimal Point with *showpoint*

The showpoint flag forces the output of floating point numbers to include the decimal point and the trailing zeros to fill the maximum number of decimal places as set by setprecision. This flag is necessary because the decimal point and the trailing zeros may be omitted otherwise.

Outputting Numbers in Exponential Format with *scientific*

The scientific flag specifies that floating point numbers are to be output using the exponential format.

Outputting Numbers in Fixed Point Format with *fixed*

The fixed flag is the opposite of the scientific flag, and specifies that floating point numbers are to be output using the fixed point format.

Using Character Codes

In Skill 20, you were introduced to the type char. An ASCII code, consisting of an integer number from 0 to 255, is used to represent characters. It is not important to memorize which code corresponds to which character, but you should check out the following program:

```
#include <iostream.h>
void main()                  // c8ascii.cpp
{
// This program shows the character
//       equivalent of a numeric code.
char code,choice='y';
int number;
while(choice=='y')
  {
    cout<<endl<<"Input the code you want to know:";
    cin>>number;
    code=number;
    cout<<endl<<"This code corresponds to the
                  character:"<<code;
    cout<<endl<<"Do you want to continue (y/n)?";
    cin>>choice;
  }
}
```

This program requests that you input an integer number, and it prints a character whose code corresponds to the number that you input. Notice that code was declared as a character, while number was declared as an integer number. When you output a character, the computer understands that you don't want to print the number, but, instead, that you want to print the character whose code is represented by that number. Thus, even though both code and number may be equal to 65, when you output number, you will see the number *65*, but when you output code, you will see the character *A*.

The program above simply reads an integer number, copies that number to a character variable (code), and then outputs the character variable.

N **NOTE**   If you want to make it clear that the integer value is converted to a character, you can cast the type in the assignment by using code= (char) number;. However, this is done automatically by the compiler.

Using *ask, askwords, yesno,* and Boxes

The functions ask, askwords, and yesno, as well as the Box objects, were very useful for handling input and output. Although you cannot use the Windows graphic interface with the standard C++ input and output streams, I am providing an alternative that will let you still make limited use of these functions and boxes.

The *nofranca.h* Header File

The nofranca.h header file allows you to use the functions listed above and boxes in your programs, even though you are not using franca.h anymore. All you have to do is to use the following directive:

```
#include "nofranca.h"
```

You must include this header file before you attempt to include franca.h. Once this new header file is included in your program, it will prevent the standard franca.h from also being included. Any calls to these functions and the use of boxes will be interpreted by this new version, and simulated in the text interface provided by C++.

You may benefit from looking at this header file. By now, you should be able to understand the complete program. Notice the directive that tests FRANCA_H and _CANVAS_H. This directive prevents the header file franca.h from being loaded.

The Complete Code

Here is the complete code for nofranca.h:

```
#ifndef NOFRANCA_H
#define NOFRANCA_H
#define FRANCA_H
#define _CANVAS_H
#include <iostream.h>
#include <string.h>
```

```
#include <stdlib.h>
#include <iomanip.h>

float ask(char question[])
{
   float answer;
   cout<<endl<<"Asking: "<<question;
   cin>>answer;
   return answer;
}

void askwords(char sentence[],int size,char question[])
{
   cout<<endl<<"Asking (sentence): "<<question;
   cin>>sentence;
}

int yesno(char question[])
{
   char answer;
   cout<<endl<<"yes or no: "<<question;
   cout<<endl<<"Please enter y or n: ";
   cin>>answer;
   if (answer=='y') return 1;
   return 0;
}


class Box
{
  char title[40];
  char message[40];
 public:
  Box();
  Box(char alabel[]);
  void say(float);
  void say(char msg[]);
  void label(int);
  void label(char msg[]);
  void place(int x,int y);
};

void Box::Box()
{
  strcpy(title,"");
  strcpy(message,"");
}
void Box::Box(char msg[])
```

```
{
  strcpy(title,msg);
}
void Box::place(int x,int y)
{

}
void Box::say(float value)
{
  cout<<endl<<title;
  cout<<endl<<setprecision(2)<<setiosflags(ios::showpoint);
  cout<<setiosflags(ios::fixed)<<value;
}

void Box::say(char msg[])
{
  cout<<endl<<title;
  cout<<endl<<msg;
}
void Box::label(char msg[])
{
  strcpy(title,msg);
}
void Box::label(int value)
{
  itoa(value,title,10);
}
#endif
```

Try These for Fun. . .

- Modify the program `c8ascii.cpp` to read a character and display the corresponding numeric code.

- Write a program to display a table that uses two columns: the first column should contain integers starting with zero and going up to 255. The second column should contain characters corresponding to the codes displayed in the first column.

- Modify the program above to display the table in 10 groups of two columns, so all the codes can fit on a single screen.

Are You Experienced?

Now you can. . .

- ☑ Survive in the real world without the franca.h software
- ☑ Use stream input and output
- ☑ Format input and output

SKILL

twenty-three

23

Using Files

- ❏ Understanding and using files
- ❏ Using preprocessor directives
- ❏ Making a class for text files
- ❏ Inputting and displaying files
- ❏ Understanding basic file operations

In Skill 23, you will develop the ability to use files with your data. You will learn how to use the stream files available in standard C++. You will also learn how to develop a class of your own to handle files. Finally, you will become familiar with the most common file operations—searching and matching. You will use these techniques to further improve the point-of-sale terminal in the next Skill.

Understanding and Using Files

Since the beginning of the book, you have stored your programs on the computer's hard drive, so that you don't have to retype them every time you need them. In general, any set of information that is stored and that can be used later is called a *file*. In this section, you learn how to store data in files, so you can read them later or transfer them to another computer.

You work with files in essentially the same way that you have been working with the display and the keyboard. Of course, since you are already experienced with program files, you know that there are some subtle differences between working with files and working with the display and the keyboard:

- A file is identified by its name on the disk.

- You can write information (output from the computer) or read information (input to the computer) using the same file.

Since you choose the file name, it is not possible for the compiler to declare a file object beforehand. Input and output stream objects were declared with `cin` and `cout`, because you couldn't choose their names. You used `cin` for input and `cout` for output. When it comes to files, however, it is different. There may be several files you want to deal with, instead of just one file for input and one file for output. Therefore, you must declare your files as objects of the class `fstream` and give them names.

Once an object is declared, you can use member functions of the class `fstream`, and you can establish an input and/or output stream using the file in the same way that you used `cin` and `cout`. Even the manipulators and the flags can be used!

Here is an example:

```
#include <fstream.h>
void main()
```

```
{
 fstream myfile;
 myfile.open("list.txt",ios::out);
 myfile<<"Anything goes.";
 myfile.close();
 }
```

This program creates a file with the name `list.txt`, and writes the string `Anything goes.` in it.

NOTE   To use files, you must include the header file `fstream.h`.

You can run this program and look at the contents of the file `list.txt` using any word processor. You can also print the contents of the file from any word processor. Since we did not specify the directory in which the file will be located, it will be created in the current directory.

Manipulating Files

You can manipulate two kinds of files:

- Text files

- Binary files

Text files are organized in lines, and each line is marked with an *end of line* (`endl`). Data remain in readable form, and blank spaces separate each data field, so you can easily understand the file's contents. On the other hand, binary files are not organized in lines. One piece of information is written after another piece, and numeric values are stored in the way they are operated on in the computer memory—in binary notation. These numbers are not converted to a sequence of decimal digits so that you can easily read them. As a result, the printout of a binary file is not easily understood. In this book, we will deal exclusively with text files.

To use a file, the file must first be declared like any other object.

File Declaration

Since files are objects of the class `fstream`, the declaration is very simple:

```
fstream    identifier  ;
```

Skill 23

The *identifier* is simply a name that you use in your program to refer to the file—it is not the name stored on the disk! The correspondence between this identifier and the file name on the disk will be left for the open( ) member function.

Once a file is declared, we can use member functions to perform operations with it. The most important member functions are as follows:

- open( )
- close( )
- eof( )

The *open()* Member Function

The following fstream member function:

```
open(char filename[], int access_mode);
```

establishes a correspondence between the file object used in your program and data on the disk. It also establishes how the file will be used: to input, output, append, etc. This function takes two arguments: a character string (filename), which determines the file name on the disk, and a flag (access_mode), which indicates the access mode.

File Name   The file name is a null-terminated string. It can contain a full path to the file, including the drive, the directory, etc. However, when you include backslashes (\) in the string, they must be replaced by two backslashes (\\).

Access Mode   The access mode will be one of the following modes:

ios::out	open file for output (write)
ios::in	open file for input (read)
ios::app	append file (start at the end of the file and write)
ios::nocreate	open file only if it exists (do *not* create it)

For example:

```
// This opens a file list.txt located on drive a,
//      directory \franca for input:
   myfile.open("a:\\franca\\list.txt",ios::in);
// This opens a file whose name is contained in the
//      character array "filename" for output:
   myfile.open(filename,ios::out);
```

Open attributes can be combined by using a logical or operator (|). For example:

```
yourfile.open("roster.txt", ios::nocreate|ios::in);
```

In this case, the system tries to open the file roster.txt for input (ios::in). If this file is not found in the current directory, it is *not* created and the open will fail.

> **NOTE**   Microsoft compilers usually create a new file if you try to open a nonexistent file. To avoid this, you must use the ios::nocreate option. Borland compilers will not create a new file if you try to open a nonexistent file.

Testing Whether the File Was Successfully Opened   It is a good practice to test whether the file was successfully opened. For example, a file may fail to open if an input file does not exist where specified, or if an output file cannot be created. This test is performed differently by Microsoft and Borland compilers.

With Microsoft compilers, you can test whether a file was correctly opened by invoking the is_open() member function after trying to open the file. If the function returns a zero, there was a problem opening the file. For example:

```
yourfile.open("roster",ios::in|ios::nocreate);
if( yourfile.is_open()==0 ) cout <<"Error: File was not open";
```

With Borland compilers, you must compare the fstream object with a *NULL*. If this comparison is true, the file is not open. For example:

```
yourfile.open("roster",ios::in|ios::nocreate);
if(yourfile==NULL) cout<<"Error: File was not open";
```

The *close()* Member Function

The close() member function is used to make sure that all data are written to the disk. In many situations, the data are not immediately written to the disk, and if the file is not properly closed, some data may be lost. There are no arguments to this member function.

The *eof()* Member Function

The eof() member function is very useful for inputting files. It returns a 1 if you try to read past the last data in the file. This end-of-file (eof) condition is very handy, because in most cases, you don't know beforehand how many pieces of data will be present in the file. What is the solution? Keep reading until eof() is reached.

Skill 23

NOTE   When you read the last piece of information in the file, you will not cause eof( ). It is only when you try to read *past* the last piece of information that you cause eof( ).

Example—Reading and Printing Personnel Information   The file c8persnl .txt contains personnel information. You can use any word processor to read and print the contents of this file. Each line in this file contains a numeric identification, a first name and a last name, and a floating point number representing the hourly wage of the employee.

The contents of this file should look as follows:

```
 1  Clark Kent      20.00
 2  Alfred Newman    6.00
 3  Oliver Twist    15.00
 4  Huck Finn       17.00
 7  James Bond      32.00
10  Saint Nick      22.00
```

Notice that the identification numbers do not contain a complete sequence (some numbers, such as 5, 6, 8, and 9, are missing), which is the usual case in most files. In real life, you don't really know how many employees you will be reading. Therefore, you must check for *end of file*.

We will now write a program to list the employees, their ID numbers, and their hourly wages. Although it is a simple program, it requires that you pay attention to formatting. The approach is simple:

1. Declare the file and the variables.

2. Read the employee information until the end of the file is reached.

3. Display the ID number, the first and last name, and the hourly wage of each employee.

In fact, we can start the program by including the steps above as comments, and then inserting the appropriate code:

```cpp
#include <fstream.h>    // c8wage.cpp
#include <iomanip.h>

void main()
{
  // Declare the file and the variables:
   char filename[]="c8persnl.txt";
   int id;
```

```
    char fname[20],lname[20];
    float wage;
    fstream employees;
    employees.open(filename,ios::in|ios::nocreate);
// Read the employee information until
//       the end of the file is reached:
    for (;;)
       {
          employees>>id;
          if (employees.eof()) break;
          employees>>fname>>lname>>wage;
// Display the data of each employee:
          cout<<endl;
          cout<<setw(5)<<setiosflags(ios::right)<<id
              <<setw(20)<<setiosflags(ios::left)<<fname
              <<setw(20)<<lname
              <<setw(6)<<setprecision(2)<<setiosflags(ios::fixed)

<<resetiosflags(ios::left)<<setiosflags(ios::showpoint)<<wage;
       }
       char choice;
       cout<<endl<<"Enter any character to finish";
       cin>>choice;
    }
```

Notice the following items in the code above:

- We initialized the character array `filename` with the file name. This works only if the file is in the same directory as your program. Otherwise, you have to specify the full path name.

- We did not check whether the file was successfully opened.

- We detected the end-of-file condition—it is important that you check the end-of-file condition after you attempt to read the beginning of new employee data. Remember that the end-of-file condition is set only after you try to read *past* the last information. If you check the end-of-file condition at the beginning of the loop (including by using a `while (!employees.eof()...)` statement), you will work with invalid data on the last loop iteration.

- We formatted the output—it is a laborious task to format the output, because sometimes you have to align the data to the left (names), and sometimes you have to align them to the right (numbers). Microsoft compilers require you to reset the left flag, instead of simply allowing you to set the right flag. Also, it is important that you set the fixed flag so that Microsoft compilers show decimal zeros.

Skill 23

- The last three lines are optional. Some compilers erase the screen soon after the program is run. When this happens, you barely have time to see the output. If you request the user to type anything, you will force the computer to wait until you are done reading.

It may still be desirable to add a couple of features to this program:

- Check whether the file was opened successfully.

- Format the first and last names.

To check whether the file was opened successfully, you could include an `if` statement, which would be different according to the compiler you are using. With a Borland compiler, you could use

```
if(employee==NULL) cout<<"Error: file does not open";
else ...
```

With a Microsoft compiler, you could use

```
if(employee.is_open()==0) cout<<"Error: file does not open";
else ...
```

Notice that only the condition inside the `if` statement is different.

Isn't it disturbing that you may have to modify the code according to the compiler you are using?

In fact, one of the benefits of using a programming language like C++ is programs that do not have to be modified from one machine to another machine, or from one compiler to another compiler. However, many compilers have minor discrepancies in the way they implement a few features.

There is still hope—you will soon learn how to use the preprocessor to ease the pains of dealing with different compilers.

The output of the program above may still not be satisfactory, because the first name and the last name are printed in separate columns. We can fix this by copying the first name to a new character array, and then appending a blank space followed by the last name. For example:

```
char full_name[40];
...
strcpy(full_name,fname);
strcat(full_name," ");
strcat(full_name,lname);
```

After we use this sequence, the character array `full_name` will contain the full name of the employee, which we can print instead of the first and last names. In the next example, there is a complete implementation.

Example—Representing Employees with Objects   Another implementation of the program above is shown below. This new version uses an object to represent the employee; the formatting is embedded in the member function display(). To illustrate an alternative approach, the object was implemented using a struct instead of a class. The class hired_person can be implemented as follows:

```
#include <fstream.h>
#include <iomanip.h>
#include <string.h>
struct hired_person
{
    int id;
    char fname[20],lname[20];
    float wage;
    void display();
};
void hired_person::display()
{
    char full_name[40];
    strcpy(full_name,fname);
    strcat(full_name," ");
    strcat(full_name,lname);
    cout<<setiosflags(ios::right)<<setw(6)<<id<<"   "<<setw(40)
        <<setiosflags(ios::left)<<full_name
        <<setw(6)<<setprecision(2)<<resetiosflags(ios::left)
        <<setiosflags(ios::right)
        <<setiosflags(ios::fixed)
        <<setiosflags(ios::showpoint)<<wage;
}
```

The main program can be adapted as follows to use this class in the c8wage1 .cpp program:

```
void main()                          // c8wage1.cpp
{
  // Declare the variables:
  char filename[]="c:\\franca\\c8persnl.txt";
  hired_person worker;
  fstream employees;
  // Open the file for input:
  employees.open(filename,ios::in);
  // Loop through all the employees:
  {
      for (;;)
      {
       // Read the employee data:
       employees>>worker.id;
```

Skill 23

```
                // Check whether it's the end of the file:
                if (employees.eof()) break;
                employees>>worker.fname>>worker.lname>>worker.wage;
                cout<<endl;
                // Print the employee data:
                worker.display();
                }
                cout<<endl<<endl<<"Enter any character to finish:";
                char enter;
                cin>>enter;
        }
    }
```

If you move display() into a member function, you will simplify the main program—not only in its conception, but also in its maintenance—because, if the file information is changed, the main program will be less affected. However, to fully benefit from this, all operations with the file should be encapsulated in the class itself, or, at least, the reading should be moved from the main program into the class.

> **NOTE**   Some programmers prefer the shorter form, if(!employees.is_open()) cout<<"Error opening file";, instead of if(employees.is_open()==0) cout<<"Error opening file"; Both forms produce the same result.

Using the Preprocessor to Overcome Incompatibilities

You will now learn a few more compiler directives:

- #define
- #ifdef
- #ifndef
- #endif

These directives can be useful in several situations, but our main goal in this section is to use them to overcome differences in compiler implementations.

Keep in mind, however, that the preprocessor is a program that manipulates your source program *before* it is compiled. The task of the preprocessor is not accomplished while your program is running.

The *#define* Directive   The #define directive can be used to replace a given identifier with a given string. For example, if we use

```
#define pi 3.1416
```

the preprocessor will search the rest of the program for the identifier pi and change it to the sequence of digits 3.1416. The result is the same as the result of the following statement:

```
const float pi=3.1416;
```

However, you can do much more than this—you can replace any identifier with any string, as long as the string does not contain blank spaces. For example, you can use

```
#define condition1 employee.is_open()
#define condition2 employee==NULL
```

and, later in your program, you can have

```
if(condition1) cout<<"Error";
```

However, you still have to use either condition1 or condition2. Wouldn't it be nice if you could somehow choose which condition to use? Hold on!

The *#ifdef* Directive   The #ifdef directive checks whether a given identifier was defined by a #define directive. It does not matter *how* it was defined, only *whether* it was defined. For example, if you are going to use a Borland compiler, you could use

```
#define Borland
```

If you are going to use a Microsoft compiler, you could use

```
#define Microsoft
```

If you then define one or the other, you can later determine which compiler is in use by simply checking whether the appropriate identifier was defined. For example:

```
#ifdef Borland
    #define condition employee==NULL
#endif
#ifdef Microsoft
    #define condition employee.is_open()==0
#endif
```

Skill 23

The *#endif* Directive   In C++, we use braces ({}) to indicate where the if statement starts and where it ends. In the preprocessor, the if statement starts immediately after #ifdef and ends at the first #endif. This is why it was necessary to
include the two #endif directives above.

If the identifier Borland was defined, the condition will be defined as employee
==NULL, which is precisely what we want inside an if statement when using a
Borland compiler. If Borland was not defined, the preprocessor will skip through
the program until the #endif. At that point, it will check whether the identifier
Microsoft was defined.

The identifier condition will be set to either

    employee==NULL

or

    employee .is_open()==0,

according to which compiler was indicated.

Therefore, you could use the following statement later in the program:

    if (condition) cout<<"Error";

What if neither option was defined?

In that case, the condition will not be defined and your program will cause an
error. If you don't want this to happen, you may consider setting the condition
to a string that will never be true. Then, if neither Borland nor Microsoft were
defined, you will simply skip the test. For example:

```
#define condition 0!=0
#ifdef Borland
    #define condition employee==NULL
#endif
#ifdef Microsoft
    #define condition employee.is_open()==0
#endif
```

NOTE   The #ifndef directive works the opposite of how the #ifdef directive works. If
the identifier is *not* defined, the preprocessor will work on the lines that follow.
If the identifier *is* defined, the preprocessor will skip to the next #endif.

Testing Whether Different Files Were Successfully Opened   Our preprocessor technique to check whether a file is open has one major inconvenience: it only checks a given file (employee). What if you need a different file? What if you use several files?

In these cases, it is a good idea to combine the preprocessor directives with a function in which you pass the file as a parameter.

This function, which I named fileopen, will check whether a given file is open and will return either a 1 (yes, it is open) or a zero (no, it is not open).

Here is a possible implementation:

```
#include <fstream.h>
int fileopen(fstream & datafile)
{
    int yesopen=1;
    #ifdef Microsoft
        yesopen=datafile.is_open();
    #endif
    #ifdef Borland
        yesopen=!(datafile==NULL);
    #endif
    return yesopen;
}
```

You could also make this function an inline function.

When you compile this function, the preprocessor will check whether you defined either Borland or Microsoft (don't define both!). If you chose Borland, the Microsoft code will be skipped. Your function will look as follows:

```
int yesopen=1;
    yesopen=!(datafile==NULL);
return yesopen;
```

If you chose Microsoft, the Borland code will be skipped.

All you have to do is to invoke the fileopen function in the program:

```
if(fileopen(employee)==0) cout<<"Error";
```

The code for this function is included in c8tfile.h, and is used by the textfile class, which will be discussed in the next section.

Skill 23

Try This for Fun. . .

- Modify the program c8wage1.cpp by moving the *read* operation into the class. Include a member function read to read the information of the next employee from the file. This function should test for the end-of-file condition, and return a 1 if data were successfully read and a zero if otherwise.

Making Classes to Deal with Files— the *textfile* Class

After you have used files in a couple of applications, you may wonder whether you can reuse part of your work to deal with different kinds of text files. You *can* define a class to deal with text files that handle all the operations we have used so far.

You should remove all operations that depend on files in general and on the record structure from the main function in particular. An object of the new class textfile (or of a class derived from this class) will be able to operate by itself.

In our payroll example, if a class workers (derived from textfile) is available, the operation of the main function will look as follows:

```
{
 workers staff; // Declare an object of class workers
 for(;;)
 {
   if (staff.read()==0) break;
   staff.display();
 }
}
```

Did you notice what this class gives you?

- You don't have to open the file—it will be automatically opened by the constructor when you declare an object.

- You don't have to mention an fstream object in your program, or perform file operations at all.

- The main function does not have to know the structure of the records. You don't have to read each field like you did before. You can use the member function read to read one complete record at a time.

- The member function `read` can be designed so that an integer is returned as a result. If the function returns a zero, the end-of-file condition has been reached.

Of course, the structure of each record will be different for each kind of file with which you work. What should you do? If you use inheritance, you can design a class that deals with an empty structure, and then redefine the member functions as needed in your files.

You can also implement in this class the ability to locate a record if you are given the value of the first field (which acts like a key). For example, you can ask your file object to locate the employee whose ID number is 7.

The `textfile` class is completely implemented in this section. I hope that this class will be useful in your programs. However, it is most important that you understand how to use classes to manipulate files and reuse your work. The code for this class, as well as for the `fileopen` function, is included in `c8tfile.h`.

For the sake of convenience, the `textfile` class uses the header file `nofranca.h`, which was presented in a previous Skill. There are two advantages to using `nofranca.h`:

- You can use the functions `askwords`, `yesno`, etc.

- You can choose either the plain, text interface of C++ or the graphic interface of `franca.h`. If you want to use the plain interface, do nothing. If you want to use `franca.h`, all you have to do is to use `#include "franca.h"` in your program before you include `c8tfile.h`. The files `franca.h` and `nofranca.h` are exclusive. Whichever file you include first will prevail and prevent the other file from being included.

Class Declaration

Here is the declaration for our `textfile` class:

```
class textfile
{
  protected:
   fstream data;
   char datafile[40];
   int filemode;
  public:
   char id[40];
   textfile();
   textfile(char filename[],int mode=ios::in|ios::app|ios::nocreate);
```

Skill 23

```
    ~textfile();
    void display();
    virtual int read();
    int find(char id[]);
    int input();
    void write();
};
```

Data Members

Three data members are protected, because you may want to use them in the classes you derive from `textfile`:

- `data` is an `fstream` object. It is clear that you need one of these objects to handle the file operations.

- `datafile` is a character array that holds the name of the file you will be using on the disk.

- `filemode` is an integer that holds information about what is being done with the file.

There is a public data member `id`, which is a character array that holds the ID field (key) of the record being examined. It is public, because any piece of program can access it.

Member Functions

Most member functions have a straightforward purpose:

- `textfile` has two constructors—the parameterless, default constructor asks you for the file name to be used. The other constructor takes the file name as a parameter.

- `~textfile` is a special member function called a *destructor*. In most cases, you do not have to include a destructor in a class. Destructors are invoked automatically when the object you declared is discarded. In this case, the destructor will be used to close the file. Destructors work in an opposite way from constructors.

- `display()` is a function that displays the contents of the current record on the screen.

- `input()` is a function that inputs contents to a record from the keyboard.

- `find()` is a function that searches the file for a record whose first field matches the parameter. Notice that the parameter is a character string. This case is a very general case, because, in a text file, any kind of data is represented by a character string. The only restrictions that we impose are the size of the key (39 characters) and the position of the key (the key must be the first field in the record).

- `write()` is a function that writes the current record to the file.

- `read()` is a function that reads a record from the disk.

Constructors

Here is the code for the constructors:

```
#include "nofranca.h"
textfile::textfile()
{
    askwords(datafile,40,"enter the file name:");
    filemode=ios::in|ios::app|ios::nocreate;
    data.open(datafile,filemode);
    if(fileopen(data)==0)
    {
        if(yesno("File not open, create?"))
        {
            filemode=ios::out;
            data.open(datafile,filemode);
            if(fileopen(data)==0) // This tests whether the file is now open
            {
                yesno("Sorry, file does not open!");
                exit(0);
            }
            else;
        }
        else exit(0);
    }
}

textfile::textfile(char filename[],int mode)
{
    if(sizeof (datafile)>strlen(filename))
            strcpy(datafile,filename);
```

```
data.open(datafile,mode);
filemode=mode;
if(fileopen(data)==0)
{
    yesno("Error in opening, will you check?");
    exit(0);
}
}
```

TIP   The functions in the listing above use nofranca.h, which allows you to use the functions askwords and yesno. If you would like to use the graphic interface, all you have to do is to use #include "franca.h" before you include c8tfile.h. Also, remember that if you use franca.h, your main program is mainprog, not main.

NOTE   When you use franca.h, you cannot use formatting in cin and cout. Use boxes instead.

The exit(0) function can be used in an extreme error situation to terminate the program.

The constructors obtain the file name, and open the file for inputting and appending.

NOTE   The expression ios::in|ios::app may seem strange to you. The vertical bar represents the logical or operator. It allows you to use the file either for inputting or for appending.

Destructor

The code for the destructor is also very simple:

```
textfile::~textfile()
{
    data.close();
}
```

Inputting from the Keyboard and Displaying to the Screen

The code for the display() and input() functions is very interesting:

```
void textfile::display()
{

}
int textfile::input()
{
    askwords(id,40,"Enter id code");
    if(id[0]=='0') return 0;
    return 1;
}
```

What happens in these functions? The display() function does not show any-thing! Does it look right? Where are the IDs, names, and hourly wages?

Remember that you cannot solve all problems at once. If you include names, hourly wages, and other information in your class, it will not be reusable! (In other applications, you may be dealing with license plates, vehicle manufac-turers, etc.) You should use the textfile class as a base from which to derive other classes. In fact, the display() function should be replaced by your own version of the display() function when you derive a new class. You will then display all the data members in a format that suits you.

The input() function requests input for the ID field. You may later provide an input() function that uses the previous input() function to input the ID and continues to input the other data members, as well. Or, you can totally override the previous version of the input() function.

The input() function in the code above requests input from the keyboard and tests whether you have entered a null string (for example, if you just hit Enter). This is one way to determine that you no longer want to input data. The function then returns a 1 or a zero. If you like this idea, you should use it. If you don't like it, just use something different in your derived class!

Reading and Writing from a File

Next, we will examine the code for the read() and write() member functions:

```
int textfile::read()
{
```

```
// This function reads the next record from the file:
    data>>id;
    if (data.eof()) return 0;
    return 1;
}

void textfile::write()
{
    data.close();
    data.open(datafile,ios::app);
    if(fileopen(data)==0)
    {
      yesno("Failed reopen for append, will you check?");
      return;
    }
    data<<endl<<id<<' ';
    data.close();
    data.open(datafile,filemode);
}
```

The read() function simply reads the next ID from the file. Again, you should complement this function with a member function of your own derived class, so the other fields are also read from the file.

The write() function operates in a similar way, except that it closes the file, and then reopens it for output. Notice that a blank space is written after the ID. It is important to use blank spaces to separate fields in a text file. After the ID is written, the file is closed again, and then opened in the previous mode. You should also complement this function with a member function of your own derived class.

Finding a Given Record in a File

Finally, here is the code for the find() member function:

```
int textfile::find(char idnumber[])
{
    data.close();
    data.open(datafile,filemode);
    if(fileopen(data)==0)
    {
      yesno("Failed to reopen for find, will you check?");
      exit(0);
    }
    for(;;)
    {
```

```
   if(data.eof())break;
   if(strcmp(id,idnumber)!=0)  read();// Virtual read!
   else return 1;
   }
data.close();
data.open(datafile,filemode);
return 0;
}
```

This function simply reads all the records, and compares the key field with the ID number for which you are looking. If this record is found, the function returns a 1. Otherwise, it returns a zero. The search starts at the beginning of the file every time. It may not be the smartest way to find a record, but it is simple enough. It is necessary to close and reopen the file, so it will be positioned at the beginning.

A very important aspect of the find() function is the reading of a record. This function reads a record from the file by invoking the read() member function.

Notice there is a standard read() that comes from the original textfile class and another read() that you wrote for your derived class. Which read() am I talking about?

If you use the standard read(), as defined for textfile, only the ID field will be read, and the next attempt to read may erroneously use either a name or an hourly wage as a key. This is because each time you read something from the file, the file is positioned to read the next information recorded.

For example, if your derived class reads records that have an ID and a name, the original read() member function is not aware of the name field and will only read the ID. When you next read (using the original read()), the computer will start reading where it last stopped and read a piece of the name assuming it is the next ID.

It is imperative that you use the read() function that you defined for your derived class instead, which is why read() is a virtual function in textfile.

You will find the textfile class in the header file c8tfile.h in your directory.

WARNING If you need to pass a textfile object as an argument to a function, pass it by reference only. If you pass it by value, you will create and destroy a copy. After the copy has been destroyed, the file will be closed.

Skill 23

Try This for Fun. . .

- Derive a class from `textfile` to operate with the `workers` (`c8persnl.txt`) file. Write a program to list the file's contents.

Understanding Basic File Operations

You should have noticed by now that files are excellent for keeping information that you may need to use several times. When you use a file, you avoid retyping all the data every time you need to use them. Furthermore, it may be impossible to retype a large quantity of data. The example discussed in the previous section illustrates how you can keep employee information conveniently stored.

Notice that the employee identification as well as the first and last names are not supposed to change. The hourly wage may change, but it is unlikely that it will change very often. For this reason, the information kept in this file is somewhat permanent.

The `textfile` class provides the basic functions to

- Input data from the keyboard

- Write data to the file

- Read data from the file

- Write data to the screen

- Find and read a record from the file

This class allows us to include new employees in the file, check the data of an existing employee, etc. However, in real life, other operations are needed to maintain a file.

- What if an employee leaves the company? We should be able to remove the record from the file. This operation is called *record removal* or *delete*.

- What if an employee needs his or her hourly wage raised? We should be able to fetch the employee's record, modify the value of the wage, and write it back. This operation is called *record update*.

File Updating

It is regrettable that the *update* operation is not easily performed in a text file. Why not? The records of each employee may have different sizes. Although this may not seem like a problem when you regard each record as a line on a page, it is a real problem in the file, because the lines are written one after the other. Therefore, if the updated record exceeds the size of the previous record, there is no way to fit it in the same place. Besides, each time you read from the file, the computer gets ready to read from or write to the next available position. You must then make sure that you rewrite the record in the same place from which it was read.

However, it is possible to implement update operations in text files. The easiest solution is to create a second file with the updated information, so you do not update data in place, but instead, you update data to the new file. On the other hand, binary files can be a little easier to deal with in this situation, if you constrain all the records to fit in a given size.

> **TIP**   You will benefit from forcing your files to have records of fixed lengths.

File Matching

Another important operation that you may want to perform in a file is *matching*. You use matching when you have to operate on two or more files, and when you fetch a record from one file and need to find a record in the second file that matches it.

For example, consider a file `workhours`, which contains an employee code and the number of hours the employee worked. To compute the value of the paycheck, you have to look into each record of the `workhours` file, and then use the employee code to find a match in the `worker` file to determine the name and the hourly wage of that employee. With this information in hand, you can compute the value of the paycheck.

The file-matching operation is simple when you use `textfile`, because the member function `find()` can locate a record with a given code.

In this example, we will produce the payroll. We are given two files:

- `c8persnl.txt` contains the employee code, the first name, the last name, and the hourly wage.

- `c8payrll.txt` contains the employee code and the number of hours the employee worked.

Our task is to display a list of all the employees that are to be paid, with their personal data and the amount to which they are entitled. Since the hourly wage and the number of hours worked are located in different files, it is necessary to match the employee record from one file with its record in the other file.

It is possible to get each record from the payroll file, and then find a match in the worker file, or to get each record from the worker file, and, then find a match in the payroll file. It is very likely that you will read the file that contains transient information (in this case, the payroll file), and update the permanent file (the worker file).

We have to do the following things for each record we read from the payroll file:

- Get the ID code and the number of hours worked for this employee.

- Find a record in the worker file with the same ID code.

- Compute the paycheck value for this employee.

Of course, we have to decide on the action to be taken when there is no match. We will greatly simplify the matching operation if we use the hired_person class to handle the worker file, because the find() member function can be used to locate an employee's record, if we are given the ID code.

The payroll file has not been defined in a class, but it can easily be derived from the textfile class. It will be a very simple task, because we have to include only one data member—the number of hours worked—and one member function. All we actually need to do is to read from this file. There is no need to code the functions for displaying, writing, inputting, or finding!

Example—the *payfile* Class

One implementation for the class that handles the payroll file could be as follows:

```
#include "nofranca.h"
class payfile: public textfile
{
    public:
     float hours;
     virtual int read();
};
int payfile::read()
{
    if(textfile::read()==0)return 0;
    data>>hours;
    return 1;
}
```

The read() function that is implemented for the payfile class calls the read() function of the base class textfile. It is always possible to do this. All you have to do to explain that you are not using the member function of the current class is to fully qualify the function name. How do you do this? Use the class name, two colons, and the function name:

```
class name ::  function name  ( );
```

For example:

```
if(textfile::read()==0)return 0;
```

When both file classes are available, the payroll program becomes quite simple:

```
void main()                         // c8payrll.cpp
{
 // Declare the variables:
    char filename[40];
    cout<<"Opening the employee's file:";
    hired_person worker;
    cout<<"Opening the payroll file:";
    payfile workhours;
    float paycheck,payroll=0;
    char idnumber[40];

 // Loop through the primary file:
        for (;;)
        {
         // Read the record from workhours
         //      if not eof:
         if( workhours.read()==0) break;
         // Find the employee data in the worker file:
         if( worker.find(workhours.id))
         {
            paycheck=worker.wage*workhours.hours;
            payroll=payroll+paycheck;
            worker.display();
            cout<<"  $"<<setw(12)
                <<setiosflags(ios::fixed)<<paycheck;
         }
         else
           cout<<endl<<"No record found for worker:"
               <<worker.id;
        }
        cout<<endl<<"Payroll total: $"<<setw(12)<<payroll;
}
```

Try This for Fun...

- Implement the member functions `input()`, `write()`, and `display()` for the payroll file. In your implementation, all records should be written to have exactly the same size (use blank spaces to fill space, if necessary).

Are You Experienced?

Now you can...

☑ Store data in files

☑ Use the preprocessor directives *#define*, *#ifdef*, *#ifndef*, and *#endif*

☑ Develop special classes to deal with your files

☑ Read and write files in your applications

☑ Develop applications that handle more than one file

Implementing a Real-World Point-of-Sale Terminal

- ❑ Enhancing the point-of-sale terminal
- ❑ Manipulating a catalog on disk file
- ❑ Reusing previously defined classes

To further improve your skills in developing applications, you will work on a real-world implementation of the point-of-sale terminal. This new terminal will get the product code from the keyboard and locate the product description and price in a file.

Revisiting the Point-of-Sale Terminal

The point-of-sale terminal implemented in Skill 21 was inconvenient because the entire parts catalog had to be input for each program execution. By keeping the data in a disk file instead of in memory, it is possible to reuse the same data after shutting down the computer and restarting it.

This implementation uses the same terminal, but, this time, you will implement the catalog using a disk file.

Implementing the New Features

If you carefully examine the latest version of the point-of-sale terminal, you may notice that the `catalog` class encapsulates all the catalog operations. In fact, if you alter the `catalog` class to keep the data in a disk file as opposed to in an array, the problem will be solved.

Why do unnecessary work? All we have to do is to design an alternative `catalog` class!

Since you have undoubtedly become an enthusiast of inheritance, you may think of deriving a new class from `catalog` and using it in this implementation. Indeed, this can be done.

However, the existing `catalog` class contains a few things that we don't really need. For example, why would we need an array if all the data are already in a disk file? In this case, it may be worthwhile to redesign the `catalog` class.

ABSTRACT CLASSES

If both `catalog` classes are needed, the smart thing to do would be to design a `catalog` class whose functions are virtual and inoperative (such as the `display` member function in the `textfile` class) and then derive

continued ▶

two classes from it, `arraycatalog` and `filecatalog`, for example. Both classes can still be regarded as catalogs, but each one has a distinctive way of operating. The base class, in this case, will never be used to create an object; it is what we call an *abstract* class.

Deriving the *catalog* Class from *textfile*

You can easily derive the `catalog` class from `textfile`. Consider the following declaration:

```
struct product
{
    char code[40];
    char description[40];
    float price;
};

class catalog: public textfile
{
    product saleitem;
    virtual int read();
    void write();
  public:
    virtual product find(char part_number[]);
    virtual product find(int somecode);
};
```

Two *find()* Functions?   You may be wondering why we declared two functions with the name `find()`. Indeed, the `textfile` class needs only one function to handle a character array as the key. However, the terminal program that is already working uses an integer as the key. If you include this new function, you provide compatibility with the current terminal, without having to change the code!

Another Look at Virtual Functions   Even though virtual functions were first introduced in Skill 17 and were used again in the `textfile` class, it may be a good idea to review them here.

When you first learned about virtual functions, you had a runner and a skater that could run. Each one ran in a particular way. So, if you had

```
runner julia;
skater mike;
julia.run();
mike.run();
```

when your program was compiled, the compiler translated these with no trouble. The compiler made sure that `julia` used the `run()` function defined for a runner and that `mike` used the `run()` function defined for a skater. Therefore, as long as the compiler knew which kind of object would use the function, it could easily determine which function to call in each place.

However, there are situations in which it is impossible for the compiler to determine which class of object will be used. Only when the program is actually executing will the true nature of the object be known. By then, however, the compiler is long done with its task!

The example in Skill 17 was a function that received a parameter of the class `runner`:

```
void march(runner volunteer)
{
    volunteer.run();
}
```

The problem is that due to inheritance, you can actually receive a runner or a skater (since a skater is also a runner, by inheritance). In fact, since this is a function, you can use it sometimes with a runner and sometimes with a skater. The compiler needs to bind one `run()` function, but the compiler does not know whether you will use a runner or a skater (or any other class you may decide to create).

When you declare a function to be virtual, the compiler postpones the actual binding of the code to the appropriate function until your program executes. The compiler simply adds extra code to determine at runtime which function to use. While your program runs, this extra code determines the appropriate function to bind (this is also called *late binding*).

Ideally, all functions should behave as virtual functions to implement perfect polymorphism. Why do we have to state that the function is virtual then?

For practical reasons. The extra code needed for the late binding makes your programs longer and slower, and, as long as the compiler can determine the class of the object, the virtual attribute is not really needed. Therefore, C++ gives the programmer the burden of specifying which functions need to have the late binding treatment.

An interesting situation in which late binding (a virtual function) is needed occurs in the `textfile` class. The `find` function calls the `read()` function at some point to read the next record. Remember there is an original `read()` function that only reads the ID field, and there may be other functions that read additional fields. You need to read the complete record, not only the ID. However, inside the find function, you have no idea which kind of object with which you are dealing. Well, it does not matter. If the read() function is virtual, the late binding will figure out which one to use.

Displaying and Inputting

Classes derived from textfile should provide their own versions of displaying and inputting. Where are they?

Nowhere! You don't really need to input data to the catalog, nor do you need to display data. You can input data and check them using any word processor. A sample file, c8parts.txt, is included with some items. You can use this file, or you can add more items to the list.

The Constructor

There is no need to specify a constructor. The standard constructor for the textfile class can be used—it will ask for the file name to be used and then open it.

The *read()* and *write()* Functions

The read() and write() functions transfer the contents of the current record, the structure saleitem, to and from the disk file. Here is the code for these functions:

```
int catalog::read()
{
  int testeof=1;
  testeof=textfile::read();
  if(testeof==0) strcpy(id,"");
  strcpy(saleitem.code,id);
  data>>saleitem.description;
  data>>saleitem.price;
  return testeof;
}
void catalog::write()
{
  textfile::write();
  data<<' '<<saleitem.description;
  data<<' '<<saleitem.price;
}
```

Notice that both functions use their base class counterparts (textfile::read() and textfile::write()). It is not strictly necessary, but it is a good idea to reuse existing code. In this case, the product code is duplicated, because `catalog` inherited the character array `id` from `textfile` and the structure defines a product code. For this reason, whenever you read information into the structure, the code is also copied to `id`.

Finding the Parts

Finally, the functions to locate a record when the product code is given are listed below:

```
product catalog::find(char part_number[])
{
  int kfind;
  kfind=textfile::find(part_number);
  if (kfind==0)
  {
    saleitem.code[0]=0;
    id[0]=0;
  }
  return saleitem;
}

product catalog::find(int somecode)
{
  char thecode[40];
  itoa(somecode,thecode,10);
  return find(thecode);
}
```

You will find the complete code for this project in the files `c8catlg.h` and `c8term.h`. The program `c8term.cpp` uses `franca.h` and the Windows graphic interface.

```
// Choose either:              c8term.cpp
//       #define Microsoft
//       or
//       #define Borland
#include "franca.h"
#include "c8catlg.h"
#include "c8term.h"
void mainprog()
{
   saleterm cashregister;
   cashregister.operate();
}
```

You should use the appropriate #define for your compiler to check that the files were successfully opened. You can also use the program above with the standard nongraphic interface. All you have to do is to remove #include "franca.h" and change mainprog to main.

Are You Experienced?

Now you can. . .

☑ **Manipulate a catalog on disk file**

☑ **Reuse previously defined classes**

PART IX

What a Life!

In Part IX, you will be exposed to some of the common problems a computer programmer has to face, and you will develop another application using object-oriented programming.

Finally, you must realize that it is not possible to learn everything about C++ in an introductory book, much less about computer programming in general. We will discuss the relevant skills that you may want to develop during your career.

Developing Applications with Object-Oriented Programming

- ❑ Understanding object-oriented programming

- ❑ Reusing software

- ❑ Completing a small project—a spelling game

- ❑ Implementing this project with object-oriented programming

In this Skill, we will summarize the important techniques of object-oriented programming (OOP), and we will propose, discuss, and implement a short project using these techniques.

The recommendations you will find here are not meant to be followed by the letter. There are several different opinions on how to design and maintain software. You should read this material and use your own judgment when the issue is brought to your professional attention.

The OOP Mentality

Object-oriented programming provides tools that make it easier for the programmer to complete his or her professional work. However, a new tool is useless until you understand how to use it. Keep in mind that a piece of software that you write today may be used again in the future. The more this software is reused, the more time and money you will save! Make your software easy to use, easy to expand (preferably, by using inheritance), and easy to maintain.

An efficient programmer can develop a reliable piece of code in a short amount of time. How can we significantly improve programming efficiency? Of course, being experienced and smart will help, but what else can you do?

You can save a significant amount of time in development and maintenance by reusing software. The following sections examine two interesting aspects of reuse:

- Reuse what is available.

- Build for reuse.

There are other, more limited ways of using a piece of software that has already been developed: software redoing and software recycling.

Redoing, Recycling, and Reusing Software

Suppose you wrote a piece of software that reads words from the keyboard and stores them in a disk file. A few months later, someone asks you to develop software that, among other things, reads words from the keyboard and stores them in a disk file.

Here are some of the actions that programmers may choose:

- Sit in front of the computer and write a piece of program. It is just an easy piece after all, and can be done in a couple of hours! You may think that this is *not* a good idea. Indeed, it is not. However, it is what most programmers end up doing. There is no established terminology to denote this approach. For our discussion, we will call this *software redoing*.

- Remember that a similar piece of program was written some time ago. Locate this piece of program on the disk, copy it to your new program, and take the opportunity to make it a little better. We call this *software recycling*.

- If the previous piece of software was built for reuse, it was probably stored in a header file. Include this file in the program, and reuse it in this new project. We call this *software reusing*.

- Another possibility may occur: the previous piece of software was built for reuse, but what you need now is slightly different from what you had then. If you can still use what was previously available, it is still reuse, as long as you do not make any changes to the original software that was available on the disk. You may derive new classes from it and even add them to the original file, as long as the original classes remain intact.

Redoing Software instead of Recycling

This is, regrettably, what most programmers end up doing. After all, the purpose of a programmer is to program, not to dig through buried code! The harm of redoing is twofold:

1. A programmer's memory is not as reliable as he or she thinks it is. In the process of redoing a program, a programmer may spend the same amount of time as when they first developed it. Even during the second time around, bugs (often the same bugs) appear and consume time.

2. If you continue with this type of approach, it may yield projects with several pieces of code that are not exactly the same, but that end up doing the same things. If maintenance is required, all these pieces will have to be located, examined, and changed.

Recycling essentially eliminates the first inconvenience of redoing, because it saves the programmer time and may jump directly to a tested version of the software. Still, it does not do much for maintenance.

Reusing Pieces of Software

Reuse really helps with maintenance. As a reusable piece of software is updated, it becomes relatively easy to promote this update throughout all the software projects. Any improvements in the reused pieces can promptly benefit all the software.

What is software reuse? We say that software is reused if the same piece of code is used over and over. It could be in the same program, in the same package, or in completely unrelated software.

Indeed, software reuse started with the use of functions (or *subroutines*, in the early nomenclature). Instead of developing a piece of code all the time, programmers learned to use functions from a library to speed up their work. Reuse not only made programming faster, but also resulted in more reliable programs. Why? Since these functions were extensively used, they were subjected to more exhaustive testing than a unique piece of program.

Objects introduced a new dimension to reuse. If you had functions in a library and you wanted something slightly different, you could not use them anymore. Either you had to modify them (using different, untested code) or you had to redo them. Also, you could use any data with any function. There was no way to prevent your data from being inappropriately modified.

With classes, it became possible to limit the use of data and to modify part of the operations while inheriting the rest.

Extensive reuse requires strict discipline. A significant amount of time can be consumed just checking for software that can be used. Worse than this, some class libraries are really difficult to understand, and the programmer will be tempted to develop his own solution, instead of losing time while learning how somebody else solved the problem. Management must use good judgment in these cases. It is true that a programmer may often come up with a piece of code in less time than would have been needed to learn how the available software works.

The problem is maintenance. Chances are it will cost more to maintain software built out of pieces that are not reusable. It is just like maintaining a house built out of custom-sized windows and doors!

An interesting compromise, when you are tempted to build your own solution, is to build your own reusable solution. Instead of only developing something that fits your current need, develop something that can also be reused.

Investing instead of Spending   It may take a little longer in the beginning to build your library, since you will be trying to solve your current problem as well as some of your future problems. It is an investment, though. As more tasks are assigned to you, you will start using your class library and be able to finish your job earlier!

Not to mention that your software will become more tested and reliable each time.

BUILDING FOR REUSE

Some programmers think they are reusing a great deal just because they use a class library. This is not the whole story! They will still lose a lot of time redoing things that could already have been done. It is OK to be too lazy to use the keyboard, but never be too lazy to think!

Anytime you are asked to do a task, think of the future. Chances are someone will come up with a similar task again. Can you create a class that will be useful to that problem? Can you make this class easy to upgrade? Can you keep your own class library?

Short Project—Spelling Game

In this section, we will describe a project and its implementation. This project requires a computer with a sound board. The purpose is to develop software to assist children in checking their spelling abilities.

This software plays the sound of a word that has been previously digitized and stored in a file. Then, a message box requests the player to type the word that was heard. If the spelling is correct, the player will be notified and the score will be updated. The time the player takes to respond is also kept.

This procedure is repeated for several words. When the list of words is completed, a score with the number of hits and misses and the total time consumed is displayed.

The program can also play the sound and show the spelling of the corresponding word once before it starts to ask questions.

Suggested Implementation

Use your sound board to record each word in a separate file. Restrict yourself to words that are less than eight characters, which simplifies the problem.

You can keep the list of words in an array of characters in memory or in a disk file. Consider storing them in a disk file and loading them to an array. If you use up to only eight characters, you will be able to use the same word to identify the file where the sound is kept.

You can input the list of words directly into your file using any word processor. Later, you may want to allow your program to request words from the keyboard, as well.

Procedure

Here is a general outline of the algorithm:

1. Consider *wordnumber*—the total number of words (and sound files) available.

2. Consider *testnumber*—the total number of words per spelling test (typically, from 6 to 20).

3. Load the words from the file into the memory array.

4. For each word in the array:

    a. Display the word in a box for a few seconds.

    b. Play the corresponding sound.

5. Repeat the following items *testnumber* times:

    a. Choose a random number from 1 to *wordnumber*.

    b. Play the sound corresponding to the word in position *wordnumber*–1 in the array.

    c. Start a timer.

    d. Request the player to spell the word.

    e. Check the time spent.

    f. Check whether spelling is correct and notify the player.

    g. Update the score.

6. Inform the player of the score and the time spent.

Extensions

Once this software is developed and runs satisfactorily, you may improve it by

*   Avoiding the repetition of words already spelled correctly

- Graphically illustrating the progress by either building a picture when spelling is correct or building a picture when spelling is incorrect

For example, you can build pieces of a hangman when spelling is incorrect. Another suggestion, which is implemented, is to build one pile of coins when spelling is correct and another pile when spelling is incorrect.

User Interface

In this case, the user interface may be the key factor in determining the success of your product. Assume that users are supposed to be in grade school. Be cool! If you illustrate the session with pictures and sounds, you will grab the attention of your users. If you forget this fact for a few seconds, your players will be bored and will turn your product off!

Figure 25.1 shows the computer screen after a session. Each green coin (in the left-hand pile) represents one word spelled correctly, and each red coin (in the right-hand pile) represents one word spelled incorrectly. In addition, every time the student hits a correct spelling, a cheerful *Alright!* is played.

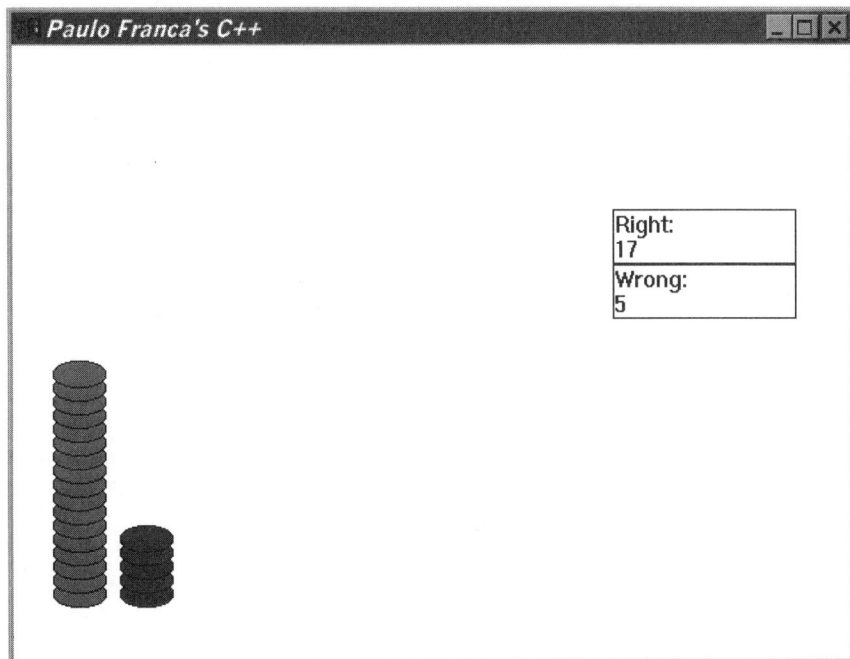

FIGURE 25.1: The result of a spelling session

Object-Oriented Implementation

The development of a software project using the object-oriented approach does not have to follow any specific rules. Nevertheless, some steps can assist you:

1. Never fear getting started. Explain how you think the problem can be solved. Review this explanation. Change it and expand it—do whatever you need to make it a good description of how to solve the problem.

2. Split the program into smaller pieces until you can comfortably deal with each piece. If you try to employ reusable pieces, either you will use pieces that you already know or you will build pieces in the hope they can be reused.

   • Remember that anytime something is reused, you save a lot of time and, presumably, have a more reliable solution. You must identify classes of objects that are available and that can be used in your project. You must also identify classes of objects that may be useful, even if they are not available—you can develop new classes of your own.

   • Allow some generality and room for expansion when you design your new classes. Do not solve the problem that you face today. On the fly, prepare to solve the problems that you may face in the future.

3. Write the class declarations once you have a good idea of the classes you will use.

   • The class declarations establish how other pieces of software interact with the classes. You can write the code for the functions later.

4. Work on the algorithm of the software that uses objects of the classes that you selected.

   • At this point, you can write the code for the program.

5. Write the class definitions—the actual code for the member functions.

However, software development is not a sequential process. Often, you may need to review some previous steps. Whatever you do to write more reliable and readable code is worth it. It will cost you much more to fix something once the software is on the market!

Developing the Project

We can use the project description that was provided as our initial step. We may try to identify useful objects that we can develop to solve the problem. Some objects available in `franca.h`, such as boxes and Screen Objects, will definitely be useful. These objects, of course, will not be enough. Should we identify new classes of objects that we can use?

If we examine the problem and try to split it into reusable pieces (according to step 2), we may end up with some objects that, when they are put together, will handle the problem.

If we imagine how this situation would work in real life, we may picture a teacher testing a student. The teacher has a list of words, which have possibly come from a dictionary, and she dictates these words to the student.

> **NOTE** The resulting code for this project is included in `c9spell.cpp`. The sound files are assumed to be in the subdirectory sounds.

Working with Words

This imagining could give us the idea to use an object of the class `teacher` that would read the words and administer the tests. The essential operations that `teacher` would perform are as follows:

- Display all the words in the test.

- Pronounce all the words in the test.

- Administer the test.

The list of words will come from somewhere, possibly from a dictionary. It would be interesting to allow the teacher to draw words from different lists. We could also devise an object that is a mix of a dictionary and a jukebox, since we have recorded sounds. The jukebox keeps a list of words (both in written format and in sound format), and should be able to

- Pronounce a given word

- Spell a word

- Give the number of words available in the list

The teacher class will, of course, use this jukebox to retrieve the spelling and to pronounce each word.

It may prove very useful in the future to implement a class of jukebox objects. There may be several situations in which we could use an object that can pronounce words kept in a list.

Since we will often deal with character arrays of size 9, the following type definition will be useful:

```
typedef char words[9];
```

Consider the following declaration for this class:

```
class jukebox
{
    protected:
        char directory[30],filename[40];// Stores directory path
                                        //        and full path
        int wordnumber;
        words list[40];
        void whatfile(words name);      // Generates file name
    public:
        int howmanywords();
        void pronounce(words thisword);
        void pronounce(int whichword);
        void spell(int which,words spelled);
        jukebox(char path[]);
        jukebox();
        int find(words whichone);
};
```

Notice there are two member functions with the name pronounce. One of them takes the word in a character array and pronounces it (by playing the file with the same name). The other one takes an integer that is an index to the list of words. The function howmanywords() simply gives the number of words available in the list.

The function spell() has an argument that is an index to the list of words. This function retrieves the character array that contains the spelling of the word and then copies it into the second argument.

As you can see, given the integer value, let's use k, the teacher can pronounce a word that is in position k in the list and can also pronounce the same word using the jukebox member functions.

Using Constructors

In addition, there are two constructors for jukebox, which initialize it. The argument to one of the constructors is a character array containing the path to the

directory where the sound files are recorded. For example, `c:\\franca\\`
`sounds\\` (remember that, in a literal string, backslashes are represented by double backslashes). This string prefixes the file name when `jukebox` tries to play a
sound. It is important to include the parameterless constructor in this case,
because `teacher` class declares `jukebox` without parameters. If this constructor is
not available, `jukebox` can not be created in this case.

TIP   If the sound files are located in the subdirectory sounds of the current directory,
the path can be sounds\\.

The function `whatfile()` puts together the directory path, the file, and the
suffix to give a string a full path name. This cfull path name is stored in the character array `filename`. This function is not public, because we intend to make it
available only for the other member functions.

Instead of declaring private members, I declare protected members, so that any
descendent classes can access them without needing to update the source code. If
we suppose objects of the class `jukebox` are available, we can define the `teacher`
class to use `jukebox`.

Declaring Classes

Objects of the class `teacher` should be able to write and play each word in the list
and to administer the test. Teachers may need a clock to keep track of time and a
place to write the words and scores. We could consider also creating an object
such as a blackboard, where `teacher` could write these things. However, the
available `Box` objects could serve just as well.

As data members, `teacher` will have three boxes: `yourword` (to display the
spelling of a word), `plus` (to display the number of correct answers), and `wrong`
(to display the number of incorrect answers). A `jukebox` is also needed, so that
`teacher` can operate with the words.

The *teacher* Class Declaration   Here is the declaration for the class `teacher`:

```
class teacher
{
  bank FirstNational;
  Box yourword;
  Clock myclock;
  Box plus,minus;
  jukebox speaker;
  int right,wrong;
```

```
public:
  void playlist();
  void test();
  teacher(jukebox &neon);
};
```

The constructor for `teacher` has an argument that is a `jukebox`. This means that a teacher must have a jukebox to work! Why is the argument passed as a reference? Just to avoid an unnecessary copy.

How about the data member that happens to be a bank? It is an idea that came up to help students visualize their performance. I thought of displaying green and red coins to illustrate progress. Since we may need similar tools in other educational software, I thought it would be a good idea to use a class of `bank` objects. The bank simply builds a pile of green coins (right) and a pile of red coins (wrong).

The *bank* Class Declaration   Here is the declaration for the class bank:

```
class bank
{
  protected:
    Circle greencoin,redcoin;
    float xgreen,xred;
    float nextygreen,nextyred;
  public:
    void plus();
    void minus();
    bank();
};
```

The `plus()` function adds a green coin, and the `minus()` function adds a red coin. A constructor is needed to create the coins and the initial location when the object is started.

The bank would be more reusable if we could specify the location where the coins can be piled. If you use default parameters, you will be allowed to omit the coordinates if you want.

The prototype for the constructor can then be changed to

```
bank( float x=50,float y=400);
```

Once the member functions become available, the main program can be as simple as this:

```
void mainprog()
{
```

```
        jukebox speaker("sounds\\");
        teacher MrRoberts(speaker);
        MrRoberts.playlist();
        MrRoberts.test();
        speaker.pronounce("allright");
        speaker.pronounce("byebye");
    }
```

Pay attention to the declarations for the `jukebox` and `teacher` objects. The `jukebox` is informed of the path to follow to find the sound files. This path is stored in the `jukebox`, so that all sounds are retrieved from that directory.

The `teacher` object has one argument, which is the `jukebox` we just created. This argument makes sure that this `teacher` will use this particular `jukebox` to administer the test.

Storing Words in Separate Directories

Finally, a couple of words, *alright* and *bye-bye*, are pronounced to indicate that the test is completed. It is clear that these words must be available in digital form in the same directory to which the jukebox `speaker` was assigned. What if you want to keep these words in a different place? After all, you may want to perform spelling tests with different sets of words, and it would be a great idea to have one set in a separate directory. Do we need to have a copy of `allright` and bye-bye in all these directories?

Of course not! Suppose you want the test words in the directory `c:\franca\ sounds\test1\` and the greetings in the directory `c:\franca\sounds\`. What can you do?

It is simple. All you need to do is to create two jukeboxes: one associated with the words to test and another associated with the greetings:

```
        jukebox speaker("c:\\franca\\test1\\");
        jukebox greeting("c:\\franca\\sounds1\\");
```

The `speaker` jukebox will be attached to the `teacher`, as before. The `greeting` jukebox will be used instead of `speaker` in the last couple of statements to pronounce the words *alright* and *bye-bye*.

NOTE   In the current implementation, the teacher also pronounces the word *alright* when the student spells a word correctly. This uses the same jukebox, and assumes that this word is in the same directory as the other words.

Defining Classes

Now that we have settled on which objects to use and specified all the functions in the declarations, we can define the functions for each of the classes. Still, at this stage, we will manually load the list of words in the jukebox.

The *jukebox* Class Definition   Here is the definition for the class jukebox:

```
jukebox::jukebox()
{
    wordnumber=0;
    directory[0]=0;
}
jukebox::jukebox(char path[])
{
    fstream wordlist;
    if(strlen(directory)>30)directory[0]=0;
    strcpy(directory,path);          // Directory
    strcpy(filename,directory);
    strcat(filename,"list");
    strcat(filename,".txt");
    wordlist.open(filename,ios::in|ios::nocreate);// File name
    if(fileopen(wordlist)==0)
    {                                // Check whether file is available
      Box errormsg("Error:");
      errormsg.say("No List!");
      exit(0);
    }
    for (int k=0;k<100;k++)
    {                                // Read words
      if(wordlist.eof()) break;
      wordlist>>list[k];
    }
    wordnumber=k;                    // Number of words
}

int jukebox::howmanywords()
{
    return wordnumber;
}

void jukebox::spell(int which,words spelled)
{
    if (which>=wordnumber)
    {
      strcpy(spelled,"");            // Restrict size!
      return;
```

```
            }
            strcpy(spelled,list[which]);     // Copy to spelled
    }

    void jukebox::whatfile(words list)
    {
        strcpy(filename,directory);     // Prefix
        strcat(filename,list);          // Name
        strcat(filename,".wav");        // Suffix
    }
    void jukebox::pronounce(int whichword)
    {
        whatfile(list[whichword]);
        sound(filename);
    }
    void jukebox::pronounce(words thisword)
    {
        whatfile(thisword);
        sound(filename);
    }
```

N NOTE

You should choose either #define Microsoft or #define Borland so that the appropriate test for determining whether a file was opened successfully can be applied. This definition must be right at the beginning of the program.

The *bank* Class Definition   Here is the definition for the class bank:

```
    bank::bank(float x,float y)
    {
        xgreen=x;
        xred=x+50;
        nextygreen=y;
        nextyred=y;
        greencoin.resize(20,40);
        greencoin.color(2,7);
        redcoin.resize(20,40);
        redcoin.color(1,7);
    }

    void bank::plus()
    {
        greencoin.place(xgreen,nextygreen);
        greencoin.show();
        nextygreen=nextygreen-10;
    }
```

```
void bank::minus()
{
   redcoin.place(xred,nextyred);
   redcoin.show();
   nextyred=nextyred-10;
}
```

The *teacher* Class Definition   Finally, here is the definition for the class teacher:

```
teacher::teacher(jukebox &neon)
{
  speaker=neon;                        // Copy to teacher's jukebox
  right=wrong=0;
  plus.label("Right:");
  plus.say(right);
  minus.label("Wrong:");
  minus.say(wrong);
}
void teacher::playlist()
{
  words oneword;
  int n=speaker.howmanywords();
  for (int k=0;k<n;k++)
    {
      speaker.spell(k,oneword);
      yourword.say(oneword);
      speaker.pronounce(k);
      myclock.wait(2);
      yourword.erase();
    }
}

void teacher::test()
{
  char spelling[20];                   // Student's word
  char correct[20];                    // Correct word
  int j;
  int count=2*speaker.howmanywords();// Number of questions
  for(int k=1;k<=count;k++)
    {
      j=rand()%speaker.howmanywords();
      strcpy(spelling,"");             // Clear display
      speaker.pronounce(j);
      askwords(spelling,9,"Please spell:");
      speaker.spell(j,correct);
      if(stricmp(spelling,correct)==0)
```

```
        {
            speaker.pronounce("allright");
            plus.say(++right);
            FirstNational.plus();
        }
        else
        {
            yesno("Wrong! Will you study harder?");
            minus.say(++wrong);
            FirstNational.minus();
        }
    }
}
```

Are You Experienced?

Now you can. . .

- ☑ **Approach application development in an object-oriented way**
- ☑ **Reuse software**
- ☑ **Understand more of the design issues involved in developing an application**
- ☑ **Implement a simple object-oriented application**

Introducing the Missing
C++ Skills

☐ Understanding what else there is in C++

☐ Understanding what else there is in computer
programming

The main goal of this book is to teach you how to solve problems using a computer and the C++ programming language. As you progress in your career, you will notice that it is far more important to devise algorithms than it is to memorize programming recipes.

The concepts you learn while developing algorithms will help you even if you need to program in another language.

To keep things simple for your learning process, some features of C++ were not covered in this beginner's book. As you develop more programs, you may want to find a more advanced text or to experiment with advanced features by yourself.

In this last Skill, some of these missing features are summarized. Also, there is much more to learn about computer programming than what you can learn in one programming book. Issues that may interest you for future learning are also mentioned.

What Else Is There in C++?

This book does not cover all the features of the C++ programming language. Several features were deliberately omitted. In this section, we will briefly discuss some of them.

Pointers

Pointers are variables that hold the addresses of other variables in the computer's memory. There are several applications of pointers in C++. However, you can deal with some of these applications by using arrays (which, in fact, use pointers) and by passing parameters by reference. In C, it is not possible to pass a parameter by reference, and, for this reason, it is extremely important to know how to deal with pointers.

If you use pointers, it will require a lot of attention and may result in hard-to-read code.

An Application of Pointers

An interesting application of pointers can be found in the implementation of the class Stage in franca.h. An object of class Stage is a Screen Object (derived from ScreenObj) that has an array of pointers to Screen Objects. Every time you insert an object in a Stage object, the address of this new object is copied into the array. Calls to member functions cause all objects in the array (one at a time) to invoke the same member function. For example, a call to the show() member function simply loops through the whole array and shows each object. A similar thing happens with the other member functions.

Combined Operators

There is a special set of assignment operators that you can use when updating a variable. They are as follows:

```
+=
−=
*=
/=
%=
```

For example, you can use

```
x+=5;
```

instead of

```
x=x+5;
```

If you use these operators, you may indeed save a few keyboard strokes. There is nothing much to gain otherwise, and the readability of your program may suffer. Nevertheless, they are very popular constructs that you may find in other programs, and they are not difficult to understand.

Operator Overloading

One of the most interesting features allowed by C++, but not covered in this book, is *operator overloading*. It is possible to define the behavior of any of the operators used in C++. For example, the operator + is defined in C++ to operate with integers and floating point numbers. It is not defined for any other type or class of variables.

You can define classes of your own: strings, complex numbers, coordinates, matrices, or even screen objects. If you do this, you can define a member function operator+ that will explain how the operator + will be used when one (or both) operands are objects of the new classes. This allows us to operate with strings.

```
if (stringA == stringB) stringA="a copy";
```

will work if you overload the operators == and = to operate with the string class you defined.

AN EXAMPLE OF OPERATOR OVERLOADING

In franca.h, you can insert a Screen Object into a Stage object by invoking the insert() member function. For example:

```
Stage soldier;
soldier.insert(rightarm);
soldier.insert(leftarm);
```

Or, you can use the << operator:

```
soldier<<rightarm;
soldier<<leftarm;
```

This is because a member function, such as Stage operator<< (ScreenObj &something), is also defined to belong to the Stage class.

The operator functions explain what should be done if the particular operator (in this case, <<) shows up between an object of the given class (in this case, Stage) and an object of the class defined for the parameter (in this case, ScreenObj). In practice, all this function does is call the insert member function.

Templates

Templates are another useful C++ feature. In the same way that you can make your functions more versatile by using arguments, you can make your classes more versatile by using *templates*.

A SIMPLE APPLICATION OF TEMPLATES

The `textfile` class had a restriction that the ID field had to be an alphanumeric string of up to 40 characters. The ID field was declared to be part of the class:

```
class textfile
{
   ...
   public:
   char id[40];
```

If you want to have an ID field whose size you can determine for each program, you can use a template:

```
template<int size>
class textfile
{
       ...
    char id[size];
```

Then, in your program, declare your class:

```
textfile myfile<65>;
```

This would work as if you had made your classes using the constant *65* to declare the size of the ID field.

However, the power of templates goes far beyond this simple example. Not only can you change the value of a number, you can also change the type or class of the data with which you are working. Therefore, instead of having ID as a type char, you could have it as any generic type:

```
...
anytype id;
```

continued ▶

> Keep in mind, however, that the work done by templates is limited to sub-stituting what is in the template for what you provide in the class declaration. Since character arrays are compared with strcmp and values are compared with the relational operators, you may still have some work left.

Templates are very powerful tools to build reusable software, since you can define classes in a generic way and customize them to a specific need.

Friend Functions and Classes

Well, who said C++ is not friendly? At least, it is the only programming language that I know that allows "friends" in the software. *Friends* are honorary members of a class. In a class declaration, class *A* can specify that class *B* is a friend. If class *B* is a friend class, all the member functions of class *B* can access private and protected data members of class *A*. A similar effect happens when a class declares a function to be a friend.

Multiple Inheritance

You can derive a class from more than one base class. In this case, data members and member functions of both base classes will be inherited by the derived class.

Memory Allocation

Throughout this book, we have dealt with only one mechanism to allocate the computer's memory to accommodate our variables and objects. This mechanism was the so-called *automatic allocation*. If you use this mechanism, the variable is created, and space is allocated when the program reaches the point where the variable is declared. When the variable goes out of scope, its contents are discarded, and the space is made available for other variables.

There are other ways to allocate memory space. Static variables remain in existence even when they go out of scope.

It is also possible, by using pointers, to dynamically allocate space for a variable during program execution. Suppose you need an array, but you do not know beforehand how many elements the array will use. Instead of allocating a maximum number, you can start the program—only after the program figures out how many elements are needed, your program requests the computer to allocate the space.

Logical Operators

Special operators are available to perform the logical operations *and*, *or*, and *not* with corresponding pieces of variables. **&&** stands for *and*, **||** stands for *or*, and **!** stands for *not*.

What Else Is There in Computer Programming?

There is no way to learn how to ride a bike by using just a blackboard. If you simply learn all the features of a programming language, it will not make you a great programmer. Knowing how to organize your data, carefully examining the most adequate algorithms, and developing good programming habits are key elements for a successful programmer.

Use your computer, and program! Be curious, and experiment!

Software Engineering Principles

One can still argue whether software development is mostly science or engineering. One may even argue that it involves art, as well! No matter which view you adopt, you must agree that there is a substantial amount of engineering-like requirements when developing software.

It is important that you meet deadlines, budgets, and performance specifications. It is no use to develop the most wonderful software in the world if it is not available when it is needed, or if no one can afford to buy it!

There are several principles that were established to help software development become more efficient. A slightly more difficult problem for you to understand is the problem of software maintenance. I bet you would rather be given programs to develop than be given programs to fix that somebody else developed. Am I right?

Nevertheless, as a programmer, you may spend most of your professional life maintaining software, instead of developing it. Software has to be maintained not only because it was wrong, but also in response to external events—the market has changed, the laws have changed, the problem has changed….

If the software is easy to maintain, the maintenance costs will be lower. How do we make software easy to maintain?

It is not a simple question. You may have noticed, though, that readable code, reuse of software components, and good documentation help a lot. When you develop your software, if you can foresee some of the possible needs for modifications, you can make your software easier to maintain.

Are You Experienced?

Now you can. . .

☑ Understand what else there is in C++

☑ Understand what else there is in computer programming

Index

Note to the Reader: Throughout this index **boldface** page numbers indicate primary discussions of a topic. *Italic* page numbers indicate illustrations.

d

To use this book, you need an IBM-compatible computer, with either Windows 3.1 or Windows 95 and one of the following compilers:

- Borland Turbo C++ 4.5 for Windows

- Borland C++ 4 for Windows

- Borland C++ 5 for Windows

- Microsoft Visual C++ 1.56 for Windows

- Microsoft Visual C++ 4 for Windows

- Microsoft Visual C++ 5 for Windows

In addition, you must download the support file from the Sybex Web site at http://www.sybex.com. Click the No experience required link, then the C++: No experience required link, and then, finally, Download. There may be updated instructions for downloading the support software.

The file CPPNER.EXE is a self-expanding, compressed file that contains all the support software. You should create a directory FRANCA in the root directory of your drive C:. Once you execute CPPNER.EXE, the following files should be in your directory:

- General purpose files (FRANCA.H, NOFRANCA.H, and PAULO.RC)

- Sample programs, header files, and text files (with .CPP, .H, and .TXT extensions)

- Files for supporting the various compilers (FRANCA45, FRANCA40, FRANCA50, FRANCAM1, FRANMS4, and FRANMS5—with various extensions)

- Sound files for multimedia projects in the subdirectory /SOUNDS (with .WAV extensions)